Annals of a Publishing House

THE

PUBLISHING HOUSE

OF

BLACKWOOD

Annals of a Publishing House

JOHN BLACKWOOD

HIS DAUGHTER

MRS GERALD PORTER

THE THIRD VOLUME OF

WILLIAM BLACKWOOD AND HIS SONS
THEIR MAGAZINE AND FRIENDS

WILLIAM BLACKWOOD AND SONS
EDINBURGH AND LONDON
MDCCCXCVIII

Annals of a Publishing House

JOHN BLACKWOOD

BY

HIS DAUGHTER

MRS GERALD PORTER

THE THIRD VOLUME OF

WILLIAM BLACKWOOD AND HIS SONS

THEIR MAGAZINE AND FRIENDS

WILLIAM BLACKWOOD AND SONS
EDINBURGH AND LONDON
MDCCCXCVIII

INTRODUCTION.

In the preceding volumes have been given the history of the founding of 'Blackwood's Magazine' and the publishing house by William Blackwood, and the story of the life and work of himself and of the sons who immediately succeeded him. In this volume it was the intention of their late lamented biographer, Mrs Oliphant, to trace the life and work of John Blackwood, the youngest of the sons to follow their father's profession, and the one to whom was granted a longer span of life in which to develop the talents and industry that distinguished them all. His association with most of the best known writers of our day has invested his name with a special interest, which his nephew and surviving partner, William Blackwood, has thought demanded a more detailed account of his life and work and of the many happy social relations which subsisted between him and his contributors.

The able and graceful pen which should have furnished this memoir is, alas! laid aside for ever, and the task has fallen to her who was to have aided Mrs Oliphant, by supplying a daughter's recollections of the years spent in daily companionship with the subject of the narrative, and whose knowledge of his character and aims has grown with her life.

MARY PORTER.

3 RANDOLPH CRESCENT, EDINBURGH,
September 1898.

CONTENTS OF THE THIRD VOLUME.

CHAPTER I.

EARLY LIFE OF JOHN BLACKWOOD.

CHAPTER II.

GEORGE ELIOT'S EARLY NOVELS.

CHAPTER III.

EDINBURGH AND LONDON.

CHAPTER IV.

A. W. KINGLAKE AND 'THE INVASION OF THE CRIMEA.'

CHAPTER V.

LAURENCE OLIPHANT.

CHAPTER VI.

THE EDITORIAL SANCTUM.

CHAPTER VII.

STRATHTYRUM.

CHAPTER VIII.

CHARLES LEVER.

CHAPTER IX.

"THE MILITARY STAFF OF BLACKWOOD."

CHAPTER X.

THE EDITOR ABROAD.

CHAPTER XI.

MRS OLIPHANT AND NEW RECRUITS.

PLATES.

JOHN. BLACKWOOD.

CHAPTER I.

EARLY LIFE OF JOHN BLACKWOOD.

SCHOOL AND COLLEGE DAYS—FIRST POLITICAL FIGHT—"THE GRAND TOUR"
—ROME—ESTABLISHED IN PALL MALL—FRIENDSHIP WITH JOHN DELANE
—AN EVER-WIDENING CIRCLE OF CONTRIBUTORS—RECALLED TO EDIN-
BURGH — BECOMES EDITOR OF 'BLACKWOOD'—LITERARY SOCIETY IN
EDINBURGH — WILLIAM EDMONDSTOUNE AYTOUN—"BON GAULTIER"—
A FACETIOUS SHERIFF—ST ANDREWS IN THE "FIFTIES"—JOHN BLACK-
WOOD'S MARRIAGE—PROFESSOR BLACKIE—REV. JAMES WHITE—A MEM-
ORABLE DAY WITH TENNYSON — COLONEL HAMLEY AT LEITH FORT—
THACKERAY'S VISIT.

IN order to place satisfactorily before the readers of
this volume the life and work of John Blackwood,
a short retrospect is necessary. Without touching
upon the matters which have already been fully dealt
with in the first and second volumes, we must re-
capitulate briefly the events that led him onward
from youth and early manhood, through the different
stages of preparation, to the position of head of the
house and editor of the Magazine which bears the
family name,—a position in which he worked faithfully and successfully for thirty years.

VOL. III.   A

The pleasant home where John Blackwood's young days were passed was at Newington, then a country village just outside Edinburgh, now an overgrown suburb of the town. The white stone house which his father, William Blackwood, had built for his bride, now partly covered with ivy, is still standing at the corner of Salisbury Road. It commanded, and still commands, an uninterrupted view of Arthur's Seat and the Salisbury Craigs. In the foreground Edinburgh lies in a gentle haze, all imperfections blurred over by the blue mists of smoke, the well-known features of the town showing up bravely,— the Castle Rock, the Calton Hill, and other characteristic landmarks, towering over the unsightly chimneys and other unpicturesque objects which crept into the scene long after William Blackwood built his house. The cheerful sunny garden which his wife loved is still an attractive spot; and the elms and chestnut trees which she planted, with a fine scorn for anything of smaller growth, now pleasantly shade the walks.

Here John Blackwood was born on the 7th December 1818, the sixth son of a family of seven sons and two daughters. They were all fond of their early home, and one of John Blackwood's favourite drives in after years was round by Newington, where he could get a sight of the old house. These were the occasions on which he described to me the life he led there, and I seem to see him now before me, a happy, pleasant-natured little child, delighted when he could escape from the feminine sway to trot along hand in hand with his father for an expedition to Edinburgh, or a glorious scrambling walk over the

Braid Hills. I see him later on, more serious, a little schoolboy with a bundle of books, walking to and from Edinburgh,—sometimes, he has told me, led into a row with the street boys, who would follow him as he turned down the Salisbury Road; for my grandfather's home and family were well known, and even when not under the influence of political excitement they would run after him, shouting, "See the wee Tory, see to him!" with other derisive remarks, which he tried to support with as much dignity as possible. But one day he could stand it no longer, and, throwing down his books, squared up to his tormentors, great big lads, by whom he was handled very roughly. His torn clothes and bleeding face, however, won for him the respect of his assailants, who, discovering he was not to be lightly interfered with, henceforth let him alone, while his father and elder brothers were delighted with the prowess of this worthy chip of the old block. This was his first political fight, the forerunner of many another, though I never heard that he came to fisticuffs again.

When about ten or eleven years old he was sent to the High School, a large public school for boys, which occupied a foremost position as a school where a good classical education could be acquired: in that and many other respects it more resembled an English public school than others of the same date in Scotland. The playgrounds are spacious, and all kinds of games were freely encouraged. At school he appears to have worked well, and to have obtained several prizes. Latin was his strong point, and history, of which he was extremely fond. A few years before his death he alludes to those school-days in a letter to the Rev. Lucas Collins, when complimenting him on his volume 'Livy,' contributed to the series of "Ancient Classics for English Readers": "At school my chief occupation was reading the ancient tales of Greece and Rome, with a book carefully concealed under the form in front of me; and Livy, of course, when I came to know him, was a prime favourite." His father evidently encouraged him in his studies by presenting little supplementary prizes of his own, as we find books with the inscription, To John Blackwood from his father, for being dux in such-and-such a year, in the hope that he will be dux the following.

After he left the High School his education was continued by a private tutor, who taught him and his brother Archie, who afterwards, like his brother William, entered the Indian army. This tutor, Mr William Hay, an exceedingly clever and accomplished man, had himself made many contributions to literature, and combined a great amount of information of all kinds with a strong love of classic lore, which he tried his best to instil into his pupils, and in the case of John with considerable success. Besides studying with Mr Hay, he also attended classes at Edinburgh University, and we find the Professor of Logic, Mr D. Ritchie, writing that he "had reason to be satisfied with his talents and diligence."

At a very early age William Blackwood and his eldest son, Alexander, discovered in John signs and indications which led them to suppose that of all the family he was the one most likely in years to come to assist in lightening their labours, the one on whom most naturally the family mantle would fall; and in very early days, from his love of reading and the remarks he made on what he read, he was called jokingly "the little Editor." The turn which events took later forced him onwards while still young; and the companionship of his accomplished brother Alexander for two years, while they were abroad together, tended also in this direction. After their father's death in 1834, Alexander, who was a martyr to asthma, was obliged to go to the South of Europe for his health, and, leaving the next brother Robert in charge of the business, he started off accompanied by "Johnnie," as he always called my father, to whom the foreign travel, he thought, would be of great advantage, and whose education was still to be continued by Mr Hay, who went with them. The advantages to the younger brother, from an educational point of view, were fully as great as the improvement derived by Alexander in health. The facility with which John acquired languages is remarked on in many of the letters by Alexander and the tutor; while the sound training he had had in Edinburgh brought him with a mind well stored, and an intelligence already ripened and eager, into the fresh field of classic ground awaiting them in Italy. Not long after their arrival in Nice, Mr Hay writes: "We have sent Johnnie to an Italian teacher to learn to speak the language. I do not think that will give him much trouble." And again, a little later: "Johnnie and I are forgetting our English." This may have been to impress the brothers and sisters at home with an idea of their devotion to study; but it was true, nevertheless, that John soon

distanced his brother and the tutor in his knowledge
of French and Italian.   The idioms he learned so
readily seemed to stick to him well through life, and
I was often struck in later years, when he had
occasion to speak French, by seeing how easily he fell
into the old familiar tongue.   Their tour has been
fully dealt with in the second volume; but where
we find any special mention characteristic of John, or
letters from him which indicate what he was in those
early days, we may permit ourselves a brief look back
to what was an important era in his life, and one
which he considered gave him the early knowledge
of men and cities which was of considerable advantage
in his profession.

How new and strange everything must have seemed
to the young Scotsmen! the quaint houses, the
climate, the unaccustomed food.   Their bills, which
have been carefully preserved all these sixty odd
years, are not uninteresting reading.   At first we
find them steadily ordering "bif-teaks," "côtelettes
de mouton," no doubt in the hope of discovering
the familiar British mutton-chop.   Their drink was
beer and other heroic beverages.   But after a time
they settled down to the time-honoured poulets of
France and the wines of the country.   The modest
rent they paid for their charming villa at Cimiez for
six months will cause a thrill of envy in the minds of
those accustomed to the extortionate Riviera charges
of to-day—1000 francs for the season was then considered sufficient.   Their major-domo received 80
francs a-month, and the old *bonne* who helped him got
20.   After they had been there a few weeks, we learn
from Mr Hay's letters that Alexander's health had

improved—"He is first out of bed in the morning, first at breakfast, which he devours like a tiger, goes out on horseback at twelve, and rides like a savage till three o'clock." The same chronicler tells us how they assisted at the carnival and all the festivities of *mardi gras*. John had attired himself in a new suit of clothes and bought a new hat—a foolish investment for that occasion; but then "Johnnie" was young, and this was his first carnival. It proved a favourite mark for the *confetti* of his fair acquaintances, who pelted him well, *le cadet* coming in for the lion's share of their attentions. He says: "In this loving warfare the English distinguished themselves 'much,' and the Scotch 'most.'" The handsome daughters of Mr Johnstone of Alva are often alluded to as always being in the midst of all the gaiety that was going on, one of them being just engaged to a son of Lord Lorton—"a good man and a Tory," the writer adds.

The first move, after Nice, was made by the old Corniche road to Genoa, whither they travelled in their own carriage according to the comfortable fashion of those days. Proceeding thus in a leisurely manner to the Italian lakes when at Cadenabbia, a long halt was made. Occasionally John had to quit this paradise for Milan, where he was sent to hunt for letters and papers, and performed the journey in the diligence, which he describes as an "infernal machine containing sixteen greasy ruffians, packed as tight as herrings in a barrel, on a hot, smoking evening"—a contrast to their own comfortable carriage which was resting with Alexander at Como.

After a summer spent in the cooler regions of

Switzerland they recrossed the Alps and continued southward, with Rome for their destination. The route after Florence lay by the shores of Lake Trasimene, and the enthusiasm of the brothers was fairly aroused by the beauty of the scene, the heights from which Hannibal descended into the foggy valley upon the Romans being easily discernible. John remarks, "The postilion was most circumstantial in his account; but unluckily became so particular in the details, as in pointing out the house where Hannibal slept after the battle, that he left some not unreasonable doubts as to his correctness." The papal customhouse was then situated exactly on the scene of action, and John alludes to the "holy" *douaniers* offering for sale bits of rusty iron as coin picked up in the district. "It must be said for them," he adds, "they could not keep from laughing at their own impudence." The first view of the Tiber was disappointing to him, as it is to most travellers, and he writes, evidently with a pang of disappointment, that "association is everything, for it must be confessed so near the source it was a small and even muddy-looking river. No white oxen were to be seen by the shores of the Clitanus. It flowed most beautifully clear, but filthy beggars, anything but white, were the only cattle to be seen in or about the elegant little temple of the river-god." Of Spoleto and Foligno he says, "The description will do for a magnificent mountain site with fine towers and battlements, and within dirt and wretchedness."

At Terni John left his companions and set out to walk to Civita Castellana. This, though he says nothing of the fatigue, was a considerable performance, and is best described by himself in his own happy manner, his health and spirits being evidently in the best possible trim. He writes :—

On reaching Otricoli, I again caught sight of the course of the Tiber running along the broad vale, but a thick haze hanging over it obscured the actual river. The heat of the sun was intense, so that by the time I reached the bridge built by Augustus I was pretty well done up. The happy thought of a bathe instantly struck me, and getting to the bank, I was soon over head and ears in the waters of the Tiber. I was obliged to plunge in a sheltered creek, for the river was deep and rapid from the recent rains, and might have carried me to Rome swifter than the papal *poste*. From the same reason it was even of a more dingy yellow than usual, but nothing could have been more refreshing, and on coming out I felt as strong as a lion. Sitting on the bank with the bright sun shining and a fresh air from the river blowing, I could almost have been poetic. I certainly could not have had a more glorious introduction to the far-famed river. After this I strode merrily forward, and soon passed Borghetto, a miserable hamlet with a most picturesque old castle. I entered Civita Castellana by a bridge over the dark precipitous ravine that encircles the town. My reception at the hotel [della Posta] was anything but flattering, for I was covered with mud, and the savages had not the discrimination to see it was the classic slime of old Father Tiber. I was shown into all manner of back dens, but at last by dint of bullying I got the best rooms they could boast. The others arrived half an hour afterwards, and were rather surprised to see me seated at my ease, and made sundry derogatory insinuations as to my fatigue, &c., but the dinner I ate showed my jaws were not tired anyhow. Terni to Civita Castellana thirty-one miles.

This is the only allusion he makes to the distance he had walked, and it is made in the diary in the usual way, at the end of the day's entry. The next day they started on their last stage to Rome by

Nervi, Monterosi, and Bacciano, with, he writes,
"as severe a frost as ever I felt in Scotland at the
same season — roads as hard as iron and pools all
frozen over."

In Rome the young traveller's time was fully occupied with his German and Italian masters, and sightseeing, and the long rides which he and Alexander
both loved. Society also made some demands upon
them as their acquaintance increased. Alexander in
one letter expresses disappointment that they were
unable to enter more into Italian society, as
"Johnnie" now spoke the language so well. But
that they visited some of the Italian families who
were entertaining that winter we gather from finding, amongst old cards and memoranda, cards from the
Duchessa Torlonia inviting the "Signore Giovanni
Blackwood" to a ball, and other invitations from less
well-known names. In a letter to his brother Archie
he describes the sort of evening parties which were
then prevalent in Rome, and from which he suffered
acutely :—

"Swarrees" (as Sam Weller says) have been our other
amusement. I don't think you have had the fortune, or
rather misfortune, to encounter one of these: it means going
to a house where you sit or stand for two or three hours and are
regaled with villanous tea, hear a great many remarks upon the
weather, &c. Perhaps some one strums away upon the piano, or
one most inveterate fellow, a German (speaking broken English),
talks away in a loud voice about the antiquities or the fine
arts. Such are almost all the "swarrees" I have seen, and
dreadfully tiresome you may guess they are.

He appears, however, to have appreciated the
Roman carnival. He gives his brother Robert a
description of the last ball of the carnival :—

John Blackwood to his Brother Robert.

ROME, *March* 1838.

Yesterday evening there was the last masked ball. Lauder [the artist] was at our rooms, and would insist upon my putting on a legal wig and gown he had; with this and a pair of spectacles I went in the character of an advocate. It disguised me perfectly; no one recognised me. Alexander was there; but I gave him the cut direct, for to have been seen speaking to him would at once have betrayed my base pretensions. Raineaud had been most industrious in powdering my wig, and to some purpose apparently; for as I was going along with the most dignified legal air you can imagine, I heard a ruffian behind saying, " E un farinajuolo " ("He is a meal-monger," or rather "flour-monger ").

The usual expeditions were made in the neighbourhood of Rome, many of them in company with Baron Stockhausen, whose acquaintance they had made the previous year at Genoa. Referring to the luncheon after one of these long days, John says :—

Alexander and I did wonders, but we dwindled to nothing before the Baron; but as he is about six feet high, and with shoulders about three and a half feet broad, and calves to match, we must console ourselves with our inferiority. We had a most pleasant evening, and there was a considerable charge in the next morning's bill for extra sugar. The Baron is a most capital fellow, and a very big swell; he is chamberlain to the King of Prussia. . . . There is such an expression of jollity and good-humour about his gigantic face that Alexander and I took a perfect liking to him at Genoa, though we hardly spoke to him above a few times.

On their return drive to Rome they met with an adventure which, though it had no bad results, was sufficiently serious at the time.

John Blackwood to his Mother.

After this we went on our way most merry and comfortable. A coolish wind had just begun to rise, and we had wrapped our cloaks most snugly about. I had clasped that big Spanish affair of Alexander's about my neck, when we came in sight of what seemed like a great lake covering the road for nearly a quarter of a mile. The coachman wanted to stop, but the Baron peremptorily ordered him to follow his nose. Well, hardly had we gone a few steps when one horse went a little to the side; the beast funked, and turned his horses round, when down they went up to the neck. The carriage was on the point of following them, when Alexander sprang out and the Baron after him ; they went up to their middle upon the road. . . . I thought it best to get rid of the big heavy cloak first—I feared it might strangle me ; . . . and the vehicle being by this time nearly down the little brae by the roadside, and seeming likely to upset, jumped for it, and went slap up to the armpits, but I quickly scrambled up on to the road. The coachman was all this time on the box. Never did I see such an expression of fright on any face. He shouted, "Help me, signori, for the sake of the Madonna! I am lost! we are all in the Tiber!" However, he got out with nothing but a ducking. We left the horses and vehicle to be drawn out by a lot of peasants who rushed up, and walked on to keep ourselves warm; but it soon overtook us, and we drove into Rome in as great spirits as ever. No colds or other bad effects, but it might have been most serious.

This letter and others like it, which have been carefully preserved all these years, though not perhaps interesting in themselves as descriptions to those who know their Rome as well as, or better than, they know London, serve the purpose, and indeed are the only means we have, of showing what John Blackwood was at this age. The picture of himself which he thus unconsciously reveals in the letters and diaries, only intended for his mother and other relatives, shows him full of boyish delight and enthusiasm for the scenes he was visiting for the first time, and to which he came evidently with a well-informed mind and an intellect already capable of forming very sound opinions on men and matters. The knowledge and information he possessed show out with an easy air of familiarity that makes the letters and diaries very pleasant reading, the fun and humour which distinguished him all his life never being far absent. This gay genial humour seemed to creep naturally into his pen, and removed from his writing as from his conversation any dash of pedantry. The letters were evidently a source of great pleasure to those at home—his former tutor, who had now left him, taking a pardonable pride in his pupil, as will be seen in the following letter :—

DEAR MISS BLACKWOOD,—With many thanks I return you Johnnie's letter, which gives me both pleasure and regret—pleasure, inasmuch as it shows that the grand objects he has seen have made a very proper and scholarlike impression on his mind[1]; and regret—a selfish one to be sure, but not unnatural—that I was not there to see. . . . I am glad, however, that Johnnie is not —— ——, who wrote a letter from Rome about as interesting as Janet Mucklebackit might have sent to Janet M'Nab, the fishwife of Fisherrow, on the subject of garvies.—Yours very faithfully, WILLIAM HAY.

-----

[1] *I* taught the boy.

They had been staying at Salerno :—

John Blackwood to his Brother Archie.

Next morning we started in a rowing-boat for Sorrento. It was a very fine forenoon, and we enjoyed the beauties of Amalfi greatly ; but hardly had we passed it when the wind began to blow right in our teeth, and it became rather rough. Our boatmen made hardly any progress, and declared they would not get to the point before midnight, so run us into a little creek, where they declared we should find donkeys and everything to carry our traps. But on inquiring from some sort of savages that inhabited the place, we found there was nothing of the sort, and on looking round saw the horrid rascals of boatmen scudding back with the favourable wind to Salerno. Like noodles, we had paid them. So we had nothing to do for it but climb the high cliffs: it was regular steep step-and-stair work, and we had more than two hours of it before we got to anything like decent habitations. It was a most horrid thing for Alexander. As Raineaud expressed it to me, " Je suis en désespoir pour monsieur." You can conceive what a rage Alexander himself was in. Many a blessing the boatmen got. If our good wishes availed, they would have foundered that night. Even at this little village the people seemed to be in a state of savage nature, speaking a dialect perfectly incomprehensible. We wandered about looking for a donkey, but all in vain: at last an old crone said she would get us a seat (*sedia*). That seemed of little importance, but I thought it might have some provincial meaning and said, " Is it an animal?" At this she got into a perfect fury and spluttered forth, " No, no; they are four Christians!" and, sure enough, in a little four as queer-looking Christians as ever you saw made their appearance, and with —of all things in the world to find in such a place—a regular sedan-chair. Alexander was speedily hoisted into this, and away we set over the Monte Sant' Angelo, a pass about 4000 feet high. It was very steep too, and the way the fellows carried Alexander in his chair of state swinging upon their necks was quite incomprehensible. Our tramp began at seven, and it was nearly midnight when we reached Castella. A most picturesque effect we must have had, for we had a tail of about seven porters of one sort or other. We found a most excellent hotel, and you may guess there was a pretty onslaught upon the victuals after our wander among the savages.

On the 2nd of May they set their faces northwards, returning by Rome, where they rested till the 8th

May, when the next entry in John's diary is made in large letters :—

May 8, 1838.—Left Rome. Were to have started at 5 A.M., but, owing to the carelessness of the police about our passports, it was mid-day when we drove through the Porta del Popolo. We gazed across the beautiful Piazza and up the long line of the Corso to the Capitol, and turned our backs upon the Eternal City—most probably for ever.

This is all that he permits himself in the way of regrets, but to those who can read between the lines it is evident he felt the adieu to Rome was the closing of a pleasant chapter in his life,—that busy, hard-working life which lay before him rendering his speedy return to these distant scenes very improbable ; and as a matter of fact, though one of his most ardent wishes was to spend again a few months at Rome, he literally never had time to do so until the year before his death, when his medical advisers urged a journey to the South for the benefit of his health. His work during all these years, though not (generally) irksome to him, may well be described as incessant.

The benefit to Alexander's health had more than surpassed their expectations, and not the least part of his (Alexander's) satisfaction lay in the manner his young brother had profited by his two years on "grand tour," the impress of which really stamped his life, and gave him at an early age the *aplomb* and confidence which materially assisted his career from the outset. He returned with the familiar knowledge of foreign languages and foreign lands which is only successfully acquired at first hand, and which transformed the clever schoolboy into an accomplished man of the world.

The next step in the preparation of John Blackwood for his life's work was one which his elders deemed necessary, though to him it was eminently less agreeable than the system of education he had just undergone abroad. This was to place him in London in the well-known house of Messrs Whitaker, there to learn the practical details and working of the publishing business. Thither he went in November 1838, having passed the autumn with his mother and the rest of the family near Edinburgh. This was a phase of his existence at which he often used to laugh as a crotchet of his elder brother's to which he was bound to defer, but the usefulness of which was never quite apparent to him. It seemed part of the well-established prejudices of a former generation that a business was better learnt under the auspices of another firm, and with other methods than those nearer home, which might be true of some professions, but hardly that of publishing, which John Blackwood always said could only be learnt by "doing" it.

The following winter, his brothers having satisfied their business consciences that he had received sufficient instruction at the hands of Messrs Whitaker, his pupilage there was allowed to cease, and in 1840 he went to take charge of the branch of the business which Alexander and Robert had started in Pall Mall. Then began the really onerous part of his life, when at the age of twenty-two he was left to himself to carry on and develop the undertaking begun by his brothers, with only an occasional visit of surveillance from them. This was the period when he first

became known to the literary world as the representative of a well-known name, and formed acquaintances and literary connections which resulted
in most cases in ties of the closest and happiest
friendship.   At this time he saw a good deal of
Mr John Delane.   In 1841 Mr Delane, who was at
the bar, but had for some time worked on the staff of
the 'Times,' became its editor.   John Blackwood was
one of the first to hear this important news, and has
described Delane rushing into his rooms late one
night, throwing himself into a chair, with the startling
announcement, "I am editor of the 'Times'!"   Being
nearly of the same age, and in the same line of life,
they had much in common, and met nearly every
day.   John Blackwood has often said many of his
happiest associations were connected with Delane in
these early days of his hard-working youth.   Delane's
was the unremitting toil of editing the great leading
daily paper—toil which could not be said to begin or
end at any particular hour of the night or morning.
After a busy day and an evening spent at some social
entertainment, they would wish each other good-night,
and Delane, nodding cheerily to his friend, would say,
"Now my work is just beginning," as he turned off
towards Printing House Square about 12 P.M.   His
talents and sagacity inspired the highest admiration
in young Blackwood, and the apparently careless ease
with which he bore his heavy burden of responsibility
was another point of sympathy.

John Blackwood's own real work as an editor did
not begin until a few years later; but all this time
he was gaining knowledge and experience, and in the
companionship of men like John Delane he was kept

constantly near the fountain-head of all that was interesting the world politically and socially, both at home and abroad. The literary connections he was forming and 'the steady attention he bestowed to business, while in no wise secluding himself from entertainments and the acquaintance of any persons congenial to his age and tastes, have been described in the second volume through the medium of his letters to his elder brothers and of theirs to him. The correspondence sets forth how the grist was being brought to the mill by the younger brother in his coign of vantage in Pall Mall, each year adding fresh names to the treasure-trove, while cementing the links formed with those who had already made their mark in the literary world. Samuel Warren, Landor, Bulwer Lytton, and the Rev. James White were all writing for the Magazine, and the heads of the house were kept well informed of all that was important for them to know by their young and vigorous *aide*, who was in the thick of the throng, and taking his information from the head and centre of the world of letters. His ready deference to the two older men and their pride and confidence in him are pleasing features in this family association, and left an unclouded retrospect of happy, useful years for the one who was soon to be single-handed in the undertaking.

In 1845 Alexander, the eldest brother, died. This was the first break in the family since their father's death, and was fraught with great changes in the conduct of the House, for Alexander had been the head, and editor of the Magazine. Alexander was the one who had first guided John in the early days

of youth and inexperience, and his lenient judgments
and kindly encouragement had smoothed over difficulties and made the harness of work easy for him. I
have often heard my father describe the half eagerness,
half diffidence, with which he used to take MSS. to
his elder brothers, thinking he had got hold of a good
thing, and not quite sure how it would be received,
only to be reassured by Alexander's slow smile and
gentle half-humorous greeting. One of the contributions he brought to them in those early days was
received with shouts of laughter. " Egad! Johnnie's
brought us a sermon this time," was somewhat discon-
certing; but John stood his ground, and stoutly maintained that the writer, whom he had heard preach the
sermon, would some day make his mark. So the
sermon was published, and his prediction was fully
justified by the then unknown preacher, who was .no
other than Archibald Campbell Tait, afterwards Archbishop of Canterbury.

Now all this was changed. John was summoned to
Edinburgh by his brother Robert, whose health was
not strong, and who found the cares and responsibilities of his position press too heavily upon him now
he was alone. From this time they two worked
the business together in Edinburgh, John Blackwood
undertaking the management of the Magazine, which
he continued to edit until his death, so that at
twenty-eight years of age he found himself practically the head of a large business, which required
constant attention and energetic diligence to ensure
its continued success. When speaking of this time,
I have never heard him refer to it otherwise than
as a period in which he, so to speak, found his own

level, and felt himself perfectly well able to cope with
the changed circumstances of his life.

The move to Edinburgh was not entirely to his
mind. He had lived away from it ever since
his boyhood. Even the summer holiday with his
mother and the rest of the family was passed in the
country, so that Edinburgh was like a strange place
to him, in the society and interests of which he had
but little part. His work, however, gave him plenty
of occupation, and that of a kind which threw him
into the society of those most congenial to him. Professor Wilson, "Delta," George Moir, Henry Stephens
(author of the 'Book of the Farm'), De Quincey,
Aytoun, Lord Neaves, were all *habitués* of the house.
With Aytoun John Blackwood was soon on terms of
intimacy and friendship, which formed one of the
pleasantest features of his life in Edinburgh. Their
houses were in adjoining streets. Randolph Crescent,
where Mrs Blackwood and her sons lived, led out of
Great Stuart Street, where Aytoun resided, and not
a day passed, I have often heard, without their meeting—often not an evening; for when no other engagement occupied either of them, John Blackwood's
after-dinner cigar was generally smoked in Aytoun's
library, where Mrs Aytoun, the youngest daughter
of Christopher North, made him very welcome. Even
their visits to London, journeys abroad, and excursions to different parts of Scotland, seem to have
been taken together; for we find Aytoun going to
the Derby and to Ascot in company with the Editor
and his friends, who arranged dinners at Greenwich
for him, at which the Bard of the North found himself
the centre of a pleasant company, whose wit and mirth

formed a sauce as piquant as any with which the fish was dressed.

His London friends and acquaintances all looked forward to the Editor's visits, which used to take place once or twice a-year for some weeks at a time. These were generally made occasions for numerous dinners and other entertainments. John Blackwood had earned the reputation of a good host, and the skill with which he arranged his dinner - parties made them very popular. The old friends were never forgotten, but their numbers were being perpetually reinforced by new acquaintances,—by no means all in the same line of life or of the same opinions; for the one thing he dreaded —nay, positively disliked—was any tendency to a groove. A magazine with him was a magazine, meaning a collection of everything, where authors, professional or non-professional, soldiers, politicians, clergymen, travellers—all might exhibit their wares, and hence to a great extent the cause of its and his own popularity. These social and literary gatherings—for the literary element was never absent— were often the hotbed where many a seed first germinated that was destined to bear good fruit. A half-originated idea would take shape in the encouraging atmosphere, and sometimes a soldier who had never distinguished himself apart from his profession, except by telling a good after-dinner story, would find himself sitting down to write a novel. Or some hard-working parson, whose literary talents had only been expended on his weekly sermons, would discover he could write able critiques on questions of the day, or pull to pieces in brilliant style the schemes

of our political opponents.   For all this their host
was mainly responsible.   Some sentence happily expressed, some chance phrase, would strike him; the
speaker would insensibly be drawn on to talk, one wit
brightening another—the ball being kept rolling by
their host, an expression he often used, and which
aptly described the sort of continuous stream of bright
and amusing talk that went on around him; never
obtruding his own conversational gifts in the slightest
degree, but imperceptibly directing the rest, and getting the best out of every one.

When John Blackwood came to Edinburgh in 1845
Aytoun was in the heyday of his powers.   Writing
on almost every conceivable subject and winning
success in very widely different fields of literature—
poems, novels, magazine articles — he exhibited a
versatility that constituted him a veritable mine of
talent, invaluable to the editor of a magazine.   His
mind had been stored in early youth by his mother
(a devoted adherent of the White Rose) with the
old picturesque stories of Scottish history and Border
romance.   Devotion to the Stuarts and admiration
for their gallant adherents were bound up in his mind
with the love of his country, which was one of his
strongest characteristics.   The patriotism which inspired him with a love deep and passionate for the
mountains and glens of Scotland turned his sympathies to the chivalrous spirits who espoused the
cause of the Stuarts; and perhaps no finer expression
has been given to that picturesque period of Scottish
history than Aytoun's ' Lays of the Scottish Cavaliers,'
of which " The Execution of Montrose" and " The
Burial March of Dundee" would alone have made

a reputation. In his earlier writings we have the
more mirthful side of his nature, as in the " Bon
Gaultier Ballads," many of which were written in
conjunction with his friend Theodore Martin, while
others were exclusively his own. "The Queen in
France" is a wonderful imitation of the old Scottish
ballad. Others we could name are easily recognisable as clever parodies of Macaulay's 'Lays,' Mrs
Browning, Tennyson, and Wordsworth. The ring
of the different cadences is unmistakable, and the
popularity the collection obtained surprised the
authors themselves, who had dashed off the verses
without any serious intentions, but with such an
admirable fidelity to the spirit of the originals as in
itself to convey a compliment to the characteristics
parodied. John Blackwood, writing to Aytoun, and
sending him and Martin a further instalment. of
the fruits of their labours, describes the volume as
a "lively little bit of property," which no doubt it
was.

Nor were Aytoun's prose writings less diversified
in character than his poetry. His lively humour and
versatility never seemed at a loss, and he appeared
to have a way of regarding everything with a view to
a possible Magazine article. Reviews of books, plays,
poems, and papers on the political questions of the
day, besides short stories (the grand test of a good
all-round writer), frequently appeared from his pen,
and there can be few readers of the 'Tales from
Blackwood' who have not laughed over his " Glenmutchkin Railway," and the story of "How I became
a Yeoman." A few extracts from his letters to my
father will give some idea of the varied nature of

his contributions to literature, besides those more important works which bore his name. His criticisms were often written in a spirit of drollery, not always to be taken *au pied de la lettre*, though no doubt containing the truth which is often spoken in jest. For example, Aytoun's feeling for Tennyson was one of genuine admiration, but the great poet sometimes appears to have excited a mirthful and whimsical mood in his " brother bard," as Aytoun liked to call himself, into which no feelings of reverent awe were allowed to enter, as in a letter proposing a review of ' Maud.' He writes to John Blackwood :—

You know how I have stuck up for Alfred through thick and thin, and will readily believe I have not come to this conclusion without a pang; but poetic justice must be done, else the small fry who are occasionally served up as whitebait for the gluttons of the Magazine would have just cause for complaint. He shall not, however, have his scalp lifted by an ignoble hand; that of a brother bard shall wield the tomahawk, and already I have in fancy worn his top-lock on my moccasins.

After reading of these bloodthirsty intentions it is satisfactory to find that the first of the Idylls brought him back to his allegiance, for we find him writing to my father : " About Tennyson, I have as yet only read the first of the series, ' Enid,' which I sipped like cream. It is *very good.*"

In 1852 Professor Aytoun was appointed Sheriff of the Orkneys, and in a letter to John Blackwood he writes :—

KIRKWALL, *July* 27, 1852.

I am much impressed in favour of my dominions, though perhaps the heat of an election is not the best time for ascending the throne. It is a funny scene. Inglis [afterwards Lord President of the Court of Session] and his party have been cruising through the Isles ever since the day of nomination, and, I hear, with good effect. I suppose we shall have a very stormy spectacle on Friday when the polling begins. I, of course, have a good deal to do in the way of making arrangements, and between whiles advising processes, of which I have now nearly mastered the area. I have not yet put pen to paper, but hope ere long to find or invent the subject for a vaudeville. . . .

He goes on to urge the importance of fresh political organisation for the party, and ends—

My only fear is, that after this spurt we shall all go to sleep again, in which case we shall deserve, when dead, to be carried to Landale's bosom.[1] On the whole, things seem to promise fairly well for Ministers. I am glad to hear that Lytton is in, and hope to hear shortly—for accounts are conflicting—that Sir G. Grey is out: that would be a very serious blow to the Whigs. Laing's return for the Northern Burghs is a good thing: he will give no factious opposition to Lord Derby, and he supplants a bitter Whig and Sutherland nominee. The Tories have generally given him their support, and I hope he will be mindful of this. . . . We expect to sail for Zetland on Aug. 7th. . . . Remember me to all friends. I write as if I were in the shoes of Robinson Crusoe, whereas I am in a highly civilised country, though between ourselves I suspect the natives have not an insuperable objection to *speerrits.*—Yours always,

W. EDMONDSTOUNE AYTOUN.

There is in one of Aytoun's letters a description of St Andrews as it appeared to him in those days—a small, old-world St Andrews which we should hardly recognise now, but infinitely amusing when approached in the right spirit. It appears to have been the one place in the world where he found it impossible to write. The cheery household of Professor Ferrier

---

[1] A Conservative agent with whom he was not satisfied.

had too many distractions — Mrs Ferrier and her charming daughters, Lady Grant and Mrs Rhoades, just growing up.   Mrs Ferrier, a daughter of Professor Wilson, was for many years a well-known figure at St Andrews, possessing in a marked degree many of the characteristics of her father, notably the wit and sense of fun, which, with her high spirits and love of hospitality, made her the life of the place and the joy of all her friends.   The drawbacks of a visit there, as whimsically described by Aytoun, might well have stood for the Magazine article for which he was excusing himself to the Editor, to whom he writes :—

Professor Aytoun to John Blackwood.

May 25, 1855

I got no satisfaction at St Andrews.   Bones of Sharpe! what a week we spent there!   [Then follows an account of his sufferings, how the Professor's youngest son made a point of sending a golf-ball at his head if he went into the garden to smoke a meditative cigar, thus driving him into the house, where in the drawing-room he had to remain] imbibing with qualified delight the domestic history of most of the families of St Andrews, including that one of Mrs Muffin or Methven, who may be, for aught I know, as fabulous a character as Mrs Harris.   [His dressing-room was an impossible refuge, as] the east wind came jauntily in by a hole in the window made by another promising young swiper of the Links.   I never spent such a week in my life.   Did I go into the dining-room after breakfast, valorously determined to write, C. was at her French lessons.   Did I cross to the College, I was instantly in the paws of Pyper.   So I surrendered myself to the popular current, and very soon began to find a mysterious interest in the household concerns of Mrs Muffin and her compeers grow upon my soul, and I verily believe that I at present upon earth know a great deal more regarding the economy of his tutelary city than St Andrew who is in Paradise.

Another letter gives an amusing account of his residence in Shetland.

Professor Aytoun to John Blackwood.

I leave Zetland on this day week. . . . This is a strange country, but on the whole I like it much. It is the most primitive part of H. Majesty's dominions, and, but for the language, has no affinity whatever with Scotland. I have seen Sumburgh Head and Fitful Head, and eat dulse without anchovy toast, and swilled water for lack of brandy, and performed divers other feats too marvellous and fish-like to be here recounted. I am gradually becoming web-footed, walk uneasily on my hinder fins, and when I cough the sound is as the cry of a cormorant. I have a wild craving for sillocks, and of an evening we play at nothing but hot cockles. Good-bye, I am just going to the beach to gather limpets.—Yours always,

W. E. A.

The following letter, written to the Editor on the departure of his brother, Captain Archibald Blackwood, to join his regiment on the outbreak of the Indian Mutiny, is a good example of Aytoun's graphic style when writing on any subject which he felt keenly. It reads as much to the point now (1898), when the Eastern Question is thrust so prominently before us, as it did when written forty years ago.

Professor Aytoun to John Blackwood.

KIRKWALL, 26*th September* 1857.

The Captain's departure must be a source of great anxiety to you all, particularly as it is against the advice of Burt;[1] but for himself perhaps it is a wise step, as he would to a certainty fret at being absent in such a time. The whole Indian story

---

[1] The medical adviser and valued friend of the family.

is hideous and revolting to the last degree. I am no more easy than yourself with regard to the course of European affairs. Here again is a notable instance of *Einigkeit*, for I too have been haunted by the meeting of the Emperors, one of whom is a mere blackguard, and the other sworn to revenge. Alexander is very dangerous, for he has a high moral position. He is the head of that great section of Christian Europe which maintains the old principle of hostility to the Mussulman at all hazards. The Greek Church has undeviatingly adhered to that, and the Romish Church has never renounced it. We, on the other hand, have no fixed religious principle of any kind with regard to external policy, but profess to regulate our motions so as to maintain the balance of political power. We have been maintaining Mahomet in Europe, and in return, the standard of the prophet of Mecca is flying on the walls of Delhi. I believe from the bottom of my soul that the Crusaders were substantially in the right. Now if that mysterious character Louis Napoleon should see his way to the possibility of making a Christian alliance, and combining the Greek and Roman elements, without losing his hold on France, where are we?

It is impossible to enumerate anything like the different subjects on which Aytoun was writing at this time. Nothing seemed to come amiss to him— a Magazine article would be manufactured out of the materials that came nearest to hand. In the Orkneys, in Edinburgh, London, or when travelling abroad, he could always be relied upon for something good. In the Orkneys he was sometimes slightly at a loss, as on one occasion he writes to my father from Kirkwall: "We are most comfortably settled here, and were it not for that old woman Maga I should be having a jolly time of it, but I have been trying to write, which is the devil in this country."

Fishing and shooting were easily obtained in these wilds, and the Professor, a keen sportsman, found

much to console him for the loss of a daily post in
this "Island of Peat-mos," as he called it. In one
letter to my father he says :—

I have not yet got out any kind of tackle or visited my
favourite "lies," so that I cannot gratify you by the recital of any
astonishing feats, but there is a good time coming. We have
got two ponies—a very pretty chestnut one for Mrs Aytoun,
which we have not yet named, and a bay horse, which formerly
carried a deceased minister of the Establishment. His trot is
of the hard Calvinistic kind, distressing to the bones, and
jolting like the divisions of a fast-day discourse. I have to
rise perpendicularly in the stirrups at his fifteenthly. But
I have purveyed me a strong Episcopal whip, and in the
course of a few days I hope to teach Ecclesiastes some prelati-
cal paces.

This appointment of Professor Aytoun's led in-
directly to an important event in John Blackwood's
life. It was while on a visit to him in these distant
islands that he met for the first time the lady who
was destined to become his wife. In the autumn of
1853 he was on board the Aberdeen steamer to Kirkwall, and encountered amongst the throng of tourists,
sportsmen, drovers, &c., a party of English strangers,
amongst whom he found Mrs Scott of Draycott
(married to a cousin of Sir Walter's), with her
brother, Mr Jessop, and other friends, bound on a
visit to the Orkneys after leaving their shooting
quarters in Kincardineshire. With them was my
mother, paying a first visit to Scotland under their
care. Arrived in the Orkneys, an introduction to the
Sheriff followed, with whom and the young Editor
many pleasant days were passed, they doing the
honours of the islands to the visitors. The acquaint-

ance thus pleasantly begun with the Scotts ripened into a warm friendship, and in the following winter John Blackwood married the young English lady he had first met in these northern regions. She was the youngest daughter, of the Rev. Joseph Blandford, rector of Kirton, in Notts.

Blackwood's home was still at 3 Randolph Crescent, Edinburgh, where he had continued to reside after his mother's death, and thither he took his bride, after a visit to London and Paris, in the winter of 1854. In June of that year one of his sisters-in-law, Miss Mary Blandford, came to visit them, and in her diaries there is an account of them and the circle surrounding them at Randolph Crescent. Amongst others she mentions meeting Principal Forbes, Professor Aytoun and his wife, Mr Van de Velde, and Professor Blackie. Blackie in those days must have produced by his appearance even a stronger impression on the Saxon stranger than in our time, when he became a well-known figure in Edinburgh. My aunt says he appeared at dinner with his hair in the wildest disorder ; but, in spite of his unconventional appearance, there was no mistaking his cleverness nor the keenness of his bright eyes flashing under the long mane, and he kept the dinner-table in fits of laughter.

From the same source we hear of another summer spent at Torwood House on the banks overlooking the Tay at Birnam, and among others who visited them there was the Rev. James White and his family. These were dear friends of the Blackwoods from the old days when John was working alone in London, and their pleasant home, whether in London or the Isle of Wight where they generally lived, was always open to him. Mr White's contributions to literature have been effectively mentioned in the second volume, together with the delightful social qualities which made him popular with such men as Dickens and Tennyson. His nationality was always impressed upon our memories by a speech of the old gardener at Torwood, who possessed a strong belief in his own and his nation's superiority. One day my father happened to be walking round the garden with Mr White, when they came across this old worthy, to whom he introduced Mr White, remarking that he was a fellow-countryman although a clergyman of the Church of England. "Ou, aye," said the old man, looking at him complacently, "gairdners or meenisters, ony kind o' heid wark, they maun aye come tae us."

Mr White's friendship with the Tennysons gave him the opportunity of making his Scotch friends acquainted with the poet while they were visiting him once at Bonchurch, when a never-to-be-forgotten day was spent with the Tennysons at Freshwater, of which the following description has been preserved :—

John Blackwood to his Brother, Major William Blackwood.

BONCHURCH, *May* 1858.

We had a delightful expedition to Freshwater yesterday. We were received by Mrs Tennyson very cordially. The Bard was in his study, and White went up and soon fetched him down. He is a striking-looking man, with a shyish, almost awkward, but manly and not unbecoming manner. He became very pleasant, and I should think him a very good fellow indeed. He evidently lives in a little world of his own, and takes things on hearsay from his satellites. Mrs Tennyson is a very pleasing woman, I believe "my cousin Amy," who did not play the part represented in the poem. After a comfortable lunch or early dinner, White and I went up to the attic which constitutes his study, and had a social pipe. He is under the impression that the Magazine is always saying unkind things of him. He said something of the kind, and I asked him how he imagined such a thing possible. He confessed he never saw the Magazine, but people told him it was so. White and I corrected him on this point. At first he was not disposed to go out at all, but then became quite keen for a walk, and finally he, White, Julia [Mrs John Blackwood], and I started over the downs to the extreme west point of the island overlooking the Needles. We had a delightful walk of about three hours—Julia chiefly in charge of the bard, with whom she was charmed. White cut off about midway, but we went on to the very end, and finally the bard brought us sheer down the cliff by way of a short cut, Julia astonishing and pleasing him greatly by her powers of scrambling. White thinks he would have come back with us had not Mrs Tennyson been a little poorly. He promises to come to see us whenever he is in Scotland. He is good fun, quotes poetry (not his own) very appropriately in a sonorous voice, and makes puns in rivalry of White. They go on chaffing each other about the merits of their respective houses. He said to White, "I believe *part* of Bonchurch belongs to you." "The *whole* of it," says White. "He means the *hole* he lives in," replied the poet. His house is very nice, a good size, and nicely fitted up. He has some land, and is lord of the manor over the downs which stretch up to the point. The views in all directions are beautiful. We did not start to return until about half-past six, and got home to Bonchurch a little after ten, where a plenteous supper was most welcome. Altogether a delightful day. To-day we are lounging about, and White and I are just starting to have our calumet on the shore. We start about eleven to-morrow, and if you wish to enjoy a few days come down here. Hosts, country, and climate are perfect.—Ever yours affectely.

JOHN BLACKWOOD.

In November 1854 when all hearts and sympathies were with our troops in the miseries of the Crimean

Campaign, he gives his sister-in-law some news from the seat of war :—

John Blackwood to his Sister-in-law, Miss M. Blandford.

I get daily more interested in the crisis in the Crimea. I was greatly delighted the other day by receiving a regular account of the early part of the campaign from my friend Captain Hamley. He dates before Sebastopol, Oct. 27th. He is not particularly sanguine, but when we go at the assault, thinks we will do it.

To the Same.

January 24, 1855.

The frost looks as if it would hold now. Fearfully cold work in the Crimea. This morning brought me a long despatch from Captain Hamley. He writes in his usual cool easy vein. He thinks we shall get into Sebastopol, but not yet a while. He has got a sort of hut, where he is much more comfortable than his neighbours. The only complaint he makes is that it is rather dark for writing and drawing, especially when, as is generally the case, he has to shut the door to keep out the storm!! He says our men bear their fearful sufferings with great fortitude.

The next mention we have of Hamley is in more peaceful scenes, he having been sent with his battery to Leith Fort. In the winter of 1856 he arrived in Edinburgh fresh from the Crimea, with all his laurels won in that grisly campaign. John Blackwood hailed with pleasure the happy chance that brought "the Gunner," as he affectionately termed him, close to his own home. The friendship between them, already begun, was speedily strengthened and cemented in the familiar intimacy and round of hospitalities which followed on Hamley's arrival in Edinburgh. There he found himself warmly welcomed as a brilliant addition to the circle of which Randolph Crescent was the centre, and where the Aytouns, Ferriers, sometimes De Quincey, who lived near Edinburgh, Lord Neaves, and others were the lights who made those mirthful evenings recall the Noctes 'of a former generation, when the wit, if more robust, was scarcely more brilliant.

Nor must we forget, amongst the new and added interests that call for remark, the visit of one staunch friend of his London days who rarely failed to look him up each autumn. Indeed it would have been considered a very blank season by John Blackwood that did not give him a few days of John Delane's pleasant company. On the first occasion of his visit he had to entertain him alone, my mother being from home at the time, and the host says he was nearly crushed by the weight of responsibility. However, Mr Delane appears to have been very pleased with everything, including his friend's little son, whom he saw for the first time.

John Blackwood to his Wife.

3 RANDOLPH CRESCENT, EDINBURGH,
October 30, 1857.

D. seems so pleased with his quarters that instead of going to-morrow he stays here until Sunday night. The little man [his son] was in great force this morning, sitting in a chair. Delane went up to see him, and was captivated with him. Our dinner went off very well yesterday, though the weight of responsibility nearly crushed me. The little doctor [Sir James Y. Simpson] was as happy as a king, and sat until eleven o'clock, regardless of repeated summonses. The magnates in the North have been worshipping Delane as usual; but I think Randolph Crescent will not be the least pleasant part of his reminiscences.

A letter from Mr Delane after this expresses very

warmly the pleasure he had in visiting his friend in his own house.

Mr John T. Delane to John Blackwood.

LINCOLN'S INN, *Nov.* 4, 1857.

MY DEAR J. B.,—I send you by parcel to-day the portrait of an old friend who has lately shared your hospitality, and who was delighted to find in you the same genial and kind feelings as in days long past.—Believe me to be, with all good wishes, very faithfully and truly yours,   JOHN T. DELANE.

In the winter of 1857 the pleasant Edinburgh coterie was reinforced by the addition of Thackeray, who stayed at Randolph Crescent when engaged on his lectures on the "Georges," which he gave at the Edinburgh Philosophical Institution. One can easily believe what one has heard that the winter with Thackeray in the house for two months seemed shorter than any winter would ever be again. John Blackwood's acquaintance with him had begun many years previously, and we find his first mention of him in a letter to "Delta" describing him as a young man named Thackeray, whom he met sometimes at the Garrick, and who was "beginning to write." Their friendship had come about entirely through mutual attraction and liking, and not through any literary relations. Though Thackeray, as has been stated, never wrote for the Blackwoods, he gives John Blackwood the credit of having inspired him to depict "Lord Crewe." In referring to a review in 'Maga' which had pleased him, he says :—

You yourself, by the way, are unwittingly the author of Lord Crewe. I remember over our toddy at your house in Edinburgh your saying, "None of us had ever depicted a young English

gentleman," and I thought I could and I did. . . . Are you
having a Merry Xmas? I wish I could see some of those
friendly faces of 51-2. But this year, although bidden to many
hospitable places, I have had no courage to go anywhere in consequence of my hawful state of 'ealth. I send my best regards
to Mrs Blackwood and any friend who remembers me; and am
yours, dear Blackwood, very kindly and sincerely,

W. M. THACKERAY.

Some quaintly friendly notes have been carefully
preserved, many of them invitations from Thackeray,
with the comprehensive address, "My dear Julia John,"
showing that the wife was now included in the friendship. Others include another member of the family,
James Blackwood, and begin, "My dear Julia John
James." These, with some water-colour sketches signed
Titmarsh, and some pretty pieces of china, still survive
as the cherished souvenirs of his visit. A very busy
and an interesting time this—Thackeray in the house,
Aytoun almost next door, and Hamley within a short
ride, who, when his duties for the day were over, generally made his way to 45 George Street or Randolph
Crescent.

CHAPTER II.

THE winter of 1856-57 was further memorable by the
introduction of a fresh element in the many interests
that were crowding into John Blackwood's life. At
this time began his correspondence with George Eliot,
and her first appearance in the pages of the Magazine
with the 'Scenes of Clerical Life.' It would be more
correct to say the correspondence began with Mr
G. H. Lewes, who introduced the unknown author's
writings to the Editor without explaining his identity.
Lewes himself had been a contributor for many years;
his brilliant articles on scientific, social, and other
matters were well known to the Editor, who admired
the literary ability which enabled him to give a fine
edge and brilliancy to the more solid subjects he
handled for the Magazine, as well as adding precision

and weight to his lighter contributions, making these articles as valuable in their way as the more important works that have distinguished him as an author and man of science. An introduction from him to a new contributor was likely, therefore, to be received with interest, though, as has been shown in the second volume, a certain customary caution was not dispensed with till the series had fairly set sail, and the Editor was able to stamp them with his unqualified approval. Lewes's gay and brilliant letters to him, and the amusing replies they elicited from the busy Editor, form a pleasant feature in the day's work.

John Blackwood to G. H. Lewes.

Feb. 23, 1857.

You have much reason to be proud of your literary godchild, George Eliot. My impression is that "Gilfil" will be even more generally popular than "Amos." There are differences of opinion about "Amos," and probably there always may be, but there is no mistake about the general verdict being as favourable as we expected. In his last G. Eliot expressed anxiety to hear Thackeray's opinion. From what Albert Smith said I gather that Thackeray is a serious admirer, but I expect the wandering "puller down of kings" here visiting, when doubtless I shall hear his opinion at full length. By the way, there are occasional touches in "Amos" akin to Thackeray's style of humour and feeling. The enclosed comment is from an intimate friend of mine, a remarkably clever fellow, the Rev. G. V. Swayne: you may recollect a paper of his on Respectability in the November or December number, which I daresay would hit your fancy.—Always yours truly,   JOHN BLACKWOOD.

The comment on "Amos Barton" referred to above says: "What a charming tale it is, and yet without any straining for effect or incident. It reminds me in its tender simplicity of the 'Vicar of

Wakefield' more than anything I have read for a long time."

George Eliot's diffidence as to her writings is often referred to in these early letters, and warnings given to the Editor lest he should extinguish the first "flickerings of the flame" by any injudicious remark.

G. H. Lewes to John Blackwood.

Entre nous, let me hint that unless you have any *serious* objection to make to Eliot's stories *don't* make any. He is so easily discouraged, so diffident of himself, that, not being prompted by necessity to write, he will close the series in the belief that his writing is not relished. I laugh at him for this diffidence, and tell him it's a proof he is *not* an author. But he has passed the middle of life without writing at all, and he will easily be made to give it up. *Don't allude to this hint of mine.* He wouldn't like my interfering.

He writes again to the same :—

JERSEY, *May* 1857.

Much do I regret your leaving town before our return. I had set my heart on breaking through the incognito, and bringing you and Eliot together, feeling sure that if you once saw and conversed with him, and found the sensitive, shrinking, refined creature he is, you would have your opinion of your new contributor considerably modified. Is there any chance of your being in town in the autumn?

He writes again :—

ROSA COTTAGE, JERSEY, *May* 24, 1857.

G. E. and I are comfortably settled in this pleasant fishing village, where the lanes and landscapes will enable him to meditate on man and clergymen, while the shore furnishes me with food for dissection and experiment. We are both delighted with Jersey, and intend receiving fresh inspiration therefrom— of which you will bear the burden! I am in clover. The shore is amazingly rich, and the brother-in-law of our landlord is the owner of a fishing vessel, and with him I propose interrogating

Nature in her submarine recesses. The weather is perfect, and French wines, duty free, help to "fleet the time carelessly as in the golden age." . . .

If you are not too busy when you write to pause for gossip, Eliot would be pleased to hear some pros and cons about Mr Gilfil. In London he had the satisfaction of the anonymous, and enjoyed the surmises which are ventured on there respecting the authorship. The stories seem to be frequently discussed there. He begs me to send his kind regards, and to say he shall soon be writing to you with his new clericus.

This letter drew the following reply referring to Lewes's seaside studies :—

John Blackwood to G. H. Lewes.

38 JERMYN STREET, *May* 28, 1857.

MY DEAR LEWES,—Yours of the 24th, with the touching address of Rosa Cottage, reached me to-day. I wrote to you about a week or ten days ago, addressing to St Heliers, and requesting on the cover that if you were not at the capital of Jersey, the postmaster should endeavour to find out a maniac answering to your name, hammering rocks, and dissecting seaweeds on the shore. I have no doubt the note has reached you, and if not you will find it at the post-office, St Heliers. As far as I recollect, there was nothing in my letter except compliments to George Eliot, and also to you upon the opening of your new seaside studies. I am sorry that in coming south I find a still broader piece of water than the Tweed between George Eliot and myself; but I am so confident of his merits that I am content to wait for the confirmation which preconceived ideas of intellect derive from personal acquaintance.

The next letter refers to the story "Janet's Repentance," in the 'Scenes of Clerical Life.'

John Blackwood to G. H. Lewes.

EDINBURGH, *Aug.* 4, 1857.

MY DEAR LEWES,— . . . I do not know that there was any particular call for me to read "Janet" at once, but it was an immense relief to turn to her from the other mass of papers lying on the table. Part III. is admirable. Although Parts I. and II. did not exactly hit my taste, my expectations of what was to come were very highly raised, and they are now in process of being more than answered. . . . Towards the close of the part I was in a horrid funk for poor Janet, and like herself felt rather relieved when the door was closed upon her. . . .

I am afraid you will find Richmond rather hot and dusty at present, but with such relaxations as the occasional eye of a cuttlefish to dissect, I daresay you will be able to rub on.—Ever yours truly, JOHN BLACKWOOD.

John Blackwood to G. H. Lewes.

April 2, 1858.

I have an admirable letter from George Eliot to-day. I knew that he would fear to give me a sketch of the rest of the story lest he should give me a wrong impression, and I very nearly said so when I made the request. On the whole, I think he is right. What he says of the treatment of a subject being the essence of art is very true, and a more elegant rendering of my constant reply to fellows sending lists of subjects for articles, "that any subject being suitable entirely depends upon how it is handled." I shall steal his expression the next time I wish to choke off any anxious inquirer as to the probable acceptability of his proposed little paper. I hope to receive the additional MS. to-morrow, in time to congratulate George on its merits before he leaves England.—Ever yours truly,

JOHN BLACKWOOD.

One can easily imagine the pleasure it must have been to the weary Editor, working through the many rough-hewn materials on his writing-table, to come upon the polished gem - like sentences of George Eliot.

In another letter to Mr Lewes, he refers to Mr Charles Newdigate's admiration for the 'Scenes of Clerical Life.' Mr Newdigate was the member for

South Warwickshire, and will be remembered by many in the House of Commons as the determined foe of the Jesuits. His house, Arbury, stood for the Chase in "Mr Gilfil's Love-Story," and George Eliot's choosing it for the background of one of her earliest stories was very natural, as it was probably the earliest house of that kind she remembered in her young days, and remained associated with her idea of all that was picturesque and dignified in an English country-house. Her father had been the land-agent to the Newdigate family, and her brother succeeded him. Of Mr Newdigate my father writes to Mr Lewes :—

John Blackwood to G. H. Lewes.

May 23, 1858.

Newdigate is a capital specimen of an honest, high-minded English gentleman and squire, and his opinion is excellent evidence as to the existence of the qualities he attributed to the tales. Thackeray's daughters had a soirée last night, and to be out of the way of the preparations the venerable man dined with us. He says he cannot get ahead with the 'Virginians,' and was desperately pushed with the last No., having written the last 16 pages in one day, the last he had to spare. The last two Nos. are, I think, better than their predecessors, but he must improve much or the book will not keep up his reputation. The indefatigable Albert seems pretty well done at present, and no wonder. Fancy playing on that confounded horn and telling these same stories for two thousand nights. He will be greatly the better for his trip to China, and I doubt not he will popularise China and give the public a clearer idea of the Chinese than we have hitherto derived from the tea chests and three fellows in pigtails crossing the bridge on the old blue plates. . . . —With best regards to G. E., ever yours truly,   JOHN BLACKWOOD.

The allusion to Albert Smith will recall to some readers his feat of reproducing Mount Blanc in Piccadilly, for the benefit of the Londoners, in the form of a series of pictures and lectures which he delivered himself, aided by songs and a Swiss horn. His attempt to popularise the "Monarch of Mountains" caused some amount of ridicule, inseparable from the methods employed, but the genuine earnestness and the clearness and vivacity of his descriptions drew thousands to his entertainment, and probably did much to swell the numbers of the Alpine Club besides the hordes of Cook's tourists, who have since found their way to those regions of snow and ice.

The following letter to my father from Albert Smith, who was an occasional contributor to the Magazine, refers to the exhibition he was holding, and also indicates the interesting literary society in and about the Garrick, of which he was a highly popular member :—

Feb. 1857.

Thackeray is flourishing. Forbes is very funny about him. He told him the other night at the Garrick that as he was making such a pot of money with his four Georges, he had better go on with the eight Henrys, and then the sixteen Gregorys; by which time the public would be so exhausted that he had better wind up with the *One John*—and that (as Jerrold said) a *cheap* one! Nothing has delighted me so much for a long time as that story of "Amos Barton" in the Magazine. The death of that sweet Milly made me blubber like a boy. I did not think, at forty, I had so many tears left in me; and was really glad to find, after my somewhat worn-out London life, I could still be so moved. You will be pleased to hear there is but one opinion about its excellence. Thack.'s eyes sparkled through his spectacles as he spoke of it yesterday.

All this time rumours were rife as to the authorship of the 'Scenes of Clerical Life.' The power of investing her characters with lifelike qualities has often been discussed, and in the early days before her identity was known, the most amusing speculations (quite apart from the Liggins imposture) were formed about her. On one occasion Mr Lewes writes :—

G. H. Lewes to John Blackwood.

George Eliot was both greatly amused and greatly gratified by the cabinetmaker's verdict: Having already been a clergyman of Puseyite tendencies and large family, he is now a carpenter, and doubtless will soon be a farmer and Methodist. It is a great compliment when a writer's dramatic presentation is accepted as actual experience.

Charles Dickens was one of those who was decidedly of opinion that the 'Scenes of Clerical Life' were written by a woman.

Charles Dickens to John Blackwood.

TAVISTOCK HOUSE, LONDON, W.C.,
27th January 1858.

MY DEAR SIR,—I have been very much interested by your extract from "Mr Eliot's" letter, which has given me the greatest pleasure. Also of your account of the manner in which you had the good fortune to find (I say nothing of the good sense immediately to appreciate) that admirable and charming writer.

The portions of the narrative to which you refer had not escaped my notice But their weight is very light in *my* scale, against all the references to children, and against such marvels of description as Mrs Barton sitting up in bed to mend the children's clothes. The selfish young fellow with the heart disease, in "Mr Gilfil's Love-Story," is plainly taken from a woman's point of view. Indeed I observe all the women in the book are more alive than the men, and more informed from within. As to Janet, in the last tale, I know nothing in literature done by a man like the frequent references to her grand form, and her eyes and her height and so forth; whereas I do know innumerable things of that kind in books of imagination by women. And I have not the faintest doubt that a woman described her being shut out into the street by her husband, and conceived and executed the whole idea of her following of that clergyman. If I be wrong in this, then I protest that a woman's mind has got into some man's body by a mistake that ought immediately to be corrected. I feel truly obliged to you and Mrs Blackwood for your friendly invitation; but as I do not expect to remain in Edinburgh more than one complete day, I am declining hospitalities on all hands, and have no alternative but to do the like in this case, as in a hundred others, against my will.—Faithfully yours,

CHARLES DICKENS.

Whatever may have really been John Blackwood's private opinion by this time as to the identity of George Eliot, one cannot but feel grateful for the arguments he must have used to have drawn forth so interesting and whole - hearted a statement of Dickens's views as to the sex of the writer of the 'Scenes.' The instances from which his deductions were drawn seem to us sufficiently striking and convincing; but in those days when every one else believed the writer to be a man, the acuteness of his observation stamps Dickens at once as the experienced student of human nature, even if he had never written another line in his life.

My father was then himself on the verge of discovery, having for some time, as he states in a letter, surmised correctly. On his next visit to town, a few weeks later, he was introduced to George Eliot.

John Blackwood to his Wife.

87 JERMYN STREET, *March* 1, 1858.

From him [Lord St Leonards] I drove to Richmond to see Lewes, and was introduced to George Eliot — a woman (the Mrs Lewes whom we suspected). This is to be kept a profound secret, and on all accounts it is desirable, as you will readily imagine. She is a most intelligent pleasant woman, with a face like a man, but a good expression. I am not to tell Langford the secret even. . . . Lewes says he would do ten times the work for me that he would do for any other man, and he does not think any other editor in the world would have been able to induce George Eliot to go on. It was very flattering, as his experience of editors is very great, and he is a monstrous clever fellow.

Thus the memorable first interview with George Eliot had taken place, and the secret of the authorship was now known to him. First impressions are generally lasting, and the kindly and generous enthusiasm he from the first entertained for his new contributor was only strengthened on closer acquaintance, and grew into the steady friendship which lasted all his life.

In the autumn of 1858 there is the frequent mention of a new novel by George Eliot. This was 'Adam Bede'—certainly the most interesting and lifelike of all her stories, and the one of which she herself says in her journal "Shall I ever write another book as true as 'Adam Bede'?" The doubts and diffidence alluded to by Mr Lewes still continued while writing it, in spite of the steady encouragement and helpful praise which Blackwood bestowed on the story in no stinted measure, as will be seen from his letters to the author. The interest of the narrative grew and grew, and the vivid presentment of the characters seemed to take possession of both author and publisher, and they wrote to each other of the creatures of her brain as though they were living personages.

John Blackwood to George Eliot.

St Andrews, *Oct* 4, 1858.

The story is a very striking one, and I cannot recollect anything at all of the same kind. I long to see how you will work it out. You may be sure that I shall sit down to the third volume as soon as I get the MS., and you shall have no cause for impatience to hear from me.

Hetty is a wonderful piece of painting. One seems to *see* the little villain. She is painted in such irresistible colours that I am very sorry for the well-intentioned Arthur. One feels that there is no chance of escape for any youth of his age unless he takes to his heels. I have thought a great deal over the encounter between Adam and Arthur,—indeed I daresay it is pondering over that scene which has prevented me from sooner sitting down to write to you. The picture of Adam's feelings before he gets the fatal glimpse in the wood is perfection. The point is worked up to with wonderful skill. It is very difficult to imagine what would happen between any two men brought so suddenly into such a total revulsion of feelings and change of relative positions as happens to Adam and Arthur, but on the whole I think you have hit the mark and sustained in a very trying climax the characters of the two men you are drawing. I am ashamed of myself for not feeling more sorry for Adam, but I have no doubt the sympathies will gather round him keenly when the full force of his affection comes upon him, and the tender and stern fibres in his heart of oak fairly begin to struggle. Mrs Poyser is excellent, as also her husband and the children, or rather child. I am puzzled as to what the wicked old Squire is up to. There can be no doubt that the book will be successful, but the degree of success will depend very much upon the third volume.

After reading the MS. of the third volume, he writes :—

John Blackwood to George Eliot.

EDINBURGH, *Nov.* 3, 1858.

After writing to you on Saturday I fastened upon the 3rd vol. of 'Adam Bede,' and read the whole of the MS. that afternoon. I am happy to tell you that I think it capital I never saw such wonderful effects worked out by such a succession of simple and yet delicate and minute touches. Hetty's night in the fields is marvellous. I positively shuddered for her, poor creature, and I do not think the most thoughtless lad could read that terrible picture of her feelings and hopeless sufferings without being deeply moved. Adam going to support her at the trial is a noble touch. You really make him a gentleman by that act. It is like giving him his spurs.

The laudatory opinions expressed in the foregoing letters were soon to be endorsed by the public, with whom 'Adam Bede' so speedily became a favourite that the popularity of the book appears to have been attained by leaps and bounds. By March 7th John Blackwood was writing to the author, "We may now consider the 'Bedesman' fairly round the corner, and coming in a winner at a slapping pace." A few days later they were preparing a second edition, and he was able to tell her she was a "popular" as well as a "great" author. Letters and congratulations poured in on all sides to the publishers for the unknown author, many of them from quarters where praise was praise indeed: Froude, the Carlyles, Dickens, Professor Owen, Dr John Brown, and others.

John Blackwood to George Eliot.

Your triumph is a great one, and I do heartily rejoice in it. The sale is nothing to the ring of applause I hear in all directions. The only qualm that ever came across me as to the success of the book was that really to enjoy it I required to give my mind to it, and I trembled for that large section of hard readers who have little or no mind to give, but now I think the general applause is enlisting even noodles.

When the time came for her to reap the well-deserved fruits of her work, the success of 'Adam' had been so much greater than was anticipated that the publishers proposed to give an additional £400. She wrote thus:—

George Eliot to John Blackwood.

May 21, 1859.

MY DEAR SIR,—I thank you: first, for acting with that fine integrity which makes part of my faith in you; secondly, for the material sign of that integrity. I don't know which of those two things I care for most—that people should act nobly towards me, or that I should get honest money. I certainly care a great deal for the money, as I suppose all anxious minds do that love independence and have been brought up to think debt and begging the two deepest dishonours short of crime. I look forward with quite eager expectation to seeing you—we have so much to say. Pray give us the first day at your command. The excursion, as you may imagine, is not ardently longed for in this weather, but when "merry May" is quite gone, we may surely hope for some sunshine; and then I have a pet project of rambling along by the banks of a river, not without artistic as well as hygienic purposes.

The following is the acknowledgment of her letter:—

John Blackwood to George Eliot.

SPONDON, DERBYSHIRE, *May* 25, 1859.

MY DEAR GEORGE ELIOT,—Your letter reached me safely here. In looking back upon 'Adam Bede,' one of our greatest pleasures will always be the thought that its success afforded us so legitimate a means of showing our sense of its value and of gratifying your feelings. . . .

We have lovely weather here, but still no rain. This place realises Miss Austen's pictures of an English village, and would have afforded rich materials to her or to George Eliot. As I hope to see you so soon, no more at present from yours most sincerely,   JOHN BLACKWOOD.

GEORGE ELIOT, Esq.

In writing to the Rev. Lucas Collins he gives his views on the weak and strong points of the book :—

None of the reviewers have observed what seems to me a very main feature in the book, the stern virtue with which the author has refrained from raising sympathy with the attractive Hetty. I have never read a book which was more calculated to make a young fellow mind what he was about in rustic or other flirtations. Mrs Poyser, or Mrs Poser as Mrs Blackwood calls her, is an immense favourite of mine, absolutely first-rate I think. The plot is very simple—certainly not first-rate, but there is wondrous power in the first half of the third volume. I recollect on first reading the account of Hetty's night journey in the fields I could hardly resist jumping off my seat as it were to go and save the poor creature, so vividly real is the picture. The whole of this part of the book affected me powerfully.

In the following letter the Editor touches upon an incident about which he often used to laugh as his solitary experience in the "fancy" line. George Eliot having expressed a wish to become the possessor of a pug, my father had commissioned Mr Langford to buy one for her, and Mr Langford, anxious to do his best, but to shirk all responsibility, applied to our cousin, Colonel Steuart, to find one. This was a labour after the Colonel's own heart, who having visited the haunts of all the well-known dog-fanciers in London, ultimately secured a tiny pug puppy for the modest sum of thirty pounds !

John Blackwood to Mr J. Langford.

I am quite unable to suggest what ought to be done with the invaluable pug. I think the Colonel must manage it himself until George Eliot returns. I think the seller of the bargain ought to keep it at his own risk. . . . Give my regards to him [Colonel Steuart], and tell him the Major and Jim are shouting with laughter at the idea of the thirty-pounder. 'Adam Bede' flourishes, so I grins and bears it!

The novel of 'Adam Bede' was hardly off her hands when George Eliot turned to another work of fiction, and in the spring of 1859 we find Mr Lewes writing about the 'Mill on the Floss,' of which he was shortly to send an instalment. Mr Lewes as usual wrote confidently, the author anxiously, and both eager to hear the Editor's verdict. In June 1859 he wrote to George Eliot he was "perfectly delighted with the opening of the new story," and wished it to appear in the Magazine,—there it would appear entirely on its own merits, which he thought quite strong enough to carry it through without the "magic name of George Eliot," which could not be affixed there where all writers were anonymous. However, the idea was eventually abandoned, and it appeared in book form in the following year. In February 1860 Mr Lewes writes of the 'Mill':—

G. H. Lewes to John Blackwood.

The first proofs read delightfully tempting, I think, and Mrs Lewes, strengthened and encouraged by your letter, thinks so too. There never *was* so diffident and despondent an author since the craft first began! By the way, you ought to know who *was* the first author? and who reviewed him? and what did his copyrights fetch?

Mr Lewes's Christmas greeting was written in

boisterous spirits over the 'Mill,' of which they had not quite settled if the title should be the name of the heroine " Maggie."

MY DEAR BLACKWOOD,—A dismal Christmas and a miserable New Year to you. May 'Maga' perish, and "Maggie" *not* repay perusal. *Voilà.*

The success of the 'Mill on the Floss' appears to have been as great as 'Adam Bede,' and more speedy. George Eliot mentions in her journal, 1st July, that it appeared on 4th April, when the subscription for it was 3600 (the number originally printed was 4000), and this in the old 3-volume form at 31s. 6d., and that Mudie having demanded another 1000, 2000 more were printed, and these had all disappeared by the time she was writing—little more than two months after the publication of the book.

John Blackwood to G. H. Lewes.

April 4, 1860.

I have a long critical letter from Bulwer. He objects to many things, but his admiration for Mrs Lewes's genius is as clear and genuine as could be wished, and he places the 'Mill' above 'Adam.' As you do not wish any criticisms while abroad I do not send you the letter; besides it is very bulky, being written on very thick paper and in his widest hand. There has been no review in the 'Times' yet. I hope this will find you both well, and continuing to enjoy Rome. I have not much news from London. The fight for the championship monopolises every one's attention. It is quite comical, and I cannot help feeling as keen as possible about gallant little Tom Sayers with his one arm maintaining such a fight. I am satisfied that if he had not lost the use of his right arm he would have polished off the giant. I never saw a prize-fight, and I daresay five minutes' conversation with the worthy Tom would effectually cool my enthusiasm.

The popularity of George Eliot's novels was now a well-established fact. The "hard readers," as my father described them, being enlisted on her side as well as the connoisseurs, the announcement of a new novel by her sent them off *en masse* to procure it, causing a stir and hum of expectation extending to circles far beyond what is known as the literary world. The fascination that her writings had for such a large class of readers surprised herself and those most nearly concerned in the production of her books, for be it remembered she did not write up any of the popular fads of the day nor truckle to any fashionable prejudice, and she employed only familiar materials. But readers began to find how interesting ordinary everyday matters might be when seen through her keen mental vision, which knew how to reveal the possibilities for a drama which cling to many a human existence apparently shrouded in the mere details of workaday life. The problems of life, the analysis of motives, the part played by conscience or that inner consciousness which each carries about with him, and which neglected becomes a Nemesis more terrible and far-reaching in its punishment than any other which tradition has invented for us—all these formed elements of fascinating interest, and the novel-readers took to the new food so kindly as almost to constitute George Eliot a sort of cult. This tendency, which can be traced in her earlier novels, became more pronounced and formed the main characteristic of her later works, up to which she may be said to have been training her readers.

'Silas Marner' quickly followed 'The Mill on the Floss,' and with it ended this particular style of novel, descriptive of village life in the homely Midlands of England, by which she first won her laurels and attracted the ear of perhaps the most faithful audience that ever sweetened the toil of an author by its sure and ready welcome of the fruits of his labour. 'Silas Marner' appeared the year after the 'Mill on the Floss,' and, as has been stated, closed the series. It presented many of the same characteristics as its predecessors, with perhaps a less attractive personnel, though those who cared to go beyond the surface could find the old charm at work.

John Blackwood to George Eliot.

Feb. 1861.

I have read the MS. you have sent of 'Silas Marner' with the greatest admiration. The first hundred pages are very sad, almost oppressive, but relieved by the most exquisite touches of nature and natural feelings. . . . I wish the picture had been a more cheery one, and embraced higher specimens of humanity, but you paint so naturally that in your hands the veriest earthworms become most interesting—perfect studies, in fact. The child found on the hearth replacing the poor weaver's lost treasure is a beautiful idea, and is, I hope, to be the medium of restoring the unfortunate Silas to a more Christian frame of mind. How perfectly you paint the poor creature quite at sea when his simple faith was cut from under his feet.

Then later he writes on the same subject of the pathetic association of the old man and the child and his attempts at discipline :—

Silas's attempt to inflict punishment and the "toad-hole" quite affected me, as I had a somewhat similar incident this very morning at breakfast. The children were making too much noise (a very trying thing at that time), and I shouted "Silence, or you go out of the room," in a voice that might have struck terror into a giant, when the smallest offender replied, "Naughty old Reekie" (my nickname). . . . I was in hopes you were going to introduce a clergyman to the help of Mrs Winthrop, and that we should have another picture of character, but I suppose you had not a good one at hand, as *sometimes* happens in this life.

G. H. Lewes to John Blackwood.

6th March 1861.

MY DEAR BLACKWOOD,—We were very pleased to hear your opinion of 'Silas.' In spite of my delight in the book I cannot help *occasionally* being made anxious by her persistent depreciation of what she writes. It is in vain that I remember how she always has felt so about her writing—in vain that I recall how pleased I have been on hearing it read aloud—a sort of doubt will overpower me; and when you come to my aid I rally again.—Ever yours faithfully, G. H. LEWES.

Hug that young rebel for me who answered you so appropriately.

Writing from his summer quarters in Fife to George Eliot, Blackwood alludes to the African traveller Captain Speke, who had been visiting him for the first time. He had taken the strongest possible liking to the manly soldier, who, with the simplicity of a child in all worldly matters, possessed the determination and courage which were to carry him triumphantly through all difficulties, leaving him hero of the exploit with which his name was ever afterwards associated as discoverer of the source of the Nile. He started from Gibleston with the good wishes of all the party, whose sympathies were warmly enlisted in his enterprise. This was the expedition undertaken with Captain Grant for his companion.

John Blackwood to George Eliot.

GIBLESTON, FIFE, *August* 15, 1859.

We have had a very interesting visitor, Captain Speke, lately from the Mountains of the Moon, and what he believes to be, I think with good grounds, the fountains of the Nile. He is a fine, manly, unaffected specimen of an Englishman. He is very innocent of literature, having since he went to India at 17 been devoted to wild sports and geographical discovery. He has gone through dangers and suffering enough to disgust any ordinary man with the mere thoughts of Africa, but he is determined to go back and carry out his discovery, and has got a grant for the purpose. His reply to my remonstrance against his going again was unanswerable—" Fancy my disgust if any vapouring, boasting Frenchman went and got the credit of this discovery for France."

The Leweses, as will be seen, were interested in all that concerned their friends : their children, their dogs, their daily pursuits, all come under the notice of Mr Lewes's lively pen—he was generally the scribe in those days. The following alludes to the life at Gibleston, the house already mentioned, in the part of Fife known as the East Neuk, where John Blackwood spent two summers :—

G. H. Lewes to John Blackwood.

Your picture of your daily life is suggestive of pleasant hours; but I see you don't turn the dogs to account. Four dogs! my dear fellow, how *can* four dogs be without attraction ? I would rather hear Mrs Blackwood's opinion on that point, not believing in your ability to edit a dog. Perhaps the dull dogs have wearied you with too many contributions to make you appreciate justly the genus dog. When you have seen Pug your mind will be more expanded, your sensibilities heightened.—Till then, believe me, ever your canine,

G. H. LEWES.

Their second summer (1860) there was an anxious
one, owing to the continued illness of Major William
Blackwood.   All through the long summer days John
Blackwood seems to have been going backwards and
forwards from Gibleston to Edinburgh, unable to leave
his brother, "who," he says in one of his letters, September 1, "is vexed at my remaining; but I think he
is glad of it, and I am sure it is a help to him."   In
the same letter he alludes to the departure of one of
his nephews, Charlie Blackwood, who was to join his
regiment in India, and parting with whom was a
terrible wrench to his sick father.   In the spring of
1861, just before Easter, Major William Blackwood's
long illness terminated fatally, and John had to mourn
the loss not only of a brother to whom he was deeply
attached, but also of one who, for the last thirteen
years of his life, had been his associate in business,
and the want of whose companionship was a sad
blank to him.

CHAPTER III.

EDINBURGH AND LONDON.

JOHN BLACKWOOD ASSUMES HIS NEPHEW WILLIAM AS A PARTNER—TENNY-
SON AND HIS CRITICS—SIR RICHARD BURTON—WRITERS OF TRAVEL CON-
NECTED WITH THE HOUSE—THE EDITOR'S LIFE IN LONDON—MEETINGS
WITH THACKERAY, GEORGE ELIOT, AND HAMLEY — THREE LITERARY
BROTHERS—REV. W. LUCAS COLLINS—A VISIT TO OXFORD—MRS OLIPHANT
—DAVID WINGATE, THE COLLIER POET—THE 'CHRONICLES OF CARLING-
FORD'—THE COUNT DE MONTALEMBERT'S VISIT—THE LATER WORKS OF
BULWER LYTTON—ANONYMOUS PUBLICATION OF 'THE COMING RACE'
AND 'PARISIANS' — 'ROMOLA' — DISASTROUS RESULT OF EDITORIAL
CIVILITY.

By the death of his brother, Major Blackwood, John
was once more left alone in the conduct of the
business, which by this time, as has been shown, by
the accession of well known and popular writers and
by his skill and management, he had enormously increased, and was increasing daily. His work was,
however, to be lightened and his loneliness cheered
by the assistance and companionship of his nephew
William, Major Blackwood's eldest son, who at the
time of his father's death was a young man of six-
and-twenty, and had been engaged for several years
in the business which was to be the profession of his
life. He then passed into the place his father had
filled so successfully, and henceforth the Editor's

letters and confidences are directed to his nephew,
and the frequent allusions to "the Major," with
which readers of the second volume of this book
have become familiar, drop out of sight, and their
place in the Editor's correspondence is now taken by
"My nephew," or "Willie" as he familiarly termed
him, and his name appears in the letters with the
frequency which betokens the important position he
now held, and the loving trust that was reposed in
him. In the following year his Uncle John made
him a partner, which is notified in a letter to Mrs
Oliphant.

John Blackwood to Mrs Oliphant.

May 1862.

Address your proof to Willie, here. I have made him a
partner in the old House this week, and hope he will keep the
colours flying when his aged Uncle has grown unfit for work.

John Blackwood was at that time forty-three years
of age, and in the heyday of his strength, and was
beginning to taste a measure of that success which the
toilsome years had brought him. Writing to Dean
Hook in the summer of 1861, he alludes to the circumstances which had placed him sixteen years ago in the
position of editor, and of the further loss he had now
sustained in the death of another beloved brother
and partner.

John Blackwood to Dean Hook.

STRATHTYRUM, ST ANDREWS, *July* 4, 1861.

I am extremely glad that I thought of sending a copy of the
Magazine, and that in so doing I have found an old friend of
my father. I knew that you were a relative of the author of
'Pen,' but was not aware that you were his representative. I

like the epithet " enthusiastic " which you apply to my father's
letters. He was an enthusiast in all he did, and a sanguine
and bold one, or he would not have fought his old ship ' Maga '
in the determined way he did. A hard fight he had for many
a day. You may have corresponded with my elder brothers,
who were half a generation older than me. Death has been
busy in my family. One after another my brothers have been
taken almost in their prime, until I, a sixth son, am the second
oldest left. Singularly enough my father had intended me
from boyhood to be the Editor, and my brothers, who did a
father's part by me, put me very early into the position, so
that, although an editor of sixteen years' standing, I am still
a young man.

I must tell you that you owe your review in some degree
to my wife, who had been reading your book and praising
it to me. She is an English clergyman's daughter, who dis-
likes Low and loves High Churchmen provided they are not
Puseyites. . . .

I do not agree with Tennyson and you about anonymous
criticism : of course the privilege may be, and often is, grossly
abused, but I assure you it has a better chance of being fair
than critiques with names appended could be. I do, however,
most cordially concur with you as to the intolerably impertinent
tone assumed by some critics. With every respect and admiration for Tennyson, I think he is childish about criticisms. His
adulators spoil him. Would he have people say that they
admire what they do not admire in his poetry ? Some of his
very warmest admirers, among whom I may reckon myself,
dislike some phases of his poetry, and he evidently looks upon
all such as enemies. I do not mean this as any defence of the
article in the ' Quarterly,' which was in a nasty, bad spirit, and,
as far as I recollect, unjust at the same time. . . .

I write as few letters as I can, and I would not have written
this long one to you unless yours had afforded me much
pleasure. . . . Any reference to my father goes to my heart.
Few know what a very able man he was, and *still fewer* what
a thoroughly *good one.*

Fresh names begin to creep into the correspondence

of the House, indicating the wider fields which were opening out, and the fertile sources from which John Blackwood was deriving, or about to derive, literary materials.   One line which he had latterly encouraged was that of narratives of sport and travel, both in short magazine articles and also in book form, and it is interesting to find Captain Burton (Sir Richard Burton) writing to him on this subject.   He says :—

Jan. 9, 1861.

MY DEAR BLACKWOOD,—After the long silence I take up my pen and point it to you once more.   On Jan. 1st I landed at the town of Knut the Dane, after a long trip through America, all the States, Brigham Young and the Mormons, the silver diggings and the gold diggings. . . . My object is for some months to rest, and eat my beef in the old country.   I am preparing an account of Mormonism, which, however, is an indelicate subject requiring to simmer in the mind.   Its flavour would evaporate in a decoction.   I must keep my hand in as regards Africa.

Then follows a list of various books on Africa which he proposes to boil down for magazine articles.   He then goes on to speak some words in favour of 'Harper's Magazine,' particularly that part of it which "never fails to contain a paper devoted to voyages and travels," and finishes the letter with the following : "If something of the kind be not done here, we shall soon require a 'Travellers' Magazine.'"   His suggestion may have prompted the idea of some such undertaking to my father, who went so far as to write to Mr William Smith, the author of 'Thorndale' and 'Gravenhurst,' asking him if he could edit a sort of Cyclopædia of Travel to appear in monthly parts at a popular price—the design being to make the public

acquainted with the expeditions and discoveries that
were being carried forward every day, and which were
usually published in volumes too expensive ever to
become generally known until they had become old
history. When he wrote the idea was in the air,
and he told his correspondent to keep it strictly to
himself, as it "would be eagerly snapped up by some
of those manufacturers of books who would not do
a right thing at all." Though this scheme was never
carried out, he had a considerable number of well-
known men writing whose voyages and accounts of
foreign lands formed a very large portion of their
contribution to literature. Laurence Oliphant, Admiral Sherard Osborn, Captain Charles Hope, &c.,
all distinguished themselves in this way. In the
winter of 1861, Mr Oliphant, who had written a
work called 'The Russian Shores of the Black Sea,'
was made Secretary of Legation in Japan, and just
before he went John Blackwood wrote to him.

Jan. 1864.

MY DEAR OLIPHANT,—Although I would like you to have
got something better and remain in this country, I am glad
to hear of your appointment. It puts your foot on the ladder,
and Japan may prove a great field. Certainly you will find
materials for writing, and I hope to see you turn out a valuable book on that remarkable country.

In the same letter he refers to a book by Mr Oliphant on the Chinese Embassy, and he also refers to
a book by Commander Forbes, R.N., entitled 'The
Campaign of Garibaldi in the Two Sicilies,' just then
coming out, which he says "gives a clear, lively
picture of all that passed, and is very *readable.*"

Admiral Sherard Osborn's name also occurs in connection with Oliphant's, as he also generally wrote some interesting accounts of China and Japan when his "big ship," as my father called it, took him into those waters. Captains Speke and Grant were soon to be added to the list of travellers whose narratives were published by the House, and later Andrew Wilson of Himalayan fame.

In his letters from London we have many glimpses afforded us of the Editor's busy life, and though dinners and luncheons and afternoon calls do not sound like hard work, they were the means employed for an end; and to any one who knows the strain of London life, and the alertness required in a man in order to hold his own successfully, this will be considered by no means the least onerous part of the work. Besides, a chance introduction often led to a new vein which might prove useful from a literary point of view, and when, as on the eve of some political crisis, the different *on dits* had all to be taken into consideration, it entailed a certain amount of going about to hear what was being said before 'Maga' formulated her opinions, a stray word or conversation sometimes leading the Editor to change his intentions with regard to what he meant to say in the Magazine.

John Blackwood to his Wife.

87 JERMYN STREET, *March* 1.

Our dinner at Delane's was very pleasant. He had not been able to get any one to meet us except his sisters and brother-in-law, Campbell, and Wolff [Sir Henry Drummond Wolff], who is made private secretary to Lord Malmesbury. I do not think Delane is unfriendly to the Government, but from what he said I do not expect the Palmerston and Russell lot mean to leave us quiet if they can help it. I went to Bulwer yesterday morning; nothing, except if possible greater cordiality. . , . . In the afternoon the Major and I went to Lord St Leonards'. The old fellow seemed delighted to see us, and we are to spend a day at Boyle Farm in May. It is a lovely place, opposite Hampton Court.

To the Same.

June 4, 1861.

Yesterday I spent a pleasant afternoon with Thackeray. He carried me off bodily to see the new house he is building in Kensington Gardens. It is very nice indeed, and I have named it the Palazzo Thackeray. It was pleasant to see old Thack., as delighted as a child, showing me all over it. He wishes me to rollick down to Greenwich with him, he having declined four other invitations on the plea of illness. I was going to dine at Warren's, but he made an appointment to dine with Hamley and me at the Rag. or Greenwich, and doubtless the fun will be great.

In another letter to the same, dated June 5, he alludes to a dinner given by Thackeray at the celebrated Blue Posts, where he seemed

a sort of king, and we got a dinner and wines such as I never saw in the house before. The fun was undeniable, and in the passages between Hamley and Thack. there was much greater cordiality than formerly. Nothing amused me more than the way ―― ――[1] sucked in everything that passed, wine included, but I could not induce him to utter. In such a party he evidently felt his mission was to listen—a reticence which is the next best quality to the highest wit.

To the same, alluding to the dinner at Warren's, he says :—

At Warren's there was no one but the Bishop of Limerick,

---

[1] A valued friend, but not a literary character.

a regular old trump, who had dined with my father long ago
and met the Professor — "a night he could never forget in
his life." He had the right feeling that the Professor's conversation was something beyond that of all the men he had met.
Warren was first-rate. He gave a sermon by the Master of
the Temple; you could have thought you heard the old gentleman speaking. The Bishop almost died with laughter—he had
suffered in the morning.—Ever, my dear, yours affectionately,

JOHN BLACKWOOD.

P.S.—Thackeray has just been in and has been talking during the last page of this letter.

A few days later he writes to his wife :—

June 15.

MY DEAR JULIA,—I have just returned from a most satisfactory interview with George Eliot and Lewes. . . . They
were unfeignedly glad to see me, and I was there for nearly
three hours. She is an admirable person, and a real good one I
am sure.

In a letter to my mother he alludes to a dinner-
party he had arranged for George Eliot. He writes :—

The dinner-party yesterday was all that could be desired
excepting for your absence George Eliot was extremely delighted with the whole affair, which she caused others to enjoy
so much. The Gunner [Hamley] was at his best, which cannot
easily be beat.

In a letter to Colonel E. B. Hamley he refers to
this dinner, and also, when praising his article on
" The Disruption of the Union," reproaches him for
not making more frequent use of his pen :—

EDINBURGH, *June* 25, 1861.

MY DEAR HAMLEY,—Your paper catches me at the last
moment. I am delighted with it. You hit the nail on the
head, and hit it so hard that it will go home. You have given

voice to the opinion of all thinking men on the subject, and done it in such pointed language that all will re-echo what you say. *You must write more.* Your silence is a loss to the world in general, and to yourself, and to me in particular. I saw George Eliot the day after our dinner. She was delighted with the party, and *both* highly pleased with the Gunner. You may tell Mrs Sturgis I never saw you behave better. As Moncrieff Skene phrased it, you made the running from the start and kept it to the end. Julia got your most amusing letter this morning.

The names of Mr Russell Sturgis and his family are very frequently mentioned in the letters at this time. Mr Sturgis was the American partner in Barings' house, and he and Mrs Sturgis entertained in London and also at their country-house at Walton-on-Thames a number of the best known and most distinguished of their country-people, besides attracting by their sympathy of tastes many of our own literary and artistic celebrities around them,—the Motleys, the W. W. Storys, and many others, and, as was generally the case with John Blackwood, his friends were likewise accepted by the Sturgises. Hamley, Thackeray, and the Delanes all appear to have found at Mount Felix or Carlton House Terrace the same good fellowship extended to them, thus forming additional links in the long chain of friendships which added so much to the happiness and interests of John Blackwood's life.

There were, as has been already stated, three brothers Hamley, all soldiers, and two of them colonels, and all three contributing to the Magazine at the same time. This occasionally led to some slight confusion, and my father had often to give explanations similar to the following, written

to the Rev. Lucas Collins: "We halt a night at
York with Colonel Hamley — not *the* Hamley, but
his brother in the Engineers, and a dreadfully
clever fellow." This refers to the eldest brother,
William Hamley, who was a colonel in the Royal
Engineers, and an important contributor to the Magazine on political and literary questions, as will be
shown later, besides being the author of several
novels. The second brother, Charles Hamley, a
captain in the Royal Marines, was also a man of
distinguished attainments, author of a story called
'Wassail,' and others. He also wrote most striking
accounts of the events taking place in the Baltic,
when he was serving with the fleet, and was present
at the taking of Bomarsund in 1855. His impressions,
written when on active service, supplied the Magazine with valuable and graphic information from these
northern latitudes, just as his brother Edward had
contrived to send news from his hut before Sebastopol.
His death occurred while he was yet in the prime of
life, and ere he had attained the age when freedom
from his professional duties would have given him that
leisure which, like his brothers, he would probably
have devoted to literature, and with every promise of
success. Nothing seemed to give my father greater
pleasure than when he could have all these three
brothers writing for him at the same time, as in a
letter to Colonel Edward Hamley he says:—

Dec. 9, 1861.

I wish much to have something from you this month, as
then there will be *three Hamleys in the same No.* I hope
you like Charles's story—it is very popular with us. . . . I
delight in 'Clutterbuck' [William Hamley's novel, which was

appearing in the Magazine]. You must really hit upon some plot of a novel, or *these young dogs* will get the start of you.

A little more than a year after this was written Captain Charles Hamley was dying, and my father, in a letter to Edward, expresses his anxiety for him :—

I am most truly grieved to hear this sad news about your dear brother Charles's health. ˙ Will you give him my warm regards, and say how earnestly I pray that God may restore his health. In regard to his papers in the Magazine, I consider 'Wassail' a beautiful story, and was only deterred from reprinting it by the dulness of the times.

This story, with other miscellaneous papers, was reprinted after Captain Hamley's death, and my father refers to it with pleasure as the work of " a dear and valued ally." Edward Hamley, the youngest of the three brothers, has already been introduced in these pages, and his friendship and correspondence are closely interwoven with the interests and associations of which we are writing.

The end of the year 1861 was overshadowed, as all will remember, by the calamity of the Prince Consort's death. In those dark December days, when the whole nation was mourning for him, and sorrowing with our beloved Queen, John Blackwood writes to his friend Mr Collins asking him to write for the Magazine a notice of the lamented Prince, and the following letters express his own admiration for the character and talents of Prince Albert, and the appreciation of the loss his death was to the nation :—

John Blackwood to the Rev. W. Lucas Collins.

Dec. 20, 1861.

You will, I know, feel like all the rest of us about Prince Albert's death, and I should like much if you could do a short notice of him for the Magazine.   The Prince did his part wonderfully well, and steered his difficult course with great judgment.   It would have been unwise and unconstitutional to have given him any regal title while alive; but now he is gone, I think we all look back upon our Queen's husband as one who has been among our rulers.   The general cry all over the country last Sunday was, "God help and comfort the Queen!" and that I daresay would be the main feature of your notice.

The Prince's encouragement of literature, science, and art, and the bias which he gave to all movements in a civilising and educational direction, by which it was no doubt his far-seeing intention to meet the demands of the time, had given my father, like other thinking men, the strong impression of his wisdom, and of the importance of his large-minded views in all questions where he could give effect to them.

By this time John Blackwood had made the personal acquaintance of the Rev. W. Lucas Collins, a distinguished scholar and accomplished man of letters, who had been for several years a contributor to the Magazine.   Many letters are addressed to him at first on purely business topics, and beginning with the formal "Sir," but gradually this had merged into the more familiar mode of address, and "My dear Collins" had now become what he remained to the last, a dear friend and faithful ally.   Of Mr Collins George Eliot says, after reading a review by him of one of her books :—

George Eliot to John Blackwood.

I see well he is a man whose experience and study enable him to relish parts of my book which I should despair of seeing recognised by critics in London back drawing-rooms. He has gratified me keenly by laying his finger on passages I wrote either with very strong feeling or from intimate knowledge, but which I had prepared myself to find entirely passed over by reviewers.

When the question of University Reform was being mooted, some articles on the. subject were written for the Magazine by Mr Collins which attracted considerable attention. The letters the Editor wrote to him show the line he wished the Magazine to take. This was substantially very much the same as that taken by the University authorities in the judicious reforms which they afterwards initiated themselves, without in any way gratifying the iconoclast demands of the ultra-Radicals.

John Blackwood to the Rev. W. Lucas Collins.

Oct. 21, 1853.

I enter warmly into what you say of the Oxford magnates maintaining what they imagine to be a dignified silence. In these days every man must stand and defend himself when attacked. The ignorant impudent brute who can rant upon a platform obtains more of the ear of the public, and consequently of Government, than the parties most deeply interested in and best acquainted with any problem which is attacked by the blind fury of innovators.

To the same he writes :—

Nov 15, 1853.

I trust to your good sense and thorough knowledge of your subject. It will be the greatest possible benefit for Oxford if her friends will really set to work to carry out moderate .reforms. In no other way can the efforts of her enemies to upset the whole concern be turned aside. The Tutors will, I think, be up against you, but it has always struck me that the tutorial system has grown to such a pitch as literally to supplant the University proper. Your remarks upon the reading-parties are, I think, excellent. Many a laugh have I had in the West Highlands on seeing these lads with their bottles of pickles, &c., imagining that there was some peculiar virtue for study in the keen air and tough mutton of the district.

To the same he again writes :—

April 25, 1854.

I like the tone of the article very much, and I think all the younger class of Oxonians will be pleased with it. As for pleasing the more stiff-necked old sticklers for forms and precedents, it is barely possible, and certainly not desirable, to please them. It seems to me that on the whole the University have behaved exceedingly well, no considerable section having run its head distinctly against all modification of old forms and customs. This part of the case is very neatly explained in your paper, and I have no doubt that the discretion of the Oxford authorities has greatly disappointed the Radical reformers, who wished to raise a howl against the University system altogether.

On the occasion of the Editor's second visit to Oxford some years after these letters had appeared, he was the guest at All Souls of Mr W. B. Skene, brother of his late friend Moncrieff Skene. This visit to Oxford helped, if anything were needed, to strengthen his belief in its time - honoured institutions; and he quite yielded to the charm which is at its height when " the green appears above the grey " in leafy June.

John Blackwood to his Wife.

ALL SOULS COLLEGE, OXFORD, *June* 16, 1867.

MY DEAR JULIA,—We got here all right, and the place is looking very pretty. I am quartered in the College, and a quaint picturesque old barrack it is, and very comfortable. Of all people in the world, Bishop Wordsworth read the lessons at All Souls chapel this morning, the sole audience consisting of Willy Skene, the only other fellows in College like myself having slunk to bed. Prayers were at a quarter to nine. I am glad to hear Puck is reading. This change will send me back to London quite fresh.

In another letter to the same he describes a dinner at All Souls :—

We were a party of seven at dinner, with the Warden [Leighton] at the head of the table, a perfect picture of an old don —suavity to a degree and dignity beyond measure, but extremely nice. . . . We dined in a great hall, and when thanks had been returned the Warden graciously led the way to a smaller apartment—oak panels and ceiling, with a fire blazing, lots of wax candles, and all the elements for drinking. The bottle passed nimbly to and fro, and if the pious founder could have looked down upon the scene it would have done his heart good. . . . Jowett caught hold of me as I was coming out of church and invited Skene and me to visit him at Merton, where he and another professor gave intellectual receptions on Sunday night, so we went there about eleven. There were ladies, but it was rather slow work, and we did not stay very late.

His taste for " swarrees " had evidently not improved since the old boyish days at Rome, when he denounced them so unsparingly. His friends General Hamley and Mr Sturgis were also in Oxford on this occasion, the latter with a son at Christ Church with whom they lunched—" a regular Mount Felix luncheon, his father smiling radiantly, and Harry commenting upon the hardships of student life. Afterwards we took Sturgis over All Souls : he was like to go into fits at the system and comfort of the place." After this visit the Editor vowed to his entertainers that if ever any sacrilegious hand should be raised against one of the time-honoured Oxford institutions, the thunders of 'Maga' should be immediately directed against the vandal.

Mrs Oliphant's name had been for some years flitting constantly through the letters—at first only in connection with literary matters, and then again in frequent and familiar allusions to home and family, as the ever-increasing friendship of years drew her more closely into our home circle and interests. Her early introduction to him, and her first novel, 'Katie Stewart,' have been already described very fully by herself in the second volume, and in her own happiest and most graceful fashion.

John Blackwood to the Rev. W. Lucas Collins.

Jan. 17, 1862.

The verses are by Mrs Oliphant, who has written a good many novels, and is a wonderfully clever (little) woman, as you will suppose when I tell you that she writes the Carlingford Series, as also the papers on Pugin and Turner.

The next paragraph in the letter refers to David Wingate, the collier poet, who interested him greatly, and for whom he predicted a considerable success.

I think I estimate David Wingate more highly than you do; but this may be that he is to me such an astounding contrast to the bards, especially humble ones, under whom I have suffered all my life; or it may be that, knowing him to be a collier, you unconsciously make more allowance for him in your estimate of him, for that fact than he at all requires. This is stupidly expressed, but it means that possibly you think more of your admiration arises from the fact of his being a collier than is really the case. I do not think his being a collier should make me read and re-read these poems with the greatest pleasure.—Always yours truly,

JOHN BLACKWOOD.

We are in sad distress owing to the sudden death of our dear friend James White, of whom you have heard me say so much. Poor Mrs White had only a few hours' warning of danger when all was over. . . . His daughter, poor thing, is summoned back from Florence, where she was on her bridal tour, and his son is in India. We were like one family together, and it will be a fearful blank for many a day.

The poems of David Wingate had a certain measure of success, but nothing like what Blackwood anticipated, nor what he thought their merits deserved, and the disappointment to the author was felt very keenly by the publisher, who had the strongest wish to help the collier-poet and bring him to light in every sense of the word, for he grudged to think of him toiling underground when his tastes and talents fitted him to soar aloft. He often alludes to the uncomplaining way in which Wingate bore the ups and downs of fortune. One day we find him spending the afternoon in the Editor's sanctum with him and Lord Neaves correcting his proofs for him, they working with the utmost goodwill, and he showing a patience and good sense as rare as it was admirable. The next we hear of him is back again working in the pit. My father writes of him :—

He sat with me for a day and a half correcting his proofs, and you know what a touchstone that is to a man's character. It is a tiresome task in general, as I can tell from many a weary day's experience; but the taste and good feeling this poor fellow showed in assenting to or repelling objections were so pleasing that I enjoyed the ten hours' sederunt. The fertile resource he showed was perfectly wonderful. Lord Neaves, who came in during our sitting, was equally taken with him.

In the same letter, in which he was recommending

Wingate for some post as an inspector or overseer of mines, he adds, "David is really a gentleman in his feelings, and will do his friends credit."

Wingate refers to his experience of correcting proof-sheets when congratulating his friend the Editor on taking a holiday.

David Wingate to John Blackwood.

MOTHERWELL, *May* 11, 1862.

I am just going to the doctor, and will tell him how you are engaged. I trust no human ailment will come near Strathtyrum while you remain there, and that Mrs Blackwood will enjoy her garden as much as you do your golf. I can well understand how you require such relaxation if the prostration I endured after my two days' "correcting" be a sample of the result of that sort of labour.

We cannot refrain from quoting a few sentences from some of the letters of this son of the soil, who, if he did not attain the distinction that was expected of him, justified by his character the opinions formed of him by Blackwood. He knew the liking the Editor had for him, and his honest independence made him fear that the money he received was not entirely the result of his own writings. He says: "If I could be sure the money promised to me is not a gift pure and simple, it might alter my thoughts a little; but I can't at all be easy under the thought that you should be a loser by me." When he returned to the mines, where he used to work at night in order to enable him to attend the School of Mining at Glasgow for a few hours during the day, he writes in a manly and patient style, which to his correspondents was more pathetic than any amount of self-pity.

David Wingate to William Blackwood.

WINDMILLHILL, MOTHERWELL, *April* 28, 1862.

If to toil on the upper world is not for me, I can relinquish it as I have done many another dream equally sweet, and to remain as I am is no descent. Your uncle's kindness has done me much good already, and if Fortune, with her customary fickleness, should cease to smile now, I am still a winner.— Gratefully yours,   DAVID WINGATE.

With one more extract we must leave the collier-poet :—

David Wingate to John Blackwood.

SCHOOL OF MINES, GEORGE ST., GLASGOW,
Nov. 19, 1862.

I have long ago despaired of finding language to express to you how grateful for your many kindnesses I am, and will make no further attempt now. For the hard labour of the pit, you will readily believe, I have no great love: I am also sure that I go back to it without a great grumble. . . . I trust I have wisdom enough to know that the pit is no worse for me than other men, and that the difference of working where the surface of the earth once was, and where it now is, is not so very great after all.

One feels inclined to say, "Bravo, David!" to this, and also to the postscript, in which he says of the poem his friend had this time been obliged to decline for 'Maga,' that he will send it to Dr Macleod for 'Good Words'!

We must now return to the 'Chronicles of Carlingford,' which have been constantly alluded to as appearing in the Magazine. By many readers the series was thought to be by the author of the 'Scenes.' They were represented at this time (1862) by "Salem Chapel"—which John Blackwood always referred to with pleasure as one of Mrs Oliphant's cleverest novels. In a letter to her at the time she was writing it, when he was particularly anxious, and by no means sure of its success, he expresses his satisfaction at the difficulties being overcome :—

MY DEAR MRS OLIPHANT,—Bravo! This part of "Salem" is splendid. You are winning the race. The minister's mother is matchless. I am delighted, glad upon my own account, but infinitely more so upon yours, as it is of incalculable importance to you. A relay of compositors are passing the Queen's birthday in setting it, and proofs will go to you by this post or the later one. A proof is essential, as no printer could set such MS. correctly. I do not believe any man alive could have read it at the pace I did, and I could not have done it had I not been desperately anxious—keen as if I had been playing a pitched match at golf, and no human emotions can rise higher than that. Collins has, as I expected, done a capital review of 'Irving.' He is charmed with the book. Address your proof to Willie here.

A name of some interest occurs in the letters about this time—that of Count de Montalembert, whose book, the 'Monks of the West,' was being translated by Mrs Oliphant. This was no slight undertaking, and after many letters the Count was finally persuaded to come to Scotland, and to visit John Blackwood at Strathtyrum. This visit was also to include some historical researches and inquiries into early ecclesiastical architecture, and my father, referring to this, writes to the Count: "We live in a famous district for you, and a very pretty old place about a mile from St Andrews, where the ecclesiastical ruins and records are most interesting, and there is an excellent library, very rich, I fancy, in the literature you care most about." It was evidently a branch of literature

into which the Editor himself had not plunged very
deeply, judging from the urgent messages he wrote to
his nephew William Blackwood to bring over every
sort of history and handbook of Fife he could lay his
hands on, so that they might not be found unprepared
by their learned visitor. A hurried note was dashed
off to William when the Count was supposed to be
nearing Edinburgh. "If he turns up to-morrow,
bring him and Lord Dunraven over. . . . We have
no history of St Andrews here." But he adds, "Go
to Randolph Crescent and take out of the library
there Lyon's 'History of St Andrews,' two or three
handbooks, and bring them over 'unbeknownst' to
the Monachist;" and he goes on to confess, for "deuce
a thing do I remember about the place except what
everybody else does." But this was not all,—he was
to bring also the 'Statistical Account of Fife' and
Chalmers's 'History of Dunfermline.' Thus equipped,
no doubt he felt prepared for any emergency.
Whether the Count ever caught him tripping we
do not know, but the visit passed off very pleasantly,
and in a letter to Mrs Oliphant, written afterwards,
allusions are made to the Count's delightful conversation, the charm and urbanity of his manners,
which, his host adds, would have been "perfectly
invaluable to him as an editor!"

Some allusion has been made to another novel
which George Eliot was writing, and of which she
described the scenes and characters as Florentine, of
the middle ages. The following is the interesting
account the author gave of how she heard her characters speaking, and her fine definition of the relative
value of realism and imagination in art :—

John Blackwood to his Wife.

June 13, 1861.

Her great difficulty seems to be that she, as she describes it, hears her characters talking, and there is a weight upon her mind as if Savonarola and friends ought to be speaking Italian instead of English. Her description of how she realised her characters was very marvellous. I never heard anything so good as her distinction between what is called the real and the imaginative. It amounted to this, That you could not have the former without the latter and greater quality. Any real observation of life and character must be limited, and the imagination must fill in and give life to the picture. ' Silas Marner' sprang from her childish recollection of a man with a stoop and expression of face that led her to think that he was an alien from his fellows. The dialect of Lisbeth in ' Adam Bede' arose from her occasionally hearing her father when with his brothers revert to the dialect of his native district, Derbyshire. She could not tell how the feeling and knowledge came to her, but when Lisbeth was speaking she felt it was a real language which she heard. Lewes and she are going to dine with me one day at Greenwich. . . . I saw Lord Eglinton for some time this morning, and we hit it off more thoroughly than I ever did before. The theme was Lord Derby, about whom we agreed in enthusiasm to a nicety. . . . Best regards to Aytoun, whom I hope you will have to dine with you to-morrow.

The book was ' Romola,' the only one of her novels not originally published by the Blackwoods. The reasons for this are indicated in a letter from John Blackwood to the author. His terms to all his writers were fair and liberal; but he never, I believe, gave what is called a " fancy price," and when one was offered to George Eliot for ' Romola' by another firm to give *éclat* to the recently started ' Cornhill,' he did not outbid them, and his prize was apparently drifting away from him when he wrote her the following letter, which tells its own story :—

John Blackwood to George Eliot.

EDINBURGH, *May* 1862.

MY DEAR MADAM,—I am of course sorry that your new novel is not to come out under the old colours, but I am glad to hear that you have made so satisfactory an arrangement. Hearing of the wild sums that were being offered to writers of much inferior mark to you, I thought it highly probable that offers would be made to you, and I can readily imagine that you are to receive such a price as I could not make remunerative by any machinery that I could resort to. Rest assured that I feel fully satisfied of the extreme reluctance with which you would decide upon leaving your old friend for any other publishers, however great the pecuniary consideration might be, and it would destroy my pleasure in business if I knew any friend was publishing with me when he could, or thought he could, do better for himself by going elsewhere. We have had several most successful enterprises together, and much pleasant correspondence, and I hope we shall have much more.

In a few days we go to Derbyshire, where we leave the children with their aunts, and intend to move on to London about the end of next week. I hope, therefore, to see you soon, and trust I shall find you in good health and spirits, and your work progressing.—Always your truly,

JOHN BLACKWOOD.

Of the names which call to mind some of the best known traditions of the House, there is perhaps none more familiar to an older generation than that of Sir Edward Bulwer Lytton—the "Bulwer" of *their* day. The literary achievements of the earlier portion of his career have been described in the second volume, with a well-merited and discriminating tribute to his talents as a novelist. Seen from another point of view, his talents are scarcely less remarkable, and in my father's letters the allusions to his statesmanlike qualities and the admirable manner in which he discharged his public duties show him to have been a man of action as well as of thought—practical and tactful in the conduct of his own business and of public affairs. In a letter to Mr Lewes, written when some changes in the ministry were impending, my father expresses his opinions of Bulwer Lytton's abilities, of which his intimate knowledge and experience of him had given ample opportunities for judging.

Bulwer is in great force, and I do not think he cares much whether he is to be a Cabinet Minister or not. I hope he will, as I think he has one of the best heads in the House of Commons. His views are so clear and statesmanlike. Very few have any idea what a shrewd practical man he is, and how ready to consult the opinions and wishes of others.

Any one who has been a little behind the scenes in literary matters will realise at a glance the importance of this testimony—particularly the last clause of it —on the part of a publisher towards one of his most important writers. A letter from my father to his brother, Major Blackwood, still further illustrates his opinion of these characteristics, which is also indorsed by John Delane. He writes—

D. [Delane] concurred in what I have heard from every one as to the first-rate style in which Bulwer had worked his office [he was then Colonial Secretary]. In particular he had been greatly struck by a paper of instructions he had given to a friend of his [Bowen] who was going out as a Colonial Governor. It was perfectly admirable both in expressions and sense, and he had told Bowen he wished it could be published for the instruction of all Colonial Governors, also that he [Bowen] should keep it as a memorial of the man to be published after his death.

Other letters show him as an essayist, putting into tangible shape and form some of the more profound thoughts and feelings which run through his romances, and in other cases crystallising for us with the sure and certain hand of the man of the world many of the current ideas and fancies of the day.

Lord Lytton's literary activity found, as has been already stated, many and various outlets : novels, poems, dramas, and essays, all were produced by him with that ease and vigour which caused my father, when speaking of the close of his life, to say, " It was as though a powerful engine had suddenly stopped working." One of his last books, and a remarkable one, was given to the world anonymously in 1871. This was a satirical romance entitled ' The Coming Race.' As its name indicates, this book suggests a look onwards. It gives a glimpse of another world and another race than ours, but with our weaknesses glorified and our failings improved away to just that point which enables us to recognise them and enjoy the author's satire at our expense. The " New Woman" is here introduced, radiant in health and physical beauty, a head and shoulders taller than her male, and as superior to him in intellect as she is in her physical attributes, but only, alas ! to fall a victim to the first advances of the all-mastering passion, to which these magnificent maidens seem as incapable of resistance as the weakest of the old type of heroine. Lord Lytton's style is here entirely altered. The writing, which is admirable, and carries the reader easily along, is marked by his usual literary skill and finish ; but it is another style, and completely baffled the critics. The author was in great glee, and mentions with delight that some wiseacre had attributed the book to Helps. He was, while ' The Coming Race '

was going through the press, engaged upon another
and very different work. This was 'The Parisians,'
a novel treating of modern Parisian life, and the cor-
ruption of society social, commercial, and political,
which preceded the downfall of the Third Empire.
It appeared originally in the Magazine, and was to
have been published afterwards anonymously, but
Lord Lytton's death in 1873 necessitated the divulg-
ing of the secret. Its favourable reception by the
public added still further to the renown of the distinguished author. Posthumous fame also attended
the appearance of his last and one of his best novels,
'Kenelm Chillingly.' It was all written and also
revised by him, but he was debarred by death from
any participation in the renown which this delightful
story brought to him. It depicts in his best style—but
with the modern touch, which makes it acceptable to
modern readers—an English gentleman of property and
status, and endowed with all the pleasant old-world
traditions and refinements that go toward preserving
a type, that in these hurrying money-worshipping
days runs a chance of being only met with in books.
But whether met with in books or in society, it is
one that appeals strongly to our English ideal of a
" gentleman," and Lord Lytton has earned our gratitude by leaving us this presentment of the genus,
with which, as his last contribution to literature, his
name will be always identified.

Their mutual regard, and the kindness and courtesy
which characterised all their relations with each other,
made this one of the instances where my father has
said business was a pleasure. One feature of their
friendship was those visits paid to Knebworth, when

their walks and rides in the shady Hertfordshire lanes used generally to bear fruit in some fresh literary project. On one such occasion at Knebworth in 1854 my father writes to my mother :—

MY DEAR JULIA,—This place is delightful. Sir Edward drove over with me to-day to Hatfield, Lord Salisbury's place. We had some agreeable conversation about his plans, which will, I think, bear fruit some day.

There is a medium and a table-rapper in the house here —both very agreeable in their way. Sir Edward has some fancy that mesmerism will cure all his ailments, and a character comes down from London every day to throw him into the trance, but has never succeeded.

The following extracts from letters of my father to Bulwer Lytton refer to the Essays already mentioned :—

EDINBURGH, *Dec.* 12, 1861.

MY DEAR SIR EDWARD,—I have read over the Essays again with increased admiration. The title puzzles me excessively. The papers are very suggestive, but there is a sort of awkwardness in applying that quality in your title, and the word "fancies" seems to me rather light to apply to such solid food for thought. It has occurred to me, would it do to associate the name of your own old Hall with this series ? Are you not expressing yourself rather positively when you say that the clairvoyance of imagination has never deceived you in the description of a place ? When you so beautifully, and I think truly, say that you could better describe the Nile than the lake at the foot of your park, is the feeling not partly that no description of the familiar little lake could possibly please you, just in the same way as no portrait of a loved familiar face almost ever is satisfactory ? Perhaps your own description of the lake might to another seem very real indeed.

What you say of monotony of occupation as a source of happiness is extremely good, especially the introductory remarks when you refer to the quiet incidents to which we refer in afterlife. I observe the truth of this very much with my brother, who has just returned from India. . . . We will talk by the hour of little incidents or family habits which could in no way be recognised as features, if indeed we observed their occurrence and recurrence at all in our rackety young life.

Your cordial praise of this No. of the Magazine gratifies me very much. So strong was my impression of its merits that I caused the type to be kept standing ready for a second edition, and I am not going to be disappointed.

EDINBURGH, *Nov.* 12, 1862.

MY DEAR SIR EDWARD,—By book-post I send complete revise of "Motive Power" and "Essays on Works of Imagination." The reflections in "Motive Power" are admirable, and it reads like one of your novels. . . . In case of any oversight, I have had the list of essays with their Magazine length made out, and it will be copied on to the back of this note. Looking over the list, I remember each essay, and feel how very good they nearly all are, and they surely must succeed. The present state of manners and things in Paris and France is a famous subject for you, and I hope most sincerely that you will hit upon a plot and the novel take shape. From the 'Telegraph' to-day it seems pretty clear that the French Emperor wishes to intervene in America, and that our Government are hanging back. I think the fellows themselves have had enough of it, and will be secretly glad of intervention, although they will say the reverse.—Yours most sincerely, JOHN BLACKWOOD.

EDINBURGH, *March* 28, 1863.

MY DEAR SIR EDWARD,—I am sure the Essays are telling now. The following is from one of the acutest critics I know, who wrote the Pugin paper which you admired: "How delightful are Sir Edward's Essays! One seems to see his own special creation, the accomplished man of the world, not entirely worldly, a quintessence of social wisdom and experience sweetened by imagination. I don't know whether he is actually such a man himself. I suspect not so good as Morley and the others of whom these Essays seem to me a kind of embodiment over again." I shall dispel any doubts as to the perfect excellence of your character. Your allusions to your sufferings with poor authors sending you MSS. is good. Think what I suffer. I wish you would say a word for me. If my rough sentences alongside of your finished language would not knock my teeth out of my head I would put in a footnote asking for mercy. The miscreants calling themselves friends, whose lying criticisms embolden them, excite my ire to a degree. Another thing annoys me. If I write a civil note returning MS., another packet invariably arrives by return of post, and as I cannot write anything but civil notes I am constantly forced to the most discourteous silence. The "Essays on Love and New Theories" also go with this, but I have not been able to get them read with the care they deserve.

The following suggestion of my father's for an essay is a very quaint one, and contains some theories on education which might, in these days when the schoolmaster is so much abroad, be thought very dangerous :—

Would the act and necessity of concealing one's ignorance be a good subject for an essay? It requires a good deal of knowledge to do this rightly. With me the chief result of a pretty elaborate education is a lively sense of my own ignorance and a power of feeling at once when a man is speaking or writing about a subject that he does not understand, although I may be equally in the dark myself. A well-informed man in the ordinary sense is generally a frightful bore; he would not be a bad subject.

In a letter to the Hon. R. Lytton, also written just about this time, he refers to his work, and the pleasure he took in it, the latter mainly owing to the character of most of his correspondents, of whom he reckoned Mr Lytton's father, Bulwer Lytton, as a notable example. He writes :—

The old ship, I am happy to say, holds on her course satisfactorily, and the sale is going steadily up, which, in the face of all the shilling opposition, is an immense triumph, of which I feel very proud. The constantly recurring months, with their inevitable Magazine day, steal life away very rapidly, and I can hardly believe that it is now some sixteen years since I succeeded to the editorship. A most pleasant life it is, and I would not exchange it for any avocation I know ; but it would be intolerable were not the contributors gentlemen with whom business relations are a pleasure, and among these contributors I need not say how high I reckon your father.

CHAPTER IV.

A. W. KINGLAKE AND 'THE INVASION OF THE CRIMEA.'

ANOTHER interesting name begins to appear in the
correspondence of this autumn, 1862 — that of Mr
A. W. Kinglake, the historian of the Crimean War.
His introduction has been slightly alluded to in the
second volume by Mrs Oliphant, with the mention
of the sending of the first portion of the book by
Mr Kinglake's aunt, Mrs Woodford. This was not,
however, arrived at without many preliminaries,
many inquiries from my father, and many stipula-
tions on the part of the author. My father naturally wanted to know what manner of book this was
going to be that would fill two volumes. Those were
to be its dimensions at first, and even this seemed
lengthy enough; for, as my father observed, in a

letter to the author before seeing any· of the work, "knowing how rapidly interest in the Crimean War had been obliterated by succeeding events, any success this book had would entirely hinge upon its merits as a historical and literary composition." How successfully Kinglake rose to this view of the case is well known now by all who have read or who know about his history, which, though it expanded into eight volumes, sustained its interest to the end, and established the reputation of its author as one of the most able masters of composition, and perhaps, in his own line, one of the most eminent writers of our time. After some correspondence with Kinglake, we have the following :—

John Blackwood to his Nephew William Blackwood.

Sept. 13, 1862.

Kinglake's letter implies a very hesitating but very able and good fellow. As for suggestions, he is a man quite able to fight his own ship, and the chances are he only requires to be told so by some one in whom he has confidence   I shall be very glad when I get the first volume.

As soon as he had read the first volume he made up his mind as to the excellence of the work, and wrote to Mr Kinglake :—

STRATHTYRUM, *Oct.* 6, 1862.

MY DEAR SIR,—I am happy to say that I think it all firstrate.   It is delightful reading, and in all these complicated transactions back and forwards, which in ordinary hands must have been tedious, you evolve your theory of motives and acts so clearly that you not only carry the reader along with you, but make him enter into it with hearty enjoyment.   Your picture of the brothers of the Elysée will live.   It is very perfect, and realises what one had imagined of the gang of swindlers suddenly in full swing of power, such as the wildest Leicester

Square dreams had never reached. I did not know Louis
Nap. had faltered at the crisis, but you have obviously good
ground for your statement. Who had the pistol presented at
his head ? Mr Boucicault will seize hold of the incident for a
sensation drama. I have always had a regard for Nicholas,
and believed what you so clearly put, that the language of
Lord Aberdeen and the peace party deluded him into the
belief that we would not go to war with him at any price. I
see nothing to comment upon or suggest to you. The part I
sympathise least with is the description of Lord Radcliffe's
extraordinary power, and doubt his influencing Nicholas's
conduct to such an extent, but you know much better. If
Palmerston had so much to do with throwing us into the hands
of France in that unfortunate Crimean War, he has, in my
opinion, much to answer for. We have never been free agents
since. He will, however, I should think, like what you say
very much.

When he had read further, my father writes more
fully, and points out very aptly the distinction between the writing of this book and that of 'Eothen,'
which, as the only other literary composition of
Kinglake, and admirable in its own line, was scarcely,
one would have said, likely to be the forerunner of
such a book as ' The Invasion of the Crimea.'

John Blackwood to A. W. Kinglake.

Oct. 19, 1862.

It is going to be a wonderful book, and will sell enormously,
at least I think so. There is a sort of chorus in the style, which
carries one along in a way to which I hardly know a parallel.
There was a sort of dreaminess about 'Eothen' which was exactly suited to the subject; but here, with all the flow of the
language, there is a precision that makes one pause to think
and feel that one is reading history. The book will give rise to
much interpellation and much controversy, but this could not
be otherwise if the history was to be worth anything. The
scene in the drowsy Cabinet at Richmond made me shake with

laughter, and it bears the stamp of truth. The survivors will be in a great state of mind about it, and if they deny the statement, will not be believed.

In another letter to Kinglake, Blackwood alludes to a sort of preface which states the elaborate manner in which the book had been prepared and all the authorities sifted.

John Blackwood to A. W. Kinglake.

Dec. 31, 1862.

I feel it to be a true account of the way the book has been written, and is very much what I would have said if questioned on the subject had I been gifted with the power of expression. The book gives the impression throughout that you have your authorities prompt and ready at your back, in as good order as the tobacco-flavoured despatches of the Tuileries, &c., among Lord Raglan's papers. The contents read, too, most appetisingly. I am glad to hear Mr Hayward's opinion; however much one's mind may be made up about the merits of a book, it is always pleasant to hear a confirmation from a good judge who is beyond the atmosphere of excitement which those connected with the launching of a great work naturally fall into.

The reviews and the talk about the book, when the first volume appeared, which dealt mainly with the preliminaries that led to the war, were very exciting, and the presentment of "our ally" was the principal point seized upon; and no wonder, for it was a novel and daring view of Louis Napoleon and the gang that surrounded him. Blackwood writes Kinglake soon after the appearance of the first volume: "One critic asks me, Will the French Emperor bring an action? I suppose you would not care for that. It would be a *cause célèbre* with a vengeance." The 'Quarterly' had a very fierce article upon the two first volumes,

an article which my father thought seemed as though
it had been pieced together by two or three different
hands. He says of it to Kinglake :—

As far as I can make out down here [Edinburgh], the indis-
criminate fury of the 'Quarterly' is telling in your favour,
certainly doing you no · harm. In the army generally, I think
the young men support you, while the fogies are frantic. By
young men I mean men in the prime of life; but when I get
to London, which I hope to do towards the end of this month,
I shall have ready means of getting at the general feeling about
the book.

Mr Kinglake's name is often mentioned now, but
the friendly relations which were afterwards so firmly
established seemed a few months after this to have
been somewhat strained.

John Blackwood to his Wife.

4 Burlington Gardens, W., *May* 29, 1863.

I saw Kinglake to-day, and doubt if we shall ever get on; if
so, it cannot be helped. The Magazine article[1] has stuck in
his gizzard, and he says he has not read it beyond what Lady
Raglan pointed out.

This cloud, if cloud it could be called, soon passed
away from the horizon of their friendship. Meanwhile there were other interests about this time
occupying my father's attention. To his wife he
writes, being still in London :—

May 31, 1863.

I went afterwards to Mrs Speke [Captain Speke's mother].
She has had little or rather no information of Speke beyond
what has been published. She inquired most kindly after you.

---

[1] On his first volume of the 'Invasion of the Crimea,' written by Sir
Edward Hamley.

Poor old Speke has been very ill; the anxiety has sent him to his bed. Captain Grant, Speke's companion, has written to his family that they will hardly be home before the 20th June.

In the same letter he mentions having seen the Princess of Wales for the first time when at the meet of the Four-in-hands in the Park. He adds, "She is very pretty indeed."

June 2, 1863, he mentions a pleasant afternoon with Sherard Osborn, "who," he says, "was just starting on his expedition, and in great spirits, although he has no end of difficulties before him." (I imagine it to have been the eve of the second Chinese war.) Ascot, with Hamley, Aytoun, Colonel Archie Blackwood, and General Steuart, appears to have been a rare festival. General Steuart's drag was placed near the winning-post, and we hear that "Aytoun sat upon the box and enjoyed himself highly, peering through his glasses at the Prince and Princess, who were right opposite to us." (Aytoun was short-sighted and wore eye-glasses.)

John Blackwood to his Wife.

June 5, 1863.

Strathtyrum must be looking lovely: I wish I were with you instead of in this Babel. On sauntering to the window I saw a queer little figure peering about, evidently looking for the house, and lo! it was Du Chaillu. He inquired most particularly for you and his "guardian." We have been sitting roaring and laughing for the last half hour.

Still no certain news of Speke's arrival at the Geographical Society dinner, where my father was Laurence Oliphant's guest.

Sir Roderick Murchison of course was in the chair. He was very civil, and said he supposed I was waiting to see Speke.

Speke was greatly complimented, and cheers whenever his name was mentioned, at the Society's meeting afterwards; but the friendly mention of the approaching sale of our friend little Paul's gorillas, &c., to aid his new expedition, was received with laughter.

June 15—he had been staying at Mount Felix :—

The Sturgises as pleasant as usual; no end of regrets and messages about you. There were no Yankees, which was a comfort.[1] . . . Mrs Sturgis is almost as much of a Southerner and anti-Yankee as Sturgis himself. He had been most aggravated by a letter from —— ——. A most excellent good woman, he said, but oppressed with "nigger on the brain."

In several letters there are allusions to the rebuilding of the premises at 37 Paternoster Row, whereby the old buildings were much enlarged and improved, and my father talks of himself and the "careful Langford" escaping from the door under a shower of little brickbats.

John Blackwood to his Wife.

4 BURLINGTON GARDENS, *June* 17, 1863.

I dined last night with Dallas at the Garrick Club party. Thackeray, Shirley Brooks, Paget,[2] and Charles Reade. We had capital fun. To-day the Colonel drove me out to Windsor to call upon Mrs Oliphant, and we found her in great force. She had sent off MS. of 'Carlingford' to the city, so I did not get it in time to read to-day, and as the hand is so small I am sending it off to Willie to get into type at once.

It will be seen from this and similar expressions that he was his own reader, and luckily he read MS. with great facility; but it tired his eyes as he

---

[1] His feeling about the war made him out of sympathy with many of the nation.

[2] One of the Metropolitan police magistrates, and a frequent and brilliant contributor, who died in June 1898.

grew older, and when he could, as in the case of any one like Mrs Oliphant, he had it printed before trying to read it.

At last, on June 18, Captain Speke arrived in London, and was the subject of quite a demonstration of welcome on all sides. "He is torn in pieces," my father writes. And when he could get quit of London he was to come to Strathtyrum, and there quietly work at putting his notes together for a book on the subject of his discovery.

John Blackwood to his Wife.

4 BURLINGTON GARDENS, W., *June* 18, 1863.

There is no doubt about the discovery of the source of the Nile; he saw it coming in a waterfall out of the lake, and followed it down. He describes the races he met with as very agreeable creatures and excessively civil.

Speke's visit to Strathtyrum, alluded to above, was for the purpose of putting his notes and diaries together in the shape of a book, describing the discovery of the source of the Nile. The herculean task this was to the gallant traveller, who was more accustomed to handle a gun than a pen, and the labour it entailed on my father and his nephew, and the whole staff at George Street, are most quaintly described in my father's letters. The material was all there, and right good interesting matter, but how to reduce the heterogeneous mass into an intelligible narrative was a puzzle. Poor Speke was taken over to Strathtyrum, shut up in a room, and told to write his book. The room, which was always known as "Speke's room," had a balcony over the front door, and my father describes in a letter to Charles Lever that when he smelt Speke's cigar on the balcony he used to say, "There goes Speke's flag of distress," and going up would find that he had got inextricably entangled in a sentence. This, we imagine, happened very often, as in a letter to William Blackwood my father writes :—

STRATHTYRUM, *July* 24, 1863.

I have been sweating over Speke's MS. this morning, and what is to be done I know not. Will you and Simpson think of something.

And again to the same, referring to Speke's notes, he says :—

They are written in such an unintelligible way, it is impossible to say what anybody could make of them, and yet he is full of matter, and when he talks and explains, all is right. He is eager to get what he has written into type, and is working like any galley-slave.

Eventually, with the assistance of Mr John Hill Burton, the historian, who, my father says, "was a kind fellow, and took great trouble with it," the MS. was finally got into shape, and the book published the following December.

John Blackwood to Captain Speke.

It is a great pleasure to look at the book in its finished state, especially when I think of you and myself in the room at Strathtyrum sitting staring at your first corrected proof. It was enough to funk a literary Tom Sayers. If D. B. had seen it in the first instance, I think he would have fled in terror. Now the labour is over, and I hope soon to congratulate you on the public taking to the book.—Ever yours truly,

JOHN BLACKWOOD.

In a letter to Mr Delane my father states his opinion of the book and the author :—

John Blackwood to John Delane.

EDINBURGH, *Dec.* 7, 1863.

Speke has been going about the world shooting since he was seventeen years old, and his ideas of grammar are of the most original description. However, we have done nothing to his text except by questioning him, and correcting him where he was likely to prove unintelligible. So the book is entirely in his own quaint language, and a more genuine one never was published. I daresay some will complain of the repetition from day to day, but, as he said himself, it was "the patient struggle from day to day that did the work," and I do not know how the idea of this could have been conveyed except by giving his diary in his own words. To me it realises savages and savage life in a way that nothing else ever did; but I daresay I am not a fair judge, as I seem to see and hear my modest good-natured dare-devil friend in the midst of these brutes, as quiet as if he were smoking his cigar in the woods at Strathtyrum. He is a character, with a strong dash of Robinson Crusoe about him: I never met with such a mixture of simplicity and almost childish ignorance, combined with the most indefatigable energy and the most wonderful shrewdness in his own particular way. It must have been this strange mixture of character that carried him through, and gave him such power over these creatures. . . . I hope you are well.—Ever yours truly, JOHN BLACKWOOD.

John Blackwood to his Nephew William Blackwood.

Give my best regards to Dallas, and say that I do not see that geographical knowledge signifies in reviewing Speke. What are the theories of geographers worth compared with the direct evidence of the only man who has walked through the country from end to end? That is the point, and the carpet-slipper gentry may cavil as much as they like. A notice of the wonderful achievement, with a few extracts, would do. Controversy might come after.

A few weeks later, in his usual Christmas letter to Mr Langford, is chronicled sadly the death of Thackeray.

John Blackwood to Mr Joseph Langford.

Dec. 30, 1863.

Thackeray's death would be a sad blight upon your Christmas. It is a real grief to me, and indeed to all my family; "old Thack." was a constantly recurring thought and subject of conversation with us. I am desperately distressed for the girls. Poor things, he completely made companions of them, and I cannot think how they are to recover from the blow. . . . Poor fellow, how often he has talked to me about them. To London literary men Thackeray's death is a very serious loss. He was a central figure, and his tone leavened and did good to the whole body. By all good fellows it will be thoroughly felt. If you see Shirley Brooks will you give him my best regards ? I had a very pleasant note from him, and intended to have written a jocular reply to his most amusing description of the miserable (real or supposed) Hepworth Dixon cabal when this sad news came. Writing these few words about poor Thackeray has set me athinking sadly over many a past scene of happy intercourse with him, and the afternoon has slipped away. So with all good wishes of the season, believe me, yours most sincerely, JOHN BLACKWOOD.

The following is an extract from Shirley Brooks's letter referred to above, written just before Christmas, and showing how little Thackeray's friends anticipated his death :—

There is a pleasant little war about Thackeray's not being appointed a vice-president of the Shakespeare Committee, and if you put the fact that Dickens *was* made one at once, while Thackeray was only asked to be a committee-man, and mix up with the fact that Hepworth Dixon is the activest man in that business, and is also the editor of a journal that abused Elizabeth (not the 'Exiles of Siberia'), and stew over the slow fire of literary animosities, you will comprehend the flavour of that kettle of fish. Such is life. Will you give my kindest regards to Mrs Blackwood, to whom and to family I wish all the good wishes of the coming year, and believe me, ever yours faithfully, SHIRLEY BROOKS.

Writing to a contributor who had sent a paper on Thackeray for the Magazine, John Blackwood, in declining it, gives his reason and some indication of his own high appreciation of the great novelist's characteristics. He writes:—

I do not feel that it describes Thackeray, and consequently I did not like to put it into the Magazine as our portrait and tribute to his memory. I do not much care for the stories you give. He used to tell such stories in a pitying half-mocking way in which it was impossible to say how much was sincerity and how much sham. But when he dropped that vein, and spoke with real feeling of men and things that he liked, the breadth and force of his character came out, and there was no mistake about his sincerity. None of the numerous sketches I have read give to me any real picture of the man with his fun and mixture of bitterness with warm good feeling. I have stuck in this note. Writing about old " Thack." has set me thinking about him, and all the scenes we have had together. I feel so truly about him that I am frightened to give a wrong impression of him to one who did not know him.

Meanwhile Kinglake was still going on with his History very slowly but surely. At the idea of certain suggestions being submitted to him he gives his reasons against receiving them in four sheets of letter-paper,—not, as might be imagined, because he was likely to object to them, but, on the other hand, as he tactfully explained, he was afraid he might see such cogent reasons for accepting them as would set him rewriting a portion of his volume and thus lose time. He says:—

I am almost alarmed, as it were, at the notion of receiving suggestions. I feel that hints from you might be so valuable and so important it might be madness to ask you beforehand to abstain from giving me any, but I am anxious for you to know what the dangers in the way of long delay might be, the result of even a few slight and possibly most useful suggestions. . . . You will perhaps (after what I have said) think it best not to set my mind running in a new path lest I should take to re-writing.

This was a contingency enough to strike terror into the publisher, who he probably knew was already chafing at the delays entailed by his elaborate and conscientious methods of writing. Referring to the slow way he worked, he gives in a letter some interesting reasons to account for this :—

A. W. Kinglake to John Blackwood.

Jan. 14, 1865.

MY DEAR SIR,—I have been very fairly industrious, but whether from want of method or from other defects, I get on but slowly. It is not fastidiousness, I think, or love of polish which makes me slow in *this* stage of the business; for it is after getting the proof-sheets that I am most accustomed to trouble myself in that way. The story of the events subsequent to the Alma strikes me now as capable of being made more interesting—not to say surprising—than I had at first supposed it would turn out to be. But whether I can do anything like justice to it, I shall hardly know until I see it in print. · If I were to have proof-sheets at present, I should be put into a frame of mind different from that which serves for writing, and for the present therefore I abstain from sending anything to the printer; but I should be inclined to print, as soon as I have written to the end of the battle of Balaclava.

In reply to this Blackwood writes :—

I am very glad to hear from you, and to learn that you have been at work and find the events after the Alma coming out so curious and interesting. The original advertisement that your History was to be complete in four volumes does not signify at all. The more volumes the public get from you the better they will be pleased, and such announcements as yours are never considered binding—indeed people forget all about them. The length of a book cannot be estimated like a web of cloth made to order, and it would be absurd to fetter a man to an estimate before he knew how his materials would grow under his hand. A change in the length originally contemplated is a thing of daily occurrence, or would be if histories, much less histories like yours, were an everyday occurrence. The battle of Balaclava will make a fine ending for a volume.

As we have already remarked in other letters, my father, having disposed of the matters in hand, generally goes off to other subjects, frequently affording us a characteristic if brief impression of some current topic of the day, as in the following to Kinglake. Having asked some questions regarding the progress of the book, he goes on to Mr Gladstone's disturbing influence in the Cabinet, and the no less bewildering results of his Homeric theories on the Scotch theological mind, and from this on to Froude's lecture, which entailed another amusing story.

John Blackwood to A. W. Kinglake.

EDINBURGH, *Nov.* 25, 1865.

The story here is that Gladstone is very troublesome in the Cabinet [1] already, and stipulating for a Reform Bill of his own. He (Gladstone) lectured here the other day. The chief feature of his address was the theory, older than his own book, of the Homeric theology foreshadowing Christianity. I happened to dine next day with some Scotch clergymen, one of whom spoke with great contempt of his jumbling Helen and "the Virgin Mary" together. I said, "No, no; Helen and Mary Magdalen." Mr Froude also gave a lecture about the same time. I went to hear him, and thought his language very good and the lecture generally interesting. A very serious defect struck me, however, that he stated what was really only a theory and then argued upon it as a fact. His theme was rather a ticklish one for a

---

[1] Lord Russell's Ministry.

Scotch audience—viz., "The Social Effect of the Reformation in Scotland." He got over any difficulty, however, by buttering my countrymen in the most fearless manner, which his audience applauded vociferously. "The Great Nation" loves flattery. The phrase "Great Nation," I must explain, is a favourite joke with myself and familiars here, and springs from not a bad story. The old gardener at Duddingston, in this neighbourhood, was showing an English stranger the beauties of the loch and Arthur Seat, and when the moon came over the side of the hill, wound up all by exclaiming, "There's a moon for ye! Oh, we're a great nation"!!!

Kinglake also, when the 'Crimea' was not pressing too heavily on his mind, often diverged to other topics —current politics, and the business of his constituency, Bridgewater, affording him occasion for some well-considered remarks. Though sitting on the Liberal benches, he did not scruple to launch a gentle sarcasm at his own party if he thought they deserved it. He writes once, "For a while politics interrupted history with me"; and adds, "Reform has become quite a nightmare, and it seems that even the much-patronised 'working man' is becoming tired of the subject."

In another letter, alluding to his own writing, he says to my father :—

A. W. Kinglake to John Blackwood.

My nature makes me quicker to find difficulties than to overcome or elude them. I am continually wanting to clear up something, and then I receive information which tends to expand my view. I advise myself against this over-care just as a sensible friend might do, but there is an obstinacy in my nature which won't give way to my mere opinion. I have been reduced into giving much more attention than I had ever intended to the *naval* engagement of Oct. '54; and that having opened a new field has been giving me a great deal of trouble. I am exceedingly impatient to be at the end of my MS. work, so much so that I have to put a constraint upon myself in order not to be *too* industrious—a very new thing for me.

On another occasion he writes, "Your letter was a great comfort to me, for at times I am dissatisfied with what I have done"; and he goes on to say, "I have been engaged in a correspondence with the Government about the use I make of official despatches, and I am happy to say that the correspondence has ended in a way perfectly satisfactory to me." Any one who has studied the book can fully estimate the importance of this last statement, for any interference with the sources from which he drew his information would have been fatal to the success of the History. On one occasion he writes in great perturbation from the House of Commons, detailing the loss of proof-sheets containing his remarks on Lord Cardigan. The way he lost them will recall to many friends his well-known figure on horseback as we used to see him taking his morning canter in the Park, or, as on this occasion, riding down to the House. He says :—

HOUSE OF COMMONS, *May* 11, 1868.

I have sustained to-day a very annoying misfortune. . . . I put them [the proof-sheets] in the breast-pocket of my coat, and rode down here on horseback, but found them gone. Unfortunately they are sheets containing judgment on Cardigan, and I fear the use that might be made of them if they fall into evil hands. I was getting on smoothly till this vexatious accident occurred. . . . I shall have a little additional labour, but what I think of is the mischief that may be made.

What the fate of the proof was we do not know; but no more being heard of it, we may conclude it was swept away with the London dust like any other unimportant - looking paper. The modest way in which Kinglake used to put himself, as it were, outside literature, and as not belonging to the craft, is very striking in one who was so justly entitled to hold his own with any brothers of the pen. Here is an instance. My father had the habit of drawing the attention of one contributor to the writings of another, if likely to interest, or to any specially good number of the Magazine, and Kinglake replies: " I am much obliged to you for drawing my attention to the papers you speak of in the Magazine. It was very good of you to think of it, for I am so little in the world of literature that it is a real charity to let me know now and then what there is specially worth reading." On another occasion, when the Magazine had been sent to him, he says: " The Magazine came this morning, but already and without cutting a page I have seen enough of George Eliot's address to think it capital. . . . How well she writes ! " This refers to Felix Holt's address to the working men.

The important Balaclava volume was still in hand, but nearing completion. In January 1867 Kinglake writes: " I will not fail to let you know when the happy moment arrives at which I can say that Balaclava, with all its wild blunders and heroic actions, is off my mind." Referring to what was already published, and also to the portion of the Balaclava MS. not sent, he writes :—

A. W. Kinglake to John Blackwood.

Sept. 10, 1867.

I need hardly say it is a great pleasure to me that you like the book. Your words give me encouragement, and supply me with a little of the alacrity which is needed for completing the task. It is wonderful to me that you should have been able to follow the story so well without special maps or plans. . . . As the MS. would not squeeze into one volume, it is very fortunate that it proves big enough for two. It seems hard upon the poor dear public to have to read two more of those diabolical volumes without getting further than Balaclava, but they could not have been compressed without abandoning my conception of the way in which the story must be told, and in which, too, *the lesson must be taught.* . . . The concluding scenes of the "Light Cavalry charge" are extremely curious and very little known. In the intermediate chapters, which you have not yet received, the scene will be partly in England and France, and I suppose you will say from these that I am not preparing for myself a quiet life.

When he did actually finish Balaclava : " I suppose few will ever imagine, though you seem able to do so, what trouble I have had with the 25th chapter —*i.e.*, with the Battle of Balaclava." Much of this MS. was sent in what was known as the " mahogany box," which, as Kinglake explains, had a special historic value of its own.

I am now once more offering to the public the mahogany box —Lord Fitzroy Somerset's—which contains the first twenty chapters, and the other parcel contains the main part of the 25th chapter. I set a value on the mahogany box, which used to contain the labours of the old Duke and his military secretary in the great days, so I am sure it will be taken care of.

Lord Cardigan died while the sheets referring to him were going through the press, but it was thought better to let them stand.

A. W. Kinglake to John Blackwood.
March 31, 1868.
I feel much obliged to you for your counsel in the circumstances occasioned by poor Cardigan's death, and I may say to

you that every friend to whom I have spoken on the subject takes your view, each of them saying I should let what I have printed stand, and insert a note.

In another letter, referring to the close of one stage of his labours in connection with this monumental work, he says :— ﹕

May 27, 1868.

In bringing to a close this portion of my labours I desire to thank you and your nephew most warmly, not only for your patience with me in my slow and troublesome way of writing, but for the kind encouragement and very material assistance which I have derived from you at every stage. I am going to speak in a separate note of the great help I have received from your printing staff.—Believe me, my dear Sir, very truly yours,

A. W. KINGLAKE.

The next letter gives a hint of the excitement in London in consequence of Disraeli becoming Premier on Lord Derby's resignation :—

Feb. 24, 1868.

Although the event was of course foreseen, the elevation of Dizzy comes upon London with an effect very like surprise. Will he merely pause to hold the citadel as long as he can, or undertake to become a "great Minister"? I think he has boldness and imagination enough to try for greatness. The state of Ireland gives him occasion. The Queen in her letter told him amongst other things that she chose him in great measure on account of his good temper in the House of Commons, but, as you apparently surmise, the counsel of Lord Derby to the Queen was one of the grounds of her determination.

The elections in the autumn occupied all thoughts, and Kinglake had to "snatch a moment" from the claims of the Bridgewater constituents to acknowledge the receipt of a "kind letter and an enclosure," for which he says :—

Nov. 2, 1868.

I snatch a moment to acknowledge the receipt, and to say how very pleasing it is to me to learn that the relations between us have been satisfactory and agreeable to you. I am sure I can heartily respond, for I consider myself most fortunate in being in such good hands. Your nephew, I am certain, knowing how I am pressed for moments, will accept this letter to you as an answer to his kind note.

Referring to the general election, John Blackwood writes to Kinglake :—

STRATHTYRUM, *Oct.* 28, 1868.

I hope your electioneering prospects are 'all right. There will probably not be much change in the character of the members of the first Reform Parliament, but the day will come when the struggle will be whether gentlemen or roughs are to sit at Westminster. There is such a buzz of electionary addresses, I read none of them.

The member for this county (Fife), Sir R. Anstruther, boasts he has addressed 50 public meetings. Talking of Anstruther reminds me his sister, Mrs Kinloch [now Lady Kinloch of Gilmerton], was with us lately, and she talked with tears in her eyes of what you so touchingly said of her young brother who was killed at the Alma. She was greatly interested when I mentioned that you thought Kinglake and Kinloch sound the same name.

The following letter announces his return for Bridgewater, for which he seems to think that in spite of his politics his two Tory publishers will be glad :—

Nov. 24, 1868.

I came back from my electioneering last evening. I feel sure that in your kindness to me personally, both you and your nephew will so far waive politics as to be glad that I was returned, and this the more since I think I am almost the only man who, in the midst of an intensely party-swayed struggle, has reserved his independence in a written or printed address.

Blackwood's reply shows he had not miscalculated their goodwill.

EDINBURGH, *Nov.* 27, 1868.

MY DEAR SIR,—It gave my nephew and me much pleasure to see that you had got safely through your election troubles. It was telegraphed here at first that you had been beat, and my nephew and I, scanning the list together, exclaimed, "Confound it, there is the only man on the other side that we care about defeated." If you have a spare copy of your address, I should like to look at it. Along with this I send a copy of the Magazine containing a review of your third volume, which I hope you will like upon the whole. You will see that there is to be another paper, so there is time for suggestions. We Tories have had a rough time of it in the Scotch elections, and it has been hard to keep one's temper, especially in such cases as the defeat of Sir William Stirling and the Earl of Dalkeith. I was quite surprised to hear how well the Earl spoke, and at the declaration of the poll the mob gave him a capital hearing. It was the only sign of grace I ever saw in an Edinburgh mob, that they seemed half sorry his father's son was beat. The Free Church, with the other dissenters and the hares and the rabbits, have played the devil with us in Scotland. The most surprising return perhaps is in Dumfriesshire, where they boast themselves descendants of the children of the Covenant, and have elected a Unitarian stationer in preference to the man supported by the Buccleuch influence.

Kinglake was unseated on petition. Very hard, as he says, being unseated by the Tories when he was one of the few, very few, who had reserved an independent attitude and did not stand pledged to Gladstone. His friends in Edinburgh tried to console him by reminding him that the loss of his occupation at the House of Commons would give him more time for writing his book; but they sympathised with his disappointment, and, as my father remarked, the House could ill spare such men as Kinglake, for

there was "monstrous little literature or cultivation
there"; and indeed, he said, "he did not think he
could turn a good number of the Magazine out of
the whole body"!!   He goes on to make a further
remark on Gladstone's majority, which, he said, were
"stuck together like men sworn to carry out a particular burglary, and will be glad to go after their
own pet schemes when that is over."   The vexatious
business of the election petition brought Mr Kinglake hurriedly back from a visit he was paying to the
Crimea for the purpose of refreshing his memory with
a visit to the scene of his literary labours.   His
return, however, was not too speedy to have interfered
with a visit to some of the battlefields in company
with General Kotzebue and the redoubtable Todleben.
A letter dated "Sevastopol" describes his movements.

A. W. Kinglake to John Blackwood.

MY DEAR SIR,—Here I am, you see, at last.   Upon my arrival
at Odessa the Governor-General of the province—General Kotzebue—was so good as to call upon me and give me the most
admirable facilities for my undertaking.   Captain Krapotine,
the officer who accompanied the Prince of Wales, was allowed
to come with me all the way from Odessa, and his knowledge
of the ground proved to be perfect.   All kinds of facilities were
given me by the authorities, and I can say that I employed my
time well.   My good fortune was such that General Todleben
chanced to come at the very time, and you may imagine how
deeply it interested us to be going over the ground with him
and hearing him "fight his battles o'er again."   I get so savage
with this flimsy paper that I really can't write a letter, but I
felt sure that you would be glad to know that I have most
completely attained the object of my somewhat long and toilsome journey.

The news obliging him to return to England found

him at Constantinople after his visit to the Crimea, and he states that he made the journey from the Bosphorus to Dover in six days—pretty quick travelling for a man of his leisurely habits. He adds: "I cannot say how intensely interesting my visit to the Crimea was, and I trust that the remainder of my task may be all the better for my pilgrimage to the scene of the struggle at Inkerman." All this time Inkerman was simmering in his brain, and some months later he writes proposing that the fifth volume of his History should be devoted to Inkerman. He inquired as to my father's views on the subject: "Another idea has occurred to me upon which I should like to have your opinion. I think, within a reasonable compass of time, I could bring out a fifth, or, in other words, an Inkerman volume; for I have it all in my head, and almost half written." My father replied that he was delighted with the idea, and thought "Inkerman was the word round which British interests in the war still mainly centred." When he had read a portion of it, he wrote to the author how greatly it had interested him.

John Blackwood to A. W. Kinglake.

STRATHTYRUM, *Oct.* 28, 1873.

Surely never was such a bright detail and light shed over such a misty, confused battle-field. It seems a series of little battles, the succession of which might weary, did not the vivid power of your language and the never-failing courage of our officers and men make them a succession of splendid pictures. It is trying to the temper to read how time after time, by what seemed almost like perverse ingenuity, we never had more than a few score or hundreds of men to meet any number of Russians, and it is a perfect miracle we were not driven into the sea. There is something very dramatic in the way you describe

Bosquet looking about in vain for anything like brigades or even regiments. I suppose if he had been caught in that trap on the Inkerman Tusk, it would have been all up. I fancy neither our officers nor men were very discreet or courteous to the French when they came up. The French had the merit of keeping together, and showing a front, although not so hot for battle as professed "braves" should have been. In regard to their wavering so much, are you not giving too much weight to the momentary impressions of men heated with actual fight? but you alone can judge of this, having had such a cloud of witnesses before you, and having sifted so carefully what they said. Sir G. Brown turning back Bosquet's proferred aid in the early morning was a terrible thing; but the battle ending as it did, one can only say, All for the best. I feel sorry for the blunders of Cathcart, who, I have always heard, was a fine fellow.

The interest in the Inkerman volume did not flag, and we find my father pouncing on the proofs as they returned with the author's revise, in spite of the difficulty of deciphering his corrections. He says of it :—

EDINBURGH, *March* 4, 1874.

Your proof is enough to strike terror into the soul of any but the most determined compositor that ever handled the stick, as they call their composing-rod. However, your corrections, numerous as they are, are marvellously clear. I have been amusing myself going over them before I sent the proof to the printers. It is quite a study in composition, and, much as I regret your taking such overwhelming trouble, I am bound to confess that you generally make your shots or sentences even more telling than they were at first.

He goes on to say :—

I am looking hourly with nervous interest for news from that infernal Gold Coast, and if nothing comes soon I shall repeat a walk up to one of the newspaper offices at midnight, which I have taken more than once already. I am greatly distressed to-day by hearing that Lytton [afterwards Lord Lytton, Viceroy of India] has lost his only son, a boy about two years old. I think you know both him and his charming wife.—Always yrs. truly,   JOHN BLACKWOOD.

Kinglake, when not actually in the throes of composition, was, it will be gathered from his letters, full of interest in external matters, and in all that concerned his friends, and particularly anxious to lend a helping hand to those who had literary aspirations. His sympathies in this line extended even to France, and he gives in one letter a new idea about our French neighbours. He says, " One of the favourite desires of the French at the present day is to be noticed by the English press." And he goes on to say that some French friends had entreated him to endeavour to obtain this blessing for a grandson of Lafayette (M. Lasteryie) who had translated a book illustrating some of the heart-stirring scenes of the Reign of Terror. Not a very stirring book, but Kinglake's dramatic perception had picked out the one episode which would make it capable of development. This was the short narrative told by a priest who " was present at the execution of La Maréchale de Noailles, the Duchesse d'Ayen, and the Vicomtesse de Noailles in the Reign of Terror, and who, whilst standing in the crowd, contrived to catch the eyes of the victims and give them absolution." He thought this might be worked up into an article suitable for the Magazine, and " confer that ineffable blessing of which I have spoken, and so enable M. Lasteryie and the Noailles and all the rest of them to go about Paris in a high state of exaltation, declaring that they have been mentioned

'dans le Blackwood! Oui, dans le Blackwood même!'"
He goes on to say: "I did not know before that
even under exceptional circumstances a priest could
grant absolution without having received a confession.
The whole affair is curious and interesting."

The Editor, of course, made Kinglake work up the
paper himself, in spite of his objections that this sort
of writing was new and strange to him, and of course
he did it excellently well. He afterwards wrote
saying, "You must have a power of making fruitful
suggestions, for here is my little preface of eight or
ten lines swollen out into quite an article." His
French friends were delighted with the paper, and
were anxious to ascertain the authorship; but this
was not to be divulged even to them, for Kinglake
says he might have been involved in endless though
friendly discussion as to the correctness of his theory
there expressed, that the "horrors of the French
Revolution" were caused by "Christian resignation."
He thought, perhaps, that meekness and resignation
were hardly the weapons with which to meet a "red-
cap."

The peculiar way which my father had of interesting one contributor in another had the result of
not only drawing them more closely to himself, but
of animating them with an *esprit de corps* that
seemed to bind them all together in a sort of compact
alliance, devoted to his interests, rejoicing in any
fresh literary success gained by the House. This has
been remarked upon by many of the coterie, and does
much to lessen the dark and tragic views which are
sometimes given us of literary jealousies and hatreds.
Kinglake was a notable instance of this. His letters

are full of·generous admiration for other contributors
to Blackwood, who have afforded him relaxation
and entertainment in his leisure moments. Mrs
Oliphant was one whose novels he always read with
pleasure; and as for George Eliot, he thought the
town ought to be .illuminated when she produced a
new book. Of Mrs Oliphant he says :—

To me she is charming. To read her is like being with a
delightful woman—a woman of powerful intellect, which she
veils perhaps from the eyes of many readers, though not from
mine, by her thoroughly feminine tact. And then her style
seems to me so perfect. I wish, in token of my admiration,
you would send her a copy of my new volume.

In another letter his admiration takes a still more
practical form, for he wished he could do something
towards making her works more widely known, as he
thought they were in those days (five-and-twenty
years ago) suffering, as Thackeray's did, from a tardy
recognition of their merits. And he said that gratitude to her for the pleasure her books had given him
prompted him to wish some steps could be taken to
make the "sluggish world do her justice." It is
interesting to find his friend Hayward, to whom he
had mentioned his wishes, giving effect to them in
a laudatory notice of her in the 'Edinburgh Review.'
Kinglake's mind followed with delight the description
which my father had evidently afforded him of the
way George Eliot wrote her books. He says in
answer to one of his letters :—

Nov. 15, 1874.

Another novel from Mrs Lewes is really a national blessing!
Why don't cities have illuminations for news so grateful, instead
of making believe to rejoice at some absurd " birthday " or the

accession of a new Lord Mayor? What you tell me of the
intellectual fermentation from which works like 'Middlemarch' result is very interesting, and makes one envy the
process of disciplined thought which, after the "simmering,"
passes all at once into the "irrevocable." With my kindest
regards to Mrs Blackwood and to your nephew, I remain, my
dear Blackwood, very truly yours, A. W. KINGLAKE.

His remarks on politics and politicians are given in
a very impartial spirit; and referring to the collapse
of Gladstone's Ministry in 1867, he writes—

Except as regards the evanescent officials, everybody I see
appears to be pleased at Gladstone's fall. "J'aime à croire," as
the French say, that he has fallen in consequence of the
wretched knock under to every one's policy which showed itself in the Alabama business and the entire obedience of
Gortschakoff.

And then he goes on to say he wishes the Magazine
would take some such way of improving the occasion
as by saying—

True, Old England knocked under, and we thought her
degenerate; but now we see that, though certainly very late
in the day, she has turned out the Government which disgraced
her, so perhaps there may be some go left in her yet.

From another letter, written when his literary work
had detained him in town after the usual holiday
exodus, he appears to have been enjoying an occasional talk with Sir William Harcourt, whom he
presents to us in the light of a sagacious Whig of
the old school, keenly alive to the prerogatives
of Archbishops, and a careful student of "Public
Opinion":—

I am alone in London, and am therefore of course very
innocent of all political knowledge. The last man I have

talked with is Harcourt, one of the chief *dramatis personæ* in the Church Bill affair. He, though an opponent, is on peculiarly friendly terms with Disraeli. I am rather surprised to hear that it was only at a late stage that Disraeli saw the advantage to be derived by giving his personal support to the Archbishop of Canterbury. Harcourt is a very careful, and, I think, a sagacious student of "Public Opinion," and although he did not tell me so, I have an idea that he gave Dizzy his inspiration by making him see the advantage to be gained by giving a tap to the Protestant drum. Disraeli for the present seems absolute master, for there is not one of his colleagues who (even with the support of two or three others) could break up the Government. The best thing the poor dear Liberals can do is to study 'Vivian Grey' as an inspired prophecy, and so try to make out "what will come next."

A further talk with Sir William left Kinglake still more deeply impressed with the extent of his clerical knowledge, implying weighty researches into matters of which Kinglake is obliged to confess his own entire ignorance. Thus, Sir William's idea that the hands of the Archbishop should be strengthened, resulted from his discovery that our ancestors had long ago accepted these means of antagonism to the Pope.

August 14, 1874.

That discovery of his is one of much interest. I daresay you will be evolving something from it in 'Maga.' It is curious that in their anxiety to claim divine right for the Bishops, the zealots try to run down the *Arch*bishops. Yet, as Harcourt tells me (for I never looked into the red books and clergy lists, where such things are to be found), an *Arch*bishop purports to be such by the direct "*Grace*" of the Deity, whereas a mere bishop is only such by the Deity's "*assent*."

Referring to the difference between Whig and Tory manners in the House, Kinglake says no one could fail to be impressed with the superior "answering" qualities of the Conservatives on the Treasury Bench when called upon to answer questions, and this he attributes to Disraeli's training, " the result of preparation and of a determination to answer without assuming unnecessarily any antagonistic attitude. I remember that Bright once, in a transient moment of candour I suppose, called my attention to the superiority of the Tory Treasury Bench in this respect."

The temptation is very great to go on quoting from this pleasant correspondent, whose keen-edged remarks are sprung upon us suddenly from a mass of letters dealing with the apparently unending subject of his History ; but other matters are waiting, and only one more extract must be added—*i.e.*, the following, which hints at the conclusion of his labours. Wars and rumours of wars might disturb the rest of Europe, and England herself have to face several more campaigns and warlike expeditions, but still the historian of the Crimea was discovering fresh materials for *his* campaign, and sat unmoved by the turmoil of current events steadily weaving his monumental work. He was then (in 1874) approaching the death of Lord Raglan, when he writes to Blackwood—

I cannot well say when the blessed moment for finishing the whole work will come, but my idea is that when I am clear of this Inkerman business I shall be able to dispose of the rest right down to Lord Raglan's death in one volume ; and I am not aware of any circumstances, except indeed my own infirmities as a writer, which ought to make me very long about it.—Believe me, my dear Blackwood, very truly yours,

A. W. KINGLAKE.

His " infirmities" as a writer, to which he makes almost touching allusion, are better characterised as

extreme conscientiousness and honest endeavour to
do full justice to his subject.   Not only his own
writing of the work, but the actual production of
the book, were made more difficult by his extraordinary conscientious nature.   Thus we find him
objecting to the usual method of making stereotype
plates from which to print.   The word stereotype, it
seems, had alarmed him with an irrevocable sound
fatal to all alterations or corrections, in which he
largely indulged.   He says in opposition to the
stereotyping, "I am so constituted that it would
be painful to me not to be able to satisfy the minds
of one of my heroes who might write to me in
anguish to explain that he is 'Captain Snook' and
not 'Captain Cook.'"   The foregoing conveys so
much more than is expressed of the qualities which
distinguished Kinglake, that it explains to a great
extent why writing his History was such a lengthy
process.

CHAPTER V.

LAURENCE OLIPHANT.

A STORMY PETREL—THE SCHLESWIG-HOLSTEIN WAR—"IN TREMENDOUS HOT WATER"—AN EVENING AT THE COSMOPOLITAN—'THE OWL'—"A SUPERSTITION ABOUT BEING CONSTANT TO 'MAGA'"—CAPTAIN SPEKE AND CAPTAIN GRANT—DEATH OF SPEKE—THE SUCCESS OF 'PICCADILLY'—THE PROPHET HARRIS — WORK IN AMERICA — 'TIMES' CORRESPONDENT IN PARIS — AMERICAN WAR—'MAGA'S' ATTITUDE—HER WAR CORRESPONDENTS—COLONEL VON BORCKE—THE DEATH OF AYTOUN —BIOGRAPHY BY SIR THEODORE MARTIN—THE EDITOR'S RETROSPECT.

ONE figure that flits ever and anon across the scene, the interest attaching to it only increased by the somewhat elusive character of the glimpses afforded us, is that of Laurence Oliphant. With him is associated much of the interest of that part of the correspondence dealing with travel and adventures and the wide field of foreign politics. Often not heard of for several months, he would suddenly appear in London from Japan or Poland, or wherever his latest enterprise had taken him. On his return he seemed to slip back as easily as though he had never left it into the peculiar niche he occupied in Society— Society which, as far as he was concerned, may rightly be spelt with a large S, if Prime Ministers, kings, and potentates of all kinds count for anything. They

certainly counted for a good deal in his literary
achievements, as they were the sources from which
he drew his information for the many political papers
he wrote. Thus, in one letter to my father from a
German watering-place, he says, "I am, as usual,
cradled in royalty," and goes on to say he is indifferent
to archdukes, excepting in as much as they could
supply him with materials for a new foreign political
journal he was interested in. Of his strangely fascinating personality it is easy to write, for his attractive qualities were patent to all who knew him;
but it is very much more difficult to try to describe
the elusive character of his genius. The characteristics of his writings are as complex as the motives
which prompted his different journeys and enterprises,
and an attempt to label and pigeon-hole him in any
special literary shelf would be as hopeless as to try to
classify any other phenomenal appearance which flashes
and dazzles and pleases us, but which we find it
impossible to bracket comfortably with anything
similar in our experience. "Here's Larrie at last,"
was John Blackwood's usual exclamation on fishing
up a letter from him amongst the usual pile—this
perhaps after, as in 1861, he had been speeding him
on his way to Japan. In the following letter, prior
to his departure for Poland, he calls him "a stormy
petrel" :—

MY DEAR OLIPHANT,—I enclose proof of your interesting
paper on Alcock's book. You will, I have no doubt, find
excellent materials for papers in your expedition to Poland.
You are a regular stormy petrel, but I hope this expedition will
not, like the one you made to the Crimea, be the harbinger of a
war. In regard to your papers for the Magazine, I am only

afraid of your taking too liberal and nationalistic a view for me ;
but I daresay you will be able to steer clear of the line, and at
all events I hope you will try. The great danger is that France
may take advantage of the occasion and endeavour to get the
Rhine frontier by a war with Prussia. This would be a serious
fix for us and Europe generally. At all events I hope you will
have a successful expedition, and let me hear from you.

In a couple of months he was back again. His visit
to Poland resulted in a contribution to the Magazine
highly interesting, but in its original form somewhat
too Polish for the Editor. My father writes to my
mother :—

4 BURLINGTON GARDENS, W., *May* 31, 1863.

I had a long talk with Larrie Oliphant to-day, who insisted
upon carrying me off to be introduced to the Baroness Blaze de
Bury, a sort of masculine female political *intrigante* (an awfully
clever woman). She is the great ally of Kinglake, and, comically
enough, she mentioned the review of Victor Hugo's 'Waterloo'
as the paper which has made most noise on the Continent and
excited the greatest curiosity as to authorship. So I told
her. . . . She said Hamley's was the best sketch of the career
and character of Wellington that had ever been written, but
was quite amazed when she knew of his other performances.

In the winter of 1864 the field of foreign politics
presented a very stormy outlook. The spectacle of
Denmark struggling with Prussia in Schleswig-
Holstein was not one which any of the Powers
could view with complacency ; and though no one
was inclined to interfere, yet a good deal of ink was
spilt in the internal conflicts which took place, in
this and other countries, as to the duty of interfering in the business. Laurence Oliphant's letter
to my father, written March 1864, describes what
he believed to be the feeling in Germany proper :—

I have tried by sticking in the word Federal here and there

to make my meaning clear. The truth is, there is a mighty
German nation, who all think alike in so far as opposition to
the Government of Berlin and Vienna is concerned. The
whole Prussian nation, except the Junkers and a small section
of the aristocracy, are of Liberal Austria, which is not large,
and all federal Germany think pretty much alike in the
Schleswig-Holstein question. Possibly thirty out of forty
millions are of one mind, and entirely disapprove of the
policy both of Bismarck and Rechberg. See in proof the
votes in the Chambers both in Berlin and Vienna refusing
all supplies for the war by immense majorities.

This and his next paragraph explaining why he was
so bitter against the alliance of Russia, Prussia, and
Austria, were in reply to some queries of my father,
who did not by any means always agree with his
politics :—

The reason I am so bitter against the Holy Alliance is that
while Russia is professing to stand by us in our Danish policy,
she threatens Sweden if she ventures to send a man to the
support of Denmark. She is playing a double game, and
tricking us in revenge for our Polish interference.

You ask me in what way we compelled the King of Denmark
to evacuate Holstein. I have no doubt that the despatch
advising him to do so will be published. And he could not
venture to disregard our counsel, as he was fool enough to
trust in our support. Then we positively requested Austria
and Prussia to take the matter out of the hands of the Diet,
and approved of their invading Holstein, as we supposed to
put the check on impetuous Germany. This is a purely aristo-
cratic war, undertaken by the King of Prussia against the wish
of Germany for the purpose of blooding his army, who will
come back more arrogant and overbearing than ever. I did not
hear a German during the battle of Wirssunde express any
other hope than that the Prussians might get a licking, and
nothing would give greater satisfaction to Germany than a
successful expulsion of the Danes from Dreppel.

The next letters from Oliphant refer to the effect produced in London by his papers in the Magazine on the Schleswig-Holstein question. It will be remembered that the Government (Lord Palmerston's) were thought by a section of the nation to have lowered the prestige of England by their conduct regarding this war; it will therefore be readily understood that an *exposé* of the situation was eminently unpalatable to them.

March 9, 1864.

MY DEAR BLACKWOOD,—I just write a line. I hope the Magazine is going off. I am in tremendous hot water—cut right and left by members of the Government. I never was so honoured before in my life; but it is unpleasant having society and not knowing who of your old friends is going to give you the cold shoulder. They must be in a very shaky position when it's come to that. They accuse me of ratting from a sinking ship. Anyhow, it is lucky I have given up all idea of Government employment, as I have floored myself. A friend of mine writes to know who is the author of an article in the last 'Maga' on Banking. If it is not a secret, will you tell me?

Blackwood's reply was as follows :—

EDINBURGH, *March* 10, 1864.

MY DEAR OLIPHANT,—The Government could not very well like your paper, and I am sorry they have got at the authorship; but I hope their present coldness will not injure your prospects. In the long-run such things are more apt to do good than harm. If you were a poor devil applying for a waitership, your prospects would certainly be blasted; but for any position worth while, the reputation of being able to do anything damaging to a Ministry is about as useful as being able to help it. The article has not affected the Magazine sale, but it is evidently thought of. Bulwer, who has more real head than any statesman going, writes to me of it with much consideration. He does not agree with it altogether, but speaks of

it in a very satisfactory way, showing that he looks upon the
writer as a man who has thought upon his subject, and is
thoroughly well entitled to be heard. I hope you are going on.
Let me know. The Ministerial ship is as rotten as can be, but
I do not think it is going to sink just at present, and they need
not accuse you on that score. Going out so much as you do, it
must be a bore to find a change in the customary greetings
with friends, but I hope it will pass off. It is a compliment,
but a disagreeable one, and I am rather vexed about it. They
must be in a funk, or they would not be so touchy.

The article on Banking is by Patterson, and a very good one
it is. Aytoun tells me he thinks it the best discussion of the
question that he has seen, and the Cavalier is very shrewd
upon banking subjects. He used to write upon them.—Always
yours truly,   JOHN BLACKWOOD.

A few days later Oliphant writes as follows :—

The outcry is subsiding against me, and most of my enemies
have given in and are extra civil; so I hope it is all right. As
far as employment is concerned, I have given up all idea there-
of. I want to come into Parliament, and look upon a dissolution as certain pretty soon. I wish I could be equally sure
of a constituency that would take a man of independent views
about foreign policy, but very submissive in home matters.

In July he writes :—

Do you see in to-day's 'Times' how completely they have
come round about Schleswig-Holstein? They ought to have
written that article three months ago. Look in to-day's 'Post'
for some private despatches of Bismarck's. They will be a shell
in the German camp, and corroborate the 'Owl.' I think
there is a great possibility of a dissolution, so keep your eyes
open about St Andrews.

The dissolution took place at the end of July
1865, and in the following November Lord Russell's
Government came into office.

The following from Oliphant explains, in answer to some questions from Blackwood, the reasons for his views about the Danish war :—

Laurence Oliphant to John Blackwood.

MY DEAR BLACKWOOD,—I have compromised the matter as far as possible, by beginning with the third page. The rest of the argument is essential to the case. I speak mildly to what the public would do if they understood the extent to which the Government has egregiously blundered. When you remember that I watched the affair through at Frankfort from the beginning, where I know all the leading politicians; that I have talked this matter out with Bismarck; that I know from him, and have made Buchanan, our Austrian Ambassador at Berlin, admit in argument that we really were the cause of the Austro-Prussian army being in Schleswig-Holstein when all the efforts which were made to prevent it were thwarted by the English policy; when, as I lived with the Duke of Coburg, I know what those efforts were; when I have followed the question, and been let in behind the scenes by the Crown Prince of Prussia, who has evidently opposed Bismarck, and by the Duke of Augustenburg, his personal enemy; and when at this moment I am in possession of information of which our Government is totally ignorant,—I write with an amount of knowledge and certainty which I know will not be appreciated by the ignorant public, and I am quite prepared to see the paper hostilely contradicted and abused. Nor inasmuch as much of my information is based on conversations, can I defend it. I write for the intimate few, very few. The day will come when the incompetency of the Government will be shown. Meantime the incompetency of their opponents being as great, there is nobody to show them up. I am writing against time, very incoherently, but I have toned off many of my remarks, and added some new matter. Send sometimes the Magazine to 'Public Opinion.' It has a circulation of 15,000, and will quote largely.—Yours ever, L. OLIPHANT.

P.S.—The article has given me immense trouble, and I have expended a deal of thought upon it.

A letter written several months after the foregoing articles by Laurence Oliphant shows how his predictions regarding the Danish war and the position of our Government were verified :—

John Blackwood to William Blackwood.

June 10, 1864.

I saw Sir Edward [Bulwer Lytton] this morning, who was in much better case than when I saw him last week. He was going to a meeting at Lord Derby's to-day to decide about the course the party should adopt in regard to Government and the Danish Question. Some men are for pushing matters to extremity, but those who would have the responsibility of Government are not. I hope we shall not attempt to come in to solve a mess which we did not make, and from which there is no creditable exit for this country. It would be no use going to war now, and if we did so, it would simply be said that the Tories had again plunged the country into war. My belief is that the Danes will protest, but submit to the German exactions, declaring that they cannot fight two countries ten times their own size without assistance. It is a miserable ending, and if all Lord Russell's despatches are published it will be a nice exposition. Young Lytton has just returned from Copenhagen, and I expect to have some talk with him to-morrow or next day.

In another letter to the same he describes an evening at the Cosmopolitan, which on this occasion appears more than ever to have fulfilled its mission of collecting the Lions of London, and my father chronicles with evident pleasure the interest of the room centring in his own two or three special friends. He says :—

I had a capital night at the Cosmopolitan, where Larry had appointed to meet me yesterday. I found no end of people, and Speke came in. On seeing me he "Nyanzied" at a great rate. Then Kinglake came in and sat down beside us most cordial. Then young Lytton, who, fresh from Copenhagen, is a great lion; so we became the centre of the room, which was full of celebrities of one kind or another. It is the best gathering in London. Kinglake and other Whig members expected our party to make a set at the Government to-night, and there is to be a large meeting at Lord Derby's to-day. I do not think a dead set at the Government will be made, but I am going down to the House to see. Jem goes down to-night, and will give you all the news of our doings to-morrow. Tell Burt I shall write him to-morrow. I intended to do so to-day, but am dead beat and must go, or I shall be too late to see the men going into the House.—Ever yours affectly.,

JOHN BLACKWOOD.

June 16, 1864.

MY DEAR WILLIE,—We had a most successful party at Bulwer's yesterday. Lord Ellenborough, Lord and Lady John Manners, Sir Robert and Lady Peel, the Danish representative at the Conference, &c., &c. I sat between Sir Robert Peel and the Dane. The Dane said, what was equivalent to a statement, that the line of division in Schleswig was agreed upon, and I am pretty certain that the difficulty is over—at all events, that there is to be no more fighting. I have always thought that the talk about the Scandinavian Kingdom composed of Sweden and Denmark utter bosh, so I put my impression to him as to how, from territorial position, Sweden could possibly assist Denmark in any Continental convulsion. To my surprise he quite agreed, and said that many Danes wished that they should be members of the German Confederation, and that Denmark would be the third Power in it. He continued: "I do not say I wish this, but it is better that we should do it now than remain a small Power, helpless in the event of any attack from our neighbours." This was addressed to Sir Robert Peel and me. Sir Robert thought it would be such a bad thing, and cited the instances of small kingdoms like Switzerland and Belgium (! !) remaining independent, at which the Dane and I laughed. I said at once that I thought it was the best possible solution, and that I was very glad to hear what he said. I think it is, and I believe it is what will come. Sir Robert was greatly surprised about this, but still more about the boundary line being so nearly fixed, and whispered to me that he had no idea it was so.

I sat with Kinglake for some time this morning. He was extremely pleasant, and said I was the first man who told him that we were not going to give notice of a vote of want of confidence this week, referring to our conversation on Sunday night. I said he gave me credit of more early information than I possessed; but the fact was, I had heard the question discussed in all its pros and cons, and felt that the cons must carry it in a quiet discussion.—Ever yours affectly.,

JOHN BLACKWOOD.

Garibaldi was in England this season, and Oliphant alludes to the breakdown in his health, which put a stop to his engagements, and the tide of hero-worship to which the gallant General had been subjected. "I had a talk with Garibaldi yesterday. He looked awfully worn and done." About this time Oliphant and some other bright spirits were starting a publication to be called the 'Owl,' which should appear weekly, giving in solemn and serious fashion a series of *canards* on social and political matters, so well got up, and with just such an air of *vraisemblance*, as to deceive all who were not in the secret. Oliphant wished Blackwood to be the publisher, and he appears to have been tempted by the sheer fun of the thing, but he declined for the reasons he gave in the following letter :—

EDINBURGH, *June* 30, 1864.

MY DEAR OLIPHANT,—I think decidedly that you should publish an Owlleum, and I am much pleased that you and your brother owls should wish me to be the publisher. I am excessively inclined to go into it with you, and it is with great reluctance I bring myself to think that on the whole it is better not to do so. In the first place, if a name so well known as mine was publicly responsible for the 'Owl,' any blockhead who chose to be offended at having his name taken in vain would at once take a shot at me, and although he might not get damages, he would certainly get costs. This would be a bore for me, and it would hamper you and your merry men in the future. . . . You will want some one to advise you as to paper, binding, &c., and the best thing will be for you to write to or call upon my manager at Paternoster Row, Mr Langford. You can trust him, and I will tell him to look after the thing the same as if we were the publishers.

The 'Owl' had a wonderful success. The conspirators used to meet and concoct their fabrications with the utmost secrecy, and there was just that amount of probability in their daring statements to set every one talking as to the possible authorities of this mysterious publication, which during its day was one of the wonders of a London season or two. The following winter Oliphant was in Paris, when he apologises for not writing as much as usual, and refers to the number of years he had written for 'Blackwood' with an almost superstitious dread of any falling off. The only contribution he could accomplish there was a "Ghost Story," which somewhere else he says he thinks must be good, as he got so frightened over it himself while writing it late at night.

PARIS, 10th Oct. 1864.

MY DEAR BLACKWOOD,—Many thanks for your letter. I enclose herewith the Ghost Story, but I have found it impossible in this great and wicked city to write the German article I intended. I get up too late in the day, and am too much engaged when up to sit down calmly to write politics. I hope that, notwithstanding my new review, I shall be able to send you an article now and then. I have a superstition about being

constant to the ' Maga.' There is not one of the last eleven
volumes that does not contain at least one of my effusions.

Amongst matters interesting my father at this
time was the publication of Speke and Grant's book
in April, to which the following letter refers :—

John Blackwood to William Blackwood.

May 26, 1864.

Sherard Osborn came in to breakfast, and we had a most
pleasant hour or more. Longmans have given up their interest
in his works, and he wishes us to publish them on any terms
we like. He was followed immediately by Speke, who laughed
and "Nyanzied" to a great extent. I have my work cut out
to keep him from quarrelling with the , Geographical Society,
Sir Roddie and all, whom he calls old women and humbugs.
Grant came in soon, and the two sat until near two. Speke, as
an experienced Literary man, advising Grant as to the arrangement of his books, was one of the very best scenes I ever assisted
at, and I only wish you and Simpson had been present. I
think Simpson would have lost his sense of propriety for once,
and burst out laughing. There never was such a pair, and
excellent fellows both. Grant expects to be in Edinburgh on
Sunday, but I shall write to you about this again. Speke
evidently is the chief, and his airs of literary experience were
like to kill me.

The mention of Captain (afterwards Colonel) J. A.
Grant recalls many pleasant days when the distinguished traveller was my father's guest. He never
spoke of Colonel Grant's achievements without alluding to the modesty and absence of all boastfulness
which were so noticeable in one whose love of sport
and adventure had often placed him in positions of
great peril. The next letter describes a visit to the
Zoo with Colonel Grant many years after his return
from Africa.

John Blackwood to his Wife.

14 ARLINGTON ST., *May* 25, 1876.

Jack [his son] and I then went to Grant. "Old Jem," as Speke used to call him, and his wife were most hearty. He gave us tickets for the Zoological Gardens, and when we went we most fortunately fell in with him, the best guide in the world in such a place. The affectionate way he looks at a wild beast is very comical, and the placid smile with which he pointed out the weak point behind the forearm at which to fire into a rhinoceros made me shout with laughter. He was doubtless the only man in the Gardens who had dined on rhinoceros.

The sight of the denizens of the African forest brought animation and life to his eye, and it was on occasions of this kind he would perhaps be induced to relate scenes in which he and a rhinoceros or a buffalo had been the chief actors, with a quiet ignoring of all the dangers of the chase that might have led one to suppose he was relating nothing more formidable than an encounter with a rabbit! The gentleness of his voice and manner, generally accompanied with the most amiable eulogiums on the merits of the ferocious beasts, made his narrative all the more fascinating to his hearers. This delightful admixture of simplicity of manner with highest personal courage and perseverance was alike a distinguishing trait in him and his *confrère* Speke, and gave an added charm to the interest attaching to them and their memorable discovery.

The happy association of Speke and Grant with my father and his friends, of which he writes so frequently, was soon to be clouded over by the misfortune of poor Speke's death. It was caused by the unlucky accident of his gun going off while he was getting over a fence in pursuit of nothing more deadly than the partridges on his father's

property in Somersetshire,—about the most unlikely
ending one could have predicted for the man who
had come scatheless through the dangers of African
travel and sport. His friend Laurence Oliphant
touchingly alludes to his death in the following
letter :—

Sept. 23, 1864.

MY DEAR BLACKWOOD,—I have just finished the melancholy
task of writing a letter to Mrs Speke. I don't know when I
have felt so shocked and saddened as by the announcement in
the 'Times,' which came so suddenly upon me yesterday. It
seemed so mysterious that a man should have lived through so
much to die thus at last. Poor fellow, one of the last conversations we had when we were living together in the spring
in Paris was on the subject of death. The last letter I received before leaving England was one from him asking me
to come and stay with him near Bath during the meeting of
the Association.

I think it possible I may have an article for you for
November on the present phase of the German question; but
as I am moving about so much, I cannot make certain about
having time to write it. At any rate it will not be long, but
merely putting the essential points in as few words as possible,
in the hope that at last the public may understand them.

A hint here and there occurs in Laurence Oliphant's
letters that he has a scheme for some new departure
in literature, some fresh ground to be broken up. It
was to be half-jesting, with just that vein of serious
thought running through it which should give the
idea that something was to be read between the lines;
and it was, further, to be a field for the display of
those remarkable gifts of later development in which
the satirical powers of his pen proved so effective.
Blackwood appears to have given, at any rate, a
gentle impulsion in the direction it was to take, and

quotes an idea J. G. Lockhart had once had for a book
to be called 'Pall Mall.' The following letter from
him to Oliphant gives his first impression after seeing
the first number of this book, which as 'Piccadilly'
became one of the best known and most successful
of Oliphant's writings :—

Jan. 27, 1865.

I have read the fragment you sent down, and return the
MS. The scheme is a grand one, and it opens well; but there
is not enough to enable one to judge whether your back will
bear the burden. It is a first-rate idea, and I am clear that
you should go on and finish a number, which I would get into
type, and then we could judge. It will be a very difficult
thing to carry out, about as difficult as can well be imagined,
and a failure would be abominable; but if you once get into
the vein, you will carry the public with you. I can suggest
nothing for a plot, except to take and disguise some of the usual
love and heiress-hunting stories of which every season produces
a crop. The unaccountable, generally bubble-spawned, fellows
who keep an establishment in London, and entertain every one
of note for a season or two, and then burst with some disclosure of bankruptcy or fraud, might form a feature. That
man who used to give private theatricals, and whose house was
burned down mysteriously, was a very curious case. —— ——
might be a very interesting figure to drape. I do not know
him, and he looks a snob; but he has merit in the Napoleonic
scale in which he carries out his plan of advertising. Long ago,
when I lived in London, I had many conversations with
Lockhart about a novel which he had a scheme of writing,
to be called 'Pall Mall.' His intention was to introduce Peel,
Brougham, and all the humbugs of the day. He never, that
I know of, did anything to it, but many a laugh we had over
the scenes and characters he could introduce.

'Piccadilly' ran its successful course first of all in
the pages of the Magazine, amid much talk and specu-
lation as to the author, and much merriment; for the

wicked world which he satirised took to the treatment
quite kindly, and even saw where the joke came in.
There was just that deftness and delicacy in the
handling which showed that it was done by "one of
themselves"; and numbers of that world, so full of
shams and humbug, in which he had found a new
unexpected field for his faculties of sarcasm, began to
look up and down their ranks for "the chiel amang
them takin' notes." What saved it from any real
bitterness was the absence of all attempt at portraiture. The characters were all merely types to be met
with every day, and their success was owing to the
author's perfect conversance with all the different
phases of society which produced them. When it
appeared in book form 'Piccadilly' was illustrated by
Richard Doyle, and in one of my father's letters he
says he saw no objections to any portrait appearing in
what is meant for a representative London crowd—
say, at the Foreign Office or any big gathering—when
the portraiture is not continued in the book. As a
matter of fact, however, no portraits were ever reproduced, unless the *disillusioné* figure of "the man
at the corner" was intended for Laurence Oliphant
himself. And *disillusioné* he certainly was, and just
at a time when things were going particularly well
with him. He had been returned for Parliament,
which, as has been already stated, was a strong wish
of his for some time past, and his first appearance in
the House was successful and promising. My father
wrote, after his first speech :—

I am extremely glad to see your maiden speech, which is, I
think, very good, and I am sure you are right about American
Fenianism. . . . You have made a good opening, I am sure, and

the opportunity was well chosen. People do not seem to care a brass farthing about the Reform Bill. Perhaps this apathy about it may enable it to pass, but I do not think it will.

Politics, however, were thrown aside, like the other interests which had formerly held him fast, and the advent of 'Piccadilly,' with its vista of the hollowness and disappointment of all mundane things or triumphs, was likewise the signal for Oliphant's exit from the scenes he had described so graphically. The change which came over him has been fully described in his biography, and the many notices—some more or less garbled versions—which appeared at the time of his death. It is sufficient for our purpose to say that the dissatisfaction which he experienced clamoured so loudly for a remedy that, having attacked the religious side of modern life, he seemed as though he must attach nimself to some new cult which should satisfy the higher aspirations of his nature.

In the autobiographical volume entitled 'Episodes of a Life of Adventure,' Oliphant gives in the last chapter some indication of the views which had long been underlying the outward current of his life, and also alludes to the parliamentary experiences which appear to have hastened the crisis. He says :—

Most people are, I suppose, more or less conscious of leading a sort of double life—an outside one and an inside one. The more I raced about the world, and took as active a part as I could in its dramatic performances, the more profoundly did the conviction force itself upon me that if it was indeed a stage, and all the men and women only players, there must be a real life somewhere. And I was always groping after it in a blind dumb sort of way—not likely, certainly, to find it in battle-fields or ballrooms; but yet the reflection was more likely to force itself upon me when I was among murderers or butter-

flies than at any other time. Now that I found myself among
politicians, I think it forced itself upon me more strongly
than ever. When it became clear to me that in order to
succeed, party must be put before country and self before
everything, and that success could only be purchased at the
price of convictions, which were expected to change with those
of the leader of the party—these, as it happened, were of an
extremely fluctuating character, and were never to be relied
upon from one session to another—my thirst to find something
that was not a sham or a contradiction in terms increased.
And the question occurred to me whether there might not be
latent forces in nature, by the application of which this profound moral malady might be reached. To the existence of
such forces we have the testimony of the ages. It was by the
invocation of these that Christ founded the religion of which
the popular theology has become a travesty, and it appeared to
me that it could only be by a reinvocation of these same forces
—a belief in which seemed rapidly dying out—that a restora-
tion of that religion to its pristine purity could be hoped for.

By ill luck this truth-seeking vigorous spirit, whose
one wish was to follow the precepts of a higher Power
and to give practical effect to the teaching of a divine
Master, fell under the influence of a person calling
himself the Prophet Harris, by whom he was spirited
off to America. Here he worked for the good of the
community over which Harris presided. His feelings
on the subject found expression in a speech to my
father, who often repeated it as an explanation of
Oliphant's religious beliefs. He used to say, "If
I were really to obey the teaching of Jesus Christ,
I should take my coat off before I had gone a few
steps along Piccadilly and give it to the first poor
fellow who wanted it." This being practically
impossible, he devoted himself to the good of
the community described, and no work was too

menial for him as a proof of his devotion. "The Prophet," as he called himself, after a year or two released him from the duties of farm-work and straw-berry-selling, discovering more advantageous means of utilising his convert; for apparently in this society any capital of money or brains possessed by the members was at the disposal of their leader, who was not slow to turn it to account. Oliphant was there-fore allowed to return to Europe, from whence he could more readily replenish the community's coffers, and we find him acting as special 'Times' correspon-dent during the Franco-German war. In Paris, after the Commune, he was performing the same work— but always under pledge to return to his American friends if the Prophet summoned him. The following from Kinglake alludes to the strange influence that had come into his friend's life.—

A. W. Kinglake to John Blackwood.

I have an account of Oliphant corresponding with your tid-ings. He has a real genius for alighting upon spots where the interests of the world's drama gather, and I trust with you that his charm and his cleverness will somehow deliver him from the redoubtable Harris.

Literary work was also allowed him, the Prophet being aware, no doubt, that this was for Oliphant a peculiarly remunerative branch of industry, so that after a few years of comparative inactivity in that line he appeared once more before the world with some sketches of American social and commercial life. In these his fine weapons of sarcasm were not found to have grown rusty, and his account of American stock-jobbery places before us in his most fearless fashion

the knaveries of the different "rings." Blackwood
never expresses any surprise, only pleasure, at seeing
him when he reappears. They seem always to begin
again just where they left off, Oliphant slipping into
the old accustomed modes of life as easily as he resumed his London clothes.

John Blackwood to his Wife.

14 Arlington St., W., *May* 19, 1876.

Larrie Oliphant came in immediately after breakfast, and we
talked and laughed as of old. He reports his wife and mother
well and happy as possible. He has a telegraph wire into his
bedroom, and had a chat with his wife this morning. Kinglake
says that she, by the inspiration of Harris, is devoting herself
to the rearing of poultry, and moralised over the mysterious
power that kind of saint has in knocking the mind out of the
most intelligent of women. It is fearful to hear Larrie's
account of the villany of New Yorkers. From bowie-knife
cut-throats they seem to have sunk to the most unscrupulous
of cut-purses. He found the paid agent and counsel of his
own company trying to betray him into the hands of the actual
"ring" of the opposing company.

The exposures of New York commercial roguery
which have since followed place his revelations in
rather a different light; for when written they appeared as warnings to the unwary, liable to be
doubted by ordinary respectable persons, but now
they are known to be a simple statement of facts.
Of social life on the other side of the Atlantic he
may be said to have been the first to "exploiter"
the American girl. And "Irene Macgillicuddy" was
undoubtedly the pioneer of that large army of damsels
who, in fact and fiction, have obtruded themselves so
conspicuously into all that relates to our modern life,
to the dismay and envy of their less enterprising

sisters. Her first appearance in print, however, was not of a nature to endear her author to the society whence she was drawn; for, as Oliphant says, "they are so ridiculously sensitive in America,"—so much so, in fact, that he thought it better to pause before his next sketch.

Laurence Oliphant to John Blackwood.

I cabled to you not to publish the Evolution article in consequence of letters enclosed, from which you will see that "Irene" has kicked up such a rumpus in New York society that we had better leave them a few months to recover their tranquillity before firing our second shot. My clever correspondent, who is herself a "bouncer," turned traitor, and gave me the points, is in an agony of alarm.

Other letters show him to be here and there and everywhere—sometimes engaged in matters connected with the Cable business, which he conducted with great ability; at other times with the railways, and other public matters, which took him long journeys through the length and breadth of the land. He himself must have had a consciousness of his own will-o'-the-wisp characteristics when he wrote thus:—

Laurence Oliphant to John Blackwood.

ATHENÆUM, LONDON.

MY DEAR BLACKWOOD,—Here I am again! but I left in a hurry, and I am in a hurry, and I am going back in a hurry; so, however much I might desire it, I do not see how I can come and see whether you have improved at golf (not that I am a judge) since I saw you last. Still I cannot resist, being so near you, giving you a metaphorical embrace, and assuring you, appearances to the contrary notwithstanding, that so far as I am aware I am neither married nor a maniac. After a long interval of indifference, the old feeling about 'Piccadilly' has come up so strongly that I have thought, if you and Doyle were agreeable, it might now be published, perhaps with greater effect than before. I do not want to trade on the somewhat peculiar notoriety I have since acquired, unless I do good in some form; but I think I might be justified in turning it to account for the benefit of society, so I should be quite ready to put my name on the title-page. This would relieve you of responsibility, and could not hurt me, as I am no longer damageable except by a failure in the grape crop. You will see what I have said in the few lines of preface which I enclose. Still, whatever happens, I want to assure you and Mrs Blackwood of my affectionate remembrances, and I shall be glad to see your handwriting again.—Yours very truly,

L. OLIPHANT.

Thoughts of Oliphant and his strange connection with America take us back to the American war. The following shows him as appearing in England just after one of the well-known incidents of the war had taken place :—

John Blackwood to William Blackwood.

Oliphant came yesterday in excellent force, and brings a very graphic account of Maclellan's movement by an eyewitness, Lord Edward St Maur, which will make a popular paper.

The movement here alluded to is no doubt General Maclellan's retreat to the Potomac with the Federal army of 200,000 men before a vastly inferior Confederate force under Lee,—a blunder which led Lee on in pursuit till the Federals with their large army had to take refuge behind their gunboats. The sympathies of the Magazine tended in the direction of the Southern cause—not, we imagine, from any deepseated prejudice in favour of slavery, but a good many of my father's friends, as will be shown, were with the

Southern army in the thick of the fray. Their letters and descriptions were full of the deeds of bravery and the personal courage of the Confederate officers, who also carried with them to a certain extent the sympathy that is felt for men fighting against fearful odds. In this, however, as in all civil wars, the feeling of sympathy was pretty evenly distributed on both sides, and my father's friends were by no means all Southerners, to go no further than Mr Motley, to whom he alludes in the following letter to a correspondent at Vienna, where Motley was then American Minister. He writes :—

How does Mr Motley get on ? Will you give him my best regards ? I heard at one time that he was very crazy on the subject of England and the North, but I daresay the course I have taken in the Magazine will not make him scratch me out of the list of his friends.

The author of 'The Rise of the Dutch Republic' was, as might be expected, a keen Northerner ; but my father evidently thought he might be open to conviction through the pages of 'Maga,' which had to give voice to the disapproval of the Federal tactics, these being particularly obnoxious to the Conservative party in England.

The sources whence were drawn the materials for the different Magazine articles that appeared on the incidents of the war were nearly all derived first hand from witnesses of the engagements, several of the correspondents having served in the Southern army. To one of these, Major Ross, an officer in the Austrian service, who had volunteered under General Lee, the following letter was written :—

John Blackwood to Major F. Ross.

EDINBURGH, *Nov.* 7, 1864.

I have read the account of your visit to the Confederate States with great pleasure. It is a very curious and interesting narrative, and if agreeable to you, I purpose to bring it out in the Magazine. . . . Some of the expressions amuse me exceedingly. Longstreet's "they have fought their last man, and he is running," is a very graphic description of a beaten army. And the enthusiast who is ready to accept a frozen hell for his fighting platform ought to rival the deeds of Squire Widrington. I was sorry to see that there was a want of cordiality between Lee and his subordinates. It is a noble fight the Southerners are making, and your narrative gives a very clear picture of what they have been doing.

Another correspondent, Von Borcke, a Prussian officer and a volunteer on the Southern side, also gave an account of some of the fighting, having taken a prominent part as head of General Longstreet's staff, and having brought away with him an additional order of merit in the shape of a Federal bullet in his lungs, which caused him to be regularly fêted when he visited his sympathising Editor at Strathtyrum. He was a typical specimen of the Prussian soldier, — a splendid fellow, over six feet, broad - shouldered and fair - haired. Several of the American officers came over to England after the war, and my father had an amusing evening with them, which he describes in a letter to Aytoun.

John Blackwood to W. E. Aytoun.

SPONDON, DERBY, *June* 26, 1865.

I had a very interesting scene the night before I left London. We were sitting quietly about half-past nine, Cluny [Gordon] and George [nephew] with us, when Fitzgerald Ross came in to say good-bye, and proposed us to go with him to have a drink with Colonel Latrobe, who was Longstreet's head of staff all through the war, and acting Adjutant-General of the army on the day [of] surrender. We adjourned immediately, and were received with cheers by Latrobe, Colonel Von Borcke (Stewart's head of staff and companion in all the raids and rides), and several other Confederates, all smoking and engaged in drinking and compounding strange drinks. "Now we'll have a camp reminiscence," says Latrobe; and Ross, as the greatest artist, was set smashing eggs and pouring in brandy, sherry, lemon, sugar, &c., the result being a "Tom and Jerry," and a lighter drink of sparkling and still Rhine wines, &c., called a "Jerry and a Tom." A tumbler of each was shoved before me, and I required to be cautious, as they were insidiously pleasant. Latrobe told us that in February he saw Lee's letter to Davis declaring that he could defend Richmond no longer, and proposing to retire and fight the thing out in the interior of the country; but Davis said *No*, on the ground of the moral effect of the fall of Richmond. At the last the army would have got off had not heavy rains come on, and not being able to march fast enough their supplies were intercepted and they were starving. Lee made Latrobe take the roll of the army, and they were 8500 men with muskets in their hands and about 140,000 round and about them. Latrobe had in his possession, and showed us, the original convention for the surrender signed by three Confederate generals and three Federals, acting as commissioners for their several armies. Two copies were kept by each, and on their side Lee had one and Latrobe the óther. Latrobe got away on parole, and he showed us the document, not an ordinary one, but written entirely in Grant's own hand. Latrobe and Von Borcke are two splendid specimens of soldiers, both about 6 feet 2. The scene and talk altogether were very striking, and realising wild war's reality and camp life to a degree. Latrobe was very complimentary to Ross, saying of him "that he was remarkable for two things,—that, having no personal interest in the war, no man among them all was more ready to fight and risk his life like the meanest soldier; and no Confederate could carry his drink or mix it better than Ross." Stewart was a teetotaller, and they told some capital stories of Von Borcke, after he had put his general to bed, riding over to

their tent in the adjoining camp (Longstreet's) to have his
drink, and the loud acclaim with which he was received and
Ross called upon to mix the liquor, as he was doing then.

I was very glad George was present, as it was a real military
scene telling of great events, and there was not the slightest
swagger about the fellows in telling all their stories. Cluny
said he had not tasted such *devilish mixtures* since he was at
Cambridge, but whatever amount of blue pill and black-draught
they might involve, he would not have missed the scene for the
world.

A few weeks after this Aytoun unexpectedly passed
away, and we come upon a letter which is marked with
the sadly significant words, "The last letter I ever
received from William Aytoun.—J. B." It is dated
12th July 1865, and on August 5 Aytoun died. No
more happy meetings, no more cheery letters, from
him, and for a long time his friend felt that gladness
had left him, and every letter is tinged with the sadness following on the loss of this dear comrade of his
youth, whose friendship for over twenty years had
been one of the happy features of his life. He alludes
very touchingly to his loss in a letter to his sister :—

John Blackwood to Isabella Blackwood.

EDINBURGH, *August 9, 1865.*

MY DEAR ISABELLA, — I came in from Strathtyrum last
night, and Aytoun's funeral is to be to-morrow. His death is
indeed a blow to me, and whenever I sit down to write a
line about him I hang over the desk thinking of all the merry
days we had together. Never, I suppose, were two men simi-
larly situated to whom their intercourse formed so much the
business as well as the pleasure of their lives. Of late years
the business element was comparatively nothing, but the
affection remained. His mother-in-law writes to me that
although he had been very unwell, it was only two days before

that they began to fear that the end was so near. Apparently
he did not suffer, and was quite calm and collected, joining
audibly in the communion service within an hour of death.
It is striking that the last words he ever wrote to me were a
message to Julia about the death of her uncle, not to grieve
unduly over the death of those who had "led a life of piety and
trusted to the merits of our Saviour"; and then he said, "Adieu,
my dear John." The form was an unusual one with him, and
it was his last adieu to his old ally. . . . On the very
morning he died I was thinking of him, and said to Julia, "I am
very uneasy at not hearing from Aytoun; write to-day to his
wife." She did so, and her letter was hardly gone when the
telegraph brought us the sad news. His poor sisters arrived
too late.

Also in a letter to Lever he remarks on the effect of
early association with regard to friendship, and quotes
Aytoun as an instance where his memory always re-
verts more to the pleasant everyday intercourse, the
mirth and good-fellowship, than to the more serious
aspects of real hard work in which they were
associated :—

John Blackwood to Charles Lever.

How true are your remarks in last "O'Dowd" about early
social intercourse. I was thinking of all the joyous scenes in
which Aytoun and I were together here, or roving about the
country. These scenes come before me much, much more than
all the serious work we had; but indeed we almost never had
a consultation that was not mingled with shouts of laughter.
With all his fun and fancy too he had a head such as is not to
be found among the *wise* middle-aged youths of the present
days. There is one good fellow less in the world, and such as
he can ill be spared in this age of humbug and pretension.

A suitable memorial of Aytoun was desired by John
Blackwood, and his wishes in this direction were car-

ried out by his and Aytoun's friend Martin (now Sir Theodore Martin). To Martin it was a real labour of love, and his remarks in the following show how deeply the subject interested him. During the heart-wearing process of looking over his dead friend's letters and papers, than which perhaps there is no occupation more utterly saddening, he says of some fragments of prose writings very characteristic of Aytoun :—

Theodore Martin to John Blackwood.

Dec. 1, 1865.

I think we should be able to turn out a very creditable volume, and keep together some things of his which I would be sorry to see drift into oblivion. Ah me, how my heart aches as I run these papers through, to think of the many cheery hours of intercourse he and I had over them in the pleasant old times !

And again :—

I should like to try my hand at something for old affection's sake. . . . The Memoir should be directed to showing the fine humour and genuine manliness of his character, and also his singular readiness and faculty in all the literary tasks to which he applied himself. I wish you could recall some more of his sayings. He was not a manufacturer of *bon mots*, and therefore, I suppose, we all find it difficult to recall any of the things that gave so much vivacity and drollery to his talk. The charm sometimes lay in a word which surprised you by its unexpectedness ; or by some quaint exaggeration at the bottom of which there was always a substratum of truth.

When the Memoir was completed and had been shown to Aytoun's sisters, Mr Martin writes : " I am delighted to find she and her sister are pleased, for I may say unaffectedly that to please them and your-self is all I care for in this business."

The following extracts from a letter to Mr Collins give a few points of appreciation from his old friend :—

In what you say of "Bothwell" I quite concur. I think his 'Lays' are the best modern ballads we have, and his heart was in them. With all his unceasing love of fun there was a great deal of poetical sentiment in his nature. . . . His love of a joke was innate, and I constantly find myself now, when anything absurd happens, exclaiming, "How poor Aytoun would have enjoyed that!" He was a most joyous companion, and even when his health gave way, he always cheered up after a few minutes' talk. In all our long intercourse we never had an unpleasant word, and it was no common intercourse, being, when in Edinburgh, daily; and in our jokes we never spared each other. When we met in the evening on pretext of business, the shouts of laughter coming from our rooms caused our respective mothers to think that the cigars, &c., were the chief occupation. Nevertheless, his work was always done. As a travelling companion, which is a great test, he was delightful. He often talked of addressing himself to some one long and sustained work; but as it was, he worked very hard, and I am not sure but that he might have felt cramped if he had tried to work by rule.

CHAPTER VI.

THE EDITORIAL SANCTUM.

REV. G. R. GLEIG—JOHN BLACKWOOD'S MODE OF GUIDING HIS CONTRIB-
UTORS—POLITICS IN THE "SIXTIES"—BANQUET TO DISRAELI IN
EDINBURGH—GEORGE ELIOT'S RETURN TO HER FIRST FRIEND WITH
'FELIX HOLT'—MISS E. J. HASELL—MISS ANNE MOZLEY—CRITICISM ON
J. S. MILL—'GRAVENHURST'—THE EDITOR AT HOME—HENRY STEPHENS
—SUNDAY VISITS—JOHN HILL BURTON—"SHIRLEY" AND THE HERMIT-
AGE OF BRAID—LORD NEAVES—THE UPMAKING OF THE MAGAZINE—
LORD JOHN MANNERS—DISRAELI'S FIRST GOVERNMENT.

IN the preceding volume some very interesting pages
have been devoted to chronicling the earlier work
done for the House by one of its veteran supporters,
the Rev. G. R. Gleig, the late Chaplain-General. The
years that followed the production of such works as
'The Subaltern,' &c., did not in any way dim his literary powers, though he worked at rather different subjects; and we find him in the "sixties" and "seventies"
with unabated vigour writing on any topic of the day
which occurred to his active mind, or which had been
suggested to him by his friend the Editor. "Yes,"
John Blackwood writes, "I shall have great pleasure
in handing over Dean Stanley's new work to you for
review." This was Stanley's 'Lectures on the Jewish
Church,' which seems to have inspired the "Church

militant" with a thoroughly combative tendency,—so much so, that we find the Editor, interposing on behalf of the Dean, led on by the subject in hand to express to Mr Gleig what were his own views in matters of faith.

John Blackwood to Rev. G. R. Gleig.

Sept. 14, 1866.

My own faith is very simple, and I have never been, nor cared to be, a theological student at all, so that I am not a good judge in a case like this. My impression, however, is very strong that you should soften the censure of Stanley. I cannot attach much importance to a man not being able to believe many of the stories in the Old Testament, or striving to explain them from natural causes; and believing as I do that Stanley is a religious man in all essentials, and striving hard to do good, I think we should be as gentle to him as possible when we think he is wrong. I often wonder at men perplexing and worrying themselves about the miracles, when our whole existence, the whole world, and all we see above us, is a miracle which God alone understands. It is the attempt to explain what it was never given to man to understand that leads man into errors.

However, his correspondent was a very doughty antagonist when his spear was once in the rest, and a second letter shows that he was still unconvinced; while the Editor has to confess that his championship is inspired by a liking for the Dean (in which most of us will sympathise), and the remains of a latent horror of the Shorter Catechism, that bugbear of Scottish children, which had left him for life with what Mr Gleig considered a lamentable indifference to dogma.

John Blackwood to Rev. G. R. Gleig.

Oct. 8, 1866.

I have a liking for the Dean as a man who is really religious, and working for the cause both of religion and morality, so that

I still have my doubts about the paper. My youthful sufferings under the Shorter Catechism have, I daresay, made me too
lax about formularies or points of faith. There is certainly a
very peculiar religious or anti-religious movement, which may
end in a pretty general throwing up of creeds, and good men
like Stanley would be wise to leave people to believe as much
as they can; so, on the whole, I think you are right in the
tone you have taken about his book.

Lord John Manners was here last week for a couple of
days, but had come from the Highlands, and had no news.
From something that passed, I am satisfied that Lord Derby
is not yet prepared to indicate his views about reform. I feel
that we must bring in a measure, although nobody really wants
one. We should of all things go dead for some stringent
measure to prevent bribery, and if you write anything, take
up that subject. These electioneering enquiries are the best
possible commentary on the humbug that is talked about
reform and the working man.

Politics during the stormy days that preceded the
collapse of Gladstone and Lord Russell, and the for-
mation of Lord Derby's and Disraeli's Government,
presented a favourable field for the exercise of Mr
Gleig's pen, and many a momentous crisis was entrusted to him for comment in the pages of 'Maga.'
Many warnings and cautions are given him as to
when he is to speak and when he is to be silent,
and the side-lights thrown on the topics of the hour
form strangely interesting comments on what have
become matters of our political history. The extension of the franchise was impending, together with
what seemed like a possible loss of Canada; then
there was the free importation of Spanish slave-
grown sugar, and the free introduction of foreign
rags into the paper-making industries. These Radical measures were all matters of widely different

interest, yet all formed burning questions of the day, and were keenly contested in the pages of 'Maga'; and very frequently, as will be seen, Mr Gleig is complimented on the undiminished skill and vigour of his writings.

John Blackwood to Rev. G. R. Gleig.

March 22, 1865.

I cannot help thinking that you write more vigorously and clearly now than ever you did. I do not know any of your earlier writings which I would rank as high for their qualities as these Gladstone and Russell papers.

Referring to a paper on Earl Russell, he goes on to say :—

Them's my sentiments exactly! The self-glorification of the Whigs and Free Traders is utterly intolerable. They take credit to themselves for the ordinary operations of nature, from a good harvest downwards; and as for the gold-fields, it never seems to enter their minds that without the discovery of these their measures would have made the country bankrupt. Free trade will end in making us helplessly dependent on others. The feeling that nothing is worth defending unless it can be shown at the moment that it *pays*, as evinced in the debate about the defence of Canada, is a very rotten sign of the state of the country. That debate made my blood boil. It was really an intimation to the Yankees that if they chose to take Canada we did not think it would pay to defend it.

The next letter contains John Blackwood's prediction, soon to be verified, that Gladstone had done himself harm at Oxford by his Irish Church speeches.

John Blackwood to Rev. G. R. Gleig.

April 5, 1865.

How completely Gladstone's speech about the Irish Church justifies your view of him. He must quit Oxford and take to the manufacturing districts.

The following is written after the elections of 1865, and refers to the Derby-Disraeli opposition.

John Blackwood to Rev. G. R. Gleig.

STRATHTYRUM, ST ANDREWS, *Aug.* 6, 1865.

Such a paper as you propose on the results of the elections is exactly what is wanted. By all means do it and let me have it in good time. We had Sir Hugh Cairns at St Andrews last week, and he dined with us one day. I liked him very much, and his feeling about politics I could see was much like my own—that Palmerston dying or falling aside there must be a fusion of parties, the educated men joining against the common Radical enemy. I mentioned to him what Kinglake said in a letter to me the other day, that "the country was thoroughly Conservative, but took no interest in the Derby-Dizzy opposition." He obviously felt the truth of this, at least *qua* Dizzy, and I cannot help the feeling myself.

The next letter, after prescribing severe punishment for John Bright for his Free-trading views, goes on to the pleasanter subject of Principal Tulloch, and points out that the Principal had apparently also suffered from the Shorter Catechism in early youth. The other matter alluded to was the Rev. Dr Norman Macleod's persecution by some rigid Sabbatarians for the wish which he, in common with other good and practical persons, had of lightening the austerities of a Glasgow Sunday by the introduction of music in the churches and other innovations.

In a letter to another correspondent, Blackwood refers again to the bitter hostility of a certain narrow-minded faction which had plunged Dr Macleod into such hot water about this time, 1866 : "In Scotland there has been rather a theological rumpus of late, and my friends Principal Tulloch and Norman Macleod

—two of the best and most useful men we have—are being called all sorts of names for venturing upon a little freedom of opinion."

John Blackwood to Rev. G. R. Gleig.

Dec. 2, 1865.

In regard to politics, it is pretty clear that the Government is giving in to the Radical element in its constitution, and I do not think you will have much difficulty in finding materials for comment. Bright's speech tells a tale. Pitch into the fellow for the way in which he insults the treacherously ruined West India planters and glories in that foul act, the admission of slave-grown sugar. That the same set of men should claim credit to themselves as philanthropists by abolishing slavery in our own colonies, and forthwith when they wanted their sugar cheap go and encourage an incredibly worse system of slavery by purchasing the sugar from the Spanish and other slave growers, has always seemed to me about the worst act of combined hypocrisy and greed that was ever perpetrated by a nation. I am still suffering under a plethora of MSS., but I wish a review of Robertson [Rev. Frederick Robertson], who was a very remarkable man, so go on with the paper at your leisure. Along with this I send you a pamphlet by Tulloch, Principal at St Andrews, about the best man we have in the Scotch Church. You will see that he goes in at that deadly enemy of Scotch childhood, the Shorter Catechism.

I do not admire the taste with which Norman Macleod goes at his subject, but I perfectly agree with him about the Scotch Sunday observance. These extreme Sabbatarians do a world of mischief, and if they do not take care, will bring on a revulsion of feeling likely to end in a very general disregard of the Sunday.

Lord Palmerston's death in October of the year 1865 brought about the fusion between the parties that Blackwood had been hinting at in so many of the letters.

John Blackwood to Rev. G. R. Gleig.

Oct. 19, 1865.

Do you think you could write a short notice of poor old Pam.? Your own recollections will supply ample materials, and I should like to say something cordial about him,—a general estimate of his character, and such reflections as his career naturally call forth. He held his head up frankly, like an English gentleman, and I much fear, if his party continue in power, there will be, without him, base truckling to America, or any foreign Power that chooses to bully us.

Writing again to Mr Gleig at the end of the year, he says :—

The point to press is the real indifference of the country to reform, and the desire of all sensible moderate men to unite. My own belief is that a Reform Bill of some kind or other must be carried, and all we can do is to make it as little objectionable as possible. An exposition to the Ten-Pounders of how completely any material lowering of the franchise would take the power out of their hands would be the most valuable thing.

Mrs Oliphant wrote me not a bad one of Montalembert, who was calling upon her the other day at Paris. He was lamenting the total want of rising statesmen, both in his own country and ours. She slyly suggested we had Lord Amberley to fall back upon. "I'd much rather have Lord Dundreary," said the Count.

The following letters from John Blackwood to the Rev. G. R. Gleig are all written in the winter of 1866 :—

In what he [Oliphant] says of the probable fate of that victim of philanthropy, the Negro, and also of the despotism exercised by the President in America, I think you may find matter for quotation or comment. Oliphant told me that he never met with a born American of any shade of politics who did not curse universal suffrage, and he did not believe a native-born Yankee existed who was in favour of it, but their blessed constitution ties them up. The rinderpest and Jamaica seem more likely to prove the immediate battlefields than reform. I hope to hear from you soon. Recollect there are only 28 days in February.

As to reform, I think our people are rather too busy warning Lord Russell off the rocks he is likely to split upon, and we are not called upon to say much until Lord Russell tables his scheme. ..

To the Same.

Absolute indifference seems to be the prevailing feeling in regard to the Reform Bill. Now this apathy may promote the passing of the Bill as effectually as if the majority were fervent in its favour. The real fact I believe to be that there will be no fervour in favour of reform until the Conservatives declare themselves dead against. If ever we do so, the Whigs will immediately put on the steam to get up every kind of agitation. Could we hint this in such a way as to expose the unscrupulous character of that party! You will, I doubt not, have ample means of knowing what our leaders think or intend. My own belief certainly is that the income tax would be the best and simplest basis for the franchise. If every elector was subject to that obnoxious impost, it would be the surest way of keeping it down, and also of expanding when real necessity required.

To the Same.

In reading Gladstone's speech, I was greatly struck by the folly and weakness of his statement, that he had only had time "roughly" to read the volume of returns on which he proceeded to argue as reasons for his Reform Bill. What was the hurry? These returns should have been a well-considered basis, or not built upon at all. Pitch into this, if you have not done so. It was like a man telling you he had not had time to consider a subject, and then not merely delivering an essay on it (a thing I have often met with), but asking you to act upon what he said.

These extracts from John Blackwood's letters to one of his most experienced and trusty contributors seem to us to serve the purpose of showing briefly how, though he never himself wrote for the Magazine, nor ever or very rarely put his hand to any alteration, yet he always most skilfully managed, when he wished to do so, to make the writer his mouthpiece. He struck the keynote, as it were, and the correspondent played the tune.¹ This is particularly noticeable in the letters referring to political articles, which are necessarily more or less oracular in tone, and therefore more open to controversy, and had to be carefully considered. If by any chance he thought he had given the wrong note, another letter follows by next post telling the correspondent he must change it or hold back, perhaps wait till the next month and watch for the turn of events. This subtle direction, the merest indication of the line to be taken, can be traced in most of the letters on other subjects, but the suggestions are usually so fine-drawn that the correspondents probably adopted them without perceiving they were not their own. His idea as an Editor was that the writer should be given full play for his powers, if he were worth anything at all, and not subjected to much interference, and that a suggestion, if made, was only a *suggestion* to be caught up or not. Only when he felt keenly, and wanted a thing said distinctly, did he put his full weight in the scale, and then, as these letters show, he conveyed his meaning in a nutshell.

The following extract from a letter to William Blackwood carries us on to that important epoch when Lord Derby and Disraeli came into office in 1867, and proceeded to formulate their Reform Bill, thus hoisting the Whigs with their own petard.

John Blackwood to William Blackwood:

4 BURLINGTON GARDENS, LONDON, *June* 3, 1867.

I found Gleig in great form. At the Club I saw Sir Charles Russell and Lord Colonsay, also Burnhouse. I gather that our friends are in great spirits, and that we have taken the right line in the Magazine. Colonsay said just what I have been saying, that no man alive can tell the result, but that it could not be helped. Sir Charles Russell said it was impossible to speak to a Whig. They were mad with fury. He was going to Lady Molesworth's to-night, but would not venture to open his mouth in case of getting into a personal fracas.

In the autumn a banquet had been given in Edinburgh to Disraeli, of which Blackwood, writing to Mr Gleig, says: "You cannot be too emphatic in regard to Dizzy's success here. Especially the meeting with the working men was a most marked success. It was, I think, the best speech I ever heard him make." It followed upon the banquet given to Lord Derby at Manchester. Both were the outcome of the feeling of confidence of which the tide had set in so strongly throughout the country. The measures recently carried by them had won them the approval of all sensible members of their own party, besides giving them the voice of the country. A Reform Bill of some sort being absolutely inevitable, they had, instead of employing any small piece-meal measures, struck out a bold wide scheme on a line of their own, as more likely to be successful and well received than any small ineffectual "tinkerings at the Constitution." John Blackwood strongly upheld this view of their policy, and, writing on one occasion of the Reform Bill, he says :—

It became our duty to make the best of it for the country.
. . . I rejoice to think that the measure has met with such
general support, and that the old party are determined to
come forward and work for the country under the new state
of things as under the old. I hold such conduct wiser and
bolder far than that of those (happily few in number) who,
having failed to give effect to their own opinions, throw up their
hands, and retire from the struggle.

The Conservatives having come into power, and the
affairs of the nation being once more guided on lines
more in accordance with 'Maga's' time-honoured principles, we shall leave the world of politics for a time,
and follow out some of the other threads in the literary
web which encircled the Blackwoods. Day by day,
year by year, it was being spun and spun, one literary
connection leading to another.

The severance with George Eliot was only of
short duration, and she came back to them,
only to be more closely reunited, and we find John
Blackwood announcing her return to her old friends
with the novel of 'Felix Holt' in 1866 in the following letter :—

John Blackwood to the Rev. W. Lucas Collins.

EDINBURGH, *April* 28, 1866.

From the advertisement in the Magazine, you will see that
George Eliot has returned to her first friend. The overture did
not come from me, and the whole transaction has been of the
most gratifying kind. I read the first two MS. volumes before
concluding anything, and I am delighted to say that I think the
book a marvel.

Besides such well-known authoresses as George
Eliot and Mrs Oliphant, there were other ladies at
this time who were doing excellent literary work for

the House, and whose attainments called forth many
pleasant letters from the Editor, who had always
steadily held out a helping hand to feminine literary
talent.   He was not, as will be imagined, one of
those who supported Women's Rights in the usual
acceptance of the term, and would never have approved of the pitting against each other for market-
able value of the two very widely differing qualities
of masculine and feminine brain-power.   He considered their merits perfectly distinct and apart,—
the man, in his opinion, was the stronger in every
way, and likelier to make his mark in the world,
as history has shown us, and this not entirely
on account of his superior schooling, as some would
maintain.   The woman, on the other hand, when she
has attained distinction in any line, did so, in his
opinion, *quand même*, and admiration for her performance was undoubtedly heightened a thousandfold
in his eyes by the fact that she *was* a woman, and
working under disabilities which made her achievements the more creditable.   At the time Lord Derby
published his translation of the 'Iliad' he entrusted
it to one of his feminine contributors for review, who
had first asked for the task.   This seems to be the
right moment to mention the name of Miss E. J.
Hasell, whose writings are well known to readers of
'Maga.'   Of her review of the translation the Editor
says :—

April 1, 1865.

You have, in my opinion, done it extremely well, giving a
very clear view of what the translation is, and the critical
remarks are given in a genuine, fresh spirit, with no pedantry
or unnecessary worrying about "renderings." Your scholarship
quite astonishes me. How in the world did you come to

have such a knowledge of Greek, and apparently of all other languages.

In spite of his admiration of the Greek the Editor takes occasion to soften the lady's views about Pope, who was a favourite of his.

John Blackwood to Miss E. J. Hasell.

My impression is that you rank the translation rather too high. Now, with all my devotion to our leader, I do not wish to say a single word in praise of his work more than it deserves. You will see on proof that I have deleted most of your references to Pope. Pope was a great man, and it is not right to run him down. Moreover, in regard to Homer, he has kept alive a kind of knowledge of the old Bard among Englishmen generally, which he could not have done had he not been a man of genius and a poet himself. Homer and his heroes would not be the familiar thoughts that they are to most of us, were it not for Pope, so the country owes him a debt of gratitude. Turning to compare his translation with some extracts I found, I read him on with more easy pleasure, and less effort at attention, than I did the Earl's blank verse, so I suspect with all his defects Pope's is the most readable translation yet.

The following to Mr W. W. Story, the sculptor, gives some idea of Miss Hasell's attainments:—

John Blackwood to Mr W. W. Story.

I have taken the liberty of giving a note of introduction to you to Miss Hasell of Dalemaine, near Penrith. She is a friend and contributor of mine. She is the most remarkable classical scholar I ever met with in a lady, and if you look at her paper, 'Andromache,' in the March number of the Magazine, I am pretty sure you will agree with me as to her attainments and power of writing, and she has written many such papers. Lord Derby thought her review of his Homer about the best that appeared. She has visited me once or twice, and I think Mrs and Miss Story will like her, as there is a great deal of character about her.

It will be gathered from this letter that Miss Hasell was no ordinary person, the nature of her attainments being more unusual for a lady four-and-twenty years ago than they are now. And when she, many years afterwards, wrote from her Cumberland home that lakes and mountains were not entirely substitutes for intellectual companionship, and that the literary society of the Lakes no longer existing, she proposed visiting Edinburgh for some mental refreshment, John Blackwood invited her to come and stay at Randolph Crescent. The idea of a lady who read Greek and Hebrew as easily as we read French or German, and for her lighter moments chose the Sonnets of Camoens in the original, sounded somewhat alarming; and even her host, after he had invited her, was rather dismayed at the thought of how he should live up to the high ideal which we told him no doubt she had formed of the Editor of Blackwood. He felt, as his aunt, Miss Steuart, used to express it, he could not be " on his altitudes " all day long. The evening she arrived Colonel L. Lockhart, Mr James Mure, and William Blackwood were present. And I must say we all sat in rather gloomy expectation awaiting our guest, only to find, when she did come, a most agreeable and sympathetic companion, interested in all we showed her, and delighted with her surroundings. Long drives, that ended in the dark those short December days, expeditions to Roslin and Craigmillar, I remember. We found, to our delight, she had a thoroughly feminine interest in Queen Mary, no foolish masculine wish to saddle her with political intrigues or even baser designs. At Holyrood there was no hurry-

ing over the fatal scene of Rizzio's murder, no doubts
as to the authenticity of those dark stains that were
shown on the staircase.   The old Palace had for her
the strongest dramatic interest, and as we drove past
the house that now marks the famous Kirk-o'-Field,
and about which my father always observed a certain
reticence, we were relieved to find that she asked no
awkward questions—nay, actually agreed with us that
if the Queen did blow Darnley up, he thoroughly
deserved it.

Miss Hasell visited us again at Strathtyrum, accompanied by one of her sisters.   She was one of those
women who bore out my father's constant experience,
that those really dowered with intellect and learning
were ever the most simple and unaffected in manner,
the most easy to work with, and the most really companionable.   His remarks to another accomplished
writer, Miss Mozley, point to this also.   He writes:
" You deserve a testimonial from a grateful Editor for
the patience you have shown about this paper ; but it
is a comical fact that in nine cases out of ten it is the
people who cannot write a bit who kick up the great
rows about their MSS., and wish for answers and
opinions by return of post."   The lady here alluded to
was engaged just at the time on a series of essays on
social subjects—Dress, Manners, &c.—and there are
many letters to her from John Blackwood, written
more fully and expansively than was his wont, perhaps
because he never had the opportunity of talking to
this correspondent and he was anxious to make her
understand him.

John Blackwood to Miss Anne Mozley.

Jan. 25, 1865.

The success of the book is a great triumph for you, as it is very rarely indeed that a republication of miscellaneous essays, however good, pays expenses, and when I undertook the publication, I did so because I felt it to be a highly creditable book to publish, but did not expect profit,—on the contrary, from previous experience, thought loss highly probable.

Referring to her essay on Conversation, he writes again :—

You are right in supposing that Professor Wilson is a tender subject with me, but at all events let me see your essay on Unrestraint. He certainly was a splendid example of the want of restraint, and those who knew him best will most readily agree with you about that. The doubt I have is, whether, never having heard him in familiar intercourse, you will understand the real grandeur of the old man. His conversation was something wonderful, such as I have never heard approached by any other man, and I have heard some of the best going and gone, within the last twenty - five years. The extraordinary thing about him was that he made the fun as good sitting talking with two old ladies, like my mother and aunt, as if he had been at a Noctes. . . . I quite agree with you that the vigorous, active, middle time of a man's life is that in which he is best for himself and others, and far happier than in the most gilded youth. Then it is a happiness which tones and strengthens old age, not a thing to sigh over, like Horace Walpole's retrospects of youth.

Again he writes to Miss Mozley :—

I am glad also that you denounce the practice so many modern novelists have of painting the parents fools, or worse, and the children preternaturally wise and discreet. It is against nature and right feeling. For this reason I never could enjoy Mrs Nickleby, cleverly painted as the character is. I always felt as if Nicholas himself were exposing his poor old mother as a fool.

The following letter to Miss Mozley, referring to her essay on the position of women, bears out what has been already stated as the Editor's opinions on Women's Rights, and the harm which is usually done to their prestige by unwise championship :—

Jan. 23, 1868.

I like the idea of the paper you propose on the change in the position of women during the last fifty years. The position of women in literature is very remarkable at present, and George Eliot and Mrs Oliphant are able to hold their own against all male competitors. There is a paper on Queen Caroline and another on the Queen's book in the forthcoming No. of the Magazine, both by Mrs Oliphant, which for excellence in their different ways it would be hard to beat. The authorship, of course, is secret. I always find that it is really accomplished women like yourself and those above mentioned who are least distressed about the Rights of Women. The rights of women papers that I see are almost invariably as badly composed as doubtless their unfortunate husbands' dinners are cooked.

He further relieves his mind on this subject by proposing that Stuart Mill should be scourged for his book, ' The Subjection of Women ' :—

I fear the article on Mill's 'Subjection of Women' is too dry. Confound the fellow, he argues as if mankind, male and female, were equally stocks or stones, or, if positively not equal at first, to be made so by the teaching of him—Mill. The man is blinded by arrogance, and instead of loving his fellow-creatures, he hates and would domineer over every one who did not agree with him. I wish you could throw in some fun and scourge him.

Mr William Smith, to whom a letter was written in connection with Mill's last book, was then writing a notice of Sterne. He was himself the author of several books of a dreamy metaphysical nature — of these

'Thorndale' and 'Gravenhurst' are the best known. Of the latter, Laurence Oliphant, writing from a Nile boat, says: "I have 'Gravenhurst' on board—a most comfortable book." He was often asked to write reviews and critiques, for which his peculiarly refined and scholarly habit of thought particularly fitted him. His life was usually spent in retirement, often in the English lake district amongst the hills and streams from which the lake poets drew their inspirations. His fastidious taste and the delicate accuracy of all his writings seem to belong to a school of an older generation—a school that took infinite pains.

John Blackwood to William Smith.

April 12, 1865.

I by no means think you too favourable to Sterne,—on the contrary, in some respects, I hardly think you defend him with sufficient boldness, especially from Thackeray's attacks, which were grossly overdone. I always thought that there was a certain amount of affectation in what Thackeray said about Sterne a-going in for "the large-hearted" line of business, and a sort of implying how differently I would have acted. I do not mean that Thackeray was insincere in the matter, but he had set himself to paint a "selfish sentimentalist," and the subject ran away with him, leading him to exaggerate trifles, real or imaginary, into proofs of the foulest black-heartedness. Your defence of Sterne against Dr Ferrier's attack is complete. It is astonishing how Dr Ferriers in our own day are listened to. I have seen very many instances of this sort of thing,—the ignorant and vulgar always applauding the attempt to reduce to their own level the man of cultivation and genius, who is conferring the greatest benefit upon them by fusing the literature of the past into his own writing.

John Stuart Mill's next book did not please Blackwood any better than the 'Subjection of Women,' and when handing the book over to the

scholarly author of 'Thorndale' for criticism in
'Maga,' the Editor cannot resist a few severe
"digs"—we believe he would have called them—
at Mill and his metaphysics, with whom he had no
sympathy, not only because of his doubts and dis-
beliefs, as those might be entertained by any of
us, but he considered the doubters should modestly
hide their disabilities instead of parading them to
the confusion and dismay of those who were still
on the right side of the fence.

John Blackwood to William Smith.

Dec. 11, 1865.

I enclose proof of your paper on Mill, which I like and agree
with as far as I can be said to like and agree with anything on
the subject.   There are many things hard of belief, but the external world is a tolerably potent fact, and I do not see what
Mr Mill supposes he can add to our knowledge by talking of it
as a "permanent possibility of sensation" or in calling "Life
Eternal" a negative conception.   The careful perusal of this
paper leaves me in my original belief that metaphysicians
spend their lives hunting after what is not to be found.
Their science consists mainly in giving names to emotions of
the mind or things which we all know to exist, and giving
them these hard names does not help us to understand them
a bit better.   There is an excellent passage of yours at page 13,
where you show that these men cannot argue out their theories
without accepting as facts the very things they attempt to deny.

The following to Mrs Oliphant still further exem-
plifies what has been said on this subject:—

John Blackwood to Mrs Oliphant.

July 11, 1864.

I should doubt whether —— has had time to do much of a
book of Lectures on Renan, so am not disposed for a paper
thereon, unless you think you have something you wish to
say yourself.   My feeling is always to let the heathen rage

and say nothing about them. I look upon the "good" sceptics with profound contempt as the most uncalled-for destroyers of paper going. Has not every poor devil doubts enough of his own without a posing ass of an essayist or reviewer trying to suggest others than them?

Enough, then, of the persons who obligingly supply us with doubts when our own do not make us sufficiently uncomfortable. John Blackwood would none of them! The simple faith and earnestness of conviction which is shown in so many of his father's letters remained also with him, and kept him steadfast all his life. He tells Mrs Oliphant how, in early days, he used to be bored by the attitude in writing or speaking of a certain type of Frenchmen who were determined to take up a solemn and thoughtful position with "Ce que c'est que la vie humaine, ou les veritables richesses d'un pays," &c. He apologises for his own irreverent attitude towards these profound thinkers by saying: "But I know I am a sad unbeliever in human wisdom, and if I could speak and write, which fortunately I cannot, I should be hooted off any platform in these enlightened days."

Mr John Paget, the metropolitan magistrate, was one of those who from time to time did much useful work for the Magazine. Art and artists were often the subjects of his contributions, and an article he was writing on John Leech drew the following from the Editor :—

John Blackwood to John Paget.
Nov. 14, 1865.

I enclose proof of your paper on Leech, which is, I think, very good and true. About the cartoon of the dying Russian

Emperor, I remember feeling the most intense disgust to it at the time. He was a great fellow in his way, was Nicholas, and to the dead man it was ungenerous and brutal. If Nicholas used the expression attributed to him, he did so in behalf of his own people, and I cannot see he was more to blame than if I, when a hostile army was advancing against Edinburgh, wished it buried under six feet of snow on the Lammermoors, but I would not send a cartoon to 'Punch' of the remains. Put me down for £10 for the testimonial to Cruickshank [George], for whom I have both a warm admiration and a personal regard.

As the years wear on, the central figure in these pages becomes a less shadowy personage to the writer, whose recollections of him date back to the childish days when only brief but always longed-for glimpses were to be had of him. There are many early associations connected with him and our Edinburgh home at Randolph Crescent where we lived all the winter, and which might be called the workaday time of the year, when my father used to be at 45 George Street — "45" as it was familiarly called — every day except for an occasional game of golf at Musselburgh. The time we children saw most of him was when we came down in the mornings to see him have his breakfast, when he used to divide his attentions between us and the 'Edinburgh Courant.' Without our society and that eminent Conservative organ I don't think he could have breakfasted when at home. All his movements were watched by us with the deepest interest, and after his cheery good-bye—"Now I'm off to 45"—we would rush to the window to see him lighting his cigar at the front door. Occasionally we were sent by our mother to "45" with notes or messages for him, and then we had what

ought to have been an awe - inspiring glimpse of
the Editor hard at work at his desk, with his
papers and letters around him. But there was no
feeling of awe on our part when we used to rush
up the staircase to his sanctum, where the noise
we made at the door ensured our welcome; and I
do not remember any time when my father was too
busy to answer, "Come in, come along," and smile at
us over his work. Sometimes he would accompany
us down-stairs and take us into the "old saloon," and,
leading my little brother and me round, would point
out the portraits and describe them to us, so that
they became as familiar to us as those of our own
kindred.

The original of one of these portraits, Mr Henry
Stephens, author of 'The Book of the Farm,' was a
very familiar figure to us when in Edinburgh. Venerable and picturesque-looking, with silvery hair and
olive skin and dark eyes, he was as unlike in appearance as he was in speech and manners to the people
one meets every day. The knowledge and accuracy
which made him of world - wide fame in his own
special subjects were not merely confined to agricultural subjects, but he brought them to bear on
matters of a very varied kind, the result of much
study and travel. Scientific, mechanical, musical
matters — all interested him. He was an equal
authority on the mechanism of a steam - plough
or a prima donna's voice—the German Kriegspiel or
the roasting of a pheasant. It was almost impossible to come upon any subject with which he was
not conversant, and in any discussion the "Swede's"
calm "That canna be," followed by a plain statement

of the case, generally settled the matter, and quite pleasantly; for he spoke from no love of contradiction, but only with the wish to make things clear. My father always treated him with the most tender respect, more like that of a son to a father. He was, at the time I can remember him, the only remaining contemporary of my grandfather.

Sunday in Edinburgh was always looked forward to by us with cheerful anticipation. My father at home all day, more stir in the house, more talk, more fun, the feeling we were going to have a good time extended to us children,—for it is very certain that children take much of the colour of their surroundings, and when the elders appear festively inclined, the little ones generally rise to the occasion, and we were seldom disappointed. On the return from church there was a dive made into the heap of letters, which on this day came to Randolph Crescent instead of going to "45," and the gems of the collection were brought to the luncheon-table,—the host sometimes forgetting his duties as carver in his eagerness for the mental refreshment contained in the correspondence. Oh! the shouts of laughter over one of Charles Lever's letters or "a rare bit" from Laurence Lockhart, or that other Laurence whom we used to hear my father call "Larry." How well they wrote! it was like hearing them speak. Sometimes it would be a communication from Kinglake, very sedate and carefully worded, but with just a little gentle sarcasm curled up somewhere if you knew where to look for it, and I don't think it was ever lost upon any of those who sat round that luncheon-table. The same party whom my father loved to see, assembled every Sunday for many a year—nephews and nieces, William Blackwood and his sisters, and my Uncle James for certain, and occasionally my aunt and other visitors.   If there was anything of a disquieting nature in the correspondence it did not transpire at luncheon, but was reserved for the quiet talk with William that generally followed.

These Sundays always recall certain visits that my father used to make that day on friends who lived a little way from town.   One of these was Mr John Hill Burton, the historian.   He lived in a quaint old-fashioned house on Craiglockhart Hill, a spur of the Pentlands, just outside Edinburgh.   To us children, who often accompanied him on these walks, this house was a special delight,—the winding stone-staircase, leading into narrow passages with break-neck steps in all directions, the oak floors of the apartments all bent and uneven, and books, books everywhere—books piled up to the ceiling, books scattered on the floor— while the denizen of this mansion, the veritable "Book-hunter" himself, sat in this royal confusion like a king amongst his subjects, happy and contented.   He and his visitor had much to talk about, and the short winter afternoons would begin to close in sometimes before my father would jump up with a start, exclaiming, "Bless me, I must have been here over an hour;" and then we would set off back to town, often accompanied by our host, whose slight wiry figure was equal to any amount of exercise.   Besides the 'Book-Hunter' and the 'Scot Abroad,' volumes by which his reputation became known, Mr Burton wrote various papers for the Magazine, and when settling for several pieces of literary labour the Editor says to him, in a letter which sounds refreshingly unlike business on the part of either: "If I have forgotten any Magazine articles, or made any mistake, be sure and tell me." In the same letter reference is made to the 'History of Scotland,' Mr Burton's great work, which had been on hand for some time, and was now, in 1865, nearing completion. Since the undertaking was begun, Mr Burton's reputation had been so immensely raised by his other writings that the publishers had the pleasant news for him that he was entitled to better terms, and the sooner they could advertise his History the better.

The Hermitage also was a favourite Sunday excursion. It was situated in the same picturesque region of the Braids; but whereas Craighouse, as its name implies, was situated on the top of a hill, the home of "Shirley" lay in a glen, a very sheltered and lovely spot. An afternoon there was a pleasure we all enjoyed—father, children, and dogs: even the cabman who drove us, according to Shirley's 'Recollections,' had a good time of it. The Hermitage house was modern, and had not the same weird fascination for us as Craighouse; but then it had very great external attractions. A scramble up the steep sides of the glen, with the wild possibility of a rabbit for the dogs to chase, was a joy that counted for much with us young ones, our excitement now and then breaking in upon the talk our father was enjoying with his friend as they paced along, and reminding him we had to be conveyed back to Edinburgh, and a move would be made to the house, where we found Mrs Skelton's hospitable tea-table awaiting us. By the time I allude to my father had begun to feel the dearth of literary

society in Edinburgh, and the companionship of the
few like Mr Skelton who could supply this want was
as highly appreciated by him as the lovely surroundings of their house were by us, who never needed to
be asked twice to accompany him on these memorable
expeditions.

Another visit he seldom failed to make, and which
usually finished up his Sunday afternoon, was on his
old friend and contributor, Lord Neaves, who lived
near us in Charlotte Square. He generally brought
away some good story, some original remark, from that
pleasant library. In later years Lord Neaves was
amongst the last of that older generation with whom
he still felt he could talk confidentially and unfold his
plans or unburden his mind, sure of sympathy and comprehension. Mrs Neaves has told us afterwards how
much her husband looked forward to these visits, and
to hearing the literary and political news in which by
his writings he had himself taken so brilliant a part.

The Queen's 'Journal in the Highlands' appeared
about this time, and John Blackwood writes of it with
genuine pleasure to Theodore Martin, who wished to
know how it struck him :—

Jan. 10, 1868.

Knowing how anxious you were about the Queen's 'Journal,'
I write at once to say that I am greatly pleased with it. There
is a genuine straightforward simplicity about the style, and a
good taste such as can only proceed from good feeling, which
is very taking. I see that the Royal Archers are honourably
mentioned in the 'Journal.' We had our annual winter dinner
yesterday, and at table I started the idea that if the Fenians
really knew the Queen's Body-Guard were all dining together
they would infallibly blow us up, suggesting at the same time
that two elderly gentlemen, who had won the silver arrow that

day, should be sent to patrol round the hall with their bows
and arrows. We had some laughing on the subject. It is
late in the day to write you a good New Year, but I do so
very heartily to Mrs Martin and you.

He next refers to a serious accident which Mr Martin
had sustained. While at Windsor Castle, when engaged upon his 'Life' of the Prince Consort,' he had
fallen upon the ice while watching the skating, and
twisted his leg, an infinitely more painful accident than
breaking it. "I am sorry to hear of your accident, but
I think I would almost stand a broken leg, certainly a
collar-bone, to be so tended. It was like the Queen to
send at once for Mrs Martin. How poor Aytoun would
have enjoyed your account of the Queen's kindness to
the crippled Troubadour."

And again, referring to his slow recovery: "Your
accident has, I fear, been more serious than I supposed,
but I trust the recovery will be complete and permanent, and do credit to all the kind care you have
met."

When it came to reviewing a book by the first lady
in the land, we can imagine the Editor felt it was a
work not to be lightly entrusted to any one, and in
selecting Mrs Oliphant for the gracious task he gave
it to one of his skilled "hands." From the excellence
of the book he told her she would have no difficulty
in making a good paper.

John Blackwood to Mrs Oliphant.

Jan. 13, 1868.

It is most pleasing—like the writing of a good sensible
woman, a thorough lady, kind and considerate to all. The
way "the Queen" acknowledges kindness and attention is
quite touching. It raises her enormously in my opinion, and

will, I am sure, strengthen her in the heart of the country.
I do not think you can have any difficulty in making a nice
short paper, as Englishwomen have good reason to be proud
of the simple genuine way in which their chief confides her
thoughts and feelings to her people.

From this subject he turns to Mrs Oliphant's own
novel 'Miss Marjoribanks,' which was pleasantly wend-
ing its way through the Magazine, and in a style
which it was hoped betokened its success when it
should appear in book form. It was a year or two
later that he began to express his fears that the
three-volumed novel which publishers had so long
fostered was doomed, and he writes to William
Blackwood : " I am worried excessively about the
non-sale of the 'Brownlows,' but I know not what
more a man can do. The days of three-vol. novels
are over for profit, but what is to be the substitute ?
Trollope [Anthony] was strong that their day is gone
by, but equally incapable of suggesting a remedy."

The numerous letters which John Blackwood wrote
to his nephew are particularly characteristic of the
writer as we all remember him, anxious to be *au
courant* with all that was taking place at home, and
as anxious that his correspondent should hear all that
he was doing in London. And though business was
constantly mentioned in as far as it appears in reference to the "upmaking" of the Magazine, there
were many harassing points in connection with the
"quantities" as well as quality of the number which
William had to settle the best way he could. On
one occasion the Editor writes in haste to say he
had miscalculated, and had ten pages too many, but
the error was fortunately discovered in time at George

Street.   The different characteristics of authors formed
an important item in the calculations.   Some did not
come up to time, others could not always be calculated
upon.   In the following letter we have a glimpse into
the mysteries of the making-up of a number :—

John Blackwood to William Blackwood.

You can make up " Horace " to begin ; I return the corrected
revise by book-post, along with the bulk of Mackay's paper
on Charles Kean.   You can follow "Horace" with "Fenian
Alarm " or " Linda Tressell."   " Linda Tressell " " revise " will
hardly, I think, be with you before Sunday, but he [Anthony
Trollope] alters little.   The enclosed from Gleig rather helps
us out of the difficulty of putting a quart into a pint-bottle.

After Lord John [Manners] left me, Hamley came in.   He
was, as you may imagine, most sympathetic about Burt's death.
While he was with me, Delane walked in.   He remained a long
time, and finally walked down with me to the Junior, where
his call soothed the General [Steuart], whom I had kept waiting a quarter of an hour for his dinner.

The death alluded to in the preceding was that of
Dr John Burt, mentioned in the earlier letters,—a
very intimate friend of the Blackwoods, of whom John
Blackwood writes to William : " Dear Burt's death
cuts both Julia and me to the heart.   It is a heavy
blow and misfortune to us all."   This particular
number of the Magazine above alluded to was still
occasioning them trouble, for he writes again to
William :—

I daresay we may postpone the " Horace," and if you think
that, you can make up Gleig.   I think we must postpone the
" Fenian Alarm."   That confounded paper on English Univer-
sities is weighing like a nightmare upon me.   As the proof has
not come back yet, I have a sort of faint hope that the man
may have taken the huff at my very moderate praise, but I fear

there is no such luck. I think the "Abyssinian Letters" are very nice, with the right amount of twaddle in them to make them popular.

These little *contretemps* and difficulties were by no means unusual, and the readers who greet a Magazine on the first of the month have little idea of the anxieties that attend its preparation. Sometimes a paper which had promised well would grow under the hands of the writer into something quite different from what had been intended, or at the last something would crop up which made it totally impracticable, as in the following case, which shows the usual easy-going imperturbable Editor in the phase of the "worried" Editor. There was a very admirable paper by Mrs Oliphant, which he was longing and had settled to publish for its literary excellence, when suddenly something in the tone of it struck him when he saw it in type,—something so terrible that the "whole Kirk of Scotland would be furious, and the Church of England not pleased"; it could not be deleted, "or the whole spirit of the paper would disappear." So there was no help for it—it could not be used; and he goes on to say that, independently of his annoyance at having to disappoint her, he was desperately inconvenienced by it, as he did not know when he "had been so put about and bothered" to make up a number at all to his mind, and finishes with "a much-worried Editor remains always yours faithfully, John Blackwood." When, however, these necessary but tormenting details had been disposed of, his uncle used to give William all the news that was going. The *on dits* of the Lobby of the House and the gossip of the Carlton were related at first-hand in a manner which might have aroused the envy of the professional paragraphists of to-day. A whist-party at the Carlton, or Mrs Disraeli's new satin gown of many colours, are all lightly touched off for William in the same way that he used, in his young days, to write to William's uncles in the forties.

During the winter of 1868 Lord Derby's illness, and the prospects of his successor in the Premiership, were the absorbing topics.

John Blackwood to William Blackwood.

Feb. 11, 1868.

While I was writing Lord John Manners came in. Lord Derby is still very ill, and they have no notion when he can be moved to London. He is, however, free from pain, and can speak about business, and their regret is that he is not in London. The wish of the Government, Lord John said, is to keep him at the head as long as they *possibly can*, so I imagine there is no immediate prospect of a change.

A Scottish Reform Bill was going through the House under the guidance of the Lord Advocate (Gordon), whose rough handling by the Liberal press seemed to demand a protest from his own side.

John Blackwood to William Blackwood.

Calling at the Lord Advocate's in the morning, I learned from his secretary that he was greatly bothered about an article in the 'Scotsman,' accusing him of not being even such a patriot as Sir G. Clerk or Sir George Murray. Of course I told Mr Nicholson to give Gordon my advice not to fash his head on the subject. Looking at what the 'Scotsman' had said made me feel that we should say a few words in Gordon's favour, more particularly as Delane tells me his quiet statement made a favourable impression. I therefore suggested to Gleig to put in a paragraph saying how creditably Gordon had acquitted himself, and that the votes of Baxter, M'Laren, &c., who so violently opposed the bill, excited a strong feeling in the House, that it had got quite enough of the breed, and indisposed Parliament to increase the Scottish representation.

Mr Gleig was to do the paragraph, but it did not quite satisfy himself nor the Editor, who on sending it down to Edinburgh says to William, " If you and Jem have any doubts take it along to Lord Neaves, who, I am sure, could make a capital paragraph or two on the above text." James Blackwood, though not a member of the firm, was often consulted on literary matters, where his good taste and sound judgment were always to be relied on. The writer goes on to speak of Lord Derby's illness :—

I looked in at the Carlton, where I saw Lord John Manners. He reports Lord Derby much better and attending to business; but as to his real recovery nobody can say. I had many points to discuss with Gleig in his article, and the acuteness of the old man was most amusing. He is as sharp or sharper than ever he was.

In another to William he complains of having been ill, but thought it was the languid indifference and the whole uncalled-for-ness of the Scottish Reform Bill, which had brought his bile to a climax. He goes on :—

It is not worth while going to the House for this Irish debate unless it comes to a climax to-morrow. I could go to the House of Lords to hear the Duke of Argyll's attack on Disraeli, but I do not know who is to answer him unless the Chancellor, and I am not sure that his doing so would be according to order. What a funk the little Duke would be in if Lord Derby were suddenly to rise in his place and take up the cudgels.

The next communication to William contains the

news, just learnt from his secretary, Mr Corry (Lord Rowton), that Disraeli is to be Premier, Lord Derby having resigned.

John Blackwood to William Blackwood.

THE BURLINGTON, *Feb.* 25, 1868.

I dined at the Club last night with Bourke [Lord Connemara], who had changed his note and said Dizzy was to be the chief. Calling at Downing Street to-day, I found Corry about three, who said that it will only be a secret about an hour longer. Disraeli is Premier, and is forming a Government to-day. I asked if all was going smooth, and he said modestly that he thought so. I went to the House to hear the announcement. Lord Stanley and Gladstone did their parts very briefly and nicely. I believe that Lord Cranborne has been offered the Chancellorship of Exchequer, but I do not think that he will accept. It is a very striking thing to think of Dizzy's position. Lord John Manners got me into the House and seemed in good feather.

Lord Derby [he says in the next letter to William] would have resigned on the previous week, but delayed until he should be better, and able to advise the Queen. The advice was most warm to send for Dizzy, and the Queen immediately sent General Grey to the "Impenitent," with the most gracious messages. As far as Lord John knows, things are going smoothly, and Dizzy himself is in tremendous spirits.

CHAPTER VII.

STRATHTYRUM.

STRATHTYRUM, the name which appears so often in
John Blackwood's letters, and where for the last
twenty years of his life half the year was spent, seems
to demand some special mention, some affectionate
recognition from those who associate it with bright
and happy memories, as well as the introduction
necessary for those who hear of it for the first time.
To these last the picture of the "Golfer's Paradise,"
where the Editor and Publisher loved to welcome
his friends, literary or otherwise, may perhaps appeal
with the charm of novelty. Strathtyrum was a large
old-fashioned country-house, rented by John Blackwood
from an uncle of the present owner, Mr James Cheape.
It is situated in charming grounds about a mile from

St Andrews, and possesses the only trees in the immediate neighbourhood. These shelter it so well, that
though on the top of a hill we never knew what the
east wind was doing till we got outside the big white
gates leading to the St Andrews and Cupar Road.
The woods that surrounded it have long winding walks
within sight of the sea. These, with the sunny
sheltered gardens, so full of fruit and flowers, combined
with its near proximity to the Links, constituted it a
veritable "Golfer's Paradise." The following to Mr
Newdigate expresses my father's pleasure at the idea
of his new country home : "I am delighted to say that
we migrate to Fife this afternoon, and no schoolboy
could feel happier in the prospect than I do. We have
got a really nice place now, Strathtyrum, close to the
'happy golfing-grounds' at St Andrews. I hope you
will be persuaded to look us up in the summer—we
could have some good fun." His life there, however,
was by no means all holiday. Very often he had to
be in Edinburgh for two or three days in the week,
and other days the parcel containing letters, proofs,
MS., &c., used to arrive regularly, and the day's golf
often ended in an evening's hard work, as shown by
the thick packets and long envelopes lying on the hall-
table next day ready for the post. He had an extraordinary power of getting through work quickly, which
enabled him to combine business with pleasure in a
way I have never seen any one else attempt. Of
course he liked his work, and did it with ease and satisfaction to himself ; but there were many things he liked
besides, and I know it often required a certain resolu-
tion on his part to begin to tackle it. It sometimes
cost him a pang to shut himself up in his library,

John Blackwood.
From a photograph by Rodger St Andrews

while his friends were talking and laughing, enjoying the sunshine in the porch at Strathtyrum, and he would smoke his cigar to the very end before he left them. I remember the bond of sympathy he established with me when a little child, seeing me carried off to the schoolroom : his feelings must have been the same as mine when he said, "Now papa must go and do *his* lessons, and he would much rather play golf."

The routine of life passed between Edinburgh, London, and Strathtyrum had few interruptions. Almost to a day the moves were made year by year from one place to the other. These three very different residences gave a considerable variety of society and interest, and perhaps accounted for the Editor never taking, except for two or three days' visits, a regular holiday, such as most men constantly immersed in business find necessary for their health. His work was often necessarily done at home—when at Strathtyrum, for instance. The drawing-room, with children and two or three dogs running about, was not by any means an unusual place to find him if he got tired of the seclusion of his library. Noise or even music did not disturb him when he was thoroughly absorbed in reading, and I seem to see him before me now in a big arm-chair, his brow wrinkled up in a way peculiar to him when thinking, correcting proofs with a pencil, throwing them on the floor sheet after sheet, till there was a goodly pile, when he would turn round with a sigh of relief to join in what was going on. His letters were always written in the library at Strathtyrum, which he called his writing-room. It was a large old-fashioned room with the windows facing the

table where he always sat, the walls lined with book-
cases and old engravings, a pleasant and reposeful
room for work, with the odour of sanctity inseparable
from a library, relieved by a distinct flavour of the
tobacco that he and his friends indulged in during the
evenings. He himself liked smoking out of doors, and
when the weather permitted, and often when it was
very cold, he would stroll out after dinner and smoke
in the woods or the porch, my mother and any friends
he could persuade generally accompanying him. As
we children grew older we used gladly to go with him
the inevitable walk to the point in the shrubbery
overlooking St Andrews Bay whence we could see
the revolving light of the Bell Rock lighthouse—a
never-failing source of interest to us, and apparently
to him, for I don't think he ever missed a single night
going to look for it, unless he were detained by refrac-
tory guests who objected to this cold-catching process.
In these walks he was generally accompanied by two
or three dogs, the dear friends and companions of the
family. One was named "Tickler," after the immortal
Tickler of the 'Noctes,' "for Church and for State a
determinate stickler"; and another was always called
"Tory," in honour of the political traditions of the
Blackwoods. If a Tory died he was immediately
replaced by another. My father would walk on
absorbed in thought, if alone or with us, his hands
plunged in his pockets, making no sign, only steadily
puffing his cigar. But these were the times his mind
was working very hard, and these dark quiet woods,
I believe, helped him to arrive at many a weighty
decision. I have often seen him throw off his coat,
and walk straight into the library, and without saying

a word sit down and write off the letter he had probably been turning over in his mind the whole time he had been out. That he had often difficult points to settle there can be no doubt, for publishing is not all plain sailing, nor does a Magazine appear on the first of every month without some wear and tear of mind for those concerned in its production.

St Andrews was a smaller place in the days we allude to than it is now. The happy golfing-grounds were then frequented by a pleasant company of real golfers, but not crowded, except on medal days. A person learning to play golf was an unknown sight; the true golfer appears to be born, not made, or at any rate his education began from the cradle, and the sight of a middle-aged tyro at the game "missing the globe" or smashing his clubs would have evoked contempt in the minds of those to whom golf was a sort of second nature. It is difficult to recall at this moment a single one of the Scotch *habitués* of our house who did not play the game more or less. To John Blackwood, besides the healthful exercise and skill golf demanded, not the least charm was the good fellowship inseparable from any sport of the kind. A keen but never a jealous player, cool and good-humoured, his presence was always welcomed on the Links. As soon as we arrived at St Andrews station, then situated by the side of the Links, the first person we saw was his caddy, old Bob Kirk, waiting for him, with the gratifying intelligence, "They're a' expectin' ye," and he would hurry off to get a round before dinner.

Mr Horace Hutchinson, in his admirable Golf volume of the Badminton Series, pays John Blackwood a very

graceful compliment : while not placing him in the
front rank of players, amongst whom medal holders
are found, he gives him first rank as a desirable
partner—the man of steady nerve and resource, who
might be trusted to pull off an uneven match successfully when a more brilliant player might have thrown
it up in despair.   In other words, he could play a
losing game,—not one of the least valuable of those
qualities that tend towards success where larger
issues are at stake than a game of golf, and which
often carried him triumphantly over difficulties where
less sanguine, less resourceful spirits would have given
in.   The " a'," as expressed by Bob Kirk, meant all
the golfing companions, many of them lifelong friends,
and all more or less bound up in the happy association
and *camaraderie* of the game, which gave lightness
and variety to John Blackwood's home life.

The very reiteration of the same names, the same
jokes and recurring incidents of the game, were
pleasant to him when he returned year after year.
There was one foursome in which he used to take
special delight, and which was played again and
again.   The other three who formed it were Sir A.
Kinloch and the " twa Meajors," as the caddies used
to call the late Major Boothby and Major R. Bethune
—in the days when St Andrews only possessed a
small military contingent.

The Golf Club and some of its members are happily
described in the book entitled ' Golf,' cleverly com-
piled some years ago by the late Mr R. Clark, an
old golfing friend of my father.   There is a chapter
entitled " Sutherlandia," and signed J. B., in which
Mr Clark persuaded him to contribute a few anec-

dotes of a very well-known golfer, Mr Sutherland,
a quaint type, whose solemn conviction that golf was
the business of life led to many amusing incidents
and stories of the green.   Of these we may perhaps
be permitted to quote one or two that were special
favourites :—

On a Saturday he asked us to make a match for the Monday.
We were reluctantly obliged to say that the month was getting
on, and we must work. He exclaimed, " God bless me! Are you
going to waste a Monday ? " We had to think some time before
we discovered the peculiar value of a Monday, until, with fits
of laughter, we reflected that after Sunday's rest his old sinews
must be fresher on Monday than on any other day of the week.

Henceforth any work done at Strathtyrum on that
particular day was called " *wasting* a Monday."   This
is another from the same source :—

His attention to promising young golfers was that of a father
to a son. One day, playing the last hole in, our friendly antagonist, Mr Kinloch, was about to strike off when a boy
appeared upon the bridge over the burn. Old Sutherland
shouted out, "Stop! stop! don't play upon him; he is a fine
young golfer." The warning came too late to stop Kinloch's
club, but in a convulsion of laughter over this consideration,
not for a boy but for a fine young golfer, he nearly *missed the
globe.*

One of the best players in those days, perhaps the best, was
Captain John Stewart, and when ordered out to India with his
regiment old Sutherland sorrowed in this wise: "It is a shame
for a man with such powers [golfing] to go out to India." He
always looked upon the game as a very serious business, and
we were once the subject of one of his earnest rebukes. We
had been playing a foursome in which the other two players
were quite young men, and there was an undue amount of
laughing and joking. After the match was over he was stalk-
ing gloomily about the Links, and met a friend just arrived from

Edinburgh to whom he unbosomed himself. "There was too much *levity* about our match to-day. I was not surprised at the others, but your brother John was as bad as any of them." We need not say that the old gentleman had *lost his match*, and having been his antagonist we felt the rebuke.

Another contributor to Mr Clark's book, signing himself Jonathan Oldbuck, gives the following characteristic glimpses of some of the members of the Golf Club :—

That cigar over there, which escapes under the scoop of a shepherd-plaid cap set awry on the head, is ministering its soothing balms to the Editor of 'Blackwood,' who is fresh from the revised proofs of the September Ebony, and the unconcerned-looking inheritor of some of the brightest of Scotch literary traditions. That man who has just entered with the comely face and frank bearing is Principal Tulloch.

And he goes on to mention the names of others, showing that literature was often represented on the links. "Shirley, freed from the common-places of Supervision in Edinburgh; and, mightier than the mightiest of her sex, there is just about this time of the year to be seen the biographer of Irving and the chronicler of Carlingford."

Nor would any mention of St Andrews Links be complete without including Tom Morris, beloved of all golfers—"Old" Tom, as we always heard him affectionately called. Many a match was played with him as the Editor's partner. He is, good fellow, we are sure, totally unaware how his name appears in some of John Blackwood's letters as a living illustration of what he wanted to impress upon a correspondent who was writing upon "Manners"— namely, that good manners proceed from good feeling, and that a *gentleman*, in the true sense of the word, may be found in any rank of life. He says :—

I can remember conversations with my late brothers when the sole question was, Is the fellow a gentleman, or is he not? If not, let us have nothing to do with him. Understand that I use the word "gentleman" in its best sense, meaning thereby a man whose good manners, at all events in some degree, proceed from his good sense and good feeling. . . . I know a caddy and a golf-ball maker [Tom Morris] whom we golfers all speak of as a gentleman. His manners are adapted to his station in life, but they are unmistakably good, and it is a pleasure to play the game with him.

To the same contributor, Miss Mozley, who has docketed the letter "Story of his Golfing Favourite":

Though I am in a hurry I must tell you a story about my golfing favourite Tom Morris. He was playing with an old gentleman Captain Broughton. The hole seemed utterly lost, Tom's ball lying in a whin, and the Captain called out, "You may give up." "No, no, Captain, I may hole it." "I'll bet you £50 to a shilling you don't." "Done with you, Captain," was the reply. He played and holed his ball, the chances being at least a thousand to one against such a feat. Nothing was said at the moment, but next morning the good old skipper, not a wealthy man by any means, walked into Tom's cottage and tendered the £50. Tom replied, "Na, na, Captain, we were joking—I canna tak' the money," and would not do so. Tom would only be making some 15s. a-week at this time.

Colonel (then Major) Laurence Lockhart, who seldom failed to visit Strathtyrum in autumn, generally at the time of the "Meeting," once when abroad and unable to come wrote some lines to express his disappointment. They give a very good picture of the scene and the idiosyncrasies of some well-known players, many of whom, happily, still survive, though others, alas! like the writer, have left us. The lines were very much appreciated, not only by the golfers but also by George Eliot, who makes them the occasion for paying a compliment to Lockhart's other writings in a letter to Blackwood, who quotes it when writing to Lockhart.

The "Voice from the Rhine" is intensely popular in the golfing world, and apart from that illustrious body the following is what George Eliot says in reply to a copy I sent to her: "Major Lockhart's lively letter gives me a longing for the fresh breezy life it conjures up. You must let me know when there is a fresh book of his, because when I have done my own I shall like to read something else by him. I got much pleasure out of the two books I did read." So you see you are being looked for.

The lines, which are here given, purport to be a dream!

A VOICE FROM THE RHINELAND.

(But don't be afraid; it is not a contribution.)

On board the Steamer PRINZ VON PREUSSEN
between MAYENCE *and* COLOGNE,
17th September 1875.

In the heart of the Rhineland! afloat on the Rhine!
Ho! Kellner, schnell kommen! gleich bringen sie Wein?
What? Look at the scenery? Let it go hang!
I leave that to Herr Cook and his Cockneyfied gang:
Bring the hock to the cabin, and leave me alone
Till we're moored to the jetty at fragrant Cologne.
But eight solid hours! I can't drown them in drink.
No, I've pens in my bag, also paper and ink;
And what can I better than score off a few
Correspondents at home to whom letters are due?
Strathtyrum stands first for a missive in prose,
But since I'm in verse I'll continue—here goes:

I was dreaming, dear Editor, fondly last night
Of this festival season of Scottish delight;
And its whole panorama of pleasure seemed spread
In a luminous ether enclosing my bed;
So that whithersoever my eyes chanced to move—
Right, left, or in front, or below, or above—
They met something—some vision—suggestive to me
Of joys that have been, and of joys that might be.
Here a well-driven grouse-pack swept level and low
O'er a bright bit of moorland, and blotted its glow;
Here, huge on the sky-line a stag sniffed the breeze;
There a stalker crept, cat-like, on hands and on knees.
Here "Fan" in the turnips stood firm as a rock;
There "Flo" through the covert went bustling the cock.
In a stream to the right trout and salmon arose,
Overhead pheasants rocketed thicker than crows.
To the left, o'er blue waters—all glitter and gleam—
Danced a tight little yacht with the wind on her beam;
And what was that orb of elliptical flight,
That flashed like a meteor and whizzed out of sight?
It recalled an occasion when multitudes yelled
O'er a ball by thy biceps, Tom Morris, propelled.
And what was that flash?   By my oath, 'twas the gun
Which announced to St Andrews the meeting begun.
And there, to be sure, was the usual array
Which greets one each year on the opening day.
Fair bevies of ladies awaiting the start,
Braw couples "tee'd up" and in haste to depart.
Looking on, Tom and Tommie, Kidd, Jamie, and Strath,
And all the professional children of wrath,
And armies of caddies in quest of a job—
Except, of course, swells like "The Daw" or old Bob.
The apple-faced sage, with his nostrum for all—
"Dinna hurry the swing! keep your e'e on the ball!"
And the gun it went off, and the fun it began,
And off to the "high hole" in vision I ran;
And there, where the critics and ring-men were massed,
I watched the quiet tide of the game as it passed.
And first, with a cleek-shot, the Editor stole
Like a thief in the night to the edge of the hole;
So that gallant Mount Melville (whom Time touches not)
Clapped his hands in applause and cried " Capital shot!"
Then himself played a " putt," which brought life to the eye
Of the mummified " Ancient" who hiccupped hard by.

And next came the fliers, to show them the way—
Brave Innes and Boothby and lithe Robert Hay,
And Hodge, and a man who's too free with his damns
(I don't know his name), and a couple of Lambs;
Then Elliot, who's rather a one-er to slog,
And with him Bob Bethune caressing a dog,
And stout Willie Mure with his muscular grace,
And wild David Wauchope all over the place,
And Ormsary, lyrical·son of the Gael,
With his whirligig spoon swung aloft like a flail.
And lo ! like some symbol of Rapine and War,
The torch of fierce Rufus which gleams from afar.
Last, a couple of greybeards came "papping along,"
Who with whin-bush and bunker the fun did prolong,
Till two fat men in rear, cried, "With anger we rave !
By the Lord, they've been hours, sir, in Walkinshaw's grave !"
'Twas the "Beefer" and "Burnhouse," whose anger thus rose,
Till it blazed in their cheeks with the tints of their hose;
And so fierce was the glare that the dreamer awoke,
And the phantasmagoria vanished like smoke.
But again, half asleep, at the close of the night,
As I dreamed of St Andrews and Scottish delight,
I sat up in my bed and proclaimed with a shout
I was sick of this kingdom of beer and *sauer-kraut*,
And that in the first train, this I swore by the Rood,
I'd be off to the land of the mountain and flood.
Brave words ! But some objects took shape in the dawn
Which but now on the table lay shapeless and wan.
These were mountains of foolscap, still virgin and white,
Which sent forth a voice that said Write, villain, write,
And a mean little hillock of "copy" hard by
Which could only re-echo the sinister cry.
My portmanteaus, 'tis true—taking voice from despair—
Whined, "Pack us, old fellow, we pine for home air;"
But the hungry portfolio which held 'Fair to See'
Yelled "Pack you ! Then, damn it ! pray who's to pack me ?"
The portfolio was right, though its language was strong,
And it cuts short a yarn that's already too long,
For in its fierce words the sad moral I hear,
"For me there's no fun, no Strathtyrum this year."

The "Voice from the Rhineland" was very far-
reaching, as will be gathered from John Blackwood's
letters, and it caused much amusement; but he re-

garded it as a poor substitute for the writer's company, which was always particularly congenial to him. "The neveu de son oncle," as he called Lockhart once, had become by this time one of the friends and *habitués* whom he loved to see in his house, and to be cheated of his visits for a whole summer made a blank not to be got over by any number of verses, however good. He always had so many things to tell Lockhart; every good story or jest—"how that would make Law. laugh," was his first thought. While Lockhart, on his side, provided many an evening's entertainment out of the humorous relations of his experiences yachting and travelling, &c., which all used to be reproduced for the Editor's amusement, who revelled in the wit and gay humour that Lockhart possessed, together with other qualities underlying his bright sunny nature that made him the most delightful of companions, and endeared him to all his friends. In a letter to Mr Story, after Lockhart had been to Rome, 1875, my father says :—

He [Lockhart] dwelt with much satisfaction upon having made your acquaintance. You would suit each other. It is alleged that when he comes to Strathtyrum neither he nor I do any work, but this is not true. He once shut himself up for three days and wrote a capital story, "The Strathkinahan Volunteers." Look it up in 'Maga.' It was a true story of how he found a body of volunteers all drunk at Dalmally, head of Loch Awe, and passed himself off as inspecting officer of the district. People said it was exaggerated, but in reality he toned down the facts.

The first year at Strathtyrum, the usually cheerful autumn season, which culminated in the October golf meeting, was clouded over by the terribly sudden death of Lord Eglinton, which occurred at Mount Melville, where he was staying with Mr Whyte-Melville for the "golf meeting." This sad occurrence cast a gloom over the whole neighbourhood, where he was well known and highly popular. In general society he was long remembered as the giver of the celebrated Eglinton Tournament. His name has been often mentioned in John `Blackwood's letters in connection with political matters, and always in terms of hope and confidence, and that at times when the Conservative horizon looked dark enough. The following letter to Professor Aytoun describes the sorrow caused by his death :—

John Blackwood to Professor Aytoun.

I have just read with much emotion your beautiful and touching tribute to dear Lord Eglinton. I will not venture to offer anything like criticism on a thing so delicate and moving as this, coming direct from the writer's heart. If I could suggest anything, it would be to make it more personal by introducing more directly the fact of the strong feeling of affection and respect with which he inspired all who came in contact with him, whether it was the Ayrshire peasants curling and golfing with him, Lord Derby sitting in council with him, or we ourselves. When I am walking about the Links yet, I constantly think I see the fine fellow, and hear him calling to know how the match is going, and telling of his own success or misfortune. Excuse this from a golfer.

To this letter my father has added the following postscript :—

I am not indisposed to think that you should make some reference to how he carried his high principles into the usually contaminating atmosphere of the racecourse, and fairly puzzled the "legs" by his downright honesty in always telling the true state of his horses. They could not believe him, and were fairly puzzled. This is fact.

Dr Boyd, in his volumes of St Andrews Recollections, sets before us in very attractive guise the intellectual and social life of these years amid the pleasant society of which he was one of the prominent and popular members. Principal Tulloch was an intimate friend and neighbour at St Andrews, one whose company was ever welcome, and to know the genial Principal was to appreciate him, like the other attractive features of the place. Indeed, at that time and for some years later, St Andrews could boast, besides its Links and sea and other permanent attractions, a group of clever and agreeable men, whose names were known far beyond the old grey city where they lived. Moreover, such men as Principal Tulloch and Principal Shairp drew after them congenial spirits. Amongst the summer visitors would be sometimes Dean Stanley, Jowett—in pursuit of his friend Professor Lewis Campbell—Tom Hughes, Froude, Millais, Charles Kingsley, and others, who brought with them a flavour of the strong modern current of thought and ideas to this far-away part of the " Kingdom."

Mrs Oliphant, too, was one of those who seldom forsook St Andrews, and was generally installed with her two sons in one of the cheerful houses overlooking the Links. Often we have sat with her at the window watching the matches coming in, and looking out for my father, who never failed to stop and have a chat with her on his way home. And there was much pleasant visiting and dining all round amongst the little coterie, who all knew each other. Without any difficulty a dinner-party could be got up at short notice. There was always some one anxious to meet some one else, and my father was very happy when

he could arrange a dinner under those circumstances.
The cutlet-for-cutlet system of hospitality would not
have been understood by him. He invited people
because he wished them to come, or for what might
be thought the even more unusual reason, that he
thought they wished to come themselves! We remember his "My dear, poor —— ¯looked as though
he wanted to be asked," was the reason he gave
once for some apparently inexplicable exercise of
hospitality.

The friends who were invited to John Blackwood's
summer home were not, as will be seen, by any means
all in the same line of life. There was a judicious
blending of the London element with that of the
neighbourhood, and the names that occur to one most
frequently recall both these different centres,—though,
of course, the incidents connected with the visits of
any well-known personages are more deeply impressed
on the memory than others.

One season Mrs Ferrier, then a widow, and Miss
Ferrier came to stay with us. At the same time we
had another visitor, who hailed from the other side of
the Atlantic, a son of Judge Halliburton. The Ferriers
felt interested in seeing the son of "Sam Slick," and
he felt himself in luck to have met on this, his first
visit to the old country, the daughter and grand-
daughter of Christopher North. Mrs Ferrier was
then an old lady, but her vivacity was little dimmed.
Her visit was a real pleasure and refreshment to her
hosts, bringing back a flavour of old days, old stories,
old friends, on all of which she touched with the
lightness that comes of real comprehension, the ease
of the brilliant conversationalist—the last term she

would probably have applied to herself, but which only inadequately expresses the dexterous manner in which she passed from one subject to another. My father delighted in this sort of talk. "Now, then, call up the next," was ever his cry. Any one who talked a subject threadbare was a person to be avoided like poison.

His friend, Mr John Paget, who has been already alluded to, was in Scotland one summer, and we find my father writing urgently to him thus : "Instead of going to Ireland so soon, pray come here, and if Mrs Paget is with you, so much the better—Mrs Blackwood will be delighted to see her. Do think of this. My nephew will put you up to the way of getting here, and I hope you will let him label you for Strathtyrum immediate."

Mr and Mrs Anthony Trollope's was one of these never-to-be-forgotten visits. The echo of Mr Trollope's laugh seems to come back to me as I strive to recall his genial presence, and the incidents of the visit : the walks, the games of golf he insisted on playing on the Ladies' Links, pretending to faint when he made a bad shot, his immense weight causing a sort of earthquake on the sandy ground ; his riding off with my mother for a scamper on the sands, his host and Mrs Trollope watching them set out from the doorsteps ; the dinner-parties in their honour, where the writer used to appear herself with the dessert, and come in too for a share of the fun and jokes that were flying about. Mr Trollope's big voice drowned every one else, as he chaffed my father down the length of the dinner-table. He had jested over golf, what would he not do next? He used to make daring assaults

upon the most cherished articles of the Blackwood
faith. Blind unswerving devotion to the Sovereign
was one of his favourite points of attack. "Now,
Blackwood, how could the death of the Sovereign
possibly affect *you*?" he would say. "If you heard
of it to-morrow morning you know perfectly well you
would eat just as good a breakfast—you would not
even deny yourself that second kidney." It was in
vain to protest that in face of such a calamity the
very thought of broiled kidneys was distasteful. Mr
Trollope bore everything before him, and prepared for
another attack. The Conservative party and Dizzy
was a tempting subject for a tilt. "You *know*,
Blackwood, you think exactly about Dizzy as I do;
you *know* you would be very glad to hear he had
been had up for—for shoplifting." *Tableau!* all
holding up their hands, and Mr Trollope delighted
with the sensation he had produced.

After the Trollope's visit my father and mother
agreed to go to Skye with them.

John Blackwood to Miss Mozley.

STRATHTYRUM, *August* 25, 1868.

We had a visit last week from Anthony Trollope and his
wife. They are both very pleasant, and have induced us to
promise to meet them at Inverness on Friday and go to Skye.
From the look of the weather I begin to repent of my promise.
He is great fun, and I daresay we shall enjoy the expedition,
though rain and wind may spoil the scenery.

Bathing had formed part of the holiday, and he
writes to William Blackwood, "I had a farewell bathe
with Anthony yesterday evening, and we parted
almost with tears at Loch Coruisk.

The same autumn, but later, came two other particularly welcome visitors, Mr W. W. Story, the American sculptor, and his daughter, now Mme. Peruzzi, who had come from Rome, and were making a tour in Scotland. This was their first visit to Strathtyrum, but not Mr Story's first acquaintance with John Blackwood, who had known him for several years, and some of his poems and other writings had appeared in the Magazine. When my father heard they were at Balcarres, only twelve miles off, he wrote at once to ask them to come to Strathtyrum. It is not given to every one to be a great sculptor and a poet too. Mr Story was both. The literary faculty was strong in him, and gave a voice to the poetic side of his nature, which, though always existing in every great artist, rarely finds expression in song when a whole career has been given up, as in his case, to a sister art. His wit and humour also made him a delightful companion, one after my father's own heart, and the days passed only too quickly. The other guests were, I think, Mr Francillon, author of 'Earl's Dene,' and Miss Deane, who came from St Andrews to stay with us. The strangers were shown the quaint old city that lay so near us, always ready to be shown off—to play up, as it were, for the benefit of the uninitiated who saw its grey towers and ruins for the first time. Then the Links, too, where they were taken to walk on Sunday—a pleasure that could only be safely indulged in on that day without risk of life from golf balls. I have heard my father recall Mr Story's jests over the language of golf—the strange inexplicable notices that caught his eye, together with the jargon going on around of *bunkers*, *dormy*, *stimy*, *cleeks*, and *niblicks*. "What,"

he said, " would be the impression of a crew of English
sailors shipwrecked at St Andrews, on hearing this
strange new language? They would never imagine
themselves in any part of Great Britain." In a letter
written a few weeks after this visit, my father says :
" I hope this will find you all safe in the Palazzo Barberini with nothing but pleasant memories of the old
country. Give my best remembrances to Miss Story ;
many people have compassionated me for not hearing
her sing. She must come back to us with her voice
in order." He adds that Rome and St Andrews, he
thinks, are the two places to live in—and there are
many, I daresay, who will agree with him.

Perhaps one of the incidents of the Strathtyrum
life most clearly impressed upon my childish recollections—probably from hearing it afterwards so often
alluded to—was the visit in July 1869 of Jefferson
Davis, the ex-President, the gallant leader of the
Confederate army, who for two years previously had
been languishing in prison awaiting his trial. The first
use he made of his liberty was to visit England, and
together with his friend, Dr Charles Mackay, they extended their journey to Scotland, and John Blackwood
eagerly welcomed the opportunity of seeing the hero
and entertaining him under his own roof. The day
they were to arrive we were all assembled on the
doorsteps, and as the carriage swept round to the
door we saw the ex-President slowly and very courteously raising his hat as he caught sight of his host
and hostess, in the way peculiar to those accustomed
to bow to large crowds. We felt that it was quite
like entertaining royalty, and we ought to have had
a band playing, and a guard of honour. He wore a

dark-blue military cloak, and his appearance was in every way dignified and commanding. His tall slight figure was remarkably upright, only the pale drawn face told the tale of disappointed hopes and physical suffering. His fine features were much attenuated, and he told us that the dampness of his prison had caused most frightful neuralgic pains in his face and head. He was delighted with Scotland. The bracing climate seemed to invigorate his health, and the universal courtesy and friendliness shown to him could not have been otherwise than very gratifying. One instance of this struck us very much in St Andrews. It happened one Sunday, after attending the Episcopal Church, our guest drove with us to see the Cathedral ruins, which are enclosed by a wall—part of the wall of the old monastery. After exploring it and lamenting the demolitions of John Knox's followers, my father left us to look for the carriage. When he returned he found there was a little crowd outside the wall, of fishermen and seafaring folk quietly waiting to have a glimpse of Mr Davis. The carriage was waiting for us at a door in the wall, through which the blue waters of the bay and the group of men in the foreground were framed as in a picture. As our party advanced to the open door the men began to press forward, one big bronzed fellow in his blue jersey murmuring, "I'd like fine to ha'e a grip o' yer haund." Mr Davis raised his hat very courteously in the manner peculiar to him, and then as the carriage drove off the crowd broke into loud cheers. Hardly the sort of reception one would have expected these sometimes aggressively free-born and independent Scots to accord to the champion of the Southern cause, but the result,

we supposed, of their admiration of his personal bravery
and gallant conduct throughout the war. Anyhow,
my father considered their enthusiasm did them credit,
and hastened to inform the object of it of the great
personal compliment we knew it was intended to convey. That evening Dr Robert Chambers was coming
to dine to meet our distinguished guest. I remember
how amused we were to find the dauntless Jeff peering anxiously round the hall, not caring to enter the
drawing-room, where he heard "strange" voices, and
looking as though he meditated a flight to his own
apartment. The idea of the hero of Bull's Run flying
before dear old Dr Chambers amused my father immensely. Needless to say, Jeff admitted that his
fears were groundless after an introduction to the
kindly and benevolent old gentleman, whose appearance alone would banish all dread of his proving a
Philistine. Any one who had the privilege of knowing
Davis personally could not fail to be attracted by the
straightforward manly uprightness of his character,
which was apparent in everything, and withal the
charm of his manner, a mixture of dignity and simplicity, that compelled a certain respect which his
kindly courtesy only made more impressive. His fine
figure was seen to great advantage on horseback, and
he looked like a cavalry officer all over.

In a letter written to Colonel Lockhart a few days
after this memorable visit, he writes :—

John Blackwood to Colonel L. W. M. Lockhart.

STRATHTYRUM, *Aug.* 4, 1869.
Jefferson Davis has been with me for the last four days, and
I have just seen him off by the train. He is a grand old man.
I could mount and draw sword for him at a moment's notice.

He half promises to come back, as he says he agrees in sentiment with Jemmy White, who wrote to me from the far North, " Ever since I came here I have been thinking what an idiot I was to leave Strathtyrum."

From a letter we have of Mr Davis to Dr Charles Mackay, we learn how much he had liked Scotland and his Scottish friends. He writes : " I fain would spend the balance of my days in Scotland. . . . I am glad I know Blackwood ; he is a charming and noble fellow, only equal to his excellent wife."

In September 1869 there were some bright amusing notes written from London, reminding us how time was getting on with the Editor, for he had gone up for the purpose of placing his son at school in England. His destination was with Mr H. G. Worsley, the brother of a friend and correspondent, Philip Worsley. This was a novel experience for him, to be left in charge of his young son, and he did his duty nobly by his own account. They seem to have been very happy together : Westminster Abbey, the Houses of Parliament, were all visited, unquestionably for little Jack's benefit ; also the dome of St Paul's, which, his father remarks, seems to have grown higher since the last time he was there ! He writes after a few days' companionship with his boy, " I quite understand how all the servants and every one are so fond of him."

John Blackwood to his Wife.

Jack bore up with his usual calm dignity till I said Good-bye, and as I drove off I saw Worsley put his arm over his shoulder in a caressing way as they walked back to the gate. So the little man is started for the first time away from us both, and may God's blessing accompany him.

In another letter to the same he mentions seeing in

London "dear old Jeff," as he affectionately terms
Jefferson Davis, "who was rejoiced to see us again."
Also in the same letter he adds: "Your old friend
Larrie Oliphant sent many messages. Beyond his
particular thories about the *good* life being acting, and
not professing, Christianity—in which he is not so far
wrong if he would only take it in moderation—he
seems quite sound." After this a visit to Lord Lytton
at Knebworth, on his way home, detained him from a
houseful of guests who were awaiting him at Strathtyrum. Lord Lytton, however, had been so anxious
to show him some of the MS. of his new novel, he
adds: "It would have been a pity to hurry away, as
Bulwer was first-rate about his novel, politics, Mrs
Stowe, and everything else."

One summer there came a short note from Lord
Lytton, asking to introduce his "friend, the Rev.
Julian Young, and his charming family," who were
then visiting Edinburgh. So warm a commendation
from the writer left nothing to be desired except to
see his friends. In the letter accepting the invitation
Mr Young says: "I know Strathtyrum well, and few
are the places I can say as I can say of it, that I have
known it for more than half a century. I spent three
very happy years at St Andrews during Dr Chalmers's
professorial reign, and it was the first place I intended
to take my wife and daughter to see." Of that visit it
is now impossible to recall anything but the echoes of
the mirth and laughter that prevailed in every society
where Julian Young found himself. The dramatic
talent which peeped forth in every look, in every
gesture, while causing regret, perhaps, that his hereditary tastes should not have had their legitimate scope,

nevertheless made him a brilliant conversationalist, and as a *raconteur* unrivalled. The acquaintance thus happily begun ripened into one of warm friendship with Mrs Young and her family ; but Mr Young, to our deep regret, we never saw again : this was his first and last visit to Strathtyrum. In a letter to his host, he humorously described the incidents of the journey back to Edinburgh, in those days occupying from three to four hours, with endless changes and waitings, and the final horrors of a passage across the Firth of Forth in a small steamer.

Rev. J. Young to John Blackwood.

The visit was short and sweet. It cost me a pang to leave when everything looked so bright about St Andrews, and our journey back made us so miserable that we felt inclined to parody Wordsworth's celebrated line and exclaim, "And oh! the difference to *we.*" We were five mortal hours before we got here. At Leuchars, where we had to stand umbrella-less in the wet for an hour in company with all the *crême de la crême* —*i.e.,* all the scum of the lowest wynds of Dundee—we saw, but did not dare to speak to Jowett. On getting on board the steamer there was not space in the gangways, on the roof, or even on the bowsprit, for a flea to sit; and as to the cabin (in which we *did* get a camp-stool), the accompaniment of three rabbit-hutches, four large cages with canaries and other birds, reeking mackintoshes, five squalling babies in arms, and the odours generated thereby, *operated on our stomachs as effectually as* mare magnum *itself.* Then, again, when we got to the station at Princes Street we were literally half an hour before we could get our luggage. There were three porters to 3000 people.

Any one who has made that journey during the holiday season will recognise the truth of this description. Mr Young goes on to say :—

By the bye, Dr John Brown, who has been sitting with us,

and spoke in high commendation of you—your hospitality, and your editorial ability and judgment—in answer to my comment about the pertinacious rain, said that an old laird, a friend of his, was talking to a tenant, a mumbling, grumbling old fellow, about the serious injury that this continued weather would do the crops, when the man, looking him very significantly in the face, exclaimed, "I'll tell ye what it is, sir; something must really be done aboot this weather."

During the visit of Mr and Mrs Young and their daughter, I remember that our neighbours, the Whyte-Melvilles, dined with us—father and son,—the *old school* and the *new*, between whom there existed the strongest affection and appreciation. Our old neighbour, Mr Melville, so vigorous and alert for all his eighty years; so precise in dress, so careful and punctilious in all the social and business relations of life,—always at his post in county matters, always certain to *do*, or, what is even more important sometimes, to *say*, the right thing. He was one of the best known and most justly esteemed of the circle that made St Andrews and its neighbourhood so pleasant. He and his wife, Lady Catherine, were the centre of everything there, and untiringly to the last showed the kindness and hospitality with which none of us who knew them can ever cease affectionately to associate their memory. How well we remember the satisfaction with which the old man used to announce that "George" was coming to stay with them—that son, perhaps not wholly comprehended and yet wholly loved. Beside his father he looked careworn, almost old, with his drooping figure and general air of disillusionment. This impression, however, was dispelled when he talked: then the sparkle and brilliancy of the moment shone out, recalling in a hundred ways the characteristics of his writings. The half-sad, half-dreamy expression was only the mask that concealed the eloquence and enthusiasm which gave us 'Holmby House' and 'The Queen's Maries.' John Blackwood and he were never acquainted till he lived at Strathtyrum, and Whyte-Melville never wrote a line for him, but they were sworn friends and allies, sometimes *foes*, on the golfing-green.

Many a bright Sunday afternoon was made brighter by his presence, when we could bring him back to luncheon from the church at St Andrews, where we all met. Then followed an inspection of all the pets —dogs, ponies, horses—for his benefit. There are many men who think they "know" a horse, and could ride and drive one, but surely never any one who absolutely *loved* a horse as he did. Then would follow an adjournment to the old kitchen-garden, with a raid made on the fruit, which did not seem to interfere with the pipes and tobacco. I wonder how many cigars and pipes were smoked in these long summer afternoons before any one remembered that the dinner-hour at Mount Melville was seven, and then we had to let him go, his host generally escorting him part of the way over the fields, a short road which lessened the distance from Mount Melville to about two and a half miles. We are here reminded of one very special Sunday when the Editor forsook our own "Zion," as he used to call the Episcopal Church, in order to hear Dean Stanley preach in the town church of St Andrews, the old parish kirk. It was an innovation, but one of which he highly approved, this appearance in a Presbyterian pulpit of the Dean of Westminster. The two institutions thus represented, he always considered, would stand or fall together, and anything that drew them more closely together strengthened both. As we turned in we saw George Whyte-Melville also forsaking our church and hurrying up to hear "the little Dean." He joined us in taking possession of the big old pew in the gallery labelled "Strathtyrum." That Sunday was St Bartholomew's Day, and after dwelling on many of the advantages that toleration has conferred upon the different branches of the Christian Church, the Dean applied Dr Chalmers's expression to the case of the Romish Church. "She was suffering," he said, "from the expulsive power of a new affection." While straining our ears to listen to the Dean, George Whyte-Melville was heard to whisper, "Capital phrase that, Blackwood, for the Divorce Court!!" The next few sentences of the excellent sermon were rather lost upon us, and my father declared afterwards he would never take "George" to the kirk again.

As the days wore on towards autumn the plot used to thicken. On the links the golfers kept pouring in, and grouse and partridge were forsaken for the time for the attractions which culminated in the golf meeting, held the last week in September. My father makes frequent allusions to this carnival, very dear to all golfers, and an occasion not to be missed if possible, and every one filled their houses for the week. The great event of the week, after playing for the medal, was the ball given next day, and for this he felt a special interest and responsibility the year he was captain of the club. In 1871 he was appointed captain

of the St Andrews Golf Club,—" the greatest honour,"
he says to Mr Gleig, " that can be conferred upon a
golfer.". His friends all rallied round him on this
occasion, we may be sure, golfers and non-golfers.
Mrs Oliphant dedicated a novel to him, and all
the correspondents, golfing or otherwise, seem to
have sympathised in the importance of the event.
The house party as usual comprised varied elements, and amongst them a noted golfer and old
friend, Mr Gilbert Mitchell Innes and his wife and
daughter.

A celebration of the Scott centenary took place the
same year at St Andrews at which he had to speak,
and he mentions that speaking in public was new to
him.

John Blackwood to Rev. W. Lucas Collins.

STRATHTYRUM, ST ANDREWS, *Oct.* 18, 1871.

I am much pleased that you and Mrs Collins liked my speech
so much. It has been a great success, and as I never spoke
in public before, I feel as if I had unexpectedly laid an egg.
The week before last we had the annual golf meeting, and
as I was made Captain of the Club, we had even a greater
racket here than usual on these solemn occasions. Strathtyrum was crammed in every corner. At the golf dinner I
had to speak, and my foot was on my native heath singing the
praises of golf. . . . It was pronounced the best ball that ever
came off in St Andrews. Hoping Mrs Collins and you are both
well.—I am, always yours truly,   JOHN BLACKWOOD.

Another autumn amongst the Strathtyrum guests
were Mr and Mrs Charles Tennant of The Glen, and
their two eldest daughters, just growing up, and in
all the grace of their early girlhood. The Tennant

politics, needless to say, were a subject on which
there could be no sort of agreement at Strathtyrum,
except that they were not to be discussed. Each
morning at breakfast Mr (now Sir) Charles Tennant
unfolded his 'Scotsman,'—not then, as now, a trusty
ally of our forces, but the mouthpiece of the Glad-
stonian party; while my father breakfasted off the
food provided for him in the 'Courant,' not without
many sly jokes that he was waiting to pick up any
crumbs of news that the 'Scotsman' readers might
let fall. The sneers at the 'Courant,' though at one
time well deserved, were just then hardly merited, as
it had entered upon a new era under the able editorship of Mr James Mure, brother of Colonel Mure of
Caldwell, and a man of ability and literary attainments. "It is very hard I am not allowed to enjoy my
manna in peace," he would exclaim—Mr Mure always
called it "Mr Blackwood's manna"—as he devoured it
at breakfast. The 'Courant' had long been a distress-
ful subject with my father. He had no time to work
a daily paper himself, and in the thinned ranks of
his family there was not a spare Blackwood for the
purpose, though he had often been asked by the party
in Scotland to take it in hand. Now he was always
sure of a good leading article, and this satisfactory
state of things lasted, we believe, as long as Mr
Mure was at the helm.

After the "meeting" the great press of golfers
lessened, and there remained for October a chosen
few, not fettered for time, who recognised that month
as perhaps the pleasantest of the whole year in
Scotland. The east wind, which often treats us
so roughly, relents then for a while, and we are

sometimes allowed a last taste of the departed
summer. The clear sunny autumn days used to
make us long to put off the return to Edinburgh as
late as possible, a wish in which the head of the
house heartily sympathised.

One autumn St Andrews must have been more
than usually attractive to him, for besides the friends
and neighbours who lived there, there were installed
around the Storys from Rome in one house, the
Sturgises in another, and in October I remember
that Mr Delane came to us on his way south from
Dunrobin. My father knew the pleasure it gave to
some of our neighbours to meet the great man, and
he, in good spirits and enjoying his holiday, was
ready for anything, and made himself as charming
as only those who have seen him under these circumstances knew he could be—shooting and walking all day, and not too tired to dine out or to
allow us to drag him to St Andrews one evening to
see our amateur acting. The play was written for us
by Julian and Howard Sturgis, and they and also Mr
Story's sons took part in the performance, which was
given at the house of Mr and Mrs Burn, old friends
of ours and the Sturgises, and their youngest
daughter also took part in the play. This was one
of the early efforts of the two brothers who have
since become well known in their different walks of
literature. Julian Sturgis had just left Balliol, and
Howard was still at Cambridge. The Storys, who
formed the other *dramatis personæ*, have followed
their natural artistic bent, the elder devoting himself to sculpture, and the younger, Julian, having
become well known in Continental art circles as a

painter. When all was ready for the performance
the two authors appeared to have had some qualms
as to their audience, which was to include Mr Story,
the editor of 'Blackwood,' and the editor of the
'Times.' "Now I come to think of it," said one of
them, "I cannot help admiring our assurance in inviting Mr Blackwood and Mr Delane and your father"
(turning to one of the Storys) "to come and listen
to this nonsense." It was very clever nonsense,
however, and turned out a great success; and afterwards we and our dreaded (?) audience all adjourned
for supper in Mr Burn's hospitable dining-room.

John Blackwood to Mr W. W. Story.

STRATHTYRUM, ST ANDREWS.

The breaking up at the end of the season is always a bad
business. When we break up from here I always feel that
another year has gone and very little been done in it. However, we remain for a few weeks yet. We have had some fine
bright days of late, and there could not be better weather for
golf.

Now, these words to any one who knew my
father are extremely characteristic; his correspondent
would understand and love him for them. To me
they recall that writing-room at Strathtyrum, the
tables, sofa, piano, littered with every conceivable sort
of paper, MSS., proofs, letters—all awaiting the attention they would receive sometime or other; a formidable array, enough to make the stoutest quail before
attacking them. Often I remember we used to marvel
at the quickness with which, when he really set to
work, he would reduce this chaos to order. I have
heard my mother frequently point out to him as a
matter of congratulation that he had satisfactorily

disposed of some unwieldy-looking mass of papers. "My dear, I am never satisfied with anything that I do," would be the reply, and he meant it in a way; but, as in the letter before me, the sunshine soon chased the clouds away. A bright sky overhead was sufficient often to dispel his weariness of spirit; and the inevitable discouragement that all suffer from at times was with him of short duration.

He had, in the autumn of 1871, the grief of losing his last remaining brother, James Blackwood, a constant companion and inmate of Strathtyrum, where his room was always kept for him.

John Blackwood to Rev. Lucas Collins.

STRATHTYRUM, *Oct.* 24, 1871.

I thank you for your kind expressions of feeling and sympathy for the death of my dear brother Jem. You know his quaint sterling character, and will feel the blank his loss must create amongst us. . . . This is the sixth brother I have seen go down almost in the prime of life, and I am now the last of the seven. Thank you warmly for what you say of myself. I know that in you I have a real friend.

His youngest brother, Colonel A. Blackwood, had died the year previous in India, where he had done good service. He served with distinction in the ―― Sikh Campaign, for which he received the Chillianwallah medals, and left the regiment he commanded at the time of his death — the 32nd Pioneers—in a high state of efficiency. This was the dearly loved youngest brother, of whom he wrote to Mr Lewes from Strathtyrum in 1861 : " We are in a perfect jubilee of happiness over the return from India of my brother Archie, my schoolfellow until we both went forth into the world, and the companion

of my heart all the days of my life." His nephew,
George Blackwood, was with him when he died, and
sent home the sorrowful account of his death. He,
alas! was soon to follow, and perished, fighting
bravely to the last, in General Burrows' ill-fated
force at the battle of Maiwand, ten years later.

For one week in the year the scarlet coats of the
Links may be said to have paled before the attractions of the scarlet uniform which clothed the Fife
Light Horse Volunteers. This gallant regiment
assembled for its yearly training, under Colonel Anstruther Thomson, in one of the Strathtyrum fields,
just outside the gates. With the Colonel for a guest,
and William Blackwood, who had joined the regiment,
besides various other officers of the different troops,
St Andrews, Cupar, Kirkcaldy, Dunfermline all sending their bravest and best, all coming and going,
we. found ourselves involved in military surroundings which my father said meant to him complete
idleness for the whole week. Unavailing were his
efforts to shut himself up in his writing-room, the
sounds of fife and drum penetrated every corner of the
house,—for when their regimental duties were over,
the Colonel would order the band to come and play
outside our doors, and it was difficult to compose a
letter to the strains of "Monymusk" or "Jessie,
the Flower of Dunblane." Finally messages would be
sent which proved irresistible—"Mr Blackwood must
come and see the tent-pegging;" "Mr Blackwood
really ought to see the Kirkcaldy boys at 'heads and
posts.'" So a cigar was lighted, and he would stroll
out with us to see the fun and generally to call in
those who wanted food. The dinner that ended the

day was by no means the least agreeable part of
the soldiering to the warriors, who would come in
scorched with the sun and sea wind which handled
their unaccustomed faces very roughly. It was a
gathering we all enjoyed: distant neighbours like
the Anstruther Thomsons, the Babingtons, Colonel
Babington, an ex-hussar and former officer of the
regiment, all took keen interest in the proceedings;
while the Moubrays from Otterstone, the Oswalds of
Dunnikier, Lady Rothes, Mr Waldegrave-Leslie, and
many others came from the farthest points of the
"Kingdom" to witness the martial display.

Colonel Anstruther Thomson, indefatigable in this
as in everything he undertakes, had worked hard to
make the regiment efficient. In his exertions he was
ably seconded in those days by his adjutant, the late
Captain J. A. Middleton, who took great interest in
it. And we were reminded of the many times we
had seen this popular officer and sportsman turn out
with them on his handsome charger, when we heard
that a detachment of the regiment, headed by their
Colonel, had formed the escort when poor "Jack," as
his friends affectionately styled him, was laid to rest
one sad November day of last year (1897).

John Blackwood to Rev. G. R. Gleig.

STRATHTYRUM, *July* 12, 1874.

This last week has been a tremendously military one here,
the Fife Mounted drilling in the parks at the gates, and their
Colonel and Willie, who is in the corps, staying with us. The
Colonel, Jack Anstruther Thomson, the mighty hunter, is a
famous fellow, and it was a most successful meeting. Strange
to say, we had most perfect weather, while you seem to have
been nearly drowned in the South.

The mention of Colonel Anstruther Thomson recalls the visits of another friend—Mr Charles Newdigate —who, next to hunting out a Jesuit, enjoyed fox-hunting. There were plenty of foxes in Fife for him, but we had never heard of any Jesuits being seen. He, however, was always on the look out for them, and this watchfulness was a peculiarity well known to every one.

He might have thought Strathtyrum an unlikely covert to harbour anything of the kind, but on one occasion when he came there from Charleton, the selection of guests he found at John Blackwood's dinner-table disturbed, or he pretended disturbed, him greatly. It was true that Mr Whyte - Melville and Colonel Anstruther Thomson were there to keep the balance; but then there were Mr and Mrs Adam (afterwards Sir William Adam, the Governor-General of Madras, and for many years the Liberal Whip), and equally dangerous because nearer at hand was the genial smiling countenance of Mr Cathcart of Pitcairlie, the chairman of every Radical meeting in the district. When he had looked round and fully realised the surroundings he mournfully shook his head and said to Colonel Thomson, " Oh, Jack, it's time we came here; my old friend is in a bad way." The shouts of laughter with which this was received may be well imagined, and the Jesuit's sternest foe, having uttered his protest, was content to enjoy his evening in the society of those companions whose political creeds differed so widely from that of their host. The latter, however, never allowed politics to interfere with the regard and liking he had for friends, like those I have named, with whom his only contests, except at an election time, were fought upon the golfing-ground.

Mr Delane, as has been stated, generally came at this time, but sometimes his friends in the north kept him so long that his holiday slipped away and we were cheated of the pleasure of his visit: he seldom allowed himself much more than three weeks. Once he wrote from Taymouth :—

I have hitherto been extremely fortunate in the weather, this being the first wet day, and have certainly had a pleasant time of it. My tastes, however, are strictly metropolitan: "the heather" is not "native" to my foot, which is more at home on the flags, and I confess that I shall see the gas-lamps and the move and throng of a great town again without much regret for forests and deer. I need not tell you how gorgeous this place is, but the genial spirit of both host and hostess is better than all the splendour.

In this he differed very much from my father, who had no liking for the noise and the throng and the gas-lamps that had to be encountered as the accompaniments of town life which he undertook for a certain time and for special purposes; but his objects accomplished, his correspondents seen, his only wish was to make off to the country as soon as possible.

The letters he used to write when from home all showed this longing, and he constantly refers with pleasure to the time when he should find himself in the "express" hurrying away from the noise and heat of London to the cool shades of the "Strath." We remember how delighted he was to see everything again in his beloved home: the pets, the horses, and dogs—all seemed to be looking better than ever, and the lawns and gardens at their best, on his return. Strathtyrum, as we have often seen it on a summer evening, with the last rays of the sun glinting through the trees, made as beautiful and graceful a setting for a man's home-life as could be wished, and every time he returned increased his pleasure in the well-known surroundings. The first walk, as soon as he had dined and lighted his cigar, was through the wood in sight of the sea and Bell Rock light. It felt warm and sheltered there amongst the fir trees and rhododendrons. The high winds never reached us, and we could sit and talk under the trees as comfortably as in the house. What he had to tell us about our friends and the incidents of his visits was always amusing and graphic—some little touch would be put on that brought the scene before us. Then there was often the speedy prospect of seeing some of those mentioned, sometimes old friends like Mr and Mrs Collins, Lockhart, Hamley, and others, who came nearly every year; or it might be an interesting new acquaintance who thought of visiting Scotland, and might find his way to Strathtyrum. We recollect the pleasant surprise it was to hear that Charles Reade, who was a comparative stranger to my father, had, after meeting him in London, solemnly promised to visit him that summer at Strathtyrum, and he looked forward eagerly, as we all did, to seeing and knowing the famous novelist under the familiar and intimate surroundings of a guest in our quiet country house. Mr Reade arrived in Edinburgh in the middle of July, and wrote from 10 Salisbury Road, slightly worried about a law case he was engaged in against the 'Glasgow Herald':—

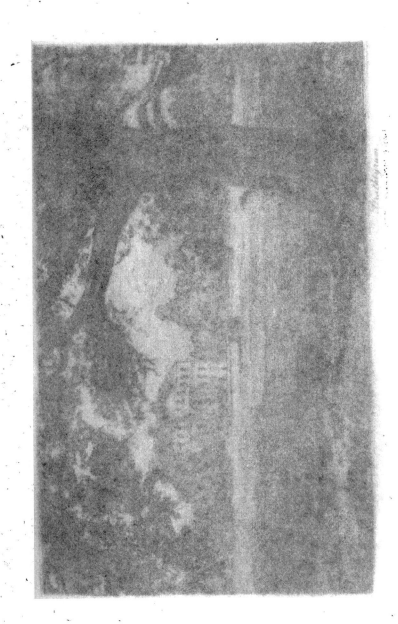

July 18, 1876.

I am old. Litigation is very agitating. I feel I shall want
48 hours in Edinburgh after the trial. By that time I hope I
may shake it all off, including a letter to some newspaper. It
is most important I should get to work again upon "The
Woman-Hater," [1] and I hope you will kindly allow my visit to
you to be a tolerably quiet one, in which the morning may be
given to that work in which we both have an interest. You
must show me the old house in Salisbury Road. It is even
now a fine situation. All the houses have gardens. Gibson's
immediate neighbour has a very fine one.—Yours very sincerely,
                                                CHARLES READE.

I attach great importance to your evidence, however short.

Having regard to his request, the visit was, I remember, a quiet one—that is, there were no visitors
staying in the house to meet him except my cousins
William Blackwood and his sister Bessie. He had
been staying, by a strange coincidence, exactly opposite my grandfather's old house in Salisbury Road.
I remember he was greatly pleased with that side of
Edinburgh, and admired the comfortable old-fashioned
houses with their big gardens. Our interest in him
had been greatly excited by the numerous letters he
wrote respecting the case of the "Hero and Martyr,"
and the fact that my father was to give evidence in it.
We were prepared to like him, and the charm of his
society stood well the test of a week's visit, in which he
was the only guest outside our own family. The heroic
ideas we had somehow associated with him, not only
from his novels but from the way he stood forward to
champion persons or causes that required redress, were
not quite reconcilable with his appearance and man-

---

[1] "The Woman-Hater" was to appear in the Magazine.

ners, which showed nothing of a fire-eating description.
On the contrary, we saw a very quiet-looking elderly
gentleman, with a particularly soft voice and courteous
manners, whose approach was rendered still more
quiet by his wearing cloth boots. Why he wore cloth
boots I cannot remember, although I believe he once
told us. We assured him they were admirably adapted
for lawn-tennis, and he straightway began to learn the
game, which was then struggling into favour. He
divided his attentions between this and the short
holes for golf we had near the house. He wrote
in his room all the morning, and we were delighted when the gong sounded that brought him
down-stairs to luncheon. Then he was like a schoolboy released from lessons, and prepared to amuse
himself and be amused for the rest of the day. He
used to say it did not matter where he sat at the
luncheon-table, there was always a warm foot-muff,
thoughtfully provided by Mrs Blackwood, in the shape
of a long-haired Scotch terrier curled up under each
chair. After luncheon a few privileged ladies came
for tea and tennis, when Mr Reade would be tempted
to try tennis or to putt, always, I must say, in a purely
frivolous spirit, but with great enjoyment to himself.
He used to say jokingly that Strathtyrum was a Palace
of Pleasure and a Castle of Indolence, and that my
father was a marvel to him, and he never could
believe he did any work at all. Everything was
there to tempt him and his friends to idleness, and
yet he saw a practical refutation of these accusations
every day in the long white packets lying on the
hall-table ready for the post.

The generous sympathy Mr Reade was ever ready to extend to any person suffering from injustice or neglect, the redress of any system that tended towards cruelty or injustice, is well known to all who were acquainted with him or his works. Like many who are warm-hearted and act with impulsive generosity, he sometimes met with disappointment and ingratitude. I remember there was a case occupying his mind and energies when at Strathtyrum, and the enthusiasm with which he pleaded the cause of his *protégé*, and his delight in winning the sympathies of my mother and my cousin Bessie Blackwood. " No, Blackwood," he would exclaim, " I am tired of talking to you. Mrs Blackwood," seizing her hand, "understands me with the instinctive sympathy of a generous mind, your niece has promised me her support, and with such friends as these," looking triumphantly at the two ladies, " I shall head a glorious list of subscriptions, and —— —— will shine through the clouds of misrepresentation and neglect that have shadowed him for years." But, alas! the kindness, the enthusiasm, the subscriptions were, I fear, all thrown away, and we felt quite crushed and so sorry for our generous-hearted friend when, a little time afterwards, my father sadly remarked that he feared the " clouds" that overshadowed —— —— were largely composed of whisky and water, and next time we saw Charles Reade we carefully avoided the subject. His visit gave us something to think of and talk of for many a long day. No one could be long in his society without seeing his was the big heart and mind ever ready to unbend where his aid and sympathy were

needed. His powerful imagination could conceive the
noblest actions arising in the most unpromising surroundings, his own genius and lofty ideals endowing
others with the qualities that tend to elevate and
beautify the poorest pathways of life. He left us,
needless to say, amid the regrets of the whole family,
one of the most strangely interesting of the many
and varied personalities that gave colour and interest
to my father's home life.

The letter he wrote after returning to Edinburgh
gives an amusing account of the trials a visitor returning from Strathtyrum had to encounter in those days,
and, as Julian Young also sets forth, without the
consoling thoughts of Strathtyrum at the end of
the journey. The envelope was addressed to " John
Blackwood, Esq. (Au Palais de Plaisir), Strathtyrum,
St Andrews." He wrote :—

10 SALISBURY ROAD, EDINBURGH, July 29.

DEAR BLACKWOOD,—I left St Andrews at 2.25, waited at
f-l-t-h-y Lucres [Leuchars] 15 minutes, at the next junction 20.
At all the stations there was a disposition on the part of the
locomotive authorities to take snuff with others of the same
kidney. At Kirkcaldy we abandoned the journey altogether for
a time, but, altering our minds, started at last and crawled down
to the pier an hour late. The steamboat people waited gravely
until our luggage came down, and then discovered we had no
coal, so they coaled the vessel before our eyes at great length.
At last we got on board and arrived in the Elysian fields [this
refers to a portion so called of the Golf Links of St Andrews],
for it was quite a smooth passage. But we landed among
bunkers, — one we made, as follows : We encountered a coal
train, and instead of standing upon our rank and going ahead,
we doffed our bonnets and set an example of retiring
modesty to the colliers. They went ahead, and we remained

inactive so long that it was 6 o'clock when we got to Waverley. In England, on these occasions, we write to the 'Times.' The 'Times' is no friend of mine, so I write to 'Blackwood.' It is really too bad. Going out to Strathtyrum this might be overlooked. The traveller knows that bunkers must end in time, and Palace of Pleasure and Castle of Indolence reward him for these impediments. But going away, it is not to be borne. —

CHAPTER VIII.

CHARLES LEVER.

RECOLLECTIONS of Strathtyrum and its visitors have
led us far ahead, and we must now take a look
backwards in order to trace the connection of Charles
Lever with the House, with which his first correspondence began in the early "sixties." His introduction to the Blackwoods led to one of those fresh
developments which are not at all unusual in the
writings of authors who have distinguished themselves in one special line, and which mark a new
stage in their career. Lord Lytton (Bulwer) gave
an example of this, his later novels being hardly
recognisable as the work of the same hand, and

George Eliot, as we shall show, was also a notable instance of this versatility. Those who associate the name of Charles Lever entirely with the racy dare-devil adventures of his early heroes will have a surprise in store for them in the perusal of his later works. Perhaps 'Jack Hinton,' 'Charles O'Malley,' and the inimitable 'Harry Lorrequer,' will always rank first with the public, who are loth to see their favourite win fresh laurels in any field save the accustomed one. There must still, however, be a balance in favour of the witty and eloquent utterances of "Cornelius O'Dowd," and the calmer and more probable, if less exciting, later novels, which gained in value by the knowledge of life and the experience of maturer years. John Blackwood, it would appear, had some doubt as to whether anything suitable for 'Maga' could come from the hands of Harry Lorrequer's author, not because of his early writings, but from a distrust of the transition from them to his later style, which had been marked by some less successful efforts. The first letter to Lever contains these opinions, though very delicately wrapped up in words which should not hurt the man whom he genuinely admired. Lever had proposed through Sir E. Bulwer Lytton to enter into correspondence regarding a serial story for 'Maga,' and John Blackwood replies thus :—

EDINBURGH, *May* 7, 1861.

Admiring your genius as cordially as I do, I still feel so doubtful as to whether what you would write would be suitable for the Magazine, that I am unwilling to make a proposition or to invite you to send MS. It would go sorely against my grain to decline anything from the friend of my youth, "Harry Lorrequer."

There is no more heard of Lever till the spring of 1863, when he sends a paper on Cavour, and the first four chapters of a novel. Cavour was immediately put into type for the Magazine, and the Editor expresses himself warmly in praise of it. The novel he thinks promising, but would like to see more of it.

John Blackwood to Charles Lever.

EDINBURGH, *April* 27, 1863.

It is a serious business to start a long serial, and I would not like to decide without seeing the bulk of the work. I do not know how you have been in the habit of writing, whether from month to month, or getting a good way ahead before the publication is commenced. If the latter is your usual plan, I have no hesitation in asking you to send me a good mass of the MS., and I will let you know as speedily as possible what I think and can propose. From these first four chapters it seems to me impossible to take a line as to the probable character of the story.

Charles Lever to John Blackwood.

HÔTEL D'ODESSA, SPEZIA, *May* 2, 1863.

MY DEAR SIR,—I hasten to answer, and thank you for your letter. I am glad you like the line I have taken on Italy. I believe it to be the true one, and I know that it is so far new. As to my story, I'd give you my whole plan in detail at once, but for this reason, which you will acknowledge to be good— that the very moment I revealed it, I should be obliged to invent another. To such an extent do I labour under this unfortunate disability, that in my own family no one even questions me as to the issue of any tale I am engaged on, well knowing that once I have discussed, I should be obliged to change it. You ask me how I write; my reply is, just as I live—from hand to mouth. I can do nothing continuously— that is, without seeing the printed part close behind me. This has been my practice for five-and-twenty years, and I don't think I could change it—at least I should deem it a rash experiment.

Again he says :—

SPEZIA, *May* 8, 1863.

As I had to own most ignominiously, I have only one way of writing, and like the gentleman mentioned in a French novel, who, having learned to dance in a room where there was an old hair-brush, never could accomplish a step without that accompaniment, so I must stick to my poor traditions, of which an old coat and an old ink-bottle, and an increasing impatience to see how my characters look in type, are chief, and I seriously believe if you cut me off from these, there's an end of me !

He goes on to say :—

I think there is material for a pleasant half-gossiping sort of paper on Social Italy : "Life in Italian Cities "—those strange wildernesses where rare plants and weeds live together on a pleasant equality, and where you may find the cowslips under a glass, and the cactus on a dunghill. Is it not strange that there is nothing so graphic about Italy as the sketches in Byron's letters ? Perhaps it was the very blending of Dirt and Levity in himself which led him to the exact appreciation.

The perfect success of the happy-go-lucky Irishman's methods was so convincing, that the Editor threw his scruples to the winds and decides there and then to go "nap."

John Blackwood to Charles Lever.

EDINBURGH, *May* 12, 1863.

After the lively and graphic picture you give of the way in which your best novels have been written, I see nothing for it but to get the first part into type, and after I have read it in proof I shall be better able to write. In the meantime I may say that I am very much disposed to plunge into the story with you, and cry, Go ahead in your own fashion if I can propose anything to suit you. I have the pleasure of enclosing a cheque in acknowledgment of your papers on Brigandage and the Italy of Cavour. The proof of the latter came back safely to-day, and I would not have objected had you added to it. They have been talking a great deal of solemn stuff in both Houses of Parliament about Italian progress and development, but our Liberal orators hardly even allude to the overwhelming influence in the country of that friend of Freedom " our ally." I like very much the idea of such a paper as you propose on Social Italy, or rather "Life in Italian Cities," and feel very confident that you will draw a very graphic picture. What you say of Byron and his letters is very good indeed.

The novel in question was 'Tony Butler,' which appeared in the Magazine. Of this story John Blackwood says :—

Your pleasant letters are always most welcome, but you give me far too much credit about Tony, as to whom I strongly feel my incompetence to advise. I am about as fit to guide his future career as his worthy mother or her coadjutor the minister. Indeed my feeling is that advice to an author in the guidance of his story should be very cautiously proffered, and is very apt to be prejudicial, to say nothing of the presumption of attempting to instruct such an artist as you.

Lever's methods when writing a story in serial form sometimes, however, occasioned amusing notes of warning from the Editor, who has to remind him that it spoils the *vraisemblance* of a story to begin to describe an interview in the winter and end it in summer. " Observe," he says, " that in the garden scene you make it a fine night, and from the morning showing before they separated, apparently the night was short ; whereas when Tony started in cold and snow for the Burnside, it was clearly winter." Similar comments draw attention to inconsistencies of this kind, which were apparently the only defects, or were all that the Editor permitted himself to criticise, and Lever took them in good part. Indeed after a few weeks of correspondence we find this successful author, whom the Editor rightly considered as one of the most distinguished novelists of the day, eagerly begging for advice and criticism.

Use your knife [he said], don't be afraid to cut. Tell me what you think of what I send you as though I was the rawest recruit in Literature. I never write with the same spirit as under such criticisms. When not too late to amend, if anything reach you that you think ill of, do not hesitate to say so at once. I can change—in fact, it is the one compensation for all the inartistic demerits of my way of work, that I can change as easily as I can talk of changing.

It must have been pleasant for the Editor to work with this powerful yet pliant mind, so strong and yet so sensitive, so frank and generous in the discussion of his own natural characteristics, taking his unknown friend into his confidence with a trustfulness which formed one of his most attractive traits. There was between these two, who had never met, some subtle bond of sympathy, inspired by instinctive comprehension of each other, a result perfectly intelligible between persons who have come face to face even only once in their lives, but very rarely inspired through the medium of paper and ink.

A few months after their correspondence began Lever lost his only son. This misfortune hit him hard, and his big heart was very sore when he wrote to John Blackwood, craving for the sympathy which he knew would be given him in full measure.

Charles Lever to John Blackwood.

CASA CAPPONI, FLORENCE, *Oct.* 1, 1863.

I was called here by telegraph, too late to see my only son alive. He died of a ruptured blood-vessel on Wednesday last. I

have for some years back had many misfortunes, and this one
fills the cup. My poor boy was twenty-six, the finest, boldest,
and cleverest fellow you ever saw, and one of the handsomest.

Referring to his novel he says, "If I had not begun
work, I would not now in justice to *you*," and goes on
to ask if the parts can be drawn out so as to give him
more time. The picture of the poor stricken author
trying to work his head while his heart was so laden
moved my father deeply, and he wrote at once the
following :—

John Blackwood to Charles Lever.

Oct. 5, 1863.

I am truly distressed to hear of the sad affliction that has
come upon you in the death of your only son. God comfort
you, and grant that your poor wife may be supported under
this heavy blow. Do not disturb yourself about your tale.
I will make any arrangement to suit a man suffering under
sorrow such as yours. We can either shorten the parts or
suspend publication at the end of the fourth part for a month
if you are not ready. All the opinions I hear of the first part
are highly favourable, and would under other circumstances
be highly gratifying to you. If I see any comments in the
press likely to interest you, I shall send them to you. All
your novels bespeak the writer a warm-hearted man, and I
think much of you in your affliction. I showed your affecting
note to my wife, who, although like myself personally a stranger
to you, joins me in warm sympathy.

After that letter Lever evidently felt he could
never use the formal "Sir" again when addressing
my father, and hereafter in all the letters he calls
him by his name. A few more touching allusions
are made to this bereavement :—

I can never forget your kind and feeling note. Broken
and crushed as I am, I am not yet insensible to such kindness.

If you only knew how we lived with our children, how much we mingled in their lives, and they in ours. It was but the other day my poor boy came back from India after seven years' absence, and the feeling that we were all together again had but just dawned on us.

He goes on to say—

It will be better for me, I believe, that I must work, and work hard. The tired head may help the heavy heart after all. From my heart I thank you for your sympathy, all the more that you included your wife in your sorrow for us.—Believe me, ever your faithful friend,   CHARLES LEVER.

Again he writes :—

It is kind of you to tell me good notices of my story. Believe me, I am far more anxious for *you* than for myself. All my ambitions are now under a small green mound where I sat yesterday, and whither I am going to sit now.

Charles Lever was at the time John Blackwood began to correspond with him British Consul at Spezia, and his visits to England were rare, nearly all his time being passed in Italy, where his residence was either at Spezia or at Florence. When at the latter, he had opportunities for obtaining insight into the tumultuous and ever-changeful tide of Italian politics, besides other foreign affairs. His views and impressions of those stirring times were embodied in a series of essays in the Magazine purporting to be written by Cornelius O'Dowd, hence the frequent allusion to him as O'Dowd. John Blackwood's admiration for the picture Lever has given us of Kenny Dodd in 'The Dodd Family Abroad' led the author into an interesting and amusing account of the composition of that inimitable character, whom he describes as typical of his nation.

Charles Lever to John Blackwood.

CASA CAPPONI, FLORENCE, *Nov.* 23, 1863.

How glad I am you like the Dodds. I know I have never done, nor ever shall do, anything one half as good, because it is original. I decanted through all the absurdity of Dodd's nature whatever I really knew of life and mankind, and it is that very mixture of shrewd sense and intense blundering that makes an Irishman. The perception and the *enjoyment* of the very domestic absurdities that overwhelm him with shame would in any other nature mean insanity, but they only make an Irishman very true to his national characteristics, and rather a pleasant fellow to talk to.

At one time he thought of reviving Kenny Dodd as the mouthpiece of these witty and sagacious papers already alluded to, but changed his mind in accordance with Blackwood's advice. "I so fully agreed with you in *not* wanting to revive Kenny Dodd that I have created a new man, Cornelius O'Dowd, whose letter is enclosed herewith, 'A Friend of Gioberti,' which caused a laugh for those who have had little mirth in their hearts of late." This paper illustrates exactly what he meant by the tragi-comic episodes, in which the comedy is so thoroughly relished that the serious aspects of the case are entirely forgotten. To any one desirous of a hearty laugh we recommend them to the volume of O'Dowd containing "A Friend of Gioberti."

Lever's work at the Consulate was never really congenial to him, and though he discharged his duties cheerfully and well, he sometimes found they interfered inconveniently with his pleasanter literary work. In the following amusing lines he sets forth some of his consular difficulties :—

I can do nothing "fictionally" for some time, though, as Heaven knows—

> I know nothing of bottomry, nothing of weight,
> Nothing of cargo, demurrage, or freight ;
> And in such a maze are my faculties wrapt in,
> That I never could say
> To this blessed day,
> Is it the Consul should pay, or the Captain ?

Having described how the type which Kenny Dodd represents is to be found all over Ireland, he on another occasion accounts for M'Casky, one of his favourite creations, who appears in ' Tony Butler.'

So you are coming round to M'Casky. I half thought you would, and said little in his defence. It certainly is not easy for any one not " bog born " to understand that composite animal which Ireland produces, and has so much of the gentleman through a regularly demoralised scampish nature — the point *d'honneur* preserved, after honour itself was gone, and the tradition of being respectable maintained after years of the sponging-house and the police courts. Believe me, I know full fifty M'Caskys, and one of them became a " Chief Justice " ! though I don't mean mine to end that way.

John Blackwood to Charles Lever.

Nov. 19, 1863.

I am afraid I am not *pro* Turk enough to take Sir Henry Bulwer's view in ' Maga.' I cannot help feeling that the Turks have no business in Europe, and always thought the Crimean war a fatal mistake, a hopeless attempt to prop up a rotten empire and a superstitious faith, which at all events it is not our business to encourage. Still we must stick to alliances, and the question always remains, Who could be trusted with Constantinople ? Sir Henry must have much curious information, and is well entitled to a hearing. Perhaps what you think of might be thrown into the form of a letter, and my private views have not been advocated in the Magazine, although I remember I was strongly tempted to back up Nicholas's little

scheme of a partition. No doubt our having Egypt would be a
great blessing to humanity, but the French at the Holy Places
gave a comical aspect to the whole proposition.

To this Lever replies :—

Nov. 23, 1863.

The sight of your handwriting is very comforting to me. I
tell you frankly I get no letters that cheer me like your own.
I quite agree with you about Turkey, and our policy has no
other defence than that it is better to leave open to contingencies
what, if we were to deal with summarily, we should finish at
once. In not negotiating with Nicholas, England was simply
giving way to one of those intermittent attacks of morality
which seize her after some aggressive paroxysm—a Kaffir war
or an annexation of Oude. We have done scores of things,
and if we live and prosper will do them again, far more repre-
hensible than a partition of Turkey.

The next letter refers to Thackeray's death, whom
he had known extremely well.

FLORENCE, *Jan.* 2, 1864.

Poor Thackeray! I cannot say how much I was shocked
at his death. He wrote his 'Irish Sketch-Book,' which he
dedicated to me, in my old house at Templorgue, and it is with
a heavy heart I think of all our long evenings together, mingling
our plans for our future with many a jest and many a story.
He was fortunate, however, to go down in the full blaze of his
genius, as so few do. The fate of most is to go on pouring
water on the lees, that people at last come to suspect that they
have never got honest liquor from the tap at all.

In complimenting Lever on one of his realistic
descriptions of an adventurer which he had written
for an O'Dowd paper, Blackwood is reminded of an
amusing character of the same sort who had haunted
him and his brother in their early travels on the
Continent. He says :—

I suppose you have a real character in view. I cannot

help feeling sorry he did not do the little Foreign Office bird.
G—— would have been a babe in his hands, and it is fortunate
he escaped.   I wish I could describe to you a splendid French
specimen of the genus whom I saw a good deal of some
twenty-five years ago.   I was a lad of eighteen, and travelling
with a brother and cousin some twelve years older.   We fell in
with him at the Hôtel de Petit Paris at Chambéry, where we
were stuck for a fortnight, and the Viscount D'Argy, as he called
himself, proved an inexhaustible source of fun, worth his dinner
and endless champagne upon all occasions.   All through Italy for
months, by some odd *chance*, he made his appearance in the
same hotel at each town as we arrived.   His naïve astonishment
at the *rencontre* was always delightful.   He has, what doubtless
was to him a most valuable natural gift, a power of growing
hair rapidly on his face such as I never saw equalled.   At
Chambéry he was in a full suit of whiskers, moustache, and
imperial; at Turin he was reduced to a modest moustache; at
Florence he was *rasé* all over, but by the time he walked into
our room at Rome he had a crop of hair that you would have
sworn was a twelvemonth's growth.   He was a devoted Royalist,
and the pleasure it had given him to seduce the mistress of
the Duc d'Orleans was consequently something wonderful.   He
made the first attempts to borrow money with a skill that
deserved better success.   He cut me afterwards in the Corso
with great dignity.   Poor D'Argy, many a laugh he has given
me, and I often wish I could give him a £5 note, but I daresay
he has long since joined his "illustrious *ancêtres*," about whom
he used to speak much at a late hour of the evening.

O'Dowd next was referring to the effects of tele-
graphy on certain branches of industry and literature, and Blackwood makes a suggestion, afterwards
adopted :—

You should touch, I think, upon the extraordinary power
which the telegraph gives to the holder of the wires.   It may
become very dangerous.   The writers of the summaries of
debates are the men most directly superseded by the telegraphic
report, but it may put an end to long speeches as effectually as

the penny post put an end to long letters. I am glad you denounce that tiresome twaddler Goldoni. I remember so well suffering under him, and feeling disgusted with my Italian instructor for grinning idiotically at passages when I could not see a vestige of fun. Your sketch of Italian character is extremely good.

The close of the letter refers to the rigours of a Scottish spring in the last days of March, and was written during a hurried sort of picnic visit to Strathtyrum :—

We have tumbled into winter here—showers of snow and a wind that cuts one in two. Mrs Blackwood came to look after the garden, but there is hardly a sign of vegetation. I shall be back in Edinburgh in a couple of days. Excuse this jumble of a note : we have only one sitting-room opened, and I am writing in a room with the children at dinner.

The rest contains a bit of advice on patronage, which, he afterwards regretfully adds, is not often needed with regard to the rewards for literature.

EDINBURGH, *April* 5, 1864.

In walking home together yesterday afternoon Aytoun and I had fits of laughter over O'Dowd. The thing that has tickled him is the victim of Cavour's eternal schemes for Italian progress, especially the plans turning up in the dead man's bureau. He agrees with me in thinking that you have completely taken second wind. I improved the occasion by commenting upon his own utter incapacity—the lazy villain has not written a line for two years. A sheriffship and a professorship are fatal to literary industry. It would be well worth while for any Government to give any man who is active in writing against them a good fat place, but it is fatal for them so to patronise their friends. God knows, however, that patronising their literary friends is a crime of which Governments are not often guilty, but I hope, with all my heart, that if we do come in; your turn, something good, will come at last.

The novel of 'Tony Butler' was all this time running its course through the Magazine, its authorship unsuspected by even such acute critics as Bulwer, so thoroughly had he changed his style. He was himself extremely anxious to preserve his incognito, which the vagaries of the post-office seriously imperilled on more than one occasion. The following is an instance of the dangers attending the transit of proofs between England and Italy, and the agitations caused thereby :—

Charles Lever to John Blackwood.

No proof has arrived, and I have a note from the Post-office, *London*, to say that a proof is detained there. This I suspected to have been one from Chapman & Hall, and wrote to them to secure it. Heaven grant it should not be T. B.; but I felt so confident that if it were yours it would be detained, if detained at all, at Edinburgh, that I wrote off without reflecting. Have I made a baste of myself?

Then follows :—

No proof. I must have made a fiasco of it in writing to C. & H. to release the proof detained in London, which they will now discover to be 'Tony'!!! Into what scrapes flunkies, messengers, *et hoc genus*, do betray us! I have offended more people in life by the awkwardness of my servants than I have done by all my "proper" shortcomings, which have not been few.

The excitement increased till the authorities at St Martin's-le-Grand gave up a packet, which, on being forwarded by Messrs Chapman & Hall to the author, he found, as he expected, contained the missing proofs of 'Tony' and "O'Dowd." Being still in doubt as to whether the contents had been examined, he wrote the following letter to Blackwood, with a threat of

vengeance not more severe than the occasion demanded :—

The proofs arrived to-day under the envelope that I forwarded. On learning from the Post-office, London, that a proof
of mine was detained there, I immediately surmised that it
must be one of my secret story hitherto, and enclosed the reference to C. & H. to release it. Now I find that it is ' Tony ' and
" O'Dowd," consequently I am in terror lest our secret be out,
and all one's hitherto care defeated by this *malladetto* messenger who " crimped the tuppence." I want you therefore to
assure me, if you can assure me, that C. & Hall's people, when
sent to St Martin's-le-Grand to release the proof, had no power
to open and examine it, nor any privilege to carry it away with
them out of the office. If this be the case, of course there is no
mischief done, and I am *quitte pour la peur;* but pray do tell
me the regulations on the subject, and for Heaven's sake and
Tony's sake, water that man's grog who posted the packet
originally, or tell me his name and I'll call my next villain by
it if I have to write another story.

In the same letter he says, " I had a pleasant
man, one of your Edinburgh professors, to dine
with me yesterday,—Scottish and medical—Professor
Bennett."

Garibaldi was to visit England in 1864, and Lever
offers to introduce him by letter to my father. He
had been able to be of some service to the hero when
he lay wounded at Spezia after his escapade at
Aspromonte. He writes : " I don't know if I ever
sent you (what I do now, at all events) a little photograph I had taken of G. when he lay wounded at
Spezia. It was ill done, but is very faithful. I
hope Mrs Blackwood will give it a place in her book
for the subject's sake." The photograph referred to
represents Garibaldi in bed, dressed in his cap and the

famous red shirt.   The curtains of the bed are looped
up around, giving him the appearance of being in a
tent.   The bullet-wound in his ankle procured him
more than even the usual amount of sympathy, and
he was the recipient of the most extraordinary offer-
ings of all kinds it is possible to imagine—clothing,
food, wine, luxuries of all kinds, many of them ludi-
crously unsuited to his requirements.   Wine, for example, he never drinking anything but water; fur-
lined coats, when he was never seen without the red
shirt; and many other luxuries principally despatched
by sympathisers in England.   An amusing account is
given of this, and of a band of English ladies determined to see him, and convey the condolences of a
large body of persons in this country — this when
Garibaldi's wounded condition demanded perfect quiet.
At last, when he had been driven into a fever from
the excitement of so many attentions, his friends persuaded a Captain Ripari to dress up in red shirt and
cap, and personate the wounded hero.   This was done
so successfully that the visitors went away delighted,
having wept over him and carried off locks of his
hair in their mistaken enthusiasm.   Referring to
Garibaldi's visit to England, John Blackwood writes
to Lever:—

April 27, 1864.

I am particularly obliged to you for the promptitude with
which you did the bit about Garibaldi.   It is, I think, the best
thing that has been written about the General, and I hope he is
worthy of it.   You will see that the Garibaldi fever has been
cut short, so that I shall have no opportunity of using the note
of introduction you so kindly sent, but I am equally obliged.
Fergusson [Sir William], the surgeon, is a very intimate friend
and old ally of mine, and I have no doubt he has given genuine

and sound advice. Garibaldi would doubtless have had innumerable invitations to No. 9 Piccadilly, and I hope the hero has not damaged himself. I have half a mind to write this joke to Ferguson and call for an explicit statement of the hero's health. Seriously, he is well away at the present crisis, and we are making sufficient fools of ourselves without this wild outbreak of hero-worship. . . .

Laurence Oliphant stayed with us for three days, and we had a "fine time." I never saw such a fellow for knowing people, pulling the wires, and being in the thick of it always. He is hand and glove with half the potentates and conspirators in Europe. Skeffy in his wildest flights is a joke to him. There is, however, no humbug about Oliphant; he is a good fellow and a good friend. He talked much of the pleasant days he had passed with you, and begged particularly to be remembered to you all. Knowing I could trust him I told him the secret, the importance of keeping which he fully appreciated, and will assist in throwing people off the scent, which 'O'Dowd' will, I think, put a good many upon. There have been surmises in the papers, but surmises are nothing. How is 'Tony' getting on, and the new "O'Dowd"? I wish, indeed, we had come across each other in earlier life; but it is no use your talking of being seedy—you are evidently as fresh as paint, and never wrote better, if so well.

The following is O'Dowd's tribute to Garibaldi referred to by the Editor :—

I really felt, if it had not been for Carlyle, I might have been a bit of a hero-worshipper myself. The grand frescoes in caricature of the popular historian have, however, given me a hearty and wholesome disgust to the whole thing; not to say that, however enthusiastic a man may feel about his idol, he must be sorely ashamed of his fellow-worshippers. "Lie down with dogs and you'll get up with fleas," says an old Irish adage; but what, in the name of all entomology, is a man to get up with who lies down with these votaries of Garibaldi?

It is not easy to conceive anything finer, simpler, more thoroughly unaffected or more truly dignified, than the man himself.

His noble head; his clear, honest, brown eye; his finely traced mouth, beautiful as a woman's, and only strung up to sternness when anything ignoble or mean had outraged him; and, last of all, his voice contains a fascination perfectly irresistible, allied, as you knew and felt these graces were, with a thoroughly pure untarnished nature. The true measure of the man lies in the fact that, though his life had been a series of the boldest and most_daring achievements, his courage is about the very last quality uppermost in your mind when you meet him. It is of the winning softness of his look and manner, his kind thoughtfulness for others, his sincere pity for all suffering, his gentleness, his modesty, his manly sense of brotherhood with the very humblest of the men who have loved him, that you think: these are the traits that throw all his heroism into shadow; and all the glory of the conqueror pales before the simple virtues of the man. He never looked to more advantage than in that humble life of Caprera, where people came and went—some, old and valued friends whose presence warmed up their host's heart; others were passing acquaintances, or, as it might be, not even that; worshippers or curiosity-seekers—living where and how they could in that many-roomed house; diving into the kitchen to boil their coffee; sallying out to the garden to pluck their radishes; down to the brook for a cress, or to the seaside to catch a fish, all more or less busy in the midst of a strange idleness: for there was not—beyond providing for the mere wants of the day—anything to be done. There was no cultivation outside that little garden where the grand old soldier delved, or rested on his spade-handle as he turned his gaze over the sea, doubtless thinking of the dear land beyond it.

At dinner—and what a strange meal it was—all met, full of the little incidents of an uneventful day. The veriest trifles they were, but of interest to those who listened, and to none more than Garibaldi himself, who liked to hear who had been over to Maddalena, and what sport they had, or whether Albanesi had taken any mullet, and who it was said he could mend the boat? and who was to paint her? Not a word was spoken of political events of the world, and every mention of them was as rigidly excluded as though a Government spy had been seated at table. He rarely spoke himself, but was a good listener—

not merely hearing with attention, but showing, by an occasional suggestion or a hint, how his mind speculated on the subject before him. If, however, led to speak of himself or his exploits, the unaffected ease and simplicity of the man became at once evident.

Cavour, who knew men thoroughly, and studied them just as closely as he studied events, understood at once that Garibaldi was the man he wanted. He needed one who should move the national heart—who, sprung from the people himself and imbued with all the instincts of his class, should yet not dissever the cause of liberty from the cause of monarchy. To attach Garibaldi to the throne was no hard task. The king, who led the van of his army, was an idol made for such worship as Garibaldi's. The monarch who could carry a knapsack and a heavy rifle over the cliffs of Monte Rosa from sunrise to sunset, and take his meal of hard bread before he "turned in" at night in a shepherd's shieling, was a king after the bold buccaneer's heart. To what end inveigh against the luxuries of a Court, its wasteful splendours, or its costly extravagance, with such an example? This strong-sinewed, big-boned, unpoetical king has been the hardest nut ever republicanism had to crack!

It might be possible to overrate the services Garibaldi has rendered to Italy—it would be totally impossible to exaggerate those he has rendered the monarchy; and out of Garibaldi's devotion to Victor Emmanuel has sprung that hearty, honest, manly appreciation of the king, which the Italians unquestionably display. A merely political head of the State, though he were gifted with the highest order of capacity, would have disappeared altogether from view in the sun-splendour of Garibaldi's exploits: not so the King Victor Emmanuel, who only shone the brighter in the reflected blaze of the hero who was so proud to serve him.

Lever and John Blackwood were still strangers to each other, as Lever had not been to England since their correspondence began; but by this time (1865) we find the Editor, in reply to a request from Lever, had sent his photograph. On receipt of it Lever says:

"I write one hurried line to thank you heartily for your photograph; it is so pleasant to see the man one talks to." In the same letter he says, "I don't know Aytoun; but, as the Cockneys say, 'I'd like to.'" The next is after receiving the photographs of his friend's children. "I like the faces of your little people greatly;" and he goes on to give his advice for the best saddle for a little boy to begin to ride on, —"A saddle, not a *pad*; a hard saddle, and not flat;" and he gives some golden advice as to the position of the stirrups for securing a good seat, and draws a sketch in the letter I have before me of the saddle he recommends for my little brother to begin riding, winding up with, "How I'd like to give the boy a lesson; who knows but I may yet?" Certainly no one was better qualified to do so than the author of 'Harry Lorrequer.' The interest he took in his unknown friend's son had in it something touching, from the fact that he had so recently lost his only son. He says in the same letter:—

I am still here. My wife has been very ill the last three days. The return of the day that took our poor boy from us was a terrible trial to her. . . . And now write soon. What scores of things you have to amuse me!—Yours most faithfully,
CHARLES LEVER.

He evidently delighted in getting letters from my father, for on another occasion about this time he writes: "You cannot believe how much your kind letters save me in colchicum. Your last two notes did more for me than an oz. of magnesia." Writing far away from England, and out of reach of any literary opinions, he probably at times grew despondent over

his work; though a glance at the brilliantly written
" O'Dowds " he was contributing to 'Maga' will show
what little reason there was for any misgivings.
Partly from his state of health, as well as from other
causes, Lever's letters at times show an amount of
depression of spirits the reverse of what one might
have expected from the buoyant writings of his
early life. It was as though he felt at times the
years had treated him unfairly, not merely in running
away with time, but in still withholding from him
some coveted good which he had thought to be
attainable, but the pursuit of which he was at
last bringing himself unwillingly to renounce. His
writings at this time leave nothing to be desired. He
had stepped successively and successfully from the
broad farce of the Irish dragoons, and what he calls
" bog born," to what is properly comedy, and the
romantic school, as in the ' Knight of Gwynn,' the
' Dodd Family,' &c. And now, in his middle age, yet
another field had opened to him, in which his knowledge of the world and politics gave him a wide scope,
not only in fiction but in the O'Dowd papers, where
we are supposed, at least when he comes to any serious matter, to be listening to Lever himself. In these,
as in some of his novels, diplomacy plays an important
part. His familiarity with the wide area which the
term " Foreign Office " implies, from the Chief Secretary down to the tiniest official in her Majesty's service, supplied him with abundant materials, which he
turned to the best possible account. His literary
reputation was thus being thoroughly maintained, but
the hard work it entailed, combined with his consular
duties, could have left him but little of the leisure

which as we grow older is, if less enjoyable, even more
than ever necessary for mind and body. Besides, there
was too, no doubt, a lingering sense of disappointment
at not getting some better post than this same con-
sulship at Spezia, which helped to depress one who
was naturally cheerful and sunny in his views, but
who, to quote his own words, "throve better on kindnesses than on kicks"; or, as he wrote once, "I am
still enough of a schoolboy to work better when praised
than caned." We can thus comprehend to some extent the comfort and encouragement he manifestly
derived from John Blackwood's letters, which used to
aid in dispelling the clouds that from time to time
overshadowed this naturally joyous temperament.

You talk of feeling old [John Blackwood says to him], but
you show no signs of it, and in some book of "Men of the Time"
I see you were born so late as 1809, only tèn years older than
I am. I now look upon you as a contemporary, and in future
shall take the liberty of addressing you as my dear Lever, the
terms in which I habitually feel and think about you.

To this Lever pleasantly replied :—

April 17, 1864.

MY DEAR BLACKWOOD,—How glad I am to be the first to say
there is to be no more "mistery" between us. I have wished
it this many a day, and have only been withheld from feeling
that I was not quite certain whether my gratitude for the cheer
and encouragement you had given me might not have run away
with my judgment, and made me forget the force of the Italian
adage, "It takes *two* to make a bargain." How lightly you talk
of ten years! Why, I was thirty years younger ten years ago.
I'd have ridden at a five-foot wall with more pluck than I can
summon now at a steep staircase! But I own to you frankly,
if I had known *you* then as I do now, it might have wiped off
some of the score of years. Even my daughters guess at breakfast when I have had a pleasant note from you.

The following letter refers to a recent "O'Dowd," and contains a suggestion to the author on the subject of duelling :—

John Blackwood to Charles Lever.

July 6, 1864.

There is a great deal of truth in the "Be always ready with the pistol," and it is particularly apposite at the present time. We have gone ridiculously far against Duelling, and God knows what you could recommend any man to do under a sudden insult. He must trust to the inspiration of the moment. There is a good side to it too, however; a bully is, I should think, less tolerated that ever he was. Gentlemen feeling themselves all equally helpless under an insult are prompt to join with the offended party, and a man committing an outrage is instantly tabooed. Men take a memorandum not to sit down again in company with a fellow who is in the habit of getting upon dangerous ground. I am not sure but that it would make your remarks more effective to allude to this phase of the question.

He goes on to say—

I think you rate the French Emperor's intellect too low. He certainly seems to understand the materials he has to work with, which is a pretty high standard of intellect. . . . I enclose a letter from the Bishop of Limerick, which I think you may like to have. He is a very nice old gentleman indeed, and I think I told you I met him at dinner in London, when he spoke very much as you spoke about Martin O'Sullivan.

Blackwood had sent the Bishop a copy of the Magazine containing allusions to O'Sullivan by Lever.

Charles Lever to John Blackwood.

FLORENCE, July 10, 1864.

MY DEAR BLACKWOOD,—What a hearty thing it was of you to send me the Bishop's letter! I hope I may keep it! Do you know that it was by the merest accident that I did not allude to *himself* in the paper, or rather it was out of deference to his apron; for one of the most brilliant evenings I ever remember in my life was having the Bishop and O'Sullivan to dine with me, with only two others. And Harry Griffin was the king of the company. Moore used to say, when complimented on his singing of the Melodies, "Ah, if you were to hear Griffin!" But why don't he recognise me? When we are ready with our vol. i. I shall ask you to send one or two, or perhaps three or four, copies to some friends. Let me beg one for the Bishop, and I'll send a note with it. I think your note *will* do me good. It has already, and I am down and hipped cruelly.

Charles Lever to John Blackwood.

VILLA MORELLI, FLORENCE,
Sept. 26, 1864.

MY DEAR BLACKWOOD,—I only knew by your nephew's letter that you were about to have a paper on old Whately, who said more stupid things and got the credit of more good ones (that were not his own) than any man of his day. He had not a grain of either wit or humour in his whole composition, and his jokes were mere *concetti*—conceits—worked out by great labour and at much cost of time and ingenuity. The last time I saw him was at Killarney, and I had the pleasure of giving him a "set down," for which I was long in his debt. It happened thus. He was there with his chaplain, West, the present Dean of St Patrick's, and Radcliffe, his Vicar-General, and we went on a ramble through some shrubberies before dinner, when Whately, discovering a large fungus under a tree, said: "This is the bread fungus; it has properties precisely like bread, and would support life for days: West, taste it." "I declare, your Grace, it is exactly like bread." "Radcliffe, eat a bit of this." "Really, your Grace, it is like wheaten bread." "Now, Mr Lever, try it—I insist." "Excuse me, I'd rather not." "Come, come, Mr Lever, you really must taste." "I cannot indeed, your Grace." "But why not?" "It would be perfectly *useless*." "Useless—useless; what do you mean by useless?" "*My* brother, my *lord*, is in the diocese of Meath, otherwise I'd eat the whole of it."

'Tony Butler' was still holding on his way in the

Magazine, the ups and downs of his career being all
as fully discussed by the author as were his own
vicissitudes of health and fortune. And Blackwood
is as solemnly asked for his advice about Tony's
marriage as if it were the matrimonial venture of one
of his children which was perplexing Lever.

> You are right [he says]. I feel it the more strongly since
> you said it, that Tony has a long way to go before he is worthy
> of Alice. But is he in this respect any worse than his neigh-
> bours? I don't believe that any man was worth the woman who
> inspired a real passion, and he only became approximately so
> by loving her, and so if T. B. turns out a good fellow it is Alice
> has done it, and not yours ever faithfully,　CHARLES LEVER.

In the few sentences just quoted the author reveals
himself to us with perfect candour, giving us his own
sentiments, and thus showing how *real* a thing his
art was to him, and how closely interwoven with his
own most cherished beliefs were the creatures of his
imagination. Tony's marriage was still troubling him
when he wrote, "If the sharks catch me, you must
finish Tony yourself, and marry him to Alice!" And
again, in despair over the matrimonial arrangements,
he says: "God help Tony, I have given her (the
heroine) to each of them every alternate day and
night for the last month; but it must be Tony, unless he should take a sudden fancy to Mrs Maxwell.
I'll send you the females very soon, and you'll have
time to say your say on it before it is irrevocable."
Developments of character appear to have turned out
as unexpected as events in the story, and over these
the author had equally no control. He describes this
in answer to some editorial remonstrances. "If I *can*
tone down M'C. I will, but Skeff's courage is, I fear,

incorrigible. Oh! Blackwood, it is not *I* that have made him but *he* himself. Not but he is a good creature, as good as any can be that has no *bone* in his *back*, and take my word for it, there is a large section of humanity that are not vertebrated animals."

This all reads very amusingly, and the Editor was well accustomed to these uncertainties; but they had their drawbacks, and we find him proposing to have the next venture with Lever rather more advanced before the outset. He says :—

> I should like to see you further forward with 'Sir Brook' before starting him, and purpose therefore not to begin until the May No. Waiting uncertain each month gives me rather more hot water than I like' in my monthly toddy. Even to such an easy-going practised Editor as I am the Magazine is no child's play, and it is an immense comfort to have a part or two of a really good thing in hand to look forward to.

'Tony's' career in the Magazine having ended, they were waiting to see what success would attend him in three-volume form, and there came a disappointment. 'Tony's' sale, alas! did not make up the required number which was to ensure the author a certain sum. Blackwood was so convinced of his merits, and so distressed for the disappointment to the author, who had taken such pains with his work, that he says—

> When, however, I saw how good 'Tony' was, and how zealously you were working at the story, I resolved that, come what might, you should have it [the £1000], and have now the pleasure of enclosing a cheque. I know that 'Tony' is good, and I am irritated beyond measure at his not selling; but never mind, look ahead, write as well as you are doing, and the fashion and the popularity will return to you.

Lever's reply to this is a lengthy and interesting
one. Amongst other items he says 'Tony' contained
the most he knew of men and women, and he did not
believe he could write anything better, though he
might hit off something more to the public taste.
"What you say of a real love story is good, but I
can't forget that Thackeray said, no old man must
prate about Love. . . . As to writing about Love
from memory, it is like counting over the bank-notes
of a bank long broken : they remind you of money, it
is true, but they're only waste-paper after all."

In 1865 Lever paid his long-promised visit to London,
and he and the friend he knew so well from their correspondence at last met face to face. He stayed at the
Burlington, and we have often heard descriptions of
the enjoyment and mirth caused by his visit, of which
the following letters give some slight indication :—

John Blackwood to Miss Mozley.

THE BURLINGTON, CORK STREET, W.,
June 4, 1865.

This place is in a greater whirl than ever, and it is with the
greatest difficulty I can get anything done. In addition to the
usual distractions I have had Cornelius O'Dowd staying in the
same house. He is a sort of fellow that comes into your room
and keeps you roaring with laughter for a couple of hours every
hour of the day. I had corresponded a great deal with him, but
had never met him before. His fun is something wonderful.

Needless to say that Lever was at once admitted
into that innermost circle of friends and associates
that formed round John Blackwood a never-to-be-
forgotten little coterie. The new-comer was sure of his
welcome before he came, and all the brightest lights
of the party—Hamley, Kinglake, Delane—did their

parts in the various social distractions that were provided for him. In writing to his nephew William Blackwood the Editor affords us some glimpses of these reunions :—

THE BURLINGTON, *May* 30, 1865.

The dinner with Lever and Kinglake went off famously. They were both first-rate, and the contrast between the two was inimitable — Kinglake making his neat little remarks extremely good, and Lever rattling on with story after story.

Then a quiet evening with him is alluded to, most of the *habitués* having gone to the Derby : " Fergie [Sir William Fergusson] and Archie were the only other two at dinner. We sat on until midnight. The sitting was mostly in the drawing-room, and Julia thought it was only eleven o'clock instead of twelve."

Another letter to William Blackwood describes Lever going out riding.

THE BURLINGTON, *June* 14, 1865.

Julia had a ride in the Park to-day with Harry Lorrequer, who had got a mount from Lord Bolingbroke. I saw a donkey-cart in Piccadilly which I thought Harry would have been tempted to clear in a flying leap. Kate [Miss K. H. Fergusson] was with them too, and they were all highly pleased with their expedition.

The following summer and autumn, his mind stored and memory refreshed by England and things English, Lever wrote some " O'Dowds" specially devoted to matters and events concerning this country. The meeting of the British Association at Bath provoked one of Cornelius's most scathing and mirth-inspiring letters on " Scientific Congresses " in the second volume of the Letters :—

Popularising science, as it is called, is like playing whist for nothing. No man ever learned *that* way, take my word for it;

but there is a worse feature in the affair than all this. We English are a very routine people, and our newspapers give a very
truthful indication of the jog-trot regularity of our lives. From
February to July we live on politics; from July to August we
go to the sea and read Kingsley's novels. Science and the
partridges come next, and a pleasant time would it be if we
could keep them each in his own sphere; but this is impossible.
The ladies who do not shoot geologise, botanise, archæologise,
entomologise, and fraternise with all the dreariest old prosers
of Europe, and bring back to their homes each day stores of
the stalest trash—the study-sweepings of the most learned and
long-winded people on the face of the globe. Now, when I
come back to a late dinner, with my eight brace of birds or
my fifteen-pound salmon, I want to see Mrs O'Dowd smiling,
civil, and complimentary; and what do I meet? a woman
overwhelmed with care, her eyes actually red with tears. It
is the coal-fields, she tells me, cannot last above twelve thousand
years longer; or it is the earth's crust—she had it from Mr
Buckland himself—is positively a seventeenth of an inch
thinner than it was in the time of Moses. I try to dispel
her gloom by talking of my day's performance, and how many
miles I have walked since breakfast, and she sneeringly tells
me "there was a time when a very different race inhabited
this earth, and when one might have seen a young Giant
walking about with a mastodon at his heels—just as we see
a butcher now with a bull-dog." This is downright offensive;
it is personal too. What right has Sir David Brewster or
Professor Faraday to fill my wife's head with speculations
about the First Man? I am, or at least I ought to be, the
first man to her; and what bones of contention are these that
these rash old crucible-heaters throw into the bosoms of families
about the age of the world, and the signs it is giving of
decrepitude?

His paper drew forth the following amusing confirmation from my father, who describes his sister-
in-law, Miss Blandford, as one of these victims of
science :—

It would have done you good if you could have heard the shouts of laughter with which your dissection of scientific congresses has been read here. There had been a good deal of joking on the subject, as my sister-in-law had come lately from Bath, and the contumely and scorn with which her scientific gleanings had been received has been a constant source of mirth. Old Sir Roddie had informed a gaping circle at her uncle's, a canon at Bristol, that "if the output of coal for one year was collected in Hyde Park, it would reach as high as Apsley House." On hearing this I replied, solemnly, that if all the fish that were ever caught at St Andrews Bay were collected, they would fill up the area of the old castle. Sir C. Lyell had informed his audience that the Bath waters were "the same heat as in the time of the Romans." We all wondered that they had not gone " off the boil." The lady about whose recent additions to her scientific knowledge I am writing has just been into my room shaking with laughter over Mrs O'Dowd's anxiety about the crust of the earth She tells me a jest about a geological young lady who was said to be " Hammerously inclined." This is good, if it is new.

The next O'Dowd letter, which is called " a grumble," gives a very good picture of a certain phase in English manners :—

As the tone of manners and observance has grown universal, so has the very expression of the features. They are intensely like each other. We are told that a shepherd will know the actual faces of all the sheep in his flock, distinguishing each from each at a glance. I am curious to know if the Bishop of London knows even the few lost sheep that browse about Rotten Row of an afternoon, and who are so familiar to us in Leech's sketches. There they are—whiskered, bearded, and bored; fine-looking animals in their way, but just as much living creatures in ' Punch ' as they are yonder. It is said that they only want the stimulus of a necessity, something of daring to tempt or something of difficulty to provoke them, to be just as bold and energetic as ever their fathers were. I don't deny it. I am only complaining of the system which makes sheep of them, reduces life to a dreary tableland, making the stupid fellows the standard, and coming down to their level for the sake of uniformity.

These letters and essays of Charles Lever form a very striking commentary upon the events of those days, and besides the lighter questions that suggested themselves to him as readily in writing as they would in conversation, weightier matters — the political clouds, the wars and rumours of wars, that were disturbing Italy in the troublous sixties—come in for a masterly handling that places before us in a nutshell the struggles of Italy and Austria, and the wire-pulling of Louis Napoleon. The issues of the war of 1866 are too well known to require description, but the causes that led to the war, and the predictions as to the results,—in particular the cession of Venice to Italy,—as set forth in the following letter, render it specially noteworthy and interesting :—

Charles Lever to John Blackwood.

May 25, 1866.

It is a most exciting time here [Florence]; every day alternates into War or No war. Of course we live amidst all sorts of lying reports, and we hear the most marvellous narratives of private table-talk of kings and kaisers. My firm conviction is that war cannot be avoided. The gentlemen are on the ground, and for decency's sake must exchange shots; but that Venice is to form part of Italy at the end of the campaign—whether the Italians get thrashed or not—is also equally clear. The crafty rascality of Louis Nap. has so jockeyed Austria that she "stands to lose," no matter how the race comes off. This trick was done in this wise. By great courtesy and attention to the Metternichs, man and wife, at Paris, he persuaded the Prince M. to represent at Vienna the favour he stood in at Paris, and how completely he enjoyed the Emperor's favour. This being fully believed, as well as the assurance solemnly given that France would remain *perfectly neutral*, Austria went forward boldly and declared that Prussia should not absorb the north of Germany. When Austria, therefore, got so compromised that she could not retire from the position she had taken without loss of prestige and honour, the Frenchman says, " I said nothing about non-intervention in Italy, and as the Italians say they are going to join Prussia, I hold myself free to send troops to their aid if I deem proper." This of course was all pre-planned, the false security and the reserve being exactly the same game that was played in '59 when L. N. pressed the Austrians to insist on the Italians disarming, and this drove the Emperor into declaring war in spite of himself. Luckily nobody asks what England thinks or says, but I was able the other day to take rather a proud stand on reading in the 'Times' that "great activity prevails in the dockyards, and the two new cranes are ordered to be got [kept] forward"!!! Hudson Hill says there will be no fight, and we have a bet upon it. I wish it were in pounds instead of francs! A telegram to-day—not yet received as very authentic—says that the Prussians have entered the Principalities. True or not, all shows us what a stupid blunder was our Crimean War, and how blindly we played the game of France throughout that lamentable episode. . . . The Italians are poorly off as regards generals; their best man is Cialdini, and he is only what Frenchmen call a *sabreur*. La Marmora is a poor creature in all but courage and loyalty of character; as a man of brains he might rank with Williams of Kars! Garibaldi will soon have sixty, some say eighty, thousand men under his command; how he is to handle such masses is another matter. The enthusiasm for him and his followers has greatly offended the French Emperor, but there was no choice. If you had not taken them as royalists they would have been republicans.

The foregoing tempts one to quote as rather apposite to this remark old Mr Sutherland, the famous golfer's, well-known and unexpected definition of the hero—" Yon Garibaldi is a *mischeevious* beast." There may have been more reason than is at first apparent

in the grim old Scotsman's sweeping denunciation of
Garibaldism.   This was no doubt one of the many
dangers and difficulties threatening Italy on all sides,
as Mr Lever goes on to say they were "terrific."
Brigandage, Bourbon plotting, bankruptcy, and the
Camorra too, had recommenced in Naples, adding new
terrors to that ill-fated province.   War, he said, was
really a lesser evil.   The Italians had been so taught
by the newspapers to believe Austria was afraid of
them, that they went gaily on to this war as to a
battue, little dreaming of the terrible lesson they
would have got had France failed them at the
last.

These letters from Mr Lever were a very great
source of interest to John Blackwood, placing him
en rapport with the wide field of foreign politics, from
which Lever gathered thus early the information
which has since become matter of history.   It was
like having a "special" private correspondent of his
own, who in any great public crisis might be depended
upon to send off an early despatch, to appear on the
breakfast-table in the ordinary guise of a letter to be
read and discussed in the familiar way we talk over
public news that has the added interest of being
conveyed through a private channel.   If letters such
as these were the result of the "colchicum" and
"magnesia" the Editor used to administer to Lever,
many must wish they knew his prescription.

The following to William Blackwood is an amusing
specimen of Lever's way of writing to younger men,
and shows, for all his sixty odd years, the *camaraderie* he felt for those who were still on the bright
side of thirty :—

MY DEAR W. B.,—I got your telegram just as I was starting for a picnic to eat of lobsters afterwards with what appetite I might. I suspect (it is mere suspicion) that chap. i. enclosed in an envelope I had borrowed from an American colleague has gone (through the words U.S. Consulate on the corner) to America, and that R. N. F. is now making the tour of the "Union." Rewriting is all very fine, but I have forgotten all I wrote, as I always do, or I should go mad! If Providence had only inflicted me with a memory in proportion to my imagination, I'd have been in Bedlam twenty years ago. I have therefore set to work to write something else. If the other turns up, you may prefer it. (You pays your money and takes your choice, as the apple - woman says.) God forgive me, but I grow less wise as I grow older. The old smock of devil-may-care that sat easily on me as a boy keeps dodging me now in grey hairs and making a fool of me. Did you ever read the German story of the fellow whose wooden leg was "possessed" and ran away with him. I haven't a wooden leg, but I have a wooden skull that plays a like freak with me.

Another letter to William Blackwood playfully reproaches him for not coming out to see him at Trieste, on the score of work detaining him.

TRIESTE, *July* 1868.

Oh B. B., what a humbug you are! Affecting to be hard worked, and galley-slaved, and the rest of it—telling this to *me* too. I tell you that on every ground—morally, æsthetically, and professionally—you *ought* to come and see me, and if you won't I'll be shot but I'll make an O'Dowd on you. . . .

As the Government are good Christians and chasteneth those they love, they have made H—— a Consul! Less beneficent countries give four or five years' hard labour and make an end of it; but there's a rare malice in sending some poor thread of a literary man, who loves the Garrick, and lobster salad, and small whist, and small flattery, to eke out existence in a dreary Continental town without society and sympathy. I'd rather be a dog and bask at the door of the Wyndham or the Alfred than spend this uneventful life of exile I am sentenced to. . . .

Well, I tell you there's a great rifle-match for all nations (even Scotch and Irish) at Vienna this month. There's another reason for coming out. You could make your Bull's eye on your way to me. You had better accede, or you may read of yourself as "the man who wouldn't come when he was axed."— Yours ever faithfully,   C. L.

After Lever was transferred to Trieste, where he was Consul from 1868 till his death in 1872, he furnished from time to time notes and comments on the events of the day; but his writings were becoming less frequent, though still displaying the vivacity and acuteness with which he always grasped the situation at home or abroad. The following gives the impression of the "situation" in Europe after the German victories over France, as it appeared to the onlooker who was hearing *on dits* of the eastern and southern parts of the Continent.

TRIESTE, *Dec.* 22, 1870.

I don't wonder that the British world is growing French in sympathy. The Prussians are doing their very utmost to disgust Europe, and with a success that cannot be disputed. I hope, if you in England mean war with Russia, that you do not count on Austria. She will not, because she cannot, help you. A Russian war here would mean the dismemberment of the empire and utter ruin. If Austria were beaten, her German provinces would become Prussian; if she were victorious, Hungary would dominate over the empire and take the supremacy at once. Which would be worse? I really cannot say. The Frenchmen I meet are full of hope and confidence, in fact they seem assured of a happy exit out of their calamities.

With this letter we must bring to an end the literary part of John Blackwood's friendship with Lever, there remaining only to tell the account of his visit to Trieste. Lever had for long been trying to persuade his friends in Edinburgh to go and visit him, and nothing but the distance and want of time had hindered the journey. In 1872, however, my father resolved that, come what might, he would make time for a run down to Trieste, which should also comprise one to Vienna, where Bulwer's son, Mr Robert Lytton (afterwards Lord Lytton and Viceroy of India), was then one of the secretaries at the British Embassy. Early in May he started, accompanied by his wife and the present writer, only too happy to escape from her lessons for this memorable expedition. From a diary, and her own very vivid, if childish, recollections, these memories are recalled of events and persons once seen but never forgotten. The journey was made first of all to Vienna, which was new ground for all of us. In outward characteristics Vienna seemed very like Paris, the wide streets, white houses, and the different "Rings," answering to the Boulevards of the French capital. We saw it under pleasant auspices, with Mr Lytton as our guide. Dinners at the Embassy, where Sir Andrew Buchanan hospitably entertained us; visits to the Grand Opera, with other entertainments, made our stay very enjoyable. The early hours for dining gave plenty of time for being out of doors afterwards, and the fashion then—it may have changed since — was to drive in the Prater after five o'clock dinner, and finish the evening at the Volksgarten, listening to Strauss's band. This sort of life seemed to amuse and suit the Editor thoroughly, for a change, and he used to sit enjoying his cigar and coffee listening to the band, while first one and then another would saunter up to have a chat, and always " Owen Meredith " at hand

to talk and laugh with him at the gay crowd throng-
ing around.

There was, however, a sad disappointment in store.
Almost the first morning intelligence had been received at the Embassy of Mr Lever's dangerous illness.
The first impulse was to start straight off to Trieste,
but it was thought wiser to wait for further tidings.
A few days later Miss Lever wrote saying her father
was rather better, and suggesting he might be able to
see us presently. So a longer stay was made in
Vienna, and an invitation accepted from Mr Lytton
to visit him and Mrs Lytton in the country. Their
house was an hour's journey by rail from Vienna. On
arriving there we found Mr and Mrs Lytton and their
two pretty little girls on the lawn awaiting us. An
hour previously they had had the shock of hearing of
the death of his uncle, Lord Dalling (Sir Henry Bulwer), to whom they were much attached. Mr Lytton
said everything he knew about diplomacy he owed to
Lord Dalling, and Mrs Lytton told us he felt his
uncle's death deeply—indeed he seemed greatly distressed. The house they rented from one of the
Esterhazys stood in a garden surrounded by fir-trees,
which, with the high hills in the distance, gave it in
the eyes of its visitors a Scottish and familiar look.
The owner had had to quit it abruptly, having gone
out of his mind, and hardly any of his personal belong-
ings had been put away. Even his hat and sticks
were left in the hall. There was also a poor dog left
by the unfortunate owner in the house, and Mr Lytton
showed the same care for this humble retainer of the
Austrian family as he did for their other possessions,
taking it out for exercise every day. It was a big

Danish boar-hound, and if by any chance he forgot it, he was miserable and never failed to return for it.

Mr Lytton was at that time writing some of his " Fables in Song," which afterwards were collected and published in a volume. During the long summer evenings, while sitting out smoking in the verandah, he would often while away the time for us by reading aloud portions of the MS. The fables and the cigarette-smoke seem all inextricably woven together in the recollections of " Owen Meredith," the name under which he was well known when a young man as the writer of many poems and verses of considerable popularity, and the name by which we habitually thought of him in those days. The time passed very quickly with walks and excursions to the pretty country villages in the district, where sometimes the Editor and the poet indulged in a game of skittles—*Kügelspiel*— with the villagers, who, like all the peasantry in that neighbourhood, were gentle-mannered and courteous. At last the good news came that Lever was better, and we set off to Trieste to see him, but not to stay in his house.

Early the morning after our arrival Miss Lever called with the welcome news that Mr Lever was much better, and she took my father back with her to see him. When he returned to us he said it was arranged we should all dine with the Levers, and shortly before four we set off to drive to their villa, which was at the top of a hill and near some public gardens—so near that we could hear the German waltzes the band played as we sat out in the Levers' own garden, which was remarkably pretty, and full of shady trees. When we arrived Lever was sitting in

a bright cheerful room with a large window, and a
balcony opening off it covered with roses and creepers.
He looked better and stronger than we had expected
to see him, and the sight of his friend seemed to bring
back a flicker of the old spirit, and he talked and
laughed gaily during the dinner, which was at four
o'clock. Lever's appearance did not give the impression of ill-health any more than it suggested the hard-
working man of letters or denizen of the Consulate,
but rather one would have imagined him to be a big,
jolly, country gentleman, with his stalwart frame and
ruddy face—his air of hearty hospitality and welcome
still further strengthening the impression. The rest
of the party were, besides his two daughters, Mr
Monson and Mr Smart.

After dinner we adjourned to the garden for coffee
and cigarettes, and Mr Lever sat up till very late.
The second evening the same pleasant party, with the
addition of the clergyman, Mr Callaghan; the same
amount of laughing and talking, perhaps rather more.
Many were the jokes about their neighbours, the society
being mainly composed of wealthy Jewish merchants
and their families; but the impression was that the
jokes were all kindly, the wit without sting, and that
the Jews had been made the best of in that cheery
happy-go-lucky household. Indeed he mentioned that
on some festive occasion Lord Dalling, in an amiable
whisper, had remarked at last, "Lever, I like your
Jews," and this, of course, made everybody feel quite
happy. My father had a great wish to see Miramar,
the home of the ill-fated Archduke Maximilian, and
Lever was as anxious to show it to him; but though
we put it off till the last day of our visit, he was

unequal to the exertion of driving so far, so Miss
Lever drove with us to the house.   It is situated on
a promontory about three miles along the coast from
Trieste—a lovely drive, and a bewitching spot for a
dwelling, built on a terrace with marble steps washed
by the sea, a luxuriance of magnolia and myrtles
surrounding it; and poor Empress Charlotte's white
doves were fluttering mournfully around, the only
signs of life we saw.   The house, with its study and
other apartments, remains just as he left it the day
he sailed away in his yacht, with the tears in his eyes
at leaving his friends and the beloved home he was
never to see again.   Miss Lever gave us a very
graphic account of his departure, the whole population of Trieste, besides his friends and acquaintances,
coming out to see him sail away.

And now comes the sad part, our last evening at
the Villa Gasteiger.   My father had dreaded this
parting: he knew his friend was not really better—
that the heart complaint he suffered from might prove
fatal at any time; but he put the thought away from
him when they were meeting every day.   It was only
now, as we approached his house for the last time,
that we felt weighed down by something impending.
Mr Lever was in the garden when we arrived, but soon
dinner was announced, and we went into the house,
the same party as the first evening.   The laughter
and chaff at dinner had been as usual, and Mr Lever
had been most delightful and amusing, the life and
soul of the party.   Afterwards we sat out in the
garden under the trees, the band over the way playing as usual.   Mr Lever said he was very proud of it.
He asked for tea to be brought out there, and when

told it was coming said, half to himself, "So is Christmas," with a smile to us. They were all smoking, and he sat in the middle of the group in an arm-chair, wearing his big shady hat, my father and mother on each side of him. He would not have the lamp they usually had in the garden, so it was nearly dark when the other guests sauntered away, leaving him alone with the friends who were soon to bid him farewell. He spoke very despairingly of himself, as though he should not recover, and said that always about that time after dinner he had a "false feeling of health," which he knew could not last. A great sadness came over us as we sat on, not talking much, listening to the band, which was playing all the time, giving an unreality to the scene, as though we were taking part in a drama. Our carriage meanwhile had come up, and had gone round to the back of the house. We heard it, but did not know how to get up and say good-bye. At last my father rose, and there was the usual stir and looking for cloaks and wraps, which seemed to help off our departure, poor Lever joking and laughing as he helped to wrap us up, and escorted us to the carriage. We shook hands with him, and said good-bye to the others there. As we drove away we looked back and saw him standing with his daughters, watching us and waving farewell. We knew it was really good-bye, and our drive was a silent one. Our apprehensions about Lever's health were only too well founded, for on our reaching Venice at five o'clock the following afternoon we were met by a telegram saying he had died during the day. My father immediately returned to Trieste by a steamer which was just starting, to be of what use he might to his friend's daughters. The journey by sea occupied twelve hours, and he wrote the next morning as follows :—

John Blackwood to his Wife.

TRIESTE, *June* 2, 1872.

I got here about seven this morning, after a not unpleasant voyage, considering the company and the circumstances. After bath and breakfast I went to Smart's room and found him and Monson. They said at once how pleased the daughters would be. They had not liked to ask me to come in the telegram, but hoped and expected I would come. I went up and sat for more than an hour with the two mourners. Poor souls! it was most affecting to hear them pouring forth about all their father's goodness and kindness. Poor Lever had sat talking about us after we left until about his usual hour, twelve. He had the usual restless night until about five, when he fell asleep. He awoke at the usual time for his letters, and after reading them and chatting he lay down to rest. They looked in from time to time as they were in the habit of doing, and found him sleeping quietly, until Miss Lever, going in towards three, found he had apparently passed away without struggle or pain. The funeral is to be at six P.M. to-morrow. . . . I hope you and Puck are getting on as well as this sad disaster will permit. It is most melancholy to think of our fine bright friend. Sitting in that drawing-room to-day looking out on the garden, I could hardly help bursting out crying. It seemed hardly realisable. However, his last evening was a bright one, and it was an end such as he had wished. (He had a perfect horror of living on weakened in body and mind, a weariness to himself and others.) There were many affectionate messages from the poor ladies to you and Puck. I have sheets of George Eliot ('Middlemarch') to read in the evening, which will be a comfort.

CHAPTER IX.

"THE MILITARY STAFF OF BLACKWOOD."

SIR EDWARD HAMLEY—'OPERATIONS OF WAR'—'OUR POOR RELATIONS'—
'SHAKESPEARE'S FUNERAL'—'VOLTAIRE'—GENERAL WILLIAM HAMLEY
—COLONEL LAURENCE LOCKHART WITH THE PRUSSIAN ARMY ON THE
RHINE—A MEMORABLE LUNCHEON PARTY—SIR ARCHIBALD ALISON—
LORD WOLSELEY — SIR HENRY BRACKENBURY — SIR HOPE GRANT—
COLONEL KNOLLYS—SIR HERBERT KITCHENER—SIR GEORGE CHESNEY
—THE 'BATTLE OF DORKING'—AN EXTRAORDINARY SUCCESS.

AROUND the name of Sir Edward Hamley centres the
interest which attaches to what John Blackwood used
to call "The Military Staff of Blackwood." This
soldierly contingent, which was for the time forsaking the sword for the pen, formed a very important element amongst the contributors, and was one
in which the Editor took special pride and pleasure.
Military matters did not by any means always occupy
their writings. Such men as the brothers Hamley,
Colonel Lockhart, Sir George Chesney, and Colonel
Conder of the Palestine Exploration Fund, wrote
equally well on matters of general interest or fiction.
So many other distinguished names occur in connection
with this branch that we feel disposed to group them
together, adding those who write on purely military
topics, such as Sir Garnet Wolseley (the Commander-

in-Chief), Sir Archibald Alison (son of the historian), Sir Patrick Macdougall, Sir John Adye, Sir D. Lysons, Colonel Charles Chesney, Sir Henry Brackenbury, Colonel Henry Knollys, and Sir Herbert Kitchener; and though he belongs to an older generation, there must be here mentioned Sir Hope Grant, a dear old friend and golfing companion of my father, who in his old age memorialised his gallant fellow-country-man Sir Colin Campbell in the ' History of the Sepoy War.'

In the second volume of these Annals we have an account of Hamley's early writings,—his novel, and the diaries he sent from the Crimea. Later years bring us down to the time when the " Captain " had become " Colonel," and so on through the experience of half a lifetime of soldiering, much of it spent in active service abroad or at the important posts he was called upon to fill in his own country. His eminent practical knowledge, together with the re-searches into the past which formed a congenial occupation to one of his literary as well as soldierly bent, led him to embody his military experience in the volume known as the ' Operations of War.' This book, which will always be associated with Hamley's name by all military students, has also a distinct literary value apart from its technical character,—the successive stages from ancient warfare up to modern times being all clearly defined, the tactics of the Black Prince and the bows and arrows of his fol-lowers coming in for their fair share of notice, down to Garnet Wolseley and the Maxim guns of our own day. Of this book the author says :—

Colonel E. B. Hamley to John Blackwood.

PARIS, *April* 6, 1866.

I do not intend the book for military men only, but, on the contrary, have sought to make it clear to the general reader. I would as soon it was reviewed by some intelligent non-professional, who having a taste for the subject and some knowledge of a general sort, might find that I had cleared up his ideas by this book, and would say so.

The American War furnished Hamley with matter for many comments and criticisms not always complimentary to our American cousins, though, as time went on, his views became considerably modified.

Colonel E. B. Hamley to John Blackwood.

SANDHURST, *Dec.* 12, 1863.

I hardly know how to return an explicit answer on such short notice. It appears to me that the calm, judicial style is altogether unsuitable to the discussion of American affairs. If their proceedings, civil, military, and popular, met the derision they deserve, they might come to a more correct estimate of their own position. But the respectful tone in which their fooleries are talked of helps to feed their conceit. I have been surprised to find the 'Times' and other papers, from the first, admitting that Wilkes would have been justified in taking the Trent to be adjudicated on by an American prize-court. I don't believe it. If she had been crammed with contraband they had no right to touch her. If they had, they have an equal right to take the Melbourne which has just sailed with troops for Canada. I don't believe they even possessed in this case the Right of Search, because all the power that right confers is to ascertain the destination of a doubtful ship.

The amount of literature which the war drew forth formed the subject of a paper on "Books on the American War," of which John Blackwood says :—

John Blackwood to Colonel E. B. Hamley.

EDINBURGH, *Nov.* 16, 1863.

I enclose proof of your paper "Books on the American War," which is very good indeed. Keep proof for a day or two in case any news should come in to influence your concluding remarks. Should the Yankees not get more credit for the energy which turns out such enormous armies operating over so vast a field of operations?

He wrote again to Hamley, giving some suggestions for a paper on military matters.

Jan. 26, 1864.

I hope you will do the paper on Crawley still, taking the general question of the ruinous effect upon military discipline of this constant interference with the authority of commanding officers. It will be interesting just now. Do you think Louis Nap. is going to have a campaign on Rhine? His silence is suspicious, but somehow I think this will soon blow past. It will be a fearful misfortune for us to be involved in a war with Germany, and it would simply be playing the French Emperor's game.

Hamley entered with great spirit into a review of some of the best known of Carlyle's works — the Latter-day Pamphlets, and also his 'Life of Frederick the Great' which he had also weighed and found wanting.

Colonel E. B. Hamley to John Blackwood.

SANDHURST, *Dec.* 1858.

If that part [the Latter-day Pamphlets] is published this month, then next month I propose to continue the subject of Carlyle — his History of Frederick — under the heading of "Carlyle, Part II." I read Lewes's notice of Frederick in Fraser, and thought it very bald and meagre, not at all what I expected from a German scholar and admirer of C.'s, and moreover so clever a man. The truth is, I fancy, that there is not much to be said about the performance in way of eulogy.

The literary power and ability which Hamley showed caused John Blackwood frequently to urge him to write more.

April 4, 1867.

I am anxious beyond measure that you should write more for the Magazine, and I wish much that I could suggest a good subject. Politics are, as you rightly imagine, a sore subject of trouble and disgust to me. What do you say to giving your views in a satirical vein on the hypocrisy and mischief of all that has been going on since Lord Russell set agoing the system of bidding for place by offers of Reform. The state of the case is simply this, that a majority of the House were dead against Reform, but being Whigs and more or less placemen, they would not join Lord Derby in opposing it. His position was that if he did not bring in a Reform measure his party would be thrown out, and that whatever sum he fixed the franchise at the majority would bid for office with a lower one. He had therefore nothing for it but to bring in a sweeping measure or throw the Government of the country into the hands of Gladstone and Bright.

The soldiers, it will be seen, were thus occasionally led into conflict : a sharp pen in their hands became as deadly a weapon as the cold steel of actual warfare, and in these rapier-like exercises Hamley particularly excelled. No bomb (to continue the warlike simile) suddenly pitched into a camp could have caused greater confusion than some of these sudden literary reprisals which John Blackwood could always call to his aid when his party or his friends required his assistance. Political subjects did not seem to appeal to Hamley very much just at this time, and he turned from them to other matters, reviews and art.

Colonel E. B. Hamley to John Blackwood.

BOARD OF MILITARY EDUCATION, *April* 11, 1867.

Many thanks for your suggestions about subjects. I have no doubt many will cast up now that I have leisure. Politics is one that I should be very diffident to write about, because it requires not only present study but a continuous attention in the past. I gave Martin yesterday what I had to say about the dear old cavalier [Aytoun]—not a great deal, for there were but few events to mark our fellowship in Scotland, but still it may be of use as the record of one who knew him so well and so greatly valued him. I saw the proofs of the Memoir so far as printed, and liked it much: it will be accepted as the work of a judicious friend, and not a mere eulogist softening away the outlines in compliance with the expectations of others till no likeness remains, as is too often the case. General Sherman has sent me a copy of his war correspondence, and a letter of his has been forwarded by the Sec. of Legation, in which he thinks I might be induced to modify my chapter on his operations in Georgia for reasons which he gives. This is a very handsome way of meeting objections, for most men who have attained to such eminence are content to wrap themselves in their dignity and make no reply, not even " d——n your eyes!" to their critics. I have always been prejudiced against Sherman on account of the barbarous way in which he made war in Georgia, but I shall, of course, write in acknowledgment of his courtesy in an equally courteous spirit.

The following, written after a visit to the Sturgises at Mount Felix, is one of Hamley's bright cheery letters, of which he wrote many to the friends with whom he was really intimate. It contains a hearty Christmas greeting and compliment to ' Maga ' :—

Colonel E. B. Hamley to John Blackwood.

DOVER CASTLE, *Jan.* 3, 1866.

I hope you have all had a pleasant Christmas, and I wish you a happy New Year. I went for the Christmas week to Mt.

Felix, where I have now passed nine of those seasons. The American Minister, Mr Adam, and his family, Sir H. and Lady Fletcher, and some American friends formed the party, and there were the usual plethora of good things and temptations to apoplexy. You will have missed our dear old friend Aytoun at this season. I don't know when I've seen a better number of 'Maga' than that with which you open the year. I feel it as a stigma to have nothing in it. Fosbrooke and O'Dowd good as ever (man at the wheel excellent); Switzerland, Von Borcke, and Robertson, all of the right sort; and 'Maga' may snap her fingers at the whole run of periodicals. I dislike the whole hocus-pocus of J. S. Mill & Co.—conjurors who put the universe like a pea under their metaphysical thimbles and tell you. it doesn't exist. It strikes me your reviewer might have scored a point against him when he (Mill) says, "If I were suddenly transported to the banks of the Hoogly, I should still have the sensations which, if now present, would lead me to affirm that Calcutta exists here and now"; for he treats the banks of the Hoogly as a real existence, and the city that stands there as an idea—showing that his own instincts lead him to express himself in terms inconsistent with his own theory.

When the first edition of the 'Operations of War' was going out of print John Blackwood wrote to the author, and when arranging for a reprint urged upon him to try his hand once more at a novel.

John Blackwood to Colonel E. B. Hamley.

Oct. 20, 1868.

I am happy to say that this edition of the 'Operations of War' is nearly out of print, so we should set about reprinting at once. You have, I hope, been correcting for a new edition. Our opinion is that we had best stick to the present size and price, but perhaps some better idea has occurred to you. 'Lady Lee' is also out of print. When you wrote 'Lady Lee' I expected many successions to keep your fame as a novelist alive. Is there soon to be another? It was a great disappointment to us not to see you at Strathtyrum this year, and there seems quite a fate against your coming to us. There is much in what you say of Kinglake, but I do not think you give him credit enough for his great labour in his anxiety to tell the truth and merit in giving such a mass of good reading to the world. The 'Edinburgh' has not yet come here, and the review there is, I suppose, yours. Thanks for your friendly expressions to myself. There is no one upon whose friendship I can more thoroughly rely at all times.

Another subject for an article suggested to Hamley by Blackwood was the Franco-Prussian war.

John Blackwood to Colonel E. B. Hamley.

Aug. 3, 1870.

We must maintain a dignified neutrality both with sword and pen as long as we can. It is impossible to sympathise really with either party. I like the Germans, and cannot help wishing that they should win, but the Prussian conduct in the last war was intolerable, and Bismarck seems as bold a liar as the French Emperor, who I see declares by his 'Journal Officiel' that France is going to war "to rescue Germany from Prussian oppression and conciliate the rights of the Princes with the legitimate desires of their people." I burst out laughing when I read that this morning. I find great division of opinion and feeling in regard to the two parties in the war, but nobody is very decided. In fact it is impossible to sympathise with either of the robbers. If, as you say, Napoleon is so averse to the war, then he must be doing it to save himself. The Prussians would not have attacked him. The best thing that could happen would be a sort of doubtful encounter, with a good deal of punishment, and the stakes Belgium and Holland drawn—that is, left in the hands of their legitimate owners. But again, if France and Prussia should make it up, perhaps their next project of a treaty would include England among the divisible spoils. Thank Heaven, we have got the Channel between us, or we might have war declared upon us any morning.

Miscellaneous writings, very varied in character,

were occupying Hamley when he had leisure for them,
— though, to the disappointment of Blackwood, he
never wrote another novel after 'Lady Lee.' One of
his cleverest efforts, of an unambitious kind, was a
small volume entitled 'Our Poor Relations.' This
little book is full of wit and quaint drollery, and the
pathos which lovers of the dumb creation will not fail
to find very fascinating. The book is intended to
enlist our sympathies in the lives of animals, particularly those which are constantly about our homes,
almost like members of the family, but, as the title
pathetically suggests, not always meeting in their
helpless dependence the kindness and friendliness to
which their sterling qualities entitle them. To all
Hamley's friends his love and tenderness for animals,
and his understanding and appreciation of their different quaint characteristics, were well-known and
charming traits, of which this volume we have described is a thorough illustration. Another and very
different piece of work, showing perhaps some of the
most brilliant qualities of his writing, is given in
'Shakespeare's Funeral,' which is supposed to represent the reception of the news of the death of Shakespeare in his native place, and the last scenes when
laying him to rest. The Warwickshire rustics and
their dialect, and the whole spirit and tone of the
surroundings, are given with a fidelity and zest which
show how thoroughly Hamley was imbued with
Shakespearian lore and his complete mastery of the
dramatic possibilities of the subject.

Another of Hamley's best known works, apart from
his military writings, was the volume on Voltaire,
which he contributed to the series of "Foreign

Classics" edited by Mrs Oliphant. John Blackwood considered this a very masterly performance, and when he asked Hamley before he began, "How will you drape the indecent old villain before presenting him to your English audience of both sexes?" it was evident he thought there might be difficulties. Hamley, however, was equal to the occasion, and availing himself of the many sides of Voltaire's character and the vast scope of his writings, succeeded in giving a perfectly new presentment of him in a brilliantly written volume, which attained the rare distinction of a small book dealing satisfactorily with a big subject.

John Blackwood to Colonel E. B. Hamley.

EDINBURGH, *Feb.* 12, 1877.

MY DEAR HAMLEY,—I have read what you send of your 'Voltaire,' and I am delighted to say that I think you have hit the mark thoroughly. To my mind it could hardly be better, and you will introduce the grand old sinner to the English public in a way in which he has never been presented. Your own grim humour fits capitally as you tell the story. I have not read anything for a long time which pleased me as much as this of you upon Voltaire. If Mrs Oliphant is as good an editor as a writer, she will feel that she has a strong man at her back. Your translations from the 'Henriade' are very good. They seem to me more Homeric and classical than the original; but it is a long time since I read the 'Henriade.'

Hamley's letters, we find, though going very direct to the point, are by no means brief, and are often extremely characteristic of him, some apt allusion or humorous remark usually redeeming the ordinary matters treated from any suspicion of commonplace. For example, a long business letter, in which he spared

himself and his correspondent no details, contains the
following refreshing glimpse of a dinner-party at the
Garrick with Mr Langford :—

Colonel E. B. Hamley to John Blackwood.

Nov. 14, 1872.

We had a pleasant dinner on Friday. _Old Joe was filled
with pride at being the chaperon of the eminent novelist
[Charles Reade], whose aspect is not of an everyday kind.
He wore a large blue coat and brass buttons, and the widest
trousers I ever saw on legs. He hasn't much address, but was
companionable, and is one who probably improves on acquaintance. Jimmy White sat by him, but that youth's intrepid
genius, though it sent forth some scintillations, hardly got free
play. Leighton the painter completed the party.

His work at the Staff College gave him plenty of
occupation ; but he never seems to have grudged the
time for writing these pleasant missives, which were
so thoroughly appreciated by John Blackwood, who
was always urging him to write. The following
alludes to a point of law regarding a bequest of
books to the College, in reference to which he had
begged Blackwood to obtain a legal opinion in Edinburgh, if possible that of Lord Neaves. He says :—

Many thanks for the trouble you have given yourself and
your legal friends about the business of the bequest. Though
I inclined to believe that I could not really be required to
obey so senseless a citation, yet the formidable language in
which it was couched left a vague apprehension that I might
ultimately become a sort of Poor Peter Peebles, old, insolvent,
making the Court of Session my dwelling-place, and incapable
of expressing myself except in the clear and simple language
of the Scottish law. To have been concerned, in ever so remote
a degree, in so occult a process as "multiplepoinding" must
always be a source of pride to me.

The following to William Blackwood refers to the death of Charles Lever :—

Colonel E. B. Hamley to W. Blackwood.

STAFF COLLEGE, *June* 6, 1872.

I saw with grief the announcement in the papers of the sudden death of Charles Lever. It would have been a sorrow to your uncle at any time, but just now, when he was making a visit to Trieste the turning-point of his journey, it must have sadly disconcerted his plans.

One of the pleasant features to my father in his London visits was the opportunity of seeing Hamley, who, when he lived in the Albany, was one of the daily visitors at the Burlington. Frequent mention is made of him in the light of an ever-welcome guest—"just then Hamley appeared, always there or thereabouts when wanted;" or it would be, "Hamley was first-rate at luncheon; he always does me good, he is such an out-and-outer;" or it might be late in the evening,—"we were just taking off our coats to have a smoke when in came Hamley, gay as a lark, and kept us laughing and talking for an hour or two." The "us" on that occasion were himself and his nephew Major George Blackwood. Sometimes, when not fettered by engagements, he would go and stay with Hamley, very often spending a Sunday with him at Sandhurst. Hamley was perhaps seen at his best on these occasions: naturally hospitable, liking to entertain his friends, his kindness and thoughtfulness made it appear as though all his arrangements were made for their comfort or amusement. Anything they once said they liked at his table used to be carefully pointed out to them next

time. The flowers they admired were gathered for
them, even the dogs had special combing and brush-
ing in their honour. The pretty house always had
every window and door hospitably open, while the
host himself on the lawn, with his dogs at his heels,
was the first to greet them with his cheery, "Here
you are at last!" His niece, Miss Barbara Hamley,
was nearly always at Sandhurst in summer when he
was entertaining friends. Her bright and graceful
presence there gave the touch wanting to his home
life, which might have been lonely without her, whose
affectionate devotion and companionship was that of
a much-loved daughter.

To see Hamley and John Blackwood together, each
so anxious to place his friend at an advantage, their
wits brightening each other, was to realise how
staunch and lasting a friendship can be between two
outwardly very dissimilar characters where there is a
perfect comprehension of each other. My father's
strong affection for him, which is breathed in every
letter where he mentions his name, was based on the
experience of over twenty years of those qualities of
straightforwardness and loyalty in his friend which
were also marked characteristics in himself. These
first essentials for friendship were in their case
enhanced by the similarity of their literary tastes
and sympathies, and the strong sense of humour
which both possessed. Sarcasm was a weapon which
both of them could use with remarkable skill. The
tendency of John Blackwood in this direction was
curbed and tempered by greater discretion—forbearance—call it what you will; but in a fair encounter
his ready wit rarely failed him, his deft rejoinders

generally finding the weak place in a foe's armour. Though given with that pleasant slow smile, and spoken with great deliberation, we always knew the bolt was going to be shot which would turn the laugh to his side. In Hamley the over-indulgence of his rapier-like wit perhaps sometimes cost him dear. But his sarcastic humour appealed so strongly to my father's sympathies, that he could seldom find it in his heart to censure what he knew really proceeded only from a love of fun.

Leaving Sir Edward Hamley with the regret one feels at parting with a trusty friend who has accompanied us a long way on our journey, we turn to his brother, General William Hamley, to whom he was deeply attached. He was a contrast to Sir Edward in many ways, and yet resembled him in others. In appearance they were both tall, broad - shouldered men, over six feet, both fair and blue-eyed, of the type which we naturally associate with the stalwart British soldier. Edward preserved his fine physique and soldierly bearing until he was struck with mortal illness; but William Hamley had suffered from the malarial influence of Bermuda, having been racked with rheumatic pains, of which his fine figure bore the traces when he returned to this country, still in the prime of life, and took up the command of the Royal Engineers' district at Manchester in 1868. He resembled his brother in his love of literature and the ability which he displayed in carrying out any literary project entrusted to him. Like him he possessed a strong sense of humour, which strengthened the bonds of sympathy between him and my father, who has already described him as " a dreadfully clever fellow."

There appears to have been a long interval elapsing between his early writings, which were produced during his brother Charles's lifetime, when all these brothers were writing, and his later and more important contributions. This was probably owing to his military duties, which kept him abroad for many years. On his return to England he resumed his literary labours with fresh zest, and became once more one of the regular contributors to the Magazine, and when in London one of the regular *habitués* of the circle that used to gather round my father at the Burlington. His writings covered a wide range of subjects : home and foreign politics and matters of general interest were all handled by him with that thoroughness and finish which were shown in everything that he or his brother Edward undertook. In one respect he differed from Edward, who never wrote but the one novel, by devoting a considerable portion of his literary activity to fiction, writing several novels which appeared in the Magazine, such as 'Traseaden Hall'; also a very amusing tale called 'Captain Clutterbuck's Champagne.' Perhaps among the most important of his miscellaneous writings was the series of papers he wrote on the events of the Franco - Prussian war, and those written on the opening of the Suez Canal, and the Turko-Russian war of 1877. The Suez Canal is an old story now, but the sad end of its engineer De Lesseps is fresh in the minds of every one, and while our ships now sail rapidly through its channels, it is not uninteresting to have recalled the difficulties which attended its early navigation.

General W. G. Hamley to John Blackwood.

CAIRO, *Nov.* 24, 1869.

You know before this that the passage of the Canal has been effected, but you will possibly be glad of the additional information that, for a first attempt, it was eminently successful, and more than fifty ships passed through with ease. The least wrong deflection of the rudder will send a ship ashore, where the width is so little and the length of the ships so great. It is not marvellous, therefore, that one or two knocked their noses, or that some of the deep ones stirred up the mud with their keels. There was a stop once or twice, but the majority of the ships floated right through. My steamer, the Principe Tomaso, never took the ground once, and would have done the transit in a day if she had been let to have her way. The sights and festivities have been very splendid, and I suppose are not yet ended. The Emperor of Austria is still here, but the Empress of the French—the star of the whole thing—is gone. I have had no rest at all since it began. Yesterday I visited the Pyramids, and to-day I go with a party I know not where. This place is crammed with people of all nations, and yet not so intolerable to Europeans as might be expected.

In another letter he says, "If old Herodotus could only get a furlough and come to look at it all!"

In the summer of 1870, during the progress of the Franco-German war, General Hamley with his wife and daughter were visiting at Strathtyrum in the month of August, when the campaign was at its height. Day after day, as soon as the post came, a rush was made for the newspapers and maps which used to appear, following the movements of the armies with astonishing rapidity, and day after day the battles were fought over again in the hall at Strathtyrum, and the blunders of the unlucky French generals traced on the maps, which were spread out over every available piece of furniture. After they left Scotland,

General Hamley began his letters on the war—a task not very easy of accomplishment, as the most unexpected and startling events were always occurring, which would upset all preconceived notions of what might probably happen.

General W. G. Hamley to John Blackwood.

Sept. 30, 1870.

I am just startled by a telegram which announces that 6000 French under Canrobert have broken out of Metz. I doubt it, but if it be so, nothing could be better for the Prussians. If the whole garrison would come out in detachments that way, they would be destroyed in detail and the beleaguering army set free.

This was one of the memorable sorties, which had for their only result a wholesale slaughter by the Prussian cannon. In 1872, when politics and the inconveniences and losses occasioned by the tyranny of trades unionism were occupying public attention, General Hamley wrote a paper called "The Reasonable Fears of the Country."

John Blackwood to General W. G. Hamley.

Jan. 30, 1872.

"The Reasonable Fears of the Country" is extremely good, and expresses, I think, the general feeling in a most readable form. I hope you will lay yourself out for going on with another political paper for next No. The opening of Parliament will certainly afford materials, although I daresay your moving will sit heavy on your mind. When are you to be made General? The change will give you much more time for writing, of which I hope you will avail yourself. That idea of yours of cutting down the fine solid reflective character which we are so fond of attributing to ourselves, may afford a test. There is something in what you say of the recoil in the national character.

And again he wrote to the same :—

March 29, 1872.

We cannot too often dwell upon the lesson taught us by France, with its heart and brains knocked out by Revolutions. How men like Dilke and others, with Paris staring them in the face, can go on as they do is a puzzle to me, as we must suppose some of them to be well-meaning idiots.

The next letter, a few months later, was written when the Ballot Bill was going through the House of Lords.

July 15, 1872.

Of the Ballot Bill I incline to say little more than that, amid the contemptuous dislike or indifference of nearly every honest man in the country, the Ballot Bill has passed. The only good I can see of it is that it may check the infernal tyranny of the trades unions.

Later events have shown that the Ballot Bill, which in its very essence was obnoxious to Conservative feeling, was in reality, as John Blackwood rightly opined it might be, the measure of all others which helped the Conservative party to obtain the working men's votes. He, however, detested the measure too heartily to derive much comfort from even this far-sighted reflection, for in his next he says—

John Blackwood to General W. G. Hamley.

April 19, 1872.

In reality nobody wants it : not that I think it would hurt our party, but I hate the principle. It converts the electoral body into a secret society with their vote as their grand masonic secret. The Masons wished to make Hogg the Ettrick Shepherd their Poet Laureate, but he declined to become a Mason, as he " would be sure to tell the secret to his wife." If Hogg was right no married man should have a vote.

Nothing has disgusted me more than Lord Granville's asking whether the American Government would be angry if the

English Government did what it thought right. At school I
have often speculated as to how far it would be safe for me to
stand up to a bigger and stronger fellow, but I should have expected and deserved a hiding if I had been weak and mean
enough to ask his advice on the subject. It is most humiliating.

The last paragraph refers to the ill - considered
conduct of the Government with regard to the
Alabama claims. On a former occasion he had
written—

The astounding impudence of these Yankee claims puts me
in a fury. Confound the scoundrels! they ought to have gone
down on their knees and thanked us for not joining the South,
which in my opinion we ought to have done.

With these extracts from John Blackwood's letters
which show us the different kind of writings on which
General Hamley employed himself, we must now leave
him and turn to the next of the friendly figures who
beckon us onwards as we pass from one to another in
the group.

He, too, is one of the soldier authors, though, unlike
some of the others, he was no longer on active service
when he began to write. Colonel Lockhart not only
filled an important niche in the literary group we are
describing, but was also one of the brightest features
in my father's friendships of later years.

A new discovery in the fields of fiction was always
a source of interest and hopeful expectation to the
Editor, and when in the early "sixties" he made
the acquaintance of Lockhart, he felt sure he had come
upon fresh ore. This member of a gifted family had
a hereditary claim upon his friendship, being the
nephew of his old friend J. G. Lockhart. In him

John Blackwood was not slow to discover evidences of literary talent, only wanting time and opportunity to develop. His early impressions of Lockhart are thus given in a letter to the Chaplain-General:—

John Blackwood to Rev. G. R. Gleig.

EDINBURGH, *April* 3, 1866.

I had a visit last week from Lockhart, and I was glad to hear that he had shown his stories to you and your son. Your opinion seems to be something like my own, but I should like to hear from you on the subject. He has all the stuff in him, and the real power of writing, which should enable him to win distinction as an author if he gets into the right groove and sticks to his work. He put me into fits of laughter with an account of an escapade in the way of a hoax he had been perpetrating on a blockhead. He is the *neveu de son oncle.*

The novels which marked Lockhart's all too brief career as a novelist begun with 'Doubles and Quits,' a story of soldier life, and the plot hinging on the incidents arising from a man being haunted by a "double," whose resemblance to him led to many ridiculous *contretemps* and adventures. This story was written with a freshness and *verve* that carried the reader laughing along with the author at the escapades he describes so gaily,—the glimpses of barrack life given being none the less palatable for a certain flavour reminding us of some of Lever's early writings.

John Blackwood to Colonel L. W. M. Lockhart.

STRATHTYRUM, ST ANDREWS, *Sept.* 7, 1868.

I have read 'Doubles and Quits' with very great pleasure. It frequently made me roar with laughter. The conversations between Dolphino and Donaldino are first-class, and Donald's disgust at mess conversation after he has gone head and ears, is to the life.   I was almost disappointed that you did not make the two worthies dine at the "Rag." . . . It gives me great pleasure to see you contributing to the Magazine, and I hope often to see your hand there.   You have a natural turn for writing, and if you settle down to your work I have no doubt about your success.   The following is an extract from a letter I had from Lady John Manners, a very clever and highly accomplished woman.   She writes, "I do wish you had seen me in perfect fits and shrieks over the second part of 'Doubles and Quits.'   What a capital story!"

In the same letter he goes on to the Abyssinian Expedition :—

What a fortunate termination of the Abyssinian Expedition. The news arrives very opportunely for the Government, and it is to be hoped Diz. has not invented the telegram.   I rather begin to feel sorry for Theodore with his Mons Meg.   He must (as Hogg said of Macculloch) have been a "stoopid savage," or he would have given us much more trouble and made better terms.

It will be remembered that King Theodore solved the difficulties of the position by shooting himself the day the English entered his capital.   Lockhart's other two novels, 'Fair to See' and 'Mine is Thine,' both appeared in the Magazine during the next few years, and are marked by a decided advance in style and power of writing; and though full of mirth and humour, these characteristics are toned down to a more sober key, in keeping with the more solid attributes of these later efforts.

In the summer of 1878, when writing to Colonel Lockhart on the subject of his last novel, my father quotes the opinion of Mr Alexander Allardyce :—

I have not heard many criticisms upon 'Mine is Thine,' but

Mr Allardyce, our new official at "45," was over here the other day, and he spoke of it most warmly, and with real discrimination. I am going to be very lucky in my selection of him (Mr Brown's successor): he is very clever, and such a nice, modest fellow.

These appreciative words must have found many an echo among the inner circle of 'Maga's' contributors, when nearly twenty years later Mr Allardyce's busy literary career was cut short by death. They also formed substantially the groundwork of an able appreciation of him which appeared in the 'Scotsman' after his death. Here the writer, after alluding to his many admirable miscellaneous compositions, and the success of his well-known novels, the 'City of Sunshine' and 'Balmoral,' dwells also upon Mr Allardyce's great modesty with regard to his own attainments, which was so attractive a feature in one of his remarkable intellectual gifts.

Reference has been made in the chapter on Strathtyrum to the charm of Lockhart's conversational powers, and some idea of his quaint humorous mode of expression may be gathered from his letters. In 1870 he was with the Prussian army on the Rhine Frontier, acting as special correspondent to the 'Times,' for which he furnished some excellent letters. To judge from the following, his private correspondence was scarcely less interesting :—

Colonel L. W. M. Lockhart to John Blackwood.

SAARLOUIS, RHEIN PROVINCES, 24*th Sept.* 1870.

I don't think I wrote to you when in front of Metz. I have just returned from a ten days' voyage *autour* that fortress, inspecting the various positions of the investments, &c. Noth-

ing is stirring there or likely to be stirring, and so after em-
bodying my observations in three letters to the 'Times'—the
best I could cook up out of scanty materials—I have telegraphed Morris that I wish to go down to Strasbourg, where
there is hotter work going on, and I am here awaiting his
answer, hourly expected. I have heard no news of a later date
than the 18th or 19th inst., so am all behind the world. We
heard of a skirmish before Paris, and that is our latest from the
metropolis, and just now I have heard that Toul has fallen.
I visited the outposts in front of Thionville, where the French
seem flourishing; but the devils fire so unreasonably at every
movement of a twig, that after crawling on all fours through a
wood I got little view of the place, but a very striking one of a
large gun staring me in the face, a ruffian beside it with his
port-fire alight, and plenty of chassepots twigging everything
on the ramparts, so I serpented my way back without much
satisfaction. I have had a very rough time of it generally,
but for the last three or four days been in clover, living with
a hospitable old fellow, General Voigts-Rheetz! commanding
the 10th Corps d'Armée. But I cannot describe to you the
horrible irksomeness of not knowing the language. We sat
down to all meals about twenty strong—all the headquarter
staff. Hardly one of them could speak passable French, and
only one a word of English. Naturally the conversation was
general in German, so just imagine what it was to sit through
all these terrible banquets (I calculated that we sat at table
seven and a half hours per diem) with an incomprehensible
gibberish yelled or sputtered all round one. My intellect
would certainly have given way if I had remained any longer.
One might every bit as well (bar the odours) have taken one's
victuals in the monkey department at the Zoologicals. But
they were all most gentleman-like and kind fellows, and no
doubt intelligent, if one could only have understood them.
"Was zee Frenchman shot?" was the question put to me
by my English-speaking friend on my return from Thionville.
Now, what could a fellow make of such a question as that?
It turned out that he meant to ask if the French had fired
at me! I have an abundant store of material for a long letter
for November, if my mind is not deranged by this sort of thing.

Once and again I have been on the point of throwing the thing up and coming home, I have had such bad attacks of illness, and am in a dilapidated condition now, but I hope to fight it out. Of course I have been entirely isolated from home news since I left Brussels a fortnight ago, but hope to hear by telegraph to-day that all goes well at home. The weather has for the last few days been glorious, but far from warm; yet the bright sun and the clear sky and the absent rain are inestimable advantages in this sort of work. I wonder what you are about. I wish you could see the hole I am writing in: more than ever natural would it appear to you that I should wish to charter a balloon and drop in to spend the evening at Strath. You would see in the 'Times' my account of the Metz balloon, a rather pathetic contrivance. Give my very affectionate regards to Mrs Blackwood, and offer the General my respectful military salute.—Believe me to be ever yours,

L. W. M. LOCKHART.

Another letter from Germany, written under the less exciting circumstances of "bath" life, will be appreciated by those who are acquainted with Homburg and its "cure":—

Colonel L. W. M. Lockhart to John Blackwood.

HÔTEL VICTORIA, HOMBURG, *July* 19, 1877.

I came here eight or nine days ago, and have been as steady as a mill-horse in the prescribed course of bathing and drinking, early hours, a restricted diet, and the other uncomfortable chastenings which belong to the place, and these things are beginning to tell. . . . The English visitors are not as yet in great numbers, but I have a good many acquaintances, though all of a strangely stupid and uninteresting sort. You can imagine that boredom is not a rare experience. However, it might be many degrees worse, and Rudd [his brother-in-law] from Aix-la-Chapelle writes in the spirit of Lazarus addressing Dives. I think the baths would have done you good. I take an effervescent sparkling one of iron and some other ingredient, which has a sort of magical effect: after ten minutes in it one

begins to whistle, in a quarter of an hour one is singing, and
at the end of the prescribed twenty minutes a delicious feeling
of being genteelly screwed on the very best champagne accom-
panies one home to breakfast with a huge appetite. All the
pleasure of intoxication is thus achieved without sin, and with
constitutional rewards instead of penalties.

You asked me about my other Tales for the series (of the
success of which I was delighted to hear), and I think I should
certainly like the "War Letter" to have an innings. I have
always thought it my very best performance. How splendidly
the 'Battle of Dorking' reads again. It is really a great
triumph of genius. I think it is even more lifelike and natural
than anything of Erckmann-Chatrian.

The following is in reply to the New Year's letter
with which Lockhart seldom failed to greet his
friend :—

John Blackwood to Colonel L. W. M. Lockhart.

EDINBURGH, *January 7*, 1874.

. MY DEAR LAW.,—Your letters are always pleasant, and I
should have felt the past year incomplete without a greeting
from you. Most cordially do I wish you all good in the
coming year and many others. All that concerns you is of
interest to me, and I am sure the more I have to pay you the
better for us both. All I can say, as that insensate female
Lady Scott said to poor Sir Walter when he was struggling like
a giant, "Write, Wattie, write." . . . Instead of entertaining at
home this New Year, we paid a visit to the Tennants at The
Glen. It is a beautiful place, one of the most perfect houses I
ever saw, and not too big. Tennant is a good fellow, and the
way he has got up that place shows that he has a head and
taste. . . .

If ever you ride along the Pont du Var look at the ditches
alongside, and imagine the feelings of a lad of eighteen who, to
the admiration of a riding-party of ladies, had been disporting
over the fields, but whose brute of a horse in jumping back on
the road missed and fell back, depositing him in the horrible

drain. I was the lad. Give my best regards to Mrs Rudd [Colonel Lockhart's sister].—Ever yours truly,

JOHN BLACKWOOD.

The following extracts from letters written when my father was in London contain many allusions to Lockhart and his ever-welcome companionship :—

John Blackwood to his Wife.

19 ARLINGTON ST., PICCADILLY, *May* 20, 1876.

This is a milder day, in fact almost warm, though the wind is still easterly. I took a turn in the Row with Law. this morning. I recognised a good many faces that looked confoundedly old, and I thought would they be thinking the same of me ? At all events, I was not got up in the *ci-devant* young style that I saw among men who, I fear, were contemporaries. . . . I dined at the Carlton yesterday. There had been no House, and the room was full of senators, who had obviously come out on pretence of the House, and instead of returning to their wives and families had seized the opportunity of dining at the club. Burnhouse [Mr G. Thomson] was quite facetious upon them. I am to dine with some selections at the Garrick to-day. I am to lunch with the Manners to-morrow, and I see I must go up to give evidence in the copyright ; so if Simpson and Willie have any suggestions to make they should write on Monday. I called on John Murray to-day. His son has just started for America. He seems to have spoken much of his visit to Strathtyrum.— Ever, my dear Julia, your affecte.   JOHN BLACKWOOD.

The amusing apprehensions as to his own appearance caused by the aged looks of some of his contemporaries here alluded to, if seriously entertained, were entirely unfounded. The striking thing about him was that, in spite of his continuous hard work and the little thought or care he bestowed on the necessity of sparing himself in any way, he always looked much younger than his years. This impression was helped by his spare wiry figure, which remained the same weight with little variation from five-and-twenty to the time we are writing of. While only a dash of grey in his whiskers betrayed signs of age, his head, with the thick dark hair, looked the same to the last.

John Blackwood to his Wife.

19 ARLINGTON ST., *May* 24, 1876.

I had caught a very severe cough, but it is passing off very quickly. Henry says it is a safety-valve, and quoted some old gentleman of his acquaintance who always looked upon a cough in that light. We had a most pleasant party, and Kinglake was very good, and evidently enjoyed himself. His deafness is a bother; but all the others were delighted to listen, and talked and looked up to him very nicely. Law. and I wandered about Westminster yesterday, and spent most of the time in the old Abbey.

The next letter refers principally to an afternoon when my father's rooms in Arlington Street received some of the cream of his literary friends, and Lockhart was summoned to assist at the festa. It was a day when even the faithful "Henry," his landlord, so well known to all our visitors at the Burlington and Arlington Street, felt the importance of the occasion.

John Blackwood to his Wife.

14 ARLINGTON ST, PICCADILLY, *June* 9, 1876.

I got a telegram from Isabella this morning, that she and Mrs Oliphant would lunch. I sent for Law. and Larrie to help me. Law. turned up, and the luncheon was charming. Towards the close of luncheon word came that Mr and Mrs Lewes were at the door. I went down and had an affectionate congratulatory interview with her. She had just sent off the last of 'Deronda,' and would not come in; but Lewes did, and was most agreeable. After he was gone Larrie turned up with his friend Von Chauvin, so the festa of intellect at 14 Arlington

St. was pretty considerable, to the great delight of Henry, who lingered at the door to catch every word that was saying.

In another letter referring to this same luncheon—

John Blackwood to his Daughter.

June 10, 1876.

Law. was here this morning in tremendous ecstasy with his luncheon-party here yesterday. The scene was like a drama. Mrs Oliphant up here, Law. and Lewes both talking first-class with her, and I for some time down-stairs speaking with George Eliot, pale and tired, in her carriage at the door. I do not think it wonderful the work should have exhausted her, and have written a line of congratulation to her to-day after reading the final proof: it is wonderful, and so new.

Those few lines give us the whole scene — one of those fortuitous meetings that, if elaborately planned, would lose half their charm.

From Lockhart we seem to turn naturally to his friend Sir Archibald Alison, both of them Scotsmen, and both hailing from the same " West Country," as we say in Scotland. Nothing used to please John Blackwood more than when he found himself able to continue literary relations between different members of the same family. Two brothers would be writing for him sometimes, as in the case of the Hamleys and Chesneys, or a father and son like the Lyttons; and amongst the military fraternity we find Sir Archibald Alison, son of the historian, following in his father's footsteps with various critical and useful papers, which appeared at different times in 'Maga' when the exigencies of his busy military career left him time for writing. His services, as we all know, have been given to his country from the days of the Mutiny, when he lost his arm, down to the Ashantee expedition and the Egyptian campaign of 1884. During the Ashantee war John Blackwood writes to a friend at the War Office : " Pray send me any news you can about Alison, and, apart from my interest in him, which is great, his mother lives near me, a frail old lady, tremulously anxious for tidings of him." The profession in which he has won so distinguished a position has naturally absorbed nearly all his time and attention,—had it been otherwise he might have followed his literary bent, and distinguished himself in another line. His contributions to the Magazine were necessarily few and far between, but always matter for congratulation from the Editor, who advised him on one occasion to reprint and give his name with a paper which had attracted considerable attention, remarking to him, " In these days a soldier has no chance unless he is able to use his pen or charter a Billy Russell to do it for him." To Sir Archibald was intrusted the difficult and delicate task, for a soldier, of reviewing the third and fourth volumes of Kinglake, which had encountered what my father called Hamley's " heaviest metal in the ' Edinburgh.' " Alison's review, while not ignoring the defects of Kinglake's narrative, which are open to military criticism, does ample justice to its literary merits and the mass of historical information and facts, which might have been so dry, but are given to us in such a charmingly readable style.

John Blackwood to Sir Archibald Alison.

Dec. 10, 1868.

Your criticism of Kinglake's opinions is very comprehensive, and hits him in a good many points of importance, but is done with so much delicacy I should say no one could feel hurt.

From Sir Archibald Alison we pass on to one whose prowess with the pen as well as with the sword enables us to rank amongst 'Maga's' Military Staff the present Commander-in-Chief, Lord Wolseley. Sir Garnet Wolseley (as he was, when my father alluded to him in letters as one of "the Military Staff of Blackwood") had begun his contributions to the Magazine by an account of his memorable expedition to quell the rebellion in the Red River Territory in 1870. The article, which was an admirable one, and remarkable for the clearness and vigour of the writing, attracted considerable attention. The Editor had always considered the expedition and the narrative equally the performances of a man of mark, and he watched his subsequent career with deepest interest.

John Blackwood to W. W. Story.

EDINBURGH, *Dec.* 1873.

This stupid Ashantee war disturbs me greatly, as I have so many friends there. Sir Garnet Wolseley is a friend and correspondent. If you did not read his account of his Red River Expedition in the Magazine a few years ago, it will be worth your while to turn that paper up. Now they are sending Alison (Sir A.) as second in command, and of course he is a most intimate friend and a good writer. It does seem a cruel and absurd thing to send our most highly instructed officers to fight naked savages in the bush. Why not empty our convict prisons and send them to fight the Ashantees, if it is necessary to fight them at all? I suppose I should be denounced if I made this suggestion, but there is a good deal in it.

The narrative of the Red River Expedition in 'Maga' was necessarily anonymous, and occasioned one of those innocent criticisms from a weekly newspaper which have often been the cause of much mirth among the inner circle of 'Blackwood.' The Editor remarks in a letter to William Blackwood: "I never felt more inclined to discard the anonymous than on reading the calm assertion that the 'writer of the Red River Expedition in 'Blackwood' knew nothing about the subject'!!" Here, then, are the slings and arrows to which the most invincible warriors expose themselves when they enter the "lists" of literature. On Sir Garnet's return to England with his well-earned laurels from the Ashantee war, my father was one of the first to go and congratulate him, and he mentions with satisfaction having been able to secure his company at luncheon, as he was "one of the busiest as well as one of the cleverest men in London." On another occasion he describes having taken his son, then a schoolboy, to see Sir Garnet.

John Blackwood to his Wife.

19 ARLINGTON STREET, *June* 5, 1876.

Then we went to Sir Garnet Wolseley's. Sir Garnet gave Jack a stick from Ashantee, the stem of a coffee-plant: it will be a historical stick, I hope.

The significant comment on the walking-stick was one of those predictions that have been more than realised. The officer who had successfully conducted the Red River Expedition had always, in John Blackwood's estimation, seemed bound to take a foremost rank in his profession, and this latest success in Ashantee only tended further to confirm his prevision of the brilliant future which lay before him.

Sir Henry Brackenbury, one of Sir Garnet's staff, has been alluded to also as a contributor. Notable amongst his writings must be accounted his brilliantly written book, 'Fantee and Ashantee,' which gives an account

of the country and people, as well as of the campaign
in which he accompanied his chief.

To turn from these campaigns of recent years to Sir
Hope Grant's history of the Sepoy war is an old story,
but it was written about this time, the fine old soldier
finishing his career with this tribute to the memory of
his friend and fellow-countryman, Sir Colin Campbell.
Sir Hope's *début* as an author was one of those surprises
which sometimes occurred amongst John Blackwood's
literary experiences, he having only known him as a
pleasant golfing companion on the St Andrews Links.

John Blackwood to General Sir Hope Grant.

EDINBURGH, *Nov.* 22, 1873.

I have read all the sheets of your book, and I now write to
congratulate you upon it. Your diary is most interesting, and
will, I feel sure, be a success. Tell Lady Grant that I am
certain it will largely increase the strong feeling of personal
regard so generally felt towards you. I was quite touched by
old Sir Colin allowing you and the others to commit the
escapade of riding all that way to see your wives. My nephew,
who has been attending to the book, is, I am sorry to say, laid
up with a hunting accident, a badly bruised ankle—a tedious
thing. The book is all in train. I have so many friends sent
out to this wretched Ashantee war that I look upon it with
perfect horror, and now I see that Alison is going. Wolseley
being a Blackwood man too, the Magazine will be very powerfully represented on the Gold Coast. The probable effects of
slight wounds in that climate is the thing that frightens me for
the officers. We came into Edinburgh for the winter a fortnight ago, and I was very sorry to leave Strathtyrum and the
happy golfing-grounds.

Colonel Knollys, who had been for many years on
Sir Hope Grant's staff, afterwards wrote an interesting memoir of his chief.

When the victories in the Sudan of Sir Herbert
Kitchener, and his entry into Khartum, have lately
(September 1898) been the subject of conversation and
congratulation in every household in England, it may
be interesting to mention that the gallant avenger of
Gordon's death was another of the military contributors to Blackwood.   As Lieutenant Kitchener we
find him in 1878 writing of "A Visit to Sofia," and
the following year he proposes a paper on Cyprus,
where he was engaged in surveying.   He says : "We
are getting on well, and my base-line came in to $\frac{3}{4}$
inch in four miles.   I have had no fever in my party,
and am exceptional in that respect."   He goes on to
ask if Blackwood would like a paper about the island,
and the result was that he wrote an excellent article,
giving much useful information about Cyprus, entitled
" Notes on Cyprus," which appeared in the Magazine
in August 1879.

Variety has always been a strong feature in the
fare provided month by month for the readers of
' Maga,' this desirable end being sometimes obtained
not merely by the introduction of a fresh contributor,
but very often by the choice of a novelty in the way
of a subject for an article.   To provide a *bonne bouche*
of this kind now and then gave the Editor great
pleasure, and his glee was unbounded when he could
say, "The whole town is talking of the Magazine."
A notable instance of this kind occurred in May 1871,
which for long afterwards in his own immediate circle
was known as the year of the " Battle of Dorking."
This celebrated *jeu d'esprit*, as its author called it,
was contributed to the Magazine by one of its
" Military Staff," the late Sir George Chesney.   At

the time he wrote it Sir George (then Colonel) Chesney was at the India Office, and had been writing for some years on different subjects—short tales and reviews. His own account of the idea of the story, which, apart from his distinguished military services, would have made his name famous, is best given in his own words :—

Colonel George Chesney to John Blackwood.

INDIA OFFICE, *Feb.* 8, 1871.

The idea has occurred to me that a useful way of bringing home to the country the necessity for thorough reorganisation might be by a tale—after the manner of Erckmann-Chatrian—describing a successful invasion of England, and the collapse of our power and commerce in consequence. An ex-volunteer in the year 1900, for example, might be telling his children his experiences of 1872, the battle of Guildford, and occupation, and humiliating terms of peace. A realistic tale after this fashion might be effective.

The Editor falling in with the notion, Colonel Chesney began his story at once, and sent a further description of it.

Colonel George Chesney to John Blackwood.

March 11, 1871.

To turn now to my proposed *jeu d'esprit,* I think I may venture to say I could give you something readable, and might contain a useful moral. If the Government [Gladstone's] had brought in a really good Army Bill, the words would have been taken out of my mouth, but as it turns out, they have left me virgin soil to work upon.

The Abolition of Purchase and the resumption of the Crown's authority over the Reserve Forces being the principal feature in Mr Cardwell's well - known measure, still left a large number of vitally needful reforms in our army organisation totally unprovided for, and this Colonel Chesney proceeds to point out. He describes the contingencies that might call away our regular forces to different parts of the globe, leaving us to be defended by brave and desperate but, alas! imperfectly trained volunteers. In the same letter he goes on to say—

We have the quarrel with America and Russia, dispersion of all our forces, followed by rising in India. Sudden appearance of Germany on the scene. Sentimental platitudes of Messrs Gladstone & Co., triming leaders in the 'Times.' Destruction of our "Field Line" by new torpedoes. Arrival of 100,000 Sanscrit-speaking Junkers brimming over with "Geist" and strategy. Hurried defence of the chalk-range by the volunteers and militia, no commissariat, line turned, total defeat, retreat on London, occupation of that place, and general smash up.

As soon as the 'Battle of Dorking' was in type my father wrote to the author, delighted with this, his first attempt at fiction, and that too of such a very interesting and novel description.

John Blackwood to Colonel George Chesney.

45 GEORGE STREET, *April* 17, 1871.

After reading the whole over again in type I am happy to say I think it extremely good, in fact a success. It reads quite naturally, and will, I believe, be found painfully interesting. You have carried out your ticklish task with so much good taste and feeling that I have almost no comments to make. We shall be accused of insulting the feelings of the British Line, but I think you bring it out very distinctly that our poor fellows fought well, and if you want to add to your chances of popularity, add a little more in that line. We are, I firmly believe, the most fighting race in the world, and we have an insatiable appetite for applause on that score.

A few days later he was able to convey to the

author some tributes to the realistic skill of the story, which had an almost startling effect. He wrote to Colonel Chesney :—

The manager here, Mr Simpson, took a proof home, and while he was still wrapt up in it was startled by his mother, a most acute old lady (who had picked up the sheets as he let them fall), exclaiming, "Surely, George, the Germans were never in England." I am much struck by what you tell me of your never having tried fiction before. I did not think you had, but when I read the 'Battle of Dorking' I thought you must have tried your hand before. Give my compliments to your wife, and tell her she is an excellent critic. Her remark first gave me much hope that you might succeed, as I had seen endless cases of really accomplished critics and essayists breaking down utterly when they tried fiction.

The following extracts from letters written at the time the 'Battle of Dorking' appeared will give us some idea of the talk and excitement the narrative caused :—

A. W. Kinglake to John Blackwood.

28 HYDE PARK PLACE, W., *April* 27, 1871.

The 'Battle of Dorking' is capitally done, and one may venture to hope that it will prove a really effective mode of conveying a much-needed warning. Throughout the imaginary record such an art of probability, and in that sense of truth, is so skilfully and so firmly maintained.

John Blackwood to William Blackwood.

STRATHTYRUM, *May* 5, 1871.

We dined at Mount Melville last night. Colonel George Moncrieff and his wife there. He was raving about the 'Battle of Dorking,'—never read anything in his life before so good and like reality.

By the time the Editor reached London a few days

later the 'Battle' had fairly caught on, and the
Magazine was soon out of print, and he tells his
nephew, writing from London—

May 13, 1871.

I found Law. [Lockhart] in immense force, talking with
Julia: he says the town is perfectly wild about the 'Battle
of Dorking,'—everybody loud in its praise.

John Blackwood to William Blackwood.

THE BURLINGTON, CORK ST., *May* 15, 1871.

We had good fun at Bulwer's last night, finding, in the first
place, the guests discussing the 'Battle of Dorking,' and the
next thing I saw was Bulwer thrusting the Magazine into
Chief-Justice Cockburn's hand and advising him to read it
when he got home. Mrs Norton was the chief feature there,
and Browning, who are both very pleasant, Mrs N. of course
perfectly charming.

He then in the same letter mentions his first
meeting with, and the pleasing impression made by,
the author of the 'Battle':—

Colonel Chesney came this morning, and I am happy to say
I think he is a first-rate one, after my own heart. We had a
very long talk, and he developed another scheme for a book.
He is a little chap, very bright and fresh-looking,—I think
considerably younger than myself. I looked in at the Carlton
afterwards and found Cluny [Gordon], who told me the universal cry is for 'Blackwood,' and that nobody can take it up
for five minutes in the club without a waiter coming to ask
if he is done with it.

The chorus went on till the Magazine was again out
of print, and in June the 'Battle of Dorking' was
reprinted in sixpenny pamphlet form, and this in a
month had attained the sale of over 80,000, and, as
my father remarked to the author in handing over

to him £250 for the reprint, there was a "pleasant prospect in store," for it soon reached the number of more than 110,000. After this remarkable success Colonel Chesney turned his attention steadily to fiction, his next novels, 'A True Reformer' and 'The Dilemma,' appearing first in the Magazine and afterwards in three-volume form, worthily maintaining his reputation as a writer whose popularity was not endangered but enhanced by pointing the dreaded moral.

CHAPTER X.

THE EDITOR ABROAD.

WITH LAURENCE OLIPHANT IN PARIS — AN ASTONISHING AND EXCITING
LIFE — MR FREDERIC MARSHALL — M. DE BLOWITZ — MR SIMPSON'S
ILLNESS—MR RUDOLPH LINDAU—MR P. G. HAMERTON—AT THE JAPAN-
ESE LEGATION—SHAKESPEARIAN READING AT SIR THEODORE MARTIN'S
—TENNYSON—LORD CRANBROOK—MR HERBERT COWELL—MRS OLIPHANT
AS A LITERARY GOD-MOTHER—ROME AGAIN—W. W. STORY, SCULPTOR
AND POET—THE PALAZZO BARBERINI—MISS BREWSTER—AN ORIGINAL
VIEW AS TO THE CAUSE OF THE POTATO DISEASE — A GOLF CADDIE'S
ART CRITICISM—HOMEWARD BOUND.

In 1871 Laurence Oliphant, who had been living more
or less apart from European interests during the last
few preceding years, appeared in Paris just after
the war. His temporary freedom from the Prophet's
thrall was signalised by his brilliant correspondence
in the 'Times,' giving in his wonderful word-pictures
accounts of the shifting drama from week to week and
from day to day what was going on within its walls.
Knowing how keenly interested John Blackwood was
in the events which had recently taken place, he
invited him to come over and visit him, and see for
himself the fearful devastation the Parisians had
wreaked on their beautiful city. My father's letters
are full of the disgust and indignation he felt at the

pitiful sights, and a never - ceasing wonder at the characteristics of the French nation.

John Blackwood to his Wife.

HÔTEL CHATHAM, *November* 30, 1871.

Soon after I came down Oliphant appeared, and we have been driving about the town until it is close on post-time. It is a most striking scene. As I surveyed the different wrecks, "The beasts!" were the most frequent words on my lips. Larrie is in great force, and I am going to stay with him, so you can address 9 Rue du Centre. He is up near the Arcade l'Étoile. . . . I hope this will find you and Puck safe in Randolph Crescent after a not very disagreeable crossing. Lady Oliphant is very well, and both send their warm regards.—Ever, my dear, your affecte. husband, JOHN BLACKWOOD.

John Blackwood to his Wife.

9 RUE DU CENTRE, *December* 2, 1871.

Paris is a melancholy sight, and I wish all our philosophic Radicals had an opportunity of seeing it. With the Tuileries and the Hôtel de Ville gone, it looks like a city without a head, and that certainly is the state of the people. We dined with Mr Marshall yesterday, and they dine with me at a café to-day.

Mr Frederic Marshall here alluded to became a very intimate friend of John Blackwood's, and also a valuable contributor. On the visits to Paris which followed this of 1871 he was ever the first to welcome us with unvarying kindness and hospitality. His position (he was then Secretary to the Japanese Legation) in the midst of the diplomatic circle made him thoroughly *au courant* with foreign politics and the gossips of the different Embassies—a world of itself apart, and yet in touch at its different points with all the great centres of the world. His knowledge and experience of Continental life were therefore far-reaching and obtained under the most favourable conditions, of which 'Maga' reaped the benefit in many articles contributed on political and social subjects, all bearing the stamp of an accomplished man of the world, telling us just as much as he intends, with a reserve in the background, in itself an evidence of literary power of the best kind. Mr Marshall and his family had been in Paris during the Commune, and his powerful and realistic description of this second Reign of Terror appeared in the Magazine. My father considered it the best account that appeared on the subject, and alludes to it frequently in his letters.

John Blackwood to John Delane.

STRATHTYRUM, *June* 26, 1871.

I wish to draw your attention to the article on the Commune of Paris, which is, I think, singularly well done. I have read indefatigably on the subject, and this seems to me by far the clearest narrative that has appeared, and the best warning to us against similar dangers at home. The writer, who is an old resident in Paris, deserves great credit for the temperate tone in which he expresses himself, and everything that has transpired since he wrote goes to confirm what he says.

While Mr Marshall was writing this paper on the Commune, he had the misfortune to lose one of his children, a young girl, and my father alludes sympathetically to the sad trouble which had overtaken him.

John Blackwood to Frederic Marshall.

45 GEORGE STREET, *June* 22, 1871.

I am extremely sorry to hear that trouble has come upon you in the midst of your labours, and from the black border on your note I fear your anxieties have been terminated fatally. You have gone through your work most nobly in the midst of all.

I read enough of your MS. to see that it was good, and to save my eyes put it into type. I have just finished reading the proof, and congratulate you on having produced a most clear, instructive, and deeply interesting exposition of what the Commune of Paris was. People in this country did not understand it a bit, and some of the articles commiserating the wretches in papers which ought to have known better made me perfectly furious. Your tone is exactly right, temperate but very decided, and you work well up to the climax of the half-stifled city. I am so glad you expose the ' International,' and point out so distinctly the similar dangers threatening ourselves with our own communists. Everything that has transpired since you wrote confirms what you say, and I only wish you had been able to write at greater length. This, however, you can remedy by a further paper. Let me know whether you are disposed and able to take up any phase of French affairs for next month.

Frederic Marshall to John Blackwood.

PARIS, 86 BOULEVARD MALESHERBES, 1st *July* 1871.

This remuneration is so liberal that I ought, in honesty, to say how amply sufficient I think it. But I thank you still more for the sympathetic tone in which you are kind enough to write to me. In moments of trial such words as you so generously use are especially welcome. It has long been one of my objects of ambition to write for ' Blackwood,' and you have opened the door to me in so encouraging a way that the realisation of my wish brings me a double satisfaction.

Thus the acquaintance grew into friendship, and Frederic Marshall became one of those valued correspondents of whom John Blackwood has said that their friendship made half the happiness of his life. Besides Mr Marshall's thorough knowledge of French politics and public matters, his long residence in the country made him an authority on matters of social and domestic interest, and after the tragic incidents

of the war and the Commune he proposed in the
following letter to my father to turn. to something
brighter :—

Frederic Marshall to John Blackwood.

There is plenty to mourn over in this fallen country, but
there is a vast deal to laugh at, and I shall be glad to open up
the second category of matter.

The result was some lively papers on French watering-
places—Trouville and Deauville.   His well-known
collection of essays, ' French Home Life,' followed
later.   These essays, which embody nearly all that
there is to know about our " Neighbours' " home life,
— dress, manners, marriage, children, servants, &c.,
— possess the advantage of being written by an
Englishman from a Frenchman's point of view.   They
show all the differences between the manners and
customs of the two nations which would be sure to
strike an Englishman, and these are treated with
the knowledge and experience which could only be
arrived at by one who had been many years a house-
holder in France.

During his visit to Oliphant in 1871, John Blackwood
also made the acquaintance of M. De Blowitz, the well-
known 'Times' correspondent, and his family.   The
introduction had highly amused him.   In one letter
he said, " Blowitz *was* good (*i.e.*, amusing).   He had
been charmed to make the Editor of ' Blackwood's '
acquaintance.   He had said it was a grand thing to
have a great review called by your name, but it must
have its inconveniences also ; for example, " On dit,
Coupez-moi Blackwood, Prêtez-moi Blackwood, *Dé-
chirez* Blackwood ! ! " &c.

John Blackwood to his Wife.

PARIS, RUE DU CENTRE, *Dec.* 3, 1871.

Yesterday we drove away straight through Paris, calling at the Hôtel Chatham, picking up an Austrian colonel and baron. The colonel had been Austrian officer with the French army on the Loire, and afterwards in Paris, so could point out every object of interest as we drove up the boulevards, where the hottest fighting had been. There was ruin in lots, especially Théâtre St Martin. The memorandum we made was never to live in Paris in a *corner* house, as in this line every one of them was either peppered with bullets or in ruins. We passed out by the Vincennes Gate, and passing Vincennes reached Champigny, where there was the three days' fighting under Ducrot at this time last year. There was a function, the Archbishop of Paris saying High Mass for the slain buried all around. He is a venerable-looking, intelligent old man, and read a good address. I saw one girl crying bitterly. General Ducrot himself came forward and made an eloquent speech. There was a combination of impudent effrontery and courage in his doing so which tickled me. I would rather have scaled the opposite heights whence the Prussians repulsed him, when he had said he would never return to Paris unless victorious. The cries were all for *Vive la France!* and a fellow who attempted to call *Vive la République!* was denounced as an imbecile. You will see an account of the whole thing in Oliphant's letter to the 'Times' on Monday. To-day we have been to St Cloud—all in ruins and covered with marks of the different positions—and home by Neuilly and along the Grand Avenue de Neuilly, where Oliphant saw the Prussians enter. It was intensely interesting, and realises all descriptions.

He wrote again, referring to the many interesting and influential personages who, as usual, were gathered around Laurence Oliphant.

John Blackwood to his Wife.

PARIS, *Dec.* 6, 1871.

Larrie leads a most astonishing and exciting life. Every one, from the Duc d'Aumale downwards, consults him, and there is a constant buzz of comers and goers in every kind of capacity. Yesterday at *déjeuner* a card was sent in for him, and he disappeared up-stairs to see Von Arnim, the Prussian Ambassador. Then a very fine-looking fellow, who proved to be Prince George Solms, a cousin of the King of Hanover (a fierce Prussian hater), was shown into the breakfast-room. In addition there were the Vicomte de Calonne, of unknown principles, and M. and Mme. De Blowitz, whom I have described to Puck, and self, made a splendid party. . . . Larrie has a carriage with a pair of greys. *Ces chevaux gris comme ils travaillent.*

John Blackwood to William Blackwood.

PARIS, *Dec.* 5, 1871.

My intention is to leave this on Friday morning. It is impossible to be here without reflecting a great deal, and gloomily, for the future of the people. Everything seems so utterly unsettled, people frightened to say what they wish for. Gladstone should come over here and walk amongst the ruins and the communistic quarter. The sight of the result, and the unwholesome-looking, scowling-looking devils he would see, would surely warn him of the danger of tampering with Bradlaughs, &c.

On December 9, 1871, he returned to London, and found his rooms at the Burlington all ready for him, and Mr Langford, his London manager, sitting by a snug fire waiting to dine with him and hear all the news. A few days later he writes from the Burlington to his wife :—

I went down to Cooper's Hill yesterday and saw Chesney, and found him living in about the most charming house I ever saw. It is within a couple of miles of Ascot, and they are bent on you coming there at that time next year. Chesney and I walked down to Eton (five miles) and saw Jack, who is to make his appearance here to-morrow evening, with the view of being in Edinburgh on Friday night

The following year my father was again in Paris on our way home from Vienna, and the ill-fated journey to see poor Lever at Trieste. Our stay there was curtailed by the news of the serious illness of Mr George Simpson, his manager in Edinburgh, which made us hurry back to London. Arrived in London, and hearing that Mr Simpson was better, he stayed on to see several important correspondents.

John Blackwood to William Blackwood.

THE BURLINGTON, *June* 28, 1872.

We got to the Burlington soon after seven last night, having had a successful journey, barring the sufferings of these two sweet saints Julia and Puck in the crossing, which was very rough. I am quite glad that you have used the notice of Lever. As it now stands it reads very well indeed, though I say it. I shall write a line to Lord Neaves and thank him for all the kind trouble he has taken. I fear Simpson must have been very ill, and I earnestly hope that he is now getting fairly better, and will keep quiet.

Any sign of illness affecting Mr Simpson always occasioned my father great concern, well knowing how reluctantly he ever gave in to any interruption of the routine of his daily duties at George Street. His long connection with the firm, and the important position he filled at 45 George Street, have already been alluded to in the second volume of this book. My father's affection for him and appreciation of his valuable sterling qualities are shown in all the letters where his name is mentioned. Referring to some business matter which was giving trouble, he wrote to William Blackwood, " Tell Simpson I would rather know I was being robbed of a hundred pounds than he should have his well-earned holiday spoilt by this vexatious business." "The buoyant Simpson" my father calls him in a letter to Mr Collins, and this term exactly describes the able and self-reliant man who for many years was so well known a figure to the *habitués* of George Street, and whose keen insight into business matters made him so valuable an *aide*. Highly conscientious, and a lover of work for its own sake, my father always looked upon him as a marvel of industry, and frequently urged him in later years to take life more easily and give himself more holidays; but, as he would often add, "You might as well ask a steam-engine to rest." The following refers to the Alabama business, which was occupying the attention of Parliament at this time :—

John Blackwood to William Blackwood.

CARLTON CLUB, *July* 2, 1872.

I saw Bulwer to-day, and he was looking quite blooming. The upshot was that the second volume is the one about which he has most doubt as to divisions except two long ones, and he is to send that to me to be got into type that we may then judge. I think it will come to 'Mag.' as we wish, but at all events he means no one else to publish the book. I have just been down to the House and seen R. Bourke, and from what he said I fancy our people are going to accept the American business as finished. I saw the Duke of Richmond for a minute, and said I did not see that the claim was withdrawn, and he said certainly not finished as it ought to be. Kinglake is in good form, and means a new volume soon, I think.

Amongst these contributors who resided abroad was Mr Philip Hamerton, so well known to English readers by his biographies, 'Modern Frenchmen,' and his charming picture of French country life in 'Round my House.' His contributions appeared in the form

of two clever stories, 'Marmorne' and 'Wenderholme.'
The former treated of the events of the Franco-
German War, and is referred to by William Blackwood,
who was ably piloting the author through the intri-
cacies of a correspondence with Hachette and Tauch-
nitz, as a powerful, well-written story.

Another visit was paid to Paris in the spring of
1877, where, besides Mr Frederic Marshall, there now
resided another interesting contributor to the
Magazine, Mr Rudolph Lindau, who had lately been
writing short stories and papers on various matters.
Dinners, breakfasts, races, theatres, all formed one
pleasant whirl, in which Lord Lyons, the Japanese
Minister, the Marshalls, and others, hospitably contributed to our entertainment. Some delightful evenings were spent with our friend Mr Marshall and his
family, where, on one occasion, I remember we met
at dinner his chief, the Japanese Ambassador, Prince
Nakano, also Mr F. O. Adams of the English Embassy,
afterwards our Minister at Berne. It was curious to
see how the Japanese had completely, as far as we
could judge, adapted himself to his European surroundings, talking the jargon of the men of the world,
and entirely at one with them in the interests of the
diplomatic circle. Mr Marshall's two young daughters
were present, not yet introduced, but ready with all
the grace and charm of their early years to entertain
the Scottish visitors, who were deeply interested in
seeing in that familiar manner a real French household, such as Mr Marshall has described to us in
'French Home Life.'

One entertainment given us was a breakfast at the
Japanese Legation, a handsome house near the Champs-

Elysées. Prince Nakano received us at the door of
the large room, and led us to a fine reception-room,
where the other guests were assembled. Among
these were the celebrated De Blowitz, Mr F. O.
Adams, and Mr Rudolph Lindau, of the German Embassy, already alluded to as a friend, whom we knew
well through his fascinating stories, "The Philosopher's Pendulum," "Weariness," and others. There
was a gentle melancholy throughout all these stories
which did not find its counterpart in the writer, whom
we found to be one of the brightest and cheeriest of
companions. He came in with the intelligence that
Don Carlos was expelled from France, why, no one
could imagine. Before we left Prince Nakano led us
to a tray on which were laid a number of quaint
Japanese articles—fans, little combs, and ornaments
for the hair—which he gave to us, a charming souvenir
of his thoughtful kindness. Mr Marshall told us of
many excellent traits of this young Prince, to whom he
and his family were much attached. Another evening
we dined with M. and Madame De Blowitz at their
house in the Avenue Josephine; the other guests,
Mr Marshall, Mr Leonard Courtney, and Mr Lindau.
It was a very amusing evening. There was a good
deal of talk about French politics and the crisis of the
few preceding days, which had resulted in the resignation of the Ministry. A hope was expressed that there
might be a small and perfectly bloodless Revolution
before we left Paris, and it was suggested that De
Blowitz, who had professed every wish to contribute
to our entertainment, should employ his powerful
machinations to procure this experience for us!

These correspondents in foreign cities gave a variety,

and that of a very pleasing kind, to the literature which was issued by the House of Blackwood, and was a branch which appealed strongly to John Blackwood's sympathies on account of his early associations. Paris, Rome, or Florence possessed attractions enough in themselves to have drawn him abroad, but the certainty of seeing Laurence Oliphant and Frederic Marshall in Paris, or William Story in Rome, was the more likely reason, we knew, that induced him to make these occasional journeys, which formed most needed breaks in his routine of life. Edinburgh, where we passed the winter months, was very inclement at that season, and often tried his health severely. In 1878 he was advised to go to Italy for the spring. He therefore decided upon Rome, where he should see his friend Story the sculptor. But Edinburgh is a long distance from Rome; we had to get through London first, and when he once showed face there, engagements gathered round him from which it was extremely difficult to break away. Some notion of this busy, and for him, had he been in strong health, pleasurable time, may be gathered from the following letters :—

John Blackwood to William Blackwood.

LONDON, *Feb.* 22, 1878.

I came in at half-past four, intending to write various letters, and there has been a continuous stream of visitors until now, half-past six. There is naught in particular to tell, luckily, but much that was interesting with Hamleys, Shand, Lockhart, Kinglake, Francillon, &c.

The next day the rush continued. He writes to the same :—

I met him [Gathorne Hardy] to-day, and he said things are

very grave. We dine there to-night. After Langford left this morning I went to Trollope's. We dine there to-morrow. After Trollope I went on to The Priory (the Leweses), and had a most delightful luncheon. He, as well as Kinglake, inquired most warmly for Simpson, and my usual joyous response about him had a concealed grief in the background. [Mr Simpson had signified his intention, owing to health, of retiring almost immediately from business.] They also inquired most tenderly after you. Kinglake has just been here for an hour, and his visit and Sir Windham's [Anstruther] has fairly broken down my letter.

On the 21st he writes to William Blackwood on the topic that was agitating all London, Was it to be war or no war? Referring to the paper for the Magazine, he says :—

I am not quite satisfied with the paper, and do not think that the writer has said enough of Hardy's speech and its effect. You and Allardyce may add to and strengthen the paper throughout. The rumours in London are very rife this afternoon, and there ought to be something to-night to make our tone about prospects of peace less confident. . . .

We dine with the Rudds [Colonel Lockhart's sister and her husband] to-morrow, and Sturgises on Monday. Theodore Martin is to have Princess Louise and a few friends to a luncheon and Shakespearian reading on Wednesday. Shylock is the play, and his wife is to be assisted by Irving, &c.: it will be quite historical in theatricals.

Mr Gathorne Hardy (now Lord Cranbrook) was, when John Blackwood alluded to him in the preceding letter, Secretary for War. He had recently been his guest at Randolph Crescent on opening the Conservative Club at Edinburgh, the members of which had given him a banquet in the Music Hall.

John Blackwood to General W. G. Hamley.

EDINBURGH, *Dec.* 23, 1877.

I am greatly taken with Mr Hardy. He is a powerful, able man, and fit, I think, to take the helm in a storm. He felt the fall of Plevna was putting things on a new basis. The helplessness of Greece I imagine the greatest difficulty in any arrangement among the Powers.

I have often heard him express the strongest admiration for Mr Hardy's powers and usefulness. He considered him to be one of the ablest men our party had at that time, and a very great loss by his removal to the Upper House.

The war question was still uppermost when he next wrote.

John Blackwood to William Blackwood.

LONDON, *Feb.* 25, 1878.

I had a most pleasant luncheon and private talk with Lord John [Manners] yesterday. He feels as we do that the Russians cannot wish a war by which they could only suffer loss, but from their rapacity and deceitfulness the catastrophe might be brought on. His feeling evidently was that we should have acted sooner, and if we had occupied Gallipoli it would have been impregnable. Even now, if there are any Turks to defend the lines, our ships on each side of the point could quite command. He says the Turks have still an army of something like 150,000, although divided at different stations. This was Baker Pasha's information. Hardy spoke much in the same way about the Russians and their intentions on Saturday evening. It is ticklish work as can be, but I think war will tide over. We had a cheery dinner at the Trollopes' yesterday. Anthony has come back in great force : Lord John says he is like to drive them all mad at the weary Copyright Commission, going over all the ground that has been discussed in his absence. Walking up Bond Street this morning, who should I meet but old Winterhalter [a well-known courier], quite disengaged and ready to

follow Monr., Madame, and Mees to the end of the world. It
seemed so providential that we have engaged him.

On the 27th he writes to William Blackwood after
the party at Sir Theodore Martin's :—

MY DEAR WILLIE,—We have just got back from the reading
at Theodore's, which was an uncommon treat. She [Lady
Martin] was first-rate as Portia, Moritz the Hungarian—who,
they say, is to astonish the stage—Shylock, and Irving Bassanio.
I think the Hungarian will do, but it is difficult to tell in a
reading, where he could not let out his voice. He gives one
the idea of being a clever fellow. The Princess [Louise] had
a dress something like Mary's, and looked very well. Tennyson
was there, and as it broke up we had an opportunity of speaking
to him and recalling our day with him at his home at Freshwater. He hoped that we would come back if we were ever
in that part. He is looking well, and younger than I expected,
nor had he so much of a careworn look as he had.

The interest of the moment, the prospects of war,
was passing over when he next wrote to his nephew,
though not the necessity, in his opinion, of being
prepared for it. He writes :—

March 5, 1878.

The Hamleys have just left me. William has begun his
paper. Ned has heard nothing of his appointment, but every
one gives the "intelligence" to him. We are dining with the
Wolseleys to-night, and I daresay we shall hear all there is
about war news. Brackenbury [now Sir Henry] and Wolseley
were both very warlike last week, but will hardly be so much
so now. I always thought it would slip past for the present;
but it is in the air everywhere, and we should be armed to the
teeth. I have written to that effect to Cowell.

From these references to public and other matters
of interest it will be seen that though the Editor
was not writing any of the Magazine articles, he was

the mainspring of their origin, and was busily collecting every *on dit* or item of information likely to be useful to his writers, making his own notes as he went along, and shaping those opinions which were presently to be formulated in 'Maga.' This garnering of the passing thoughts and impressions of the day was an important part of his work, and for which he had a special knack. He seemed to remember a conversation, and refer to it with the same ease as if it were a letter, and having possessed himself of what was really valuable in it, he allowed the superfluous matter to drop.

Mr Herbert Cowell, whose name is mentioned in the preceding letter as writing a political article for the Magazine, was then, we may say, a well-experienced and steady contributor, and is now perhaps the oldest in the ranks of 'Maga's' band. He is a writer whose extensive knowledge of politics, gained by the close and shrewd observation of years, both in India and at home, has made him an authority in those matters, and a very valuable contributor to that branch of literature, which has always been of dominant importance in 'Blackwood.' We find a letter addressed to him as far back as 1854, and it is pleasant to read the Editor's remark on his young correspondent, then an undergraduate at Oxford, — Mr Cowell was only seventeen when he wrote this first paper, which was entitled " Conservative Reascendancy Considered," — and to find him to-day still true to his colours, and occasionally writing, as ably as ever, on the topics which have always interested him.

John Blackwood to his Brother Major William Blackwood.

Feb. 5, 1854.

From the terms of Mr Cowell's note I think he must be a very clever fellow, and I argue well of his paper from the diffidence with which he expresses himself regarding his first success.

The next refers to the approaching retirement of Mr Simpson—

John Blackwood to William Blackwood.

LONDON, *Feb.* 27, 1878.

I would have written to Simpson, but I have been sitting here all day despatching necessary notes and visitors, and one does not like to write about what one feels so much when there is an incessant rush going on. His well-known mark, G. S., across a note, indicating that something had been attended to, quite affected me this morning. It has just been announced that Bessie [his niece, Miss Blackwood] is in the drawing-room, so I shall finish now and go down to her.—Ever yrs. affecte.,

JOHN BLACKWOOD.

P.S.—Bessie is looking blooming, and had a pleasant journey up.

In the same letter he alludes to a contribution from a young writer, to whom it is evident Mrs Oliphant had stood god-mother, and was rejoicing in his good luck—

I read the "Ride Across the Peloponnesus"; it is too boyish, but it is lively and nice. Mrs Oliphant lunched with us to-day, and says the writer will go mad with delight. Of all people, he turns out to be a son of Macmillan's, and is a singularly clever, nice, modest lad. I think I remember seeing him at Eton. Mrs O. herself has no intentions for this month. She was looking very well.

From these extracts it is easy to understand that

in spite of the cold and fogs, London was very enthralling. However, we got away somehow, the last adieus were made, the letters written, and the last parting instructions were poured into the ears of Mr Langford, who accompanied us to the station, and we started on our journey to Italy the second week in March. At Florence we found the same fierce cold wind which had pursued us all along the Riviera, and my father, who was suffering from a cough and difficulty of breathing, often wished himself back in his own comfortable house. At Florence a letter from Mr Story told us that Mrs Story was in Florence, having come to see her first grandson. Miss Story had married Signor Peruzzi, the Sindic of Florence, and we found Mrs Story staying at their house in the Via dei Seragli. Mr Story wrote from Rome :—

I have engaged rooms for you at the Costanzi. . . . The Bristol was full, and General Grant is just arriving to-morrow. I know you LOVE him, and of course I supposed you would share your room with him—perhaps even your bed—still I did not so arrange it. · You must go and see my wife and daughter when you are in Florence, they are at No. 6 Via dei Seragli, and my wife will tell you all about your rooms here. . . . The spring has lost its temper within this last week and cut up rough. All winter has been like spring, gentle and mild, and now spring has put on the lion-skin of winter and roars, but it is only a moment of ill-temper. To-day is enchanting. I am sorry that the mistral fought you so on the Cornice Road.— With kindest regards to you all, ever yours,

W. W. STORY.

My father's only request had been that the rooms should be *al sole,* and as near the Barberini Palace, where Mr Story lived, as possible. The rooms he took for us at the Costanzi answered both these requirements, looking straight over a sunny garden towards the Barberini, which rose an imposing mass over the roofs of a few intervening houses. There we were installed on the 23rd March. Lord Derby's resignation, as the following letter indicates, was at this time exciting the political world in England :—

John Blackwood to William Blackwood

HÔTEL COSTANZI, ROME, *March* 30, 1878.

We have not the text of Dizzy's speech on Lord Derby's resignation. He seems to have been dignified, but we should have let him go long ago. A man who will not work kindly with you is worse than an enemy, and the greater his name the sooner should he be turned adrift.

In a letter to the same, written a few days later, he says :—

April 2, 1878.

We are still without positive information here as to what our Ministerial appointments are. I should hardly think Hardy would like being moved from the War Office at such a crisis.

The words which follow have a curious interest now, when the eyes of all Europe have but recently been centred on Greece and the disposal of Crete :—

Apparently the ground we are taking with Russia is that we cannot trust a word she says, and are consequently arming to the teeth. That is the best way of avoiding war and holding. It would be very comical if we went in with Greece upon our arm, but nothing else would give us such an easy chance of getting Crete and all the strong places we want. Greece would hand over the defence of her grand nationality to us with the greatest pleasure.

Very soon after our arrival, my father had a bad cough that kept him a prisoner to the house for many days. The effects lasted so long that they debarred

him to a great extent from the pleasure he had
anticipated in revisiting Rome — the Rome he had
longed to see again, ever since he last saw it with the
dome of St Peter's glistening in the sun as he and his
brother drove away over the Campagna more than forty
years before. One felt that he was looking upon the
same scenes, but with different eyes. He left it a boy,
with his life before him, hopeful and steadfast in his
aims no doubt, but with the future uncertain, as it
must be to all who have to make their own way in the
world,—was it to be success or failure? The readers
of these pages have probably answered that query for
themselves long ere this stage of the narrative. This
second visit to Rome found him a man in middle life,
with his intellectual powers matured, and possessed of
the culture and experience gained in a lifetime passed
in close acquaintance with some of the brightest intellects of his day. One of those whose talents and
personal charm had always greatly attracted him was
Mr W. W. Story, the American sculptor, who possessed, as we have already mentioned, the twofold gift
of song. This distinguished artist had for many years
made his home in Rome, like others of his fellow-
countrymen whom the calls of art have brought across
the Atlantic, only to identify them so closely with the
best of our Old World interests and traditions that
the country of their adoption seems to be their natural
home, and one cannot imagine them living anywhere
else. John Blackwood's acquaintance with Mr Story
dates back to old days when they used to meet at Mr
Sturgis's house, and Sir Edward Hamley was, we
believe, the first to draw his friend the Editor's attention to the sculptor's poetical gift.

Colonel E. B. Hamley to John Blackwood.

July 2, 1865.

Story's poetical sketches are quite as forcible as Browning's, and infinitely clearer and more intelligible than the fantastic productions of that queer genius.

Another charm of Story's poetry, besides its lucidity, which, as Hamley insists, must render it more acceptable to general readers, was the admirable rhythm of his verses, which runs on like music through the different poems, notably in "Giannone" and some others of the modern poems, which illustrate conspicuously his powers of versification. Most of these appeared in the Magazine, and were afterwards collected in a volume entitled 'Graffiti d'Italia.' Of the longer pieces, "Ginevra" is a touching medieval love poem, and was considered by John Blackwood an especially fine piece of writing.

John Blackwood to W. W. Story.

Feb. 24, 1866.

I enclose proof of "Ginevra," which continues to strike me as being a very beautiful and touching poem. Some passages are, I think, admirable, full of passion and power.

Referring to the length of the poem, which was its drawback for the Magazine, he decides that none of it could be spared, and they must divide it into two parts :—

This opening affords such a faithful and beautifully painted picture of the state of things which produce the catastrophe of the story, that I do not see how it could be dispensed with. . . . There is a very great merit in the air of truth you have given to the poem; one feels as if it were the sad tale of a real Ginevra of Siena. This power of giving a lifelike reality to the story you are telling inclines me to think you would succeed as a novelist if your chisel left you time.

Another of these poems, "Cleopatra," attracted much attention, not only from its own powerful originality but from its being the inspiration of the same artist who had given that splendid representation of the "Serpent of Old Nile," whose beauty formed such a memorable feature amongst the sculptures in the Great Exhibition, and is considered by many to be Story's greatest work. Amongst his writings published separately was a poem in blank verse, which had for its subject Nero, about whom he endeavoured ingeniously to weave a dramatic interest. But the subject was, as John Blackwood thought, too repellent, baffling even Story's powers to make it popular, and Blackwood wrote :—

Feb. 8, 1876.

I much fear my original impression, that nothing would make Nero popular, is to prove right. I could not get any of my friends to take up your strange pet *con amore.*

Story's views and impressions on Art were given in a series of papers entitled 'Conversations in a Studio,' in the form of conversations, which first appeared in the Magazine in 1874 and were continued at intervals. Other and very interesting matter was described by him in the 'Roba di Roma,' which, as its title implies, comprises much strange "stuff" or "matter" of an out-of-the-way and interesting description, some of it involving great research in a portion of Rome rather outside the tourist's beat, and having for its centre the gloomy castle of St Angelo. This castle, situated on the farther bank of the Tiber, once an emperor's tomb and then a medieval fortress, teems with the dark histories of the past, which lend even to this day a certain

fascinating, haunting gloom to that region of old
Rome known as Trastévere. Story's artist mind
seized upon this unspoilt portion of the city, and he
has preserved for us many traditions and old-world
stories that might have slipped out of sight, with
many of the picturesque customs and national characteristics which are fast disappearing from what was
once the most conservative city in the world. "How
quiet Rome seems to be keeping," John Blackwood
wrote to Mr Story in 1867, after the war was over.
"If I were the Pope I would stick to the Vatican
at all hazards, and if the Romans have any sense
they will keep him there." Pio Nono held the same
views, as we all know, and the "Prisoner of the
Vatican" remained in that modified seclusion, which,
like many other anomalies, has come to be accepted
as quite in the order of things. It will be seen from
these letters, and the many allusions to Mr Story,
what an important factor he was in the pleasure
which my father had promised himself in this visit
to Rome, and which only his state of health, which
was occasioning him suffering and ourselves great
anxiety, prevented him from thoroughly enjoying.
There were, however, some bright days when he was
able to enjoy his friend's society, and of them we
shall endeavour to recall the brightest portion.

As soon as he was well enough to go out he went to
Mr Story's studio to have the treat of seeing his friend
at work, one of the pleasures he had always looked
forward to. Their "conversations in a studio" would
no doubt, if printed, have been entertaining, though
not perhaps on the lines laid down by "Wilton" and
"Mallet." On that occasion I remember we found Mr

Story at work with the clay on his hands, but he left
it and took us round and showed us the treasures of
the studio. There was one room filled with lovely
women—Electra, Polyxena, Cleopatra. He told us
he employed no models for these beautiful faces—he
had an ideal in his own mind ; and certainly it seemed
to us the right way for successfully portraying these
heroines I have mentioned, whose counterparts it
would not be easy to discover amongst the herd of
models in the streets of Rome or elsewhere. For
some time after this my father was confined to the
house by a second bronchial attack, and when he
struggled out of it he was of course much weakened,
and unable for sightseeing or visiting. But many
friends came to see him. Professor George Ramsay,
Sir Augustus Paget, Mr T. A. Trollope, all used to
come and sit with him, and earned the gratitude of
his womenkind by cheering him up with their pleasant
talk. Dr Niven of the American Church was also a
frequent visitor, and Miss Hampton Brewster, a clever
American lady, a friend of the Storys. All were
grieved to find him so long a prisoner and unable to
enjoy the delights of a Roman spring. When he was
able to go out once more the drives through the
Borghese, the Doria Pamfili Gardens, and other well-
known resorts, were the greatest pleasure to him, the
day usually ending with a visit to the Palazzo
Barberini—up the long marble staircase, where he
liked to track Mr Story by the cigarette-ends he
declared must be his. There in those cool darkened
rooms one stepped out of the dust and glare of the city
into an atmosphere that was always congenial and
reposeful. My father used to heave a sigh of relief

as he sank into one of the comfortable lounges where
Mrs Story would install him, telling him in her kindly
way that having come, he must stop there and not
leave them till the sun went down.   Then she would
throw up the sun-blinds and show him the far-stretch-
ing view over the red roofs to the Campagna. The
recollection of those days, never, alas! to come again,
must be fresh in the memories of many like ourselves
who have experienced the hospitalities of Mr and Mrs
Story at the Barberini Palace.   There all that was
most interesting in Roman society seemed to be drawn
as by a magnet.

At their large receptions were to be found the chief
Italian families, English and Americans, artistic and
other celebrities there; and in these large assemblies
one might find oneself wedged in the crowd between
General Grant and a Cardinal in all his glory.
Several times a little select luncheon-party was arranged for my father.   On one occasion I remember
we met there Miss Anne Hampton Brewster, the
American authoress, already mentioned.   She had
been editress of a Boston newspaper, but had forsaken that line for the more reposeful occupation of
writing upon antiquarian matters connected with the
scavazioni continually progressing at Rome.   She
was immensely interested in meeting the Editor of
'Blackwood,' and I remember my father was drawn
on to talk by her and Story of his recollections of
famous persons, the many amusing incidents and
strange rencontres he had had during his life, in the
way he only would talk when there were but few, and
a congenial few, present.   Mr Story would take up
the thread sometimes, with the gay humour that

made whatever he said illuminate the subject in hand. Bulwer Lytton and his son the late Lord Lytton were often mentioned, and Thackeray, who was an intimate friend and *habitué* of the Storys' house. My father had a perfect horror of that bore of society the regular *raconteur*, who, as he said, dragged in his good story "by the heels" on all occasions, regardless of everything, or who rode a topic to death. His own excellent memory and way of assimilating facts and incidents that struck him enabled him to drift easily from one subject to another. Occasionally his experiences would carry him back to Scotland and his own country-people. One story of his, I remember, delighted our American friends immensely. An inquiry was once being made as to the cause of the potato disease, and a number of leading farmers and agriculturists were invited to give their views on the subject in the 'Agricultural Journal,' which the Blackwoods published. Among the many answers received for publication one took the palm: the writer said, "I thocht at first it was a dispensation of Almichty God, but now I believe it is an insect." There were shrieks of delight over this. These few quiet afternoons with his friends was all that he was able for in the way of society while in Rome, and formed the most enjoyable part of his visit. One other call he made—on an old lady, who had been a friend of Professor Aytoun's, Miss Haig of Bemersyde, the descendant of the family of whom Thomas the Rhymer sang—

> "Tyde what may betyde,
> There'll aye be Haig of Bemersyde."

She was the last of her race, and had the mournful

conviction that in her the prophecy would be defeated, when it occurred to her to adopt some one of the same name, and her choice fell on Captain Haig, the Duke of Edinburgh's equerry, and she chose him to succeed her. Her villa, not far from the Borghese gardens, was one of the prettiest of the private residences near Rome. It was surrounded by a vineyard and high walls, and the little door in the wall which admitted hardly gave one the idea of the fine gardens beyond nor the splendid views from the house. " I see Soracte every morning," the old lady said to us, " and know by his colour if it is to be a fine or a wet day." My father was delighted with the house and grounds and the fine air, which was really refreshing after Rome. And Miss Haig kindly suggested he should come and stay with her and regain his strength before setting out on his homeward journey; but he did not feel equal to that, and we made our adieus charged with many messages to Miss Aytoun and her sister Isabella and other old friends in Scotland whom she had not seen for years. On most of our sightseeing expeditions he had, to his great disappointment, been unable to accompany us; but I remember that he was with us on our first visit to the Forum, and that he pointed out to me the Via Sacra, the road the fathers of our faith had trod, and the prisons where they suffered. He always seemed to be thoroughly imbued with what one can only describe as the genius or spirit of the place. It all was real to him, so easy to live again the lives of those who have gone before, whose monuments, tombs, and statues greeted us at every turn. Marcus

Aurelius galloping down from the Capitol on his charger seemed at last a personage as real as King Umberto himself in his Victoria dashing past us on his way to the Quirinale. Meanwhile, by the end of April, it began to be very hot in Rome, and most of our friends that were birds of passage had moved off; even the denizens of the Barberini, who did not trouble themselves much about what the weather was doing outside its thick walls, were beginning to prepare for their departure, and my father became more than desirous to get off, when he wrote as follows :—

John Blackwood to William Blackwood.

HÔTEL COSTANZI, ROME, *April* 29.

MY DEAR WILLIE,— This confounded bronchitis sticks so close to me that Aitken [the doctor] will not sanction a day for us to start for Florence, and during the last day or two, although the weather is fine as can be, he makes me keep in the house.

At last the longed-for permission was given, and on the 6th May we set out on the first stage towards home, reaching Paris at the end of May. My father's health improved very much on the journey, and he wrote in very good spirits from Paris :—

John Blackwood to William Blackwood.

HÔTEL DE RIVOLI, PARIS, *May* 31, 1878.

I seem to get better as I come north, and I hope devoutly the improvement from, or in spite of, the cold weather will last. Paris is not hot—indeed yesterday we had a fire. We had a charming breakfast with Lindau at his rooms to-day, and then did the Exhibition under his guidance. Marshall is "sair hadden doun" with Japanese work,—he could not get away from the Legation to-day.

On the occasion above alluded to, when break-
fasting with Mr Lindau, I remember our admiring the
situation of his house in the Avenue Friedland. He
then described to us how he had lived there before
the war, and the strange anomaly it had seemed to
find himself with the armies of his country laying
siege to his own home, and devoutly hoping that no
shell would burst near his dwelling, and wondering
if his dog had shared the fate of many others of
its kind, perhaps forming a dinner for his servant.
After the entry of the Prussians, as soon as he could
he made his way to the house, and found, to his
delight, that his Breton servant had gone to his
home in Brittany and taken the dog with him.
He also told us of the honesty and carefulness of
this man, who could have had but slight expectation of ever being called to account by him, and yet
that he found everything as he had left it, not even
the firewood touched.

My father had recovered wonderfully by this time,
and on level ground hardly suffered from the breath-
lessness which had been such a distressing part of
his illness in Italy. He went with us one day to
have a look at the Exhibition, where Mr Lindau
constituted himself our guide, and saved us no doubt
many a weary, useless trudge round those intermin-
able halls and courts by taking us straight to what
was most worth seeing. The portraits interested my
father immensely : he gave the palm to Bonnat, and
said if any one would tempt him to sit for his portrait
it would be Bonnat. How much we wished he would
have had his portrait painted by any good artist.

The oil-painting we have of him was not good enough, and never pleased us nor any of his friends : it lacked force and expression. "It hasna the licht o' his ee," was his "caddie's" (old Bob's) criticism on it, and it was quite true. After a week in Paris we crossed over to London. It was then the middle of June, and the country looked fresh and green, undimmed then by summer drought. My father began to feel happy again,—he was on his way home, and the shadow cast by his illness was passing away. In London he did not intend to linger, all his anxiety was to get home. A few of his more intimate friends were looking out for us, and no one welcomed him more kindly than the Anthony Trollopes, who knew from their relatives how ill he had been in Rome. Mr Trollope wrote to him :—

DEAR BLACKWOOD,—I am so happy to welcome you back. Will you and Mrs Blackwood, or either, be at home at 2.30 to-day ? If so I and my Missis will call. I suppose you are not off to the races.—Yours always, A. T.

A little later he went to Edinburgh with my mother, and wrote to me very cheerfully just after his arrival :

John Blackwood to his Daughter.

3 RANDOLPH CRESCENT, *June* 14, 1878,

MY DEAR MARY,—We got down all right, although we missed you much on the journey, especially at luncheon, where your mother was rather embarrassed by the paper containing the salt, which sprinkled itself impartially all over the place. We got into Edinburgh station as the clock struck seven, and were welcomed by Willie, King [our coachman], the man with the wooden leg, and all the loungers of the place who could carry stick or travelling-bag . . . Although I coughed a bit during the night I am very well to-day. I have had two notes from Jack—short, but to the purpose. He comes over this afternoon from Fife. It will be the end of next week before we go to Strathtyrum. I am not to be allowed to play golf in the meantime, but I can walk round with a good match, which is the next highest pleasure in existence.

CHAPTER XI.

MRS OLIPHANT AND NEW RECRUITS.

WE have now introduced in these pages the names of
most of the eminent writers who stand forth prominently as having been continuously associated with
the greater part of John Blackwood's career as an
editor and publisher. There still, however, remain
to be mentioned some well-known authors who came
to him during the later years of his life. And, *place
aux dames*, there is yet much that is interesting to

be told regarding her whose indefatigable pen served
him so faithfully and so long.   Mrs Oliphant's place
in a work of this kind is difficult to determine,
for the reason that there is not a year, hardly a
month, from the date of her earliest contribution
down to her last, in which she is not represented in
the archives of the Magazine.   Following her brilliant
course up to the last article she wrote for John
Blackwood in 1879, we find that this portion alone
covers a tract of twenty-seven years.   We have
drawn attention to the opening novels of the series,
the 'Chronicles of Carlingford' and other works that
occupied her in the early "sixties."   Those early
years were marked by sorrows which for long left
their trace on Mrs Oliphant's naturally cheerful and
happy temperament.   How bravely she struggled on
in her sadness and bereavement is evinced by the
mass of work she accomplished at that time, finding, perhaps, her only relief in the toil which one
of less courageous, less disciplined mind would have
felt to be impossible.

John Blackwood to Mrs Oliphant.

EDINBURGH, *April* 15, 1864.

Your corrected proof has not turned up yet, but I am in
hopes that you may have taken it with you to Capri. . . .
The view from Capri must be something wonderful.   I recollect thinking Sorrento the most beautiful spot in the world.
You should go over there. . . .   I fully understand your feelings about returning home, and earnestly hope that change of
scene and air will do you good, and that through your remaining children comfort and happiness will find their way into
your heart again.   I shall be truly glad to see any miscellaneous paper from you, and shall welcome it heartily for many
reasons.

When Mrs Oliphant wrote the following she was thinking of going to Capri :—

Mrs Oliphant to John Blackwood.

68 CAPO LE CASE, ROME, *2nd April* 1864.

I think the story ['The Perpetual Curate,' one of the "Carlingford" series] may be wound up in two or three numbers more, which, if nothing happens to me, I will try to get done in Capri. One object in going there is for quiet—the sea has a consolatory voice. I don't think there is any likelihood that I shall see you in England this year.

She was feeling deeply discouraged by the second loss she had sustained in the death of her daughter, a child of eleven. She adds :—

I have no wish to go home. To do so, diminished and impoverished as I am, is more than I can bear. One's courage may be good for once and not answer a second time. The effect of the second blow, so sudden and unforeseen, makes it look as if this was the rule and order of my life.

The fateful note is struck here with a mournful presentiment of what was to follow in the later years when the bereaved mother had to bear still further all the sufferings which death's ruthless hand can inflict on a tender loving heart. There were, however, many bright and happy years intervening, when her sorrows were sweetened and her toils lightened by the joys of friendship and the success and renown that were accruing to her from her literary achievements.

The following to Miss Mozley again shows her hard at work, and my father striving to interest her in the remarks her writings elicited from other literati :—

John Blackwood to Miss Mozley.

The "Carlingford" novels are by Mrs Oliphant, and I am not surprised that you did not think them by the author of the "Margaret Maitland" series. She is a very remarkable woman, and I think 'Miss Marjoribanks' promises to excel all she has hitherto done. Some of her miscellaneous essays, too, are wonderfully good. She is in low spirits, having lost her only daughter, a little girl about eleven, last year, and I sent her such of your remarks as I thought might have a cheering effect. Her reply is that she was only eighteen when she wrote her first novel, and she ought to have improved by this time. She adds: "I remember that once in a time I refused to believe that Bulwer Lytton wrote 'The Caxtons.' As to your courteous critic's remarks, I am quite conscious of the 'to be sure's' and the 'naturally,' but then a faultless style is like a faultless person, highly exasperating, and if one did not leave those little things to be taken hold of perhaps one might fare worse."

John Blackwood's letters appear to have been to Mrs Oliphant, as they were to many others, sources of inspiration and hopefulness. Sometimes, even when not writing for him, Mrs Oliphant has told me, she felt impelled to ask his opinion on a piece of work, sure that she would not ask in vain for a sound and helpful criticism, and sure, too, that he would not grudge the trouble, even to the extent of sitting up at night "to gallop through it," as he expresses it. He saw on this occasion enough in his gallop to commend it at once very highly to Mr Collins, to whom he wrote next day:—

John Blackwood to Rev. W. Lucas Collins.

Along with this I send you by book post the first sheets of a 'Life of Edward Irving,' by Mrs Oliphant. The work is to be

complete in two volumes, and for her sake I wish much to have
a good review of it, especially seeing that I have never had
an opportunity of saying a word for her in 'Maga.'   Feeling in want of advice, she sent me the MS. last summer of
first half of first volume, which I read and thought perfectly
beautiful.   These sheets came yesterday, and I sat up and
galloped through them, but could not read close enough to
form any opinion worth having; but I did not fancy them as
strongly as I did the early part of the narrative.   Besides,
Irving loses my sympathy very much when he gets up to
London; but I think her part is admirably done, and when I
read the first half, which I did carefully, I thought it as fine
a bit of biography as ever I met with.

The next letter, to the Count de Montalembert,
refers to the third volume of his 'Monks of the
West,' of which, as we have stated, Mrs Oliphant
had already translated the first and second volumes.

August 23, 1865.

I make this offer under the impression that Mrs Oliphant
will undertake the translation.   This I consider important to
you also, as I am certain that *now* she could make a really
exquisite translation such as is almost never met with.

Her residence abroad, and the translation she had
been doing so effectively, seem to have turned Mrs
Oliphant's attention towards the subject of French
periodicals; but my father is not very encouraging in
that direction.

I enclose proof of your paper on French periodicals, which I
have read with much amusement and complete confirmation
of the opinion I formed of the 'Révue' when long ago (I am
not strong enough for such feats now) I read the 'Deux
Mondes' steadily for a couple of years to see if I could get any
hints on papers worth translating in the Magazine, and found
nothing except two pretty little stories, by Mme. Reybaud I

think they were   The utmost praise that can be given to them is that, in spite of their graceful command of language, more successful than the Germans in trying to be *vif*, they *have* succeeded in being heavy.

The following amusing note will find an answering chord of sympathy in the minds of any persons who have ever experienced the anxiety attendant on the non-arrival of "proofs" :—

John Blackwood to Mrs Oliphant.

EDINBURGH, *Dec.* 26, 1865.

Your proof did not get back to me until Sunday, and as the printers were clamorous for upmaking on Saturday I made up without " Miss M.," which I was sorry for when I saw your note. It may be a satisfaction to you to know that I had a horrible nightmare last night, and dreamed that the Magazine had all been made up wrong, Mr Hutchison, the manager of the printing office, having unaccountably gone and printed papers that had been used before, and I still more unaccountably never having discovered the mess until my copy of the complete No. reached Randolph Crescent. I awoke swearing furiously, and demanding of the terrified Hutchison how cancels could be managed in time. It was an Editor's dream with a vengeance, and whether the Christmas mince-pies or the leaving out of " Miss M." had most to do with it I know not. I wish I could venture upon a double number of the Magazine, and so get myself out of the fix in which I am. I used to pique myself upon the sort of instinctive skill with which I balanced my quantities, never having to reject a good article for lack of space or to accept an indifferent one to fill up. I am half inclined to tell you to do the paper upon the religious or irreligious movement in Scotland. My objection to the movement is that it unsettles the creed of old women of both sexes to no purpose, as I do not see that any of the new lights either do or can offer any substitute. Do you think you could do any good ? I was in Glasgow the other day, and met Norman Macleod. We had some good fun over the persecution he is undergoing. In addi-

tion to the theological outpourings there are songs and carica-
tures against him. It is too bad, but

> Norman is a bairn of Grace,—
> Blessings on his sonsie face—

and I have no doubt he will pull through.

My father's sympathy for Dr Macleod in the persecution he was then undergoing has already been
mentioned. It is difficult, where such a wide range
of subjects was coming under Mrs Oliphant's notice,
to take up any one paper and point to it as an example of her skill as a reviewer. We are slightly
helped out of this *embarras des richesses* when she has
grouped her subjects or given us a series of papers
illustrating the same period or the same theme. Of
the former we must give a prominent place to her
'Historical Sketches of the Reign of George II.'
These Sketches were afterwards published in two
volumes, the characteristic of each subject forming
the title of the chapter. Sir Robert Walpole, who
heads the list, figures as "The Minister," and a
very curious and interesting picture is given by
Mrs Oliphant of this remarkable man, who served
his country faithfully and yet earned but little
love or gratitude for his services. Chesterfield follows next as "The Man of the World," and formed
another remarkable piece of portraiture. Of these
two John Blackwood says to the Author, March 31,
1868, "Walpole is an admirable and beautiful sketch;
I have no doubt Chesterfield will be as good." Of
"The Sailor," Lord Anson, who pleased him, he says,
"You bring out the story of the tough determined
sailor in a very striking way." But perhaps the gem

of the series was the delightful picture Mrs Oliphant gave of Bishop Berkeley, that most lovable of philosophers, whose zealous efforts on behalf of Christianising the native population of America, if not crowned with much success, still sheds a pleasant light upon an age not much given to philanthropic endeavour.

John Blackwood to Mrs Oliphant.

EDINBURGH, *Dec.* 14, 1868.

Along with this I send proof of your sketch of Berkeley. You have made a charming paper of it. So very interesting have you made the beautiful story of his life, that I am quite interested to know what became of his children. I never heard. Do you know anything of their fate? Your last sentence contains a very beautiful and true thought. Some readers will not catch it, but I fear it will be difficult to make it plainer. As for philosophers generally you rank them more highly than I do. Grant Berkeley's theory about matter, and it does not carry an inch farther in understanding the mystery in which the whole world of knowing and being is shrouded. In this respect it is like Ferrier's "Ego," without which he maintained nothing existed. I remember that philosopher smiling grimly when one day in his garden, after he had given me a long chapter on the eternal "Ego," I exclaimed, "Why then, by your theory the world ends where each man dies," and that may explain what has always rather puzzled me, that the day of judgment should be at the end of the world, and yet immediately after death. Ferrier wrote such a beautiful clear style, that he nearly succeeded in showing that all their theories were bottles of smoke. I speak lightly, but Ferrier was, I think, about the best philosophical writer I ever read, and was nearer finding out something than any of them. On the second last slip I have marked a passage which I should wish either to be modified or deleted. It was not in the least surprising that Berkeley in those days did not think of negro emancipation or the removal of R. C. disabilities. There are many tolerably sensible people who think that the way in which our West Indian negroes were emancipated was a cruel piece of humbug. As to the removal of Roman Catholic disabilities, I think Berkeley could ask you now to show what good it has done; they will always ask for more and more, and I do not blame them for it. You will have observed that the Pope is so pleased with Scotland's support of Gladstone that he has given us a whole hierarchy.

The beautiful thought in the last sentence of Mrs Oliphant's chapter on Bishop Berkeley to which my father draws attention seems intended to point out that, though his intellectual strivings may not have been entirely effectual, yet the lesson of his life will never be lost. The words referred to are these: "Knowledge may fail, though it is everlasting; Man, the creature of a day, is the only thing on earth which lives for ever."

Of the same kind as the preceding were several sketches of authors which she did for the Magazine. The letters they evoked from the Editor give his views of the matter in hand, with sometimes a remark calculated to modify his correspondent's tone or convert her to his own. Most people who know how to take thankfully the good things the gods send us will agree with him as to the desirability of dealing gently with the weaknesses of geniuses. Considering how poor the world would be without them, it seemed to him like watering our best wine to detract in any way from their strength.

John Blackwood to Mrs Oliphant.

EDINBURGH, *Jan.* 13, 1871.

Along with this I send proof of your "Cowper," which contains many most excellent things and is most interesting reading. The prevailing defect is that you give much too harsh a view of Cowper. You make no allowance for the suffering nervous man—indeed it is really painful to read what you say of the Gentle Poet. He was not a wretch concentred all on self. On margin of proof I have made some comments. That shrinking from going through the forms necessary to secure a livelihood for himself is not an evidence of selfish laziness, but of an extreme nervousness of temperament always on the verge of insanity and entirely to be pitied. A very little alteration will make the paper first-rate. As it stands it affords a pitiable and painful picture of a man of Genius, and for the good of the world our Geniuses should always be draped as gracefully as possible.

In the following he congratulates Mrs Oliphant on giving herself time for miscellaneous writings, she having just completed her novel, 'The Brownlows.' He also alludes with satisfaction to her "Sketch" of Hume, who figures as "The Sceptic" in the historical series we have described.

John Blackwood to Mrs Oliphant.

March 31, 1869.

I am glad to hear you have cleared your decks, and are ready for miscellaneous work. I am greatly taken with the line you seem to have taken about Hume. Other sceptics are so violent that they show an uneasy consciousness that there is somebody looking after them, but he seems to have thought and digested away with a possibly vague idea that if he did no harm, no harm was likely to be done to him hereafter—a creed which in many respects is most useful, and, in spite of our national abhorrence of good works, ought to be, and is, a part of all belief.

In the same letter he tells her he has made several ineffectual attempts to read 'The Ring and the Book,' and wonders how many of his (Browning's) "most deluded admirers could read through it. The other night I was struggling away at 'The Ring and the Book,' and picked up the book Puck had left on the sofa: it was 'The Lady of the Lake,' and I had a delightful evening with my old friend in, I daresay, the hundredth reading."

Froude comes in for the weight of his indignation in regard to his treatment of Mary Queen of Scots. The celebrated chapter on the Fotheringay tragedy, with the merciless painting of the last scenes, particularly the execution, filled him with anger and disgust. He writes thus to Mrs Oliphant: "She may have had false hair, although I do not believe it, and certainly would not have mentioned it if I had." The change, too, as described in her appearance immediately after death, could not, he said, have been true, "unless we are to suppose they kept a magical Madame Rachel for her at Fotheringay." He goes on to say, "I know Froude, and he is a very pleasant fellow, but he must be severely punished for this," and Mrs Oliphant was instructed to strike and spare not.

The death of Charles Dickens in 1871 had produced much literature on the great novelist and his writings. The next letter refers to Mrs Oliphant's paper on his works, and while conveying a high compliment to her critical judgment, the Editor throws in a few of his own kindly views just to give the impression of Dickens's influence for good which he wished to have conveyed.

John Blackwood to Mrs Oliphant.

EDINBURGH, *April* 25, 1871.

It is a most admirable and convincing piece of criticism, placing Dickens, I believe, about his right level. You do not, however, give him sufficient credit for the kindly influence of all his writings, nor point out with sufficient warmth how much harm a man with such influence might have done, and I incline for more kindly praise. I quite agree with you that his pathos, and the exuberant kindliness of some of his characters, are often very maudlin; but the failing is to virtue's side, and his first little Christmas book took the country by storm. I do not, however, know how I might like it now. What you say of the low level of his characters is exceedingly true, and I could almost believe you had seen a print where poor Dickens was drawn in his chair with all his characters hovering about him after the manner of Visions of Shakespeare. It was brought in to me by Henry, the waiter at the Burlington, who said, "Is'nt it touching, sir?" The effect was horribly grotesque, and I put it away with a shudder, thinking of the dead man. I have not been able to use the "Cowper" this month, which I am vexed at, you have been so very good about it. I do not think you have ever written anything better in criticism than this on Dickens, and I think it will be accepted as the real award, so every care should be taken to have no expression which more devoted worshippers could take hold of and call harsh.

Of Mrs Oliphant's later novels, 'Valentine and his Brother,' published in the Magazine in 1873, was, John Blackwood considered, one of her very best. The setting of the novel was familiar ground to the authoress, being partly descriptive of Scottish country life and partly of Eton and school days.

John Blackwood to Mrs Oliphant.

EDIN., *March* 11, 1874.

I enclose proof of parts 4 and 5 of 'Valentine,' and they are very beautiful. It seems too long to dwell upon Valentine's boyhood, but it is all so good I could not suggest anything to be cut out. Old Mrs Moffat is very good, and the two children in the wood are delightful, quite a little Idyl. I enjoy the brothers Grender extremely. Your foot is on your native heath both in Eskside and at Eton, which is a great advantage. It is difficult to say what you are going to make of Val. himself, and I suppose you intend to keep it doubtful. The meeting at the end of part 5 promises wonderful complications.

The graceful manner in which Mrs Oliphant would

always drape the figure of any personality that
pleased or interested her, combining with it the
"touch of nature" that makes us love our kind, was
a strong element of her success as a biographer. Her
talents in this direction had been fully employed and
heartily encouraged by my father in his selection of
her as the writer of the various sketches of eminent
men we have mentioned. The following letter shows
his high appreciation of her biographical powers, and
his wish that she should devote herself more particularly to that branch of literature :—

John Blackwood to Mrs Oliphant.

EDINBURGH, *March* 16, 1876.

I enclose proof of your paper upon Norman Macleod, which
is simply beautiful. It reads like a poem, and is so true and
good all over. In reading it both last night and to-day tears
have come into my eyes repeatedly. I wish my brother Archie
and poor Janet had been alive to read it, as they were devoted
to Norman. Biography is about the greatest among your many
fortes, and I wish we could hit upon a subject where you could
write a book quite untrammelled. Montalembert should have
been, but it could not be.

Dr Norman Macleod, who is here so touchingly
alluded to as a personal friend, once contributed an
excellent "Curling Song" to the Magazine.

Another branch of work, apart from her writings,
which occupied Mrs Oliphant during the "seventies,"
was the editorship of the series known as "Foreign
Classics," which was published after the "Ancient
Classics," and was conducted on much the same lines.
The different volumes were all contributed by well-
known writers, and amongst the correspondence they
occasioned we find a very interesting letter from Mr

Hayward, who was then writing the Goethe volume. The views of such a well-known authority and essayist as to what constitutes "readability and attractiveness" are worth quoting :—

A. Hayward to John Blackwood.

8 ST JAMES STREET, *March* 6, 1878.

I am glad you like what you have seen. *That* is the essential point. I am comparatively indifferent about details, although I have carefully studied my effects. It is impossible to write about Goethe without taking into account the broad views taken by Carlyle and Lewes and others of certain portions of his life, but I agree with you that anything purely critical about either of them may be considered out of place. I have therefore struck out the concluding portion of the note at page 2, although if I only consulted my own judgment I should retain it. I am sure you must agree with me that readability and attractiveness are the grand points. I am convinced that the success of my articles (such as it is) is owing to what, strictly speaking, is their digressiveness.

The following letters refer to Mrs Oliphant's review in the Magazine of Sir Theodore Martin's ‘Life of the Prince Consort.’ This was a book which, it will be seen from John Blackwood's letters, had greatly pleased and interested him—not only on account of the subject of the Memoir, for whom, as we have stated, he felt genuine interest and admiration: he was also deeply interested in the book as a literary work, considering it a marvel of industry and research, and reflecting no small credit on the ability and good taste of his friend Sir Theodore Martin.

John Blackwood to Mrs Oliphant.

EDINBURGH, *Dec.* 4, 1874.

Along with this I send by book post the first volume of the ‘Life of Prince Albert,’ which please keep carefully out of sight until Tuesday, as there is desperate jealousy among the press about early copies. I read the volume yesterday. Take it altogether, it is a pleasant picture, and justifies the national devotion to the Queen. The Prince was evidently a good, warm-hearted man, with great trained abilities. There was apparently a sort of an English reserve about him which prevented him from making fresh friends and associates in this country. He seems more a German than an Englishman throughout, but I think none the worse of him for cleaving to his old Rosenau and his beloved family at home. I wish some , of his talk could have been given, or some of the little shades of domestic life thrown in to help the light of the picture. But Martin had a most difficult course to steer, and I think the book does immense credit to his taste and judgment.

After Mrs Oliphant had written her review my father writes :—

EDINBURGH, *Dec.* 17, 1874.

I enclose proof of the review of Prince Consort's Life, which I think you have done very well indeed. To me it is a very curious picture and touching. It proves that the pair were really good and sincere, and determined to do everything for the best in their station. It makes me understand the Queen's continued sorrow for the Prince, and it will have that effect on the public. Martin deserves immense credit. There is not a word that is fulsome or likely to turn away public sympathy, of which there was great danger in the circumstances, and there is not a thing told that can hurt the feelings of any one. If you can enlarge a little in the above direction, I think you will improve the paper, and be doing what is right. Do not burlesque the good Stockmar quite so much : a little of it is quite right, but keep your full idea of the character for a novel.

To the same :—

Jan. 18, 1875.

Yesterday I got a letter from Martin in which he says the Queen is greatly pleased with the review of the Prince Consort's Life, which she has heard is by *you.* She says, however, that it

is unjust to Stockmar, who was the last man in the world to
claim credit for anything he had done for the Prince or her,
and thought of nothing but their good.

When one turns over the pages and pages of letters
all addressed to this one correspondent, all either
suggesting subjects for her pen or accepting her own
selections, the question arises, When did she find time
to get through the mass of work they represent?
Even the inmates of her own home would find it
difficult to explain how it was accomplished.   Marvellous industry was a feature in her character, but
even that estimable trait is sometimes found to be
useless when mental exertion has to be called upon as
well.   With Mrs Oliphant perhaps the secret was to
be found in the fact of her being able to concentrate
her thoughts quickly on the matter that had to be
attended to, and her ability to do her work at any
time.   She worked early and she worked late, and
yet there was no time in the day when she could
not be seen.   She may be said to have been always
working, yet her work was never obtruded.   In her
own home the kindest and most attentive of hostesses,
she always had time to take part in anything that
was going on.   To a stranger who saw her leaning
back in her chair, her hands occupied with some
needlework, she would seem one of the most leis-
ured of women, no hurry in her speech nor in her
movements, only now and then a swift glance from
her dark eyes would tell she was quickly turning
over in her mind all that was passing.   When she
was writing at Strathtyrum we can recall many
instances of her charming adaptability to the ways
of the house.   A guest for whom naturally host and

hostess would have wished to make hours and arrangements suit, she would have nothing altered. Down in the morning in time for the golfers' early breakfast, she would wait about and see them off, and talk and work with the ladies of the party, and then quietly steal away to her room to do a good morning's work—a contrast to the solemn fuss that usually prevails when the ladies of a country house-party announce that they have "letters to write."

The time she perhaps did the greater part of her writing was during the hours which most of us consecrate to slumber, and in the quiet hush of the night I believe some of her best work was done. My father on one occasion alluded to this in writing to William Blackwood. "Make up Mrs Oliphant's 'Dunkirk' to follow 'John'; it is a wonderful piece of painting. I think she did it in a couple of nights here." "Here" means Strathtyrum, where Mrs Oliphant often occupied the room with the balcony which had witnessed the throes of poor Speke's literary composition, and was, besides, the room where Charles Reade used to spend his mornings writing 'The Woman-Hater,' and where Laurence Lockhart used to ask to be shut up when the calls of society threatened to leave him no time to finish work, and where many others we could name found a haven. In the afternoon she was ready for anything that was to be done—a drive or a walk on the Links—and was never lost sight of again till bedtime, having been the centre and mainspring of any pleasure-seeking or amusement that was going on: for this hard-working accomplished lady, who could hold her own with most of the powerful intellects of her day, was no despiser

of small things or small pleasures. A day's outing,
when she could for the time throw aside her work,
was always acceptable. It might be a day in London,
with a French play or Wagner's music at the end of it,
or a picnic to one of the quaint fishing villages on the
Fife coast—no matter where, it was always a pleasant
day if devised by her. And this recalls one special
occasion when Mrs Oliphant planned an entertainment
which attracted some attention owing to the occasion
of the festival and the interest attaching to those
who were her guests. The thought had occurred to
her to celebrate by a banquet to John Blackwood as
Editor of 'Maga' her five-and-twenty years of authorship under his banner, and to assemble together as
many of the other contributors as possible to do
honour to the occasion. The spot chosen for the
gathering was the historical island of Runnymede,
where King John met his barons and signed the
Magna Charta. The meadows that surround it are
green and luxuriant, and the island can boast, as in
the days of the barons, some fine spreading trees
which overshadow its lawns. There on a fine afternoon in June 1877 were assembled, at Mrs Oliphant's
invitation, my father and mother and many of his most
intimate friends, besides many friends and acquaintances of Mrs Oliphant. Sir Edward Hamley and his
brother General William Hamley, Mr Alex. Innes
Shand, Colonel Lockhart, and Mr Kinglake had
travelled down with us by special train from Waterloo to Wraysbury; and we found Colonel George
Chesney from Cooper's Hill, Mr R. D. Blackmore,
Mr Henry Reeve, and many other well-known persons
arriving by the boats which were in waiting to convey

the guests to the island. When all were assembled
on the lawn the Editor, as the principal guest, led
Mrs Oliphant to the marquee where luncheon was
spread, and my mother was conducted to her place
at the board by Mrs Oliphant's eldest son Cyril, then
an Oxford undergraduate about nineteen or twenty
years of age. After luncheon Cyril Oliphant gracefully proposed the health of his mother's friend the
Editor and success to the Magazine with which she
had been so happily associated for over five-and-
twenty years. One could hardly realise how long
it was, when we saw Mrs Oliphant that day looking
so well and handsome in her gown of grey silk and
her white lace bonnet, completing the pleasing picture
she made with her delicate colouring and beautiful
white hair. When her son sat down my father rose,
and his impromptu speech, in which he thanked Cyril
Oliphant for proposing his health, was most happily
and brightly expressed. He gave it just the right
turn and direction, which made it interesting to all
present, most of whom were, like Mrs Oliphant, contributors to the Magazine. In conclusion he called
forth loud applause from the other guests by alluding
to the fact that Mrs Oliphant's eyes were undimmed
by her twenty-five years' writing. And in reference
to the island where we were assembled he said he
hoped the Barons of Blackwood had not met under
the trees to dictate terms to him, but that, on the
contrary, they would always rally round for his support. There was loud applause at this from the
Barons, who certainly made a brave show. In writing to Mrs Oliphant afterwards to congratulate her
on the success of her entertainment my father says :—

John Blackwood to Mrs Oliphant.

June 21, 1877.

At the risk of praising what *pars fui*, I cannot resist writing a line to congratulate you on the perfect success of your festival. Nothing could have been more pretty or more gracefully done, and I know that feeling was answered among your guests. Hamleys, Kinglake, Lockhart, &c., &c., have been with us since, and evidently mean to remember the day. When Kinglake reached his club he regaled himself with reading one of your novels. Nothing pleased me more than the excellent way Cyril did his work. You will laugh when I say that I was glad to see that he was anxious and nervous, although he concealed it well. A young fellow is no good unless he is anxious and nervous about anything that touches his heart: he will never hole his putt without a share of that feeling. Looking at you and my merry men round the table on Tuesday, I felt that at the head of such a corps I would be ready to face and beat the best barons that ever entered a tilt-yard, and this put into my head the little joke I made about the Runnymede Barons.

Recollections of Mrs Oliphant, the friend of one's childhood and youth, tempt us to linger near her; but time presses, and with one backward loving glance we pass out of her presence.

The next step brings us to a group of ladies who have all made their mark as novelists, and whose early successes were achieved under the Blackwood banner. It has been already said, and with reason, how much John Blackwood did to foster and encourage feminine literary talent. When he found it to exist unsuspected amongst the children or relatives of any of his friends his pleasure was twofold, and we thus find him welcoming Mrs Walford, the popular authoress of 'Mr Smith' and daughter of Mr Colquhoun of Luss, the veteran sportsman and author of the 'Moor and the Loch.'

STRATHTYRUM, *July* 7, 1875.

Your father is a very old correspondent and friend of mine, and it gives me much pleasure to welcome his daughter as a contributor to 'Blackwood.'

Later he writes to her of her novel 'Pauline' :—

Sept. 11, 1877.

It is throughout very pleasing and amusing, and is, I think,. gaining in popularity, and I hope may do well as a separate publication.

Mrs Walford's first clever story, 'Mr Smith,' had scored a signal success, securing a wide popularity for its author, which her later works—notably 'Pauline' —have ably sustained.

Another authoress as a young girl achieved a success with a very different sort of novel ; for it was a love story pure and simple, entitled 'Miss Molly'— very slight and very pretty—which introduced Miss Beatrice Butt (Mrs W. Allhusen) to her audience, who have since looked with interest for its successors. 'Delicia' and other stories by her which followed are all written with the grace and charm that characterised her first successful effort, of which John Blackwood wrote thus :—

John Blackwood to Miss Butt.

April 10, 1876.

I am so pleased with the result I intend to make your share two-thirds of the profits, and my nephew has much pleasure in joining me in this change of terms. I have often laughed and said of ladies' novels that a cause of their success was sometimes their not being ladylike, and it is no small feather in your cap that a main element in the success of your little story has been that it is perfectly ladylike.

A new and interesting feature in the fiction of 'Maga' was the appearance in 1879 of 'Reata,' the first novel of the two sisters· who wrote conjointly under the name of E. D. Gerard. That original and fascinating story formed.a somewhat novel departure in English fiction, introducing us to scenes of Austrian military life and the picturesque surroundings of a country house in Poland, with the graphic realism that comes of intimate knowledge acquired in the country described. Miss Dorothea Gerard was in Edinburgh during the winter of 1878-79 with her father; Mr Gerard of Rochsoles, and one of the fresh interests John Blackwood had that winter was in making her acquaintance. These two sisters, he rightly adjudged, were going to make a name for themselves as novelists, and from the following to their cousin, Sir Archibald Alison, who had god-fathered the 'Reata' MS., it was evident he had from the first taken the deepest interest in them and their writings :—

John Blackwood to Sir Archibald Alison.

BATTS HOTEL, DOVER ST., *Feb.* 26, 1878.

After I got your letter I went gallantly at it, and have read the whole 12 or 1400 MS. folio pages. The writers are evidently very clever accomplished women, with great descriptive powers and a very good sense of humour.

After reading it in type my father was so convinced of the excellence of the story that he decided to publish it first in the Magazine.

John Blackwood to Madame de Laszowska.

STRATHTYRUM, *Oct.* 4, 1878.

I have read the first volumes of your novel in proof, and am happy to say that the reading of these two volumes in type has

more than confirmed the favourable opinion I formed of the
whole book when I read it in MS. The story will, I think,
bear division into parts, and I have been reading it now with
a view to publication in 'Blackwood' in the first instance. I
hear that your sister and fellow-worker, Miss Gerard, is in
Edinburgh for a day or two, and I am quite sorry I cannot go
to Edinburgh this week to enjoy a talk with her over 'Reata';
but my nephew, who is my partner, knows my sentiments and
shares them.

Referring to the title, about which there had been
some discussion, he says: "Still 'Reata' is not a name
which would have given any idea of the picture of
human nature, good sense, and feeling which the book
presents." The novel was finally christened 'Reata;
or, What's in a Name.'

Madame de Laszowska, the elder of the two joint
authoresses, we did not see at this time, the winter of
1879—she was in Poland then with her husband; but
we made the acquaintance of Dorothea, who with her
younger sister, Gertrude, was a constant visitor at
Randolph Crescent. My father looked forward, as
we all did, to the visits of these clever bright girls,
whose comings and goings made a pleasant variety in
days which, though they knew it not, were shadowed
to us by anxiety and the approach of sorrow. After
Miss Gerard's return to Poland John Blackwood wrote
as follows :—

John Blackwood to Miss Dorothea Gerard.

45 GEORGE STREET, *April* 1879.

I hope you have been well since you got back to Brünn, and
have not been afflicted with weather such as we still have here.
It is bitterly cold with occasional blasts of snow to-day. My
health struggles on pretty fairly, but I do not expect to feel

very lively until the sun revisits us, of which there are no signs
at present.　Your friends at Randolph Crescent are very well,
and they both send their warm regards to your sister and you.
Has she been painting much?　The portrait of "Tip" holds a
place of honour [this sister, Miss Gertrude Gerard, had painted
one of our dogs].　My nephew is in London, and has seen a good
deal of the Alisons, who are very curious to see your novel.
Sir Archibald will, I am sure, be glad to see his cousins as
fellow-contributors.　He never wrote much for me, but his
father was a great contributor in my early days.　People are
all abusing Lord Chelmsford, and I fear he has broken
down, but it is ungenerous to run him down as people are
doing.　I do not know him, but am intimate with one of
his brothers (Charles Thesiger), who is a clever fellow and
a good soldier.　Give my remembrances to your sister, and
remind her that we expect to see you both at Strathtyrum
this summer.

The success of their first novel more than realised
the expectations the Editor had formed of it, and
though he did not live to see the fulfilment of his
predictions, his encouragement and helpful criticism
no doubt tended to establish the two accomplished
writers in the line they had thus brilliantly struck
out for themselves, and which has led to the distinguished position they have since attained in the
ranks of novelists.

Prominent among the new names now appearing
in the letters, and indicating the fresh literary interests
that were gathering about John Blackwood, we find
that of Mr R. D. Blackmore.　The admiration he felt
for his writings interested him deeply in making Mr
Blackmore's personal acquaintance, and after their
first meeting he wrote to his wife, "I am greatly
taken with the author of 'Lorna Doone,' and think
we shall hit it off."

Mr Blackmore's first novel in the Magazine was 'The Maid of Sker,' a tale of Cornish fisher life, fresh as the breezes from that rocky coast, and described with a vividness that makes one smell the "brine" and feel the strong sea-winds. Referring to some portions of the story, of which the development had not seemed quite clear, John Blackwood apologises to the author for his criticism with a quotation from Burns.

John Blackwood to R. D. Blackmore.

EDINBURGH, *Feb.* 23, 1871.

I am puzzled what to say, but I think you may go on with the view that I accept the story for the Magazine. Your hand is so small that it has rather bothered my eyes, which during the last year, to my great disgust, have begun to show symptoms that they have been pretty well worked, and I have been strongly tempted to put both parts into type. The point I have most doubt upon is whether you make the old fisherman sufficiently attractive and interesting; but he is a character very lifelike, and when I see him in the block I have very little doubt I shall think you are right. Turning over Burns the other night, I came on the following lines, which, if you have forgotten them, as I partially had, will, I think, take your fancy:—

> " Our friends, the reviewers,
> Those chippers and hewers,
> Are judges of mortar and stone, sir ;
> But of meet, or unmeet,
> In a fabrick complete,
> I'll boldly pronounce they are none, sir."

It is curious to see the man of genius living out of the world as thoroughly up in the thing as if he had been reviewed in 'The Saturday,' &c., last week. The lines warn me not to say much about a work of which I have by no means seen the "fabrick complete."

When the 'Maid' appeared in type and could boast of being three (Magazine) months old there was no doubt as to her being a success.

John Blackwood to R. D. Blackmore.

STRATHTYRUM, *Oct.* 5, 1871.

Old Davy is a wonderful fellow and capitally sustained. I see that some wiseacres declare he writes better than an old sailor could, but so did Robinson Crusoe.

I went into the drawing-room just now to ask the ladies how they liked Part III., and there was quite a chorus of applause. Major Lockhart, who is sitting opposite me correcting the last part of 'Fair to See,' has not read your third part, but is loud in praise of the other parts.

The next novel of Mr Blackmore's that appeared in 'Maga' was 'Alice Lorraine,' a tale of the South Downs and the rich fruit-growing districts of Kent. Writing to the author, John Blackwood, in reference to the date of the story, gives vent to a favourite theory of his with regard to the much vaunted superiority of our day over that of any other period of civilisation :—

John Blackwood to R. D. Blackmore.

45 GEORGE STREET, *Dec.* 29, 1873.

I enclose proof of the first part of 'Alice Lorraine,' which, I am happy to say, I like very much indeed, and I have read it twice over with very great pleasure. It is extremely picturesque and full of quaint humour. Your descriptions are beautiful, and Alice, the old gentleman, and the as yet unseen Hilary are very promising. It will suit us quite well not to publish the first part until March. The story has an antique look, and, looking at your date, I am reminded that, like 'Waverley,' it is sixty years ago since the time of your story. With all our brags about progress, telegraphs, railways, &c., the world is much less changed in the years since 1811 than in the time from the days of Prince Charlie to those of Walter Scott.

The pleasant beginning with Mr Blackmore grew and prospered, and the friendship thus formed was one of the many interesting associations of my father's later years.

The introduction of Anthony Trollope to the readers of the Magazine was through one of those mysterious literary surprises to which 'Maga' has often been addicted. Anonymous writing lends itself readily to an author wishing to try a new venture ; and when the popular chronicler of the Cathedral Close forsook it for a change, he turned to 'Maga' as the open door by which to escape the reproaches of those who might have resented his departure from that pleasant neighbourhood, of which the rectory or vicarage is the rallying-point—a neighbourhood he has made so successfully his own that his accustomed readers might not have seen the reason for his trying new ground. He did so, however, and went far afield to "old" Prague, which he made the background for a clever and original story called 'Nina Balatka,' which appeared in the Magazine, and afterwards was published in one volume.

John Blackwood to J. M. Langford.

EDINBURGH, *April* 3, 1867.

I am pleased to hear of Trollope's disposition for further relations. When you see him give him my compliments, and say I am quite inclined. "Author of 'Nina Balatka'" may become a very convenient *nom de plume*, especially for such a very prolific writer as our friend. The anxiety about the authorship shows that the book is telling although not selling. I have a note from Oliphant to-day saying, "I am much questioned as to the authorship of 'Nina Balatka'; is it Trollope?" I have replied that the authorship is a secret, and playfully suggest that if he is further pestered on the subject he should hint that it is by Disraeli !

Trollope's next contribution was a story called 'Linda Tressel,' of which the scene is also laid in Germany.

John Blackwood to Anthony Trollope.

EDINBURGH, *April* 5, 1868.

'Linda' excites much interest, and there is no question as to the skill with which her sad tale is told. She is, I think, more talked of than 'Nina,' and will, I hope, find a wider audience than her predecessor; but the sale of novels is not in a satisfactory state, and I suspect we would have to smoke a great many cigars together before we could hit upon the best mode of improving matters. Remember your promise that you and Mrs Trollope should come and pay us a visit whenever it suits you.

The following winter Mr Trollope came to Edinburgh to give a lecture to the members of the Philosophical Institution in the Music Hall.

Anthony Trollope to John Blackwood.

WALTHAM HOUSE, WALTHAM CROSS, *October* 13, 1869.

Yes, I am coming to lecture at Edinburgh, but not till Friday, the 28th January—a long way—and I shall be very happy to be your guest—am indeed most thankful to you for asking me. Some learned pundit kindly offered to give me the "hospitality of the City," which, as it means a half-formal introduction to the pickled [samples?] and a visit to the public library and the like, I viewed with horror and did not accept. I lecture about Novels, and shall expect Mrs Blackwood to go and hear me. I will not be so hard upon you, however,—you must know more about novels than I can tell you.

Another piece of work of Mr Trollope's which entailed on him considerable labour, though from his letters he evidently loved doing it, was his volume 'Cæsar's Commentaries,' which he wrote for the series "Ancient Classics." Of this series, which was a favourite scheme of John Blackwood's, we shall speak presently. The following refers to this volume :—

Anthony Trollope to John Blackwood.

WALTHAM HOUSE, WALTHAM CROSS, 16*th April* 1870.

It has been a tough bit of work, but I have enjoyed it amazingly, and am very much obliged to you for having suggested it. It has been a change to the spinning of novels, and has enabled me to surround myself with books and almost to think myself a scholar.

After the pompous earnestness which sometimes characterises the industry of less renowned workers, how refreshing it is to find an author of Anthony Trollope's mark taking himself and his attainments in this pleasantly easy fashion. Another agreeable feature connected with the publication of this little book was that he made it a present to my father.

Anthony Trollope to John Blackwood.

THE ATHENÆUM, *May* 7, 1870.

I sent down the whole work corrected, having, as I think, complied with every suggestion made by you or Collins. It is a dear little book to me, and there is one other thing to be said about the little dear. I think the 1st of June is your birthday, at any rate we'll make it so for this year, and you will accept it for a little present.—Yours always, ANTHONY TROLLOPE.

Any one who knows the busy life Mr Trollope led will appreciate the compliment he paid his friend in presenting him with this book; for, small though it was, the subject required an immense amount of labour to condense it satisfactorily, besides the necessary reading. My father was greatly touched by the gift, as the following letter shows :—

John Blackwood to Anthony Trollope.

EDINBURGH, *May* 9, 1870.

I am truly grateful and touched by the very handsome manner in which you have presented me with the copyright of the 'Cæsar.' It affects me as a great personal compliment and mark of regard never to be forgotten. I did look this gift-horse most carefully in the mouth, and I can speak to its merits. My anxiety about it was double, as I felt that if I did not think your adventure into this new field not only a success but a decided one, I was bound to tell you my opinion. I carried your letter home to my wife, and I need not say how warmly she enters into my feelings of gratification. She had been rather low owing to the death of her favourite horse " Sunbeam," and your letter was quite a fillip to her.

The next letter shows Mr Trollope embarked on a long novel for the Magazine.

John Blackwood to William Blackwood.

STRATHTYRUM, *Oct.* 28, 1877.

I have read the whole of Trollope's novel, and I am happy to say the continuous interest is quite undeniable. It is like a long process, and novel in its treatment. Strange to say, the hero's character, which I had thought was going to be very taking, falls flat, but with a few softening touches may still, I think, be made more of. The great thing is that the interest of the story never flags.

This novel, 'John Caldigate,' was partly written during the author's voyage to the Cape.

Anthony Trollope to John Blackwood.

CAPE TOWN, SOUTH AFRICA, 21*st July* 1877.

MY DEAR BLACKWOOD,—I write a line on my arrival here to say that I finished my novel on my way out, and that I have sent the remainder of the MS. to Chapman. It is to be called 'John Caldigate.' I mention this especially as the name is not given in any of the parts. As I have as yet only been on shore twelve hours I am not prepared to give a full and comprehensive description of the country, but it seems to be a poor, niggery, yellow-faced, half-bred sort of a place, with an ugly Dutch flavour about it; but I shall tell you more about it by-and-by. Give my kindest regards to your wife and Mary. —Yours always sincerely, ANTHONY TROLLOPE.

A notable point about Anthony Trollope's mode of composition was the regular and systematic manner in which he accomplished his writing. He had said he would send off the rest of 'John Caldigate' as soon as he reached Cape Town, and, true to time, we find as soon as he landed the MS. was despatched. The following is an amusing account of the way he says he apportioned his time even when holiday-making abroad :—

Anthony Trollope to John Blackwood.

HÖHENTHAL, 7*th Sept.* 1878.

I have been on my legs among the hills every day for four hours, and have every day done four hours of writing. I then sleep eight hours without stirring. The other eight are divided between reading and eating, with a preponderance to the latter. It is a healthy, innocent, inexpensive life. The wines are very light, so much so as to make the water almost preferable.

In the same letter he congratulates my father on his improved health, and says : " We all send our joint loves, and are in *real truth* delighted to hear of your convalescence, and trust that you may not do any-

thing to delay it through strong-headed over-activity."
The kindly expressions in this and many other letters
from Anthony Trollope all show his affectionate solicitude for my father, between whom and himself there
existed the strongest personal regard and friendship,
and this quite apart from their business relations,
which were comparatively slight. Indeed in this case
the publishing connection may be said to have resulted
from their friendship, which John Blackwood specially
valued as one of the good and pleasant things that
came to him latterly, when the years were beginning
to steal away some of those who had been the companions of his youth.

Another interesting feature of John Blackwood's
later years was his acquaintance with Charles Reade.
Always a devoted admirer of Reade's genius, he felt
intensely pleased and interested when in 1876 the
great novelist intimated through Mr Langford his
wish to publish a story in the Magazine. This was
his well-known novel 'The Woman-Hater,' a story of
powerful and dramatic interest; and, as some of the
letters indicate, the interest was not lessened by
the storm then raging in Edinburgh between the
University authorities and the female medical
students, who were clamouring at the college gates.
Charles Reade's sympathies, needless to say, were all
on the side of the weaker sex, and his heroine Rhoda
formed as attractive and dangerous a rival as ever
struck terror to the hearts of the male members of the
medical profession. Before this stage of the story
was reached there were, however, many preliminaries.
The Editor was like a man who had invested in a

high-mettled steed, and though he greatly admired his paces, was not quite sure where they might lead him.

John Blackwood to J. M. Langford.

EDINBURGH, *March* 18, 1876.

I have read all you sent me of Charles Reade's novel, and there is no doubt as to its great merit and powerful interest. There is great fun too. The bad man and the bad girl are perhaps too transparently bad. It is very strong meat, and if it does not get too high there is no mistake about it. You have said nothing of the impression the MS. has made on you; are you puzzled? My opinion of it is very high, although I wish the tone were a shade more agreeable and like the Magazine. Speak freely what you think. I do not find that experience makes an Editor over-confident; on the contrary, I think I was bolder when I knew less. I am greatly taken with his [Reade's] letter. I hope [he adds] something may come of this correspondence, as I am very sanguine as to what the book will be, and I like the man. . . . Have you any idea how much of the novel he has written? 'A Simpleton' is a very short novel indeed, but I would leave the length to himself, as I feel that he is a straightforward fellow, and has all the pride of genius in making his work short or long as may best suit his purpose.

The first thing to be done was slightly to alter the tone, about which the Editor had qualms: this he thought was best done by removing the chief characters from the contaminating atmosphere of Homburg and the tables.

John Blackwood to Charles Reade.

EDINBURGH, *March* 15, 1876.

After what I have read I can hardly imagine that I am mistaken as to the interest, power, and humour of the tale you have to tell. In the meantime I should like to hear from you as to the future of the story. When do you mean to change the atmosphere ? I feel as if a purer air than that mixture of Frankfort and Homburg were wanted for the free grace of such characters as Harrington, Zoe, the Klosking, and even good old Ashmead, to develop freely, but do not let me mislead you as to your plans.

Charles Reade's delightfully humorous replies to this and similar suggestions are highly characteristic :—

Charles Reade to John Blackwood.

2 ALBERT TERRACE, KNIGHTSBRIDGE, *March* 19, 1876.

Many thanks for your kind and encouraging letter. I see you would be glad to leave Homburg, and for good reasons. When, however, you expressed the wish, you did not perhaps foresee that I have stayed there to do big business and present a situation of that invaluable kind which we artists call a generative situation. There are good but barren situations. But there are also good and generative situations. When Severne gambles in sight of Zoe and her friends and his own, and the Klosky takes his seat and breaks the bank, that is a generative situation which cannot do its immediate work and die. The consequences will follow the English characters on their journey, and crop up again in England. Eventually I think you will find the greater part of the tale in England, and will not regret the time I have spent in Homburg, making you thoroughly acquainted with no less than five strong characters.

The next letter shows the Editor still having an uneasy time over this story, of which the colouring seemed to him somewhat too warm :—

John Blackwood to Charles Reade.

EDINBURGH, *March* 17, 1878.

The doubts that arise in my mind *quâ* the readers of the Magazine are mainly from your love of plain-speaking and warm flesh-tints. When I see a heroine whom I like, as I do Zoe, giving way too readily to love and kisses, my feelings are something like those of Cuddie Headrigg when he saw Tom Halliday "slaverin' and kissin'" at Jenny Dennison.

To this Reade makes a protest, declaring his heroine has only had her hand respectfully saluted, and appeals for countenance to Anthony Trollope and George Eliot. What suggested this combination it is impossible to say, except that he did not know which name would have the most reassuring effect on his correspondent.

Charles Reade to John Blackwood.

2 ALBERT TERRACE, KNIGHTSBRIDGE, *March* 28, 1876.

The other matter is that the MS. in hand seems to suggest to you that Zoe gives way too readily to love and kisses. Now, Zoe and her lover are caught in a shower, and take refuge in the corner of a cow-house at a moment of great tenderness. Neither Trollope nor George Eliot would have let these two part without a kiss. But up to this date nothing of Zoe has been kissed but her hand, and that without her consent and to her blushing confusion.

Then follows an ingenious explanation of his heroine's further derelictions, so artlessly expressed that the Editor is once more silenced: "As to the girls leaning their heads on Severne's shoulders, that is different. I really did not intend to convey more than an occasional graze in which fatigue and the 'scamper' of the railway were participators." But there was worse danger ahead, and when the lady doctors appear in the next paragraph we feel sure, from the flourish with which they are introduced, that the fiery steed is off at last, and that all the resources of editorial skill will be wanted to control him :—

I send you herewith the new instalment of our story, which lands the party in England and introduces Æsculapius or the doctress and her struggles, which are a great chapter in human nature and of infant civilisation. The character is so important that I must beg you to receive it in strict confidence and sepulchral silence. New ideas of any magnitude are now very rare in fiction, and it would be a calamity if any one of my contemporaries were to get wind of Æsculapius.

An alarming note, too, is struck in the next communication, in which the author says :—

I should not like to be debarred from advancing such truths in the story, and could not afford to miss or skip the pro and con. I am anxious, therefore, to have it understood that decency in the treatment is not to imply debility. You know Sydney Smith denounces "decent debility." In a word, my honest convictions must not be fettered to please old Christison & Co. I do not think you have any such intention, but on a point so important it is best to be explicit, the more so as you must expect remonstrances from cliques when you allow your Magazine to be a vehicle of justice.

Could anything be more appalling than the prospect? My father felt no sympathy with the lady doctors, and if he did not actually disapprove of the movement, certainly thought it unnecessary. It was very hazardous, too, to suggest alterations for fear of spoiling the story; but, as will be seen, he bitted and curbed the runaway so dexterously that he did not very seriously run his head against any "body" nor prejudices.

John Blackwood to Charles Reade.

STRATHTYRUM, *July* 10, 1876.

Rhoda is not more one-sided than is natural in her story. Indeed in the circumstances imagined it is temperately told, but I do not think it would have moved me so much as it did the Woman-Hater. To begin with, I do not believe in the movement being wise or likely to be useful to any material extent. Also I do not believe in the old doctors, foozles or otherwise, taking the vulgar trades-union view of the women becoming dangerous competitors. It is nonsense to accuse these worthy men of wilfully—that is, unfairly—taking the ladies' money. My belief is that they were too complaisant at first, and so got both themselves and the ladies into a difficulty. I am not very intimate with any of them except my own Doctor Maclagan, and I do not know what view he takes; but I know they are all well-meaning men, as unlike trades-unionists as well can be. Write to me as soon as you can about this point to Edinburgh. I should most decidedly cut out Rhoda's prayer (Part VIII.), both for her own sake and still more that of the book. Her expostulations with the Unseen Power are not to edification, and remind me of a worthy old doctor under whom I sat, who always began his long prayer by holding out his fist almost in a threatening manner, exclaiming, "Thou knowest," &c. It is very reluctantly that I write anything but praise of 'The Woman-Hater,' but I hope you will excuse it and grant me these points.

After all the correspondence, of which we are only able to give a few of the main points, it is satisfactory to find from a letter of John Blackwood to Mr Langford that Charles Reade had yielded to treatment, and in the nicest, pleasantest way in the world had softened and toned down what the Editor considered were the flaws of this really powerful and interesting story :—

I am glad to say his [Reade's] corrections were exactly in the right line: two of them hit two apparently little but really important points which I longed to write about but did not, fearing to make him think me too fastidious. I shall mention the two the first time I write to him, as the alterations increase my sense of his taste, and I wish to keep his tone as light as can be.

The negotiations about the book and John Black-

wood's criticisms and suggestions about the early part
were all made before he was personally acquainted with
Charles Reade.   The following letter describes their
first meeting :—

John Blackwood to William Blackwood.

14 ARLINGTON ST., *May* 18, 1876.

I had a long and most pleasant visit to Charles Reade.   He'
is a thorough gentleman, and we shall pull together like men.
When I left I said I was so glad we had come together at
last, and he replied, " The good fortune is mine."   When I went
in he was busy writing, and said I found him like a good boy
at his work.

The next letter shows them with ' The Woman-
Hater' fairly launched, and not even the shadow of a
libel action to detract from its success :—

John Blackwood to Charles Reade.

EDINBURGH, *Nov.* 28, 1876.

I am wearying to hear from you, and I do not weary the less
because I have a strong suspicion that I am the chief defaulter
in correspondence.   What you so gracefully said about our
relations with each other was very grateful to me, and whenever
we came together I felt that we would pull well.

I hear distant mutterings of wrath or surprise and sorrow
among the doctors; but none of them have addressed me on the
much-vexed Lady question, and altogether it has passed off much
more quietly than I expected.   Had poor Russel [the editor
of the ' Scotsman'] been alive, he would have blown a blast
that would have reached the Border.   The last correspondence
I ever had with him, poor fellow, was occasioned by my writing
to him for pamphlets about the lady doctors' adventures in
Edinburgh, with which he liberally supplied me, and I told him
we would have a hearty laugh some months afterwards when he
would see why I was looking into a matter so much out of my
line.   We all read with much amusement your very accurate

description of the dress of the old lady at Strathtyrum painted by Raeburn. Have you recovered your lost dog? My daughter read out the advertisement from the 'Times.' I said, or both said, "That is very like Charles Reade," and behold it was your address.

During Charles Reade's visit to Scotland the preceding summer Mr Russel, the well - known editor of the 'Scotsman,' had died, and my father had then, in writing to Mr Reade, alluded with very real regret to the loss of one with whom, in spite of the difference of their political creeds, he had ever been on terms of personal friendliness.

John Blackwood to Charles Reade.

STRATHTYRUM, *July* 1876.

I feel upset this morning by the death of poor Russel of the 'Scotsman.' Our relative positions did not make us associates, but mutual love of fun made us friends whenever we met, and many a hearty laugh we have had together. Many years ago, when Thackeray was staying with us, he insisted on making us better acquainted, and a great night we had when late one evening the sage walked into my smoking-room bringing Russel with him. Heigh - ho! Hoping to find you in good care to-morrow—I am, yours very truly, JOHN BLACKWOOD.

Mr Russel was a keen fisher, and occasionally sent a paper to the Magazine on the subject of his favourite sport, amongst these being "An Angling Saunter in Sutherland," and another entitled "What's a Grilse?"

With the next letter we must conclude the pleasant episode of John Blackwood's friendship with Charles Reade—a friendship which, though begun when both of them had reached life's eventide, was fraught with

a stronger regard and understanding of each other
than often falls to the lot of younger men.

John Blackwood to Charles Reade.

STRATHTYRUM, ST ANDREWS, *July* 30, 1876.

You had left the enclosed inside proof of 'Woman-Hater.'
We were all so sorry to see you go away, and have cheered
ourselves since with talk of your pleasant visit and the prospect
of your return. When you left I felt that I had got another
friend in the world, which is pleasant at my time of life,
when so many who were the flowers of my forest are wede awa'.

CHAPTER XII.

GEORGE ELIOT'S LATER WORKS.

'THE SPANISH GYPSY' — "FELIX HOLT'S ADDRESS TO WORKING MEN" — DISRAELI IN EDINBURGH — HOLIDAYS ABROAD — GEORGE ELIOT IN ROME — OTHER POEMS — A FRESH EPOCH — 'MIDDLEMARCH' PUBLISHED IN BI-MONTHLY PARTS — DISCOURAGEMENT WHILE WRITING — STIMULATING EFFECT OF JOHN BLACKWOOD'S LETTERS — DEATH OF LORD LYTTON (BULWER) — GEORGE ELIOT'S PRAISE OF 'KENELM CHILLINGLY' — SUCCESS OF ''MIDDLEMARCH' — A NEW NOVEL — JOHN BLACKWOOD'S FIRST PERUSAL OF 'DANIEL DERONDA' — PERSONAL RECOLLECTIONS OF, AND VISITS TO, GEORGE ELIOT — A TRUSTY MESSENGER — A STARTLING INQUIRY — SALVINI AS OTHELLO — SIR W. FERGUSSON — JOHN BLACKWOOD'S CRITICISMS ON 'DERONDA' — A NEW DEVICE IN REPORTING A CONVERSATION — THE TRIBE OF ISRAEL — OBJECTS OF THE BOOK — ITS POPULARITY — SUCCESS IN AMERICA — DEATH OF G. H. LEWES — 'THEOPHRASTUS SUCH.'

THE story has already been told of George Eliot's introduction to the "House" and John Blackwood's correspondence with her about her first novel, and his pleasure and that of his brother, Major William Blackwood, in her early successes, of which perhaps 'Adam Bede' was the most striking. We have now to mark how the years were occupied between the production of 'Felix Holt' in 1866 and her last work, 'Theophrastus Such.' The intervening years had been fruitful, and her readers found fresh pleasure awaiting them in the poem which forms a sort of halting-ground between her. early novels and those which mark the later epoch of 'Middlemarch' and 'Deronda.' She seems to have paused for a time after leaving the sober everyday pictures of English life with which she had hitherto illustrated her text, and, seizing upon the glowing colours and dramatic possibilities of Spain, she composed a poem on the racial struggles of the Moors and Spanish gipsies. This work, 'The Spanish Gypsy,' was published in the spring of 1868, and forms another and striking illustration of her genius. Renunciation is the keynote of this poem, and whatever differences of opinion there may be as to the quality of her verse, there can be no question as to the beauty of thought and poetical feeling that inspired it, while Fedalma, the gipsy heroine, will always rank amongst the most brilliant and tragically interesting of the author's creations.

John Blackwood to George Eliot.

EDINBURGH, *Dec.* 6, 1867.

The first part of the great poem is now all in type. It is wonderful. I find myself reading and re-reading, and I feel quite incompetent to say all I think of it, especially within half an hour of post-time. You may feel satisfied that Fedalma will add another wreath to your laurels.

In the same letter John Blackwood expresses his satisfaction with "Felix Holt's Address to Working Men." It had been written at his earnest request after the publication of her novel 'Felix Holt,' which treats of working men's strikes and the tyrannies of trades-unionism.

I enclose proof of your noble address to the working men. I wish the poor fellows were capable of appreciating it. If they

were, we should be all right; but it will do great good, and is
exactly what I expected that you would write.   Your picture of
"the ignoble martyrdom of fools," which would be their fate
if they allowed the mob and mob orators to mislead them,
and destroy the class who have leisure and refinement to think
and legislate, is perfect.   According to my knowledge of working men, which is not inconsiderable, the good among them
are thoroughly up to the useless self-seeking character of
their own noisy demagogues, and I think you may say something more on that head.

In suggesting this subject to George Eliot, John
Blackwood had referred to Disraeli's visit to Edinburgh in November 1867, and the great success of
his address to the working men, of which he says:
"Disraeli's address to the working men here was the
best thing I ever heard him do.   My printers were all
there, and were highly delighted.   It strikes me that
you could do a first-rate address to the working men
on their new responsibilities."   This was just after the
extension of the franchise.

While writing 'The Spanish Gypsy' George Eliot
went to the seaside for a few weeks' quiet and rest.

George Eliot to John Blackwood.

THE PRIORY, NORTH BANK,
REGENT'S PARK, *July* 12, 1867.

We returned on Wednesday from our quiet and sea-breezes,
and can all the more feelingly congratulate you on being at
Strathtyrum again.   I hope you are enjoying your privileges
thoroughly.   Nevertheless, I am malicious enough to wish that
some chance may send you up to town again before Christmas,
as I think was the case last year, so that you may hear how
Fedalma's fortunes are being developed.

There   are   many   pleasant   letters   written   from

abroad by George Eliot to John Blackwood, which appear in her Memoirs, and describing her well-earned holidays, or " play life," as she calls it. The following is one which has never been published :—

George Eliot to John Blackwood.

                     ~ Rome, *April 6,* 1869..

We are only just settled here on our return from Naples, for even so far have we ventured in search of warmth, which is not to be found in Italy any more than in England. A certain captain whom we met on our journeying quoted as an opinion of his uncle's, that " you could not dodge March in Europe," and our experience makes us to register that opinion as a maxim for our future guidance. We shivered along the Corniche even in the few days of sunshine, and most of our days were grey and rainy. We intended always to make Rome our principal destination on the journey, but we wished to avoid the Holy Week and Easter, thinking that our one experience of the ceremonies and crowds at that season (in 1860) was enough for a life. But it happens that this year the chief festival is the commemoration of the Pope's fiftieth year of priesthood, on Apr. 11th, and the number of strangers is less reduced than usual after the end of Easter. We want to keep quite incog. and to see no acquaintances until near the time of going away ; for as I travel to see foreign objects and not to hear English views, I get impatient even of company, otherwise agreeable, when it distracts my attention from some scene or monument which I shall probably never revisit. Our last rare bit of sunshine and blue sea at Naples was utterly spoiled by an English acquaintance who found us out in the public gardens and droned his worthless observations in our ears for an hour and a half, innocently intending to be as kind as possible in offering himself as a screen between us and the wondrous light around us. Whatever else refuses to mend itself in Rome, the coachmen are improved in their manners since our former visit, and no longer torment the pedestrian " mossoo " as if he were an escaped lunatic unable to perceive his immense need of a *vettura.* The cold wind makes the *vettura* an unwelcome necessity to a sensitive "mossoo." Even at the theatre the rush of cold air from the stage when the curtain rises makes us wrap ourselves up in wintry fashion. Last night we went to see Ristori as Judith, this being advertised as her farewell performance. Even with that same deduction of shivering discomfort, and the worst company imaginable to act with her, it was a gain to see again a nobly, beautiful woman, grand and graceful in her attitudes and movements, and with a delicious deep voice. The Holofernes was a hideous burlesque, who set the whole house laughing by a drunken rant when the action was approaching the climax. We saw Salvini, the tragedian, at Genoa, and wished that human nature in the shape of actor or actress could bear the juxtaposition of merit with delight.

Of course you will not write any answer to this letter. Our play life here will last probably a fortnight or more, but everything about our movements is uncertain. I hope we shall shake hands with you in London after our return.

Five months after the publication of 'The Spanish Gypsy' they had to prepare a third edition, and the following letter shows that the popular author was holding her own with the public in spite of unfavourable criticisms :—

John Blackwood to George Eliot.

EDINBURGH, *Oct.* 20, 1868.

I am happy to tell you that the second edition of 'The Gypsy' is so nearly out of print that we ought to proceed with a reprint *at once.* The sale is very gratifying, especially considering the numbers of hostile criticisms, and I am in great hopes that the poem is working its way with the knowledge of the general public. Whether it is not too refined ever to reach the point when a cheap edition with a view to a vast sale would be desirable one cannot tell, but at present we certainly do not think it would be wise to try that plan.

After 'The Spanish Gypsy' George Eliot interspersed at different times various other poems amongst her prose writings, which were afterwards collected and published in a volume in 1874. Referring to these, John Blackwood says:—

John Blackwood to George Eliot.

EDIN., *April* 1, 1874.

The poems are very beautiful. There is a solemn cadence, almost a warning tone, about them which is very impressive. You must have been thinking, if not writing, poetry all your life, and if you have any lighter pieces written before the sense of what a great author should do for mankind came so strongly upon you, I should like much to look at them.

On the last day of the year 1870 George Eliot wrote in her journal: "I have written only 100 pages — good printed pages — of a story which I began about the opening of November, and at present mean to call 'Miss Brooke.' Poetry halts just now." This is the first mention of the beginning of 'Middlemarch,' of which the first instalment was entitled 'Miss Brooke.' The form of its publication was a new departure, at least for George Eliot's books, as it appeared in bi-monthly parts, and its appearance may also be said to mark a fresh epoch in her writings. The same charm, the same human feeling and descriptive skill, are all there, but there is something more —something to be read between the lines. George Eliot the popular author had become the popular teacher. When John Blackwood wrote to her, in reference to this book, that Dorothy Brooke was "better than any sermon," he really meant what he said. The following is his impression after seeing the first part in type:—

John Blackwood to G. H. Lewes.

STRATHTYRUM, *Oct.* 9, 1871.

Give my best regards to Mrs Lewes, and tell her that she who can administer to the world such glorious tonics as ' Middle-march' must sturdily cure herself of all ailments. I put off the re-reading in type with a sort of "slow reluctant" loving delay (which I daresay you will understand) until yesterday, when my wife, not being "too religious for family comfort," having accepted my apologies for not accompanying her to church, I sat down to the proof. I passed the greater part of the day reading, smiling, and thinking as I read. Our scheme should succeed, as this first part took me as much time to read as I would devote to many a large volume. There is a perfect wealth of thought and fun, and then it is real life. When I was transferred to the Vincy breakfast-room I almost exclaimed aloud, By Jove! she is equally at home here. If I might venture a doubt about anything, it is Mr Casaubon's letter proposing. It is exceptionally funny; but I mean, is it not too transparently so not to strike even a girl so devoted to wisdom as poor dear Dodo?

From Mr Lewes's reply it will be seen that George Eliot still experienced that strange discouragement while writing, and seemed more than ever to rely on my father's letters to stimulate and give her courage to go on.

G. H. Lewes to John Blackwood.

THE PRIORY, NORTH BANK,
REGENT'S PARK, *Thursday.*

MY DEAR BLACKWOOD,—Talk of tonics, you should have seen the stimulating effect of your letter yesterday respecting ' Miss Brooke'! She who needs encouragement so much, to give her some confidence and shake the ever-present doubt of herself and her doing, *relies* on you, and takes comfort from you to an extent you can hardly imagine. Unhappily it don't *last.* A week hence she will be as sceptical as ever! Thank God she is really improving now, though still very weak, and burning with poetic fire to be at Dodo once more.

The preceding letter is addressed "Captain" John Blackwood.

George Eliot's health, never very robust, had flagged somewhat while she was writing the end of ' Middlemarch.'

John Blackwood to George Eliot.

STRATHTYRUM, *Sept.* 7, 1872.

I am so sorry to hear from Lewes that you are still poorly, and I do wish your wonderful *picture* was ended that you might get away to health-restoring Homburg. How you do paint and dissect Bulstrode's feelings. It is a terrible picture of the attempt to love God and Mammon, for you throw in a touch of reality in the wretch's religion which removes him from the ordinary religious hypocrite of his school. In the struggle that night, he, as it were, hardly knew himself that he was committing murder when he gave the brandy. That is the impression you have left, I think. This 7th Book leaves Dr Lydgate in a terrible mesh. The gossiping Middlemarch harpies gathering to the prey is fine. It makes one's flesh creep to think of any good man's character in their hands. My own reflection reminds me of a story. A humorous old bachelor lawyer had retired from business to live about twenty miles from Edinburgh, and one Sunday had out a batch of his old lawyer cronies. Late at night, when they had ably dissected their various acquaintances, the liquor in the dining-room ran short. My friend said, " Gentlemen, there is the key of the cellar, and any of you may go and get up whatever you like, but damn me if I'll leave my character in your hands for five minutes."

In January 1873 Lord Lytton (Sir E. B. Lytton) died. A world-wide celebrity in literature and a prominent figure in politics, he was, too, a valued friend of John Blackwood, who felt his loss profoundly, and George Eliot's warm praise of his latest work was a re-echo of his own enthusiasm. The following contains the tribute to Lord Lytton's last novel, 'Kenelm Chillingly,' which she felt to be the best and most suitable closing chapter for the end of his life. She also dwells in this letter on what was well known to be a favourite theme of hers, ever since the days when she immortalised Maggie and Tom Tulliver in 'The Mill on the Floss.'

George Eliot to John Blackwood.
THE PRIORY, NORTH BANK,
REGENT'S PARK, *April* 21, 1873.

I only want to say that I have been very sorry to hear of your illness, now happily past, and then to thank you for sending me 'Kenelm Chillingly.' I was guilty of allowing a friend to run away with my copy when I had only finished the first volume, so that my reading of the other two was delayed. I have had great pleasure in the purity and elevation of its tone, —its catholic view of life, free from all snobbishness or bitterness of partisanship. Of all the author's writings that I know, there is not one that we could have felt to be more harmonious with the closing epoch of a long career. The last sentence touched me deeply.

That picnic of the young ones to Strathtyrum was very pretty, and a good enough subject for a poem. I hope that the brother and sister love each other very dearly : life might be so enriched if that relation were made the most of, as one of the highest forms of friendship. A good while ago I made a poem in the form of eleven sonnets, after the Shakespeare type, on the childhood of a brother and sister—little descriptive bits on the mutual influences in their small lives. This was always one of my best loved subjects. And I was proportionately enraged about that execrable discussion raised in relation to Byron. The deliberate insistance on the subject was a worse crime against society than the imputed fact.

Details of the success of 'Middlemarch' appear from time to time in the letters, the demand for this book having been immense in its first published form, and a year after the appearance of the first instalment the sale still continued.

John Blackwood to George Eliot.

STRATHTYRUM, *Nov.* 3, 1873.

When I last heard of 'Middlemarch' the sale was still going on. It has been most satisfactory, but I shall write to you with particulars from Edinburgh. We have had a good many visitors as usual, and among others Delane lately. His tale of the blunders through which that Ashantee war had arisen increased one's anger at the policy and administration which has sent so many fine fellows to that horrid country. Wolseley is a friend and correspondent of mine. I had a letter from his wife yesterday. She had heard from him in good health and spirits from Cape Coast. He is an able man, and will, I doubt not, do well, but who can fight with such a climate? I do not like the look of this Ashantee bush-fighting at all. The risk of our officers being picked off is very fearful. I see one of our correspondents says, " The present inclination of the Houssas is to run away when they are fired at." I suspect the correspondent shared the emotion. How little attention the terribly grave state of matters in France is attracting in this country. Edinburgh is more occupied with a confounded Water Bill, and London with that beastly Claimant, than with all the infernal drama that is going on across the Channel.

By the following year 'Middlemarch' had appeared in a new and cheaper dress, which seems to have been equally attractive; and when telling George Eliot of this, mention is also made of the success of the poems.

John Blackwood to George Eliot.

STRATHTYRUM, *Aug.* 4, 1874.

I have such good news to give of 'Middlemarch,' 'Jubal,' and also 'Spanish Gypsy,' that I write a line to report progress. Of the 7s. 6d. edition of 'Middlemarch' we printed 3150 in May and 2100 in the latter part of June. The above are all disposed of, and we have just reprinted 2100 more, of which the first

batch went off to Paternoster Row to supply orders. The
success of 'Middlemarch' has also exercised a benign influence
on the sale of the other novels. Of 'Jubal,' you are aware that
the first edition of 1609 copies is gone, and we subscribed 247
of the second edition in London. Of the 'Spanish Gypsy'
[which was by this time old as books go] I see we have sold 107
copies between December and July. This is all good, and must,
I think, make you turn to a new book with fresh confidence that
you are not writing in vain. I hope you are both enjoying this
delightful weather in the country. It is charming here. Major
Lockhart came over to us a few days ago with loud talk of
shutting himself up in his room and working. The scoundrel
has never been off the Links since his arrival. My son is at
home for the holidays, and I think you would like him. He
has a strong turn for humour, which he develops with much
gravity.

The words of good cheer that John Blackwood used
to give George Eliot, conveying not only his own
appreciation, which perhaps she valued more than any
other, but also showing to what a large extent the
public were reading her works, had the twofold
advantage of raising her spirits at the time, and
also of sending her off to her desk again; for, shortly
after the preceding letter, we find indications that
another great work is on the way : this was 'Daniel
Deronda.'

John Blackwood to George Eliot.
EDINBURGH, *Nov.* 19, 1874.

When I got back from the country last Thursday I found a
most alarming pile of letters and packets of manuscript of all
kinds awaiting me, but your pleasant despatch, with its most
welcome news, leavened the whole mass. I do long to see that
"slice of MS." which has passed into the "irrevocable." Lewes
and I are both, I believe, good critics, but it is very plain sailing when we have works such as yours to comment upon. The
leaving Strathtyrum was, as usual, a melancholy business, and

we had to leave behind Tickler, the favourite old terrier. He
was heard swearing violently as we drove through the lodge
gate to the railway. Meanwhile we are not without dogs, as
that rascal Jack brought down a fox-terrier with him from
school and left it with us. It is a perfect demon of mischief.
Its first act was to tear my own copy of the month's Magazine,
and then it tried to apologise to me by utterly demolishing a
'Cornhill.' From its supposed great value, it is not allowed to
go into the streets yet, and occupies its leisure with insane
attacks upon a bear-skin rug in the library. It will finish the
work my nephew's rifle began in the Hymmalaya—I see I
cannot spell the word in any known form, although I am printing it every month. Have you read 'The Abode of Snow'?
not that it is by my nephew—I wish it were.

The following letter is in answer to one from
William Blackwood, who had sent good news of the
new book :—

John Blackwood to William Blackwood.

3 RANDOLPH CRESCENT, *April 22, 1875.*

I had great pleasure in receiving your letter to-day. The
interview with the Leweses must have been deeply interesting,
and I only wish you could have reported her looking better.
I have seen her several times in those depressed states about
her work, but always when she fairly began to speak one felt
that there was occasion not for depression but for rejoicing.
Certainly she does seem to feel that in producing her books she
is producing a living thing, and no doubt her books will live
longer than is given to children of the flesh.

About six months after this mention of the novel,
the first portion of 'Daniel Deronda' was handed over
to William Blackwood to convey to his uncle, who
was eagerly awaiting it in Edinburgh.

John Blackwood to George Eliot.

3 RANDOLPH CRESCENT, *April* 22, 1875

Willie tells me he has had a long and most interesting visit at The Priory, the only drawback to which was that you were complaining of not feeling well and being depressed. I have seen that depression on you before, at periods when other authors would have been crowing and flapping their wings without the solid reason which, I am sure, you have for doing so. I am quite elated at the prospect of Willie bringing down so large a portion of your new novel, and I feel your sending the MS. to me in this way as a thing to be proud of. Curiously enough, I was walking about with Theodore Martin yesterday when, talking about you and Lewes, he mentioned how devoted the Queen was to your works, especially 'Adam Bede.' So I told him how you had given me the MS. of first vol. of 'Adam,' with strict injunctions not to read it until I could do so quietly at home, and how I utterly disobeyed orders by peeping into the front pages on the top of the omnibus when Lewes deposited me at Kew, and fastening upon it the moment I left King's Cross next morning until I finished my reading with delight before I reached Newcastle when night was setting in.

When George Eliot was writing the earlier parts of 'Deronda' in 1875 John Blackwood went to see her, and thus describes his visit :—

John Blackwood to his Wife.

THE BURLINGTON, *May* 19, 1875.

I went yesterday by appointment to lunch with the Leweses, where I was most cordially welcomed. She is looking pale and a little languid, but that was to be expected under the interesting circumstances, as she delivered to me a volume of MS. which I am yearning to sit down to. As I left she said, "Now bring me a particular account of Jack. Nobody is more interested in the house of Blackwood than I am." I had told her I was going to Storrington to-morrow to see him.

To the same he writes :—

May 21, 1875.

Jack is coming up to-morrow, and will be delighted to come with me to Spondon by the train due at Derby 5.27. I found him very well, and everything right except the confounded Latin Prose. Further perusal confirms my admiration of George Eliot's work. She is a living marvel. It was quite affecting to see her happiness over what I had written to her and had to say.

Lewes has just been in and found me in the act of writing to George Eliot. I showed him what I was doing. He said: "Do go on. You have no idea how much good that will do her. She has more faith in your judgment than in that of any one else." His own judgment, he says, she naturally enough considers may be biassed, but I must say I have never found him wrong on the subject.

This turning, even in the very zenith of her fame, with almost childlike longing for approval to the friend of her early efforts, had in it something touching, and gave a certain grace to all the transactions that passed between them. The following amusing post-card from Mr Lewes, dashed off in haste, confirms this impression of the way the editorial letters acted on her spirits :—

G. H. Lewes to John Blackwood.

THE PRIORY, March 3, 1876.

DEAR BLACKWOOD,—Your note has been as good as a dose of quinine. As the drooping flower revives under the beneficent rain, so did her drooping spirits under your enthusiastic words.

On one occasion when we were calling on her that summer she said she was very anxious about the safety of the MS. of 'Deronda,' and wanted to have it back, but dared not trust it to the post-office. My father said he could not bring it himself next day, but could send it by a trusty messenger (the footman). At this she quailed. "Oh, he might stop at a public-house and forget it." We assured her such a lapse had never been known to occur. "Then might he not, if he were the sort of high-minded Bayard we described, be very likely to stop and help at a fire?" This was a contingency we had never contemplated, and finally, after much laughter, we promised her that some member of the family should place the MS. in her hands, and as a matter of fact I think my mother drove over with it to her the next morning. On this, as on all occasions when I saw her, the impression was that of a person beyond all things kindly and sympathetic, ever ready to be amused and interested in all that concerned her friends. Her sense of humour, too, was extremely keen, and my father, I remember, always made her laugh. The ponderosity of her conversation and the difficulty of making any way with her, of which some visitors have complained, must, we think, have been caused by their selecting topics not really congenial to themselves simply because they were talking to George Eliot, scaling heights that were beyond them, and as a result getting crushed by a solid avalanche of learning. But if one talked with her upon music, which she loved, pictures, the play, a flower-show, or equally a horse-show, she was with you — we were all talking upon what we equally understood. But the views of the novice on the latest metaphysical puzzles of the day, or an uncertain dive into scientific research, might have involved disaster. A mind so quick as hers could not fail to see when her companion was out of his depth, and then no doubt she felt contempt for what was mere pretension.　Large numbers of people used to invade her Sunday receptions who had often small claim upon her forbearance.　We remember one ridiculous incident of two enterprising young men who sat down opposite her with the intention of eliciting her opinions on the Turko - Russian war.　They were nothing if not simple and direct, and without any preamble whatever they fired off their first shot at their gentle-mannered hostess, startling the whole room with, "Are you a Russian or a Turk?" "Neither," came the grave reply in that deep musical voice, which we may well imagine gave them their quietus for the rest of the afternoon.

John Blackwood to William Blackwood.

THE BURLINGTON, *May* 29, 1875.

Yesterday Molly and I drove up to The Priory, where we passed a most charming hour with Mrs Lewes.　She was in great spirits and talked much with Molly, inquiring if she ever intended to send her father a MS., and said impressively that writing good letters ran in the family.　In the evening we went to hear Salvini, and we took Kate Fergusson with us.　I cannot quite make up my mind what to say about the Italian. About his physical and facial power there is no doubt, but of the mental power to make a great actor I am not so sure.　I am not perhaps a fair judge, as I have always hated "the black Sam," and if I had been a Venetian noble in those days I would have stuck a dagger into him at any stage of the business. When Salvini is raging about he does not lessen this feeling, and his Iago is such a wretched slimy valet of a creature that one is impatient of his being so deceived.　Still I listened and watched most minutely every turn of the man, which is saying a good deal.　Kate saw many play-actor friends all about the house.　Her climax was when Mario, with a beautiful white beard and bald white head, bowed expressively to her from the boxes. He applauded tremendously, and doubtless is a good judge. Mario, from my recollection at Nice, is exactly my own age, and his venerable appearance touched me, but he looked very handsome.

The first volume of 'Deronda' left John Blackwood after its perusal in a state of admiration. It seemed to him to contain all the elements of human interest which go to making a good tale, besides the more profound thoughts and reflections which characterise the author's later style. His critical mind delighted to dwell on the peculiar idiosyncrasies of each character, and he knew just where to lay a finger on the subtle delineation of thought or feeling which might easily escape general criticism.

John Blackwood to George Eliot.

THE BURLINGTON, *May* 25, 1875

Reading the whole, and re-reading many parts of the first volume of 'Daniel Deronda,' has more than confirmed the admiration and delight with which I wrote and spoke to you after my first happy sitting over your MS. That first night I really felt like a glutton dallying over his feast, and not reading at all with my usual rapid stride. The first scene in the dreary gorgeous German gambling-saloon, with the gamblers all looking so like each other about the eyes and mouth, is to the life, and poor Gwendolen's "enraged resistance" is so true. That is a magnificent illustration of yours about circumstances weighing upon characters such as hers like the weather upon the harvests. There is something very impressive in the way that fear froze that wild wilful heart on the sudden fall of the panel and disclosure of that horrid picture. Grandcourt is a most original character, and he and Deronda promise to be a grand contrast in your picture. There is somewhere a passage about a false air of demoniac strength in commonplace unregulated people who know not how to direct their force, that has made a great impression on me, but if I tried to refer to all the passages that have done that I should never finish my letter.

The next letter continues the criticism on 'Deronda,' and refers also to the opinion of others who had seen the "proofs."

John Blackwood to George Eliot.

STRATHTYRUM, *Nov.* 10, 1875.

That wicked witch Gwendolen is perfectly irresistible—new and yet so true to nature, like all the other characters. Her running mental reflections after each few words she has said to Grandcourt are like what passes through the mind after each move at a game, and, as far as I know, a new device in reporting a conversation. A cautious speaker will here learn that his pauses may also give his interlocutor an advantage. The verdict among us all here is that you are fairly outdoing 'Middlemarch,' and I need say no more. These sworn "horse-coursers," my wife and nephew, suggest that poor Primrose's knees were not likely to have been broken by such a fall as you describe *in a field.*

The Jewish element standing out so strongly in the book was the only point about which my father had felt any doubts, but, as the following to Mr Langford sets forth, he refrained from making any criticism on this head to the author :—

Book VI. of 'Daniel Deronda' will clear away your doubts about Book V., about which I too felt some qualms. But the simple fact is, she is so great a giant that there is nothing for it but to accept her inspirations and leave criticism alone. Reading some of my old friends, 'The Antiquary,' 'Heart of Mid-Lothian,' &c., lately, I thought, good heavens, what a mess any man sitting down to criticise these books piecemeal would have made!

To the author he had written :—

Of Mordecai I feel that it would be presumptuous to speak until one has read more, and I daresay puzzling and thinking over that phase of the tale has been the cause of my not writing to you sooner.

George Eliot to John Blackwood.

THE PRIORY, NORTH BANK,
REGENT'S PARK, *Feb.* 25, 1876.

I thought it likely that your impressions about Mordecai would be doubtful. Perhaps when the work is finished you will see its bearings better. The effect that one strives after is an outline as strong as that of Balfour of Burley for a much more complex character and a higher strain of ideas. But such an effect is just the most difficult thing in art,—to give new elements—*i.e.*, elements not already used up—in forms as vivid as those of long familiar types. Doubtless the wider public of novel-readers must feel more interest in Sidonia than in Mordecai. But then, I was not born to paint Sidonia. We had not heard that the editor of 'Harper's Magazine' had written to you agreeably, but I suppose it is he who has diligently sent American notices in newspapers, one of which, I think, Mr Lewes said was ably done. One newspaper passeth away and another cometh. We must remember that the writing which does this brief office is often a more difficult industry than work of more lasting value. Reviewers are fellow-men towards whom I keep a Christian feeling by not reading them. But Mr Lewes thinks they have treated me very well, though Mr Langford hints a disposition to grumble.

He eventually became reconciled to Mordecai, even to the point of admiration, as we shall see.

John Blackwood to G. H. Lewes.

EDINBURGH, *March* 2, 1876.

I read Book VI. last night, and have unbounded congratulations to send to Mrs Lewes. She is *a magician.* It is a poem, a drama, and a grand novel. There is no doubt about the marvellous Mordecai, and oh, that Cohen family! The whole tribe of Israel should fall down and worship her. I must read again before venturing to write to her. When I finished the part at half-past three I grudged very much not being able to go with Deronda to see his mother. The suspense is great.

By the time Book VII. was reached the story was nearing its tragic climax, and John Blackwood tells the author that "the book is so powerful as to be very terrible," and sympathises with her on the mental strain she must have undergone in writing it, for George Eliot felt every line that she wrote.

John Blackwood to George Eliot.

EDINBURGH, *April* 17, 1876.

No wonder Deronda felt "worn" at the close of the interview with Gwendolen. I can hardly imagine any one reading without being carried away and feeling upset, and what must be the strain of thinking and writing out such a scene! Much as I know of the conscientious pain and anxiety you go through in the construction of your great works, I never felt more deeply and sympathisingly with you in your labours than I did last night in reading this Book VII. of 'Daniel.'

When John Blackwood went to London a few weeks later George Eliot was writing the last chapters of 'Deronda,' and the strain and excitement attendant on the work was great. Sometimes she had felt unequal to seeing even this sympathising friend, who writes as follows :—

John Blackwood to William Blackwood.

14 ARLINGTON STREET, *June* 6, 1876.

After we came out of the City we went to The Priory. She was not visible, being in the agonies of the wind up and suffering from faceache. We had, however, a most pleasant lunch with Lewes and Miss Helps, daughter of Arthur Helps, who was there   Lewes said his wife was writing with tears in her eyes, and I do not wonder at it. That portion of the proof which I received to-day certainly made me weep. There is a simplicity and power about it that has not been reached in my time. As we drove home we called at George St. I was taken up to see him [Sir William Fergusson]. His illness is, I fear, a fatal one, but I do not think the end is imminent. If it is the end, it is a beautiful and peaceful one, with his three girls sitting near the foot of his bed. He talked in his usual pleasant cheerful way, and only complained of weakness. It did not show in the face except in the eyes, which had a little of the strained look one always fears to see.

The touching allusion to the illness of his old friend Sir William Fergusson which we have just quoted is only one of many which appear in my father's letters with reference to Sir William that year: not a day seems to have passed without his hearing of him, and his usual cheerful budget is almost invariably saddened with the unfavourable accounts of his health.

At length the work was accomplished and the last sheets of ‘Deronda’ were handed over to John Blackwood, who thus expresses his delight over them :—

John Blackwood to G. H. Lewes.

14 ARLINGTON ST., PICCADILLY, *June* 10, 1876.

I got “The End” to-day. Grand and touching are too mild words for this book. Give the author my best love, respect, and congratulations. It troubled me to see her sitting pale and tired in her carriage at the door yesterday, and I fear I did not say half what I wished to say, but Mrs Lewes sees everything, and would, I trust, see what I felt. No wonder she felt tired and unwilling for company, but I earnestly hope that the change across the Channel is already beginning to tell for good. I intended to have gone to Scotland on Monday, but Delane, who has been very ill, presses me so earnestly to come to see him at least for a couple of days that I

cannot leave without seeing my old friend and companion. So
if you write to me address here.

'Daniel Deronda' was published in parts like
'Middlemarch,' and the following letter to Mr Lewes
shows how each succeeding number rivalled its predecessor in popularity :—

John Blackwood to G. H. Lewes.

EDINBURGH, *May* 11, 1876.

I enclose a most pleasant statistical table of the sales of
'Daniel' up to the present time. The closeness with which the
sale of the successive numbers keeps up to the sale of the First
Book indicates most satisfactorily how firm and enduring is the
hold that the work is taking. I never recollect a case in which
the sale of a work published in a serial form kept so closely up
to the first start. Many buy a first part of a popular work from
curiosity and then drop it, contenting themselves to read afterwards as opportunity may serve, but 'Deronda' has evidently
hooked his fish at the first start and is keeping him steadily on
the line all through the run. I knew that Book III. must tell
tremendously. Jews are not generally popular pictures in
fiction, but then look how they are served up. They never have
been so presented before, like human beings, with their good and
their evil, their comic and their tragic side. In the midst of
triumph it is distressing to hear of Mrs Lewes feeling so feeble.
I do hope that the expedition to Oxford will do her good.

George Eliot went abroad immediately after finishing 'Deronda,' and Mr Lewes, in an account of their
quiet pursuit of health and rest at Ragatz, gives an
amusing glimpse of his efforts to learn Hebrew.

G. H. Lewes to John Blackwood.

HOF RAGATZ, 17*th July* 1876.

Your pleasant and welcome letter found us both greatly
improved in health and spirits by our stay here. Mrs Lewes is
quite another woman, and is recovering her colour and contour

—*not* before they were wanted. Her appetite is good, and we walk four hours amid the woods and up the easy mountain-sides—bathe, eat, read, and idle—" letting the world fleet by as in the golden time." Not a single word have we exchanged with any one above the rank of a waiter or shopkeeper—and don't miss the "charms of society," about which some people talk so glibly as indispensable to existence. In the woods of a morning she has taken to instruct me in Hebrew, and we waken the echoes with our laughter sometimes at my blunders and attempts at Israelitish eloquence ! Mrs Lewes desires her very best remembrances to all (with especial thanks to Willie for his agreeable note), and hopes you have been enjoying your trip into the Highlands. I have had some notion of going there too when we come back, and visiting the Brit. Association at Glasgow, but this is at present very vague.

The press were not' unanimous in praise, it would appear from the following letters, and the Jewish element, about which John Blackwood had originally felt doubtful, appears to have been the point in the book on which opinions differed. There were, to counterbalance this, many extraordinarily interesting and striking expressions of approval from private sources, showing the deep impression the story had produced, and how widely it was being read, or rather studied.

George Eliot to John Blackwood.

THE PRIORY, NORTH BANK,
REGENT'S PARK, *Nov.* 3, 1876.

A cloud of cold having rolled off my brain, it seems clear to me that I owe you a letter. It will be rather interesting to see what is the sale of ' Deronda ' compared with ' Middle-march.' Miss Helps, who sees a great many people, and makes her one copy a sort of lending library, says that she never observed a case in which the " opinions of the press " so totally differed from the impression produced on readers. I am saved from concluding that I have exhibited my faculties in a state of decay by very delightful letters from unknown readers, and reported judgments from considerable authorities. A statesman who shall be nameless has said that I first opened to him a vision of Italian life, then of Spanish, and now I have kindled in him a quite new understanding of the Jewish people. This is what I wanted to do—to widen the English vision a little in that direction and let in a little conscience and refinement. I expected to excite more resistance of feeling than I have seen the sign of, but I did what I chose to do—not as well as I should have liked to do it, but as well as I could.

The following to William Blackwood describes one of the many letters the author used to receive from unknown correspondents, all taking the most vivid personal interest in her characters :—

George Eliot to William Blackwood.

THE HEIGHTS, WITLEY, GODALMING.

It was a very harmless breach you committed in opening my American letter, which happens to be one that I should have liked you to read. A young lady of New York expresses much gratitude for being saved, by reading 'Daniel Deronda,' from marrying a man whom she could not love, but whom she was disposed to accept for the sake of his wealth; but she is so far from being absolved by this momentous personal matter that she goes on to be still more effusive about the " enjoyment and instruction " she has had from the Jewish element in the book, and thinks the scene on the Bridge the best in the book— " flashing through one with a sort of electric sympathy," &c. Tell your uncle that America is the quarter of the world for " appreciative butter."

In the end of November 1878 Mr G. H. Lewes died. One of his last acts had been to send off to Edinburgh the MS. of George Eliot's essays entitled 'Theophrastus Such.' Without his fostering care and sympathy the thoughts of publishing a new book seemed more than ever to weigh upon her spirits. With her usual unselfish consideration for others we find her writing about the proofs, knowing the book had been put into type and fearing it might cause inconvenience to keep it standing so long, as it was not to be published for some time.

John Blackwood to George Eliot.

EDINBURGH, *January* 14, 1879.

It comes home to my heart to see your hand again, and your considerate note in the midst of all your heart-breaking trouble is so like you. Do not allow the proofs of 'Theophrastus Such' to concern you in the least—the type can wait your perfect convenience. I had it set up that the proofs might be ready to your hand when you were able to turn your thoughts that way. It is all in type now, and I shall complete your set of proofs to-morrow. I have been reading it all with great interest, and it does make one think. In the circumstances perhaps it does make me think more gravely than I otherwise would have done. There are so many things, too, that make one feel where one's own shoe pinches, especially in the weaker points of character. It brings us all in a kind of way to the confessional.

CHAPTER XIII.

LAST YEARS.

"ANCIENT CLASSICS FOR ENGLISH READERS"—"SKILLED LABOUR" AT
A POPULAR PRICE—ANTHONY TROLLOPE'S 'CÆSAR'—SIR THEODORE
MARTIN'S 'HORACE'—LORD NEAVES AND 'THE GREEK ANTHOLOGY'—
A GRATIFYING COMPLIMENT—DEATH OF SAMUEL WARREN—"HOW
JOHN WAS DRILLED"—THE DUKE AND DUCHESS OF RUTLAND—
BEFORE THE COPYRIGHT COMMISSION—INTERNATIONAL COPYRIGHT THE
GREATEST BOON TO AUTHORS AND TO LITERATURE—A RETROSPECT—
THE EARLY MAKERS OF THE MAGAZINE—THEIR SUCCESSORS—A
POWER IN THE PUBLISHING WORLD AND A FRIEND TO AUTHORS—
HIS METHODS—FINDS THE PUBLIC "A MOST EXCELLENT BEAST IN
THE MAIN"—HIS LAST GAME OF GOLF—ILLNESS—STRATHTYRUM—
AUTUMN DAYS AND SADNESS—DEATH—SOME TRIBUTES.

A SCHEME which had long been simmering in John
Blackwood's mind, and to which there are many
previous allusions of a tentative kind, at last took
shape, as we shall show by the following letters.
He had often been struck by the want of a series
of books—not school-books, nor yet exhaustive translations—which should place the ancient Greek and
Latin authors within reach of a class of readers
who knew neither Latin nor Greek, or at best had
forgotten the smattering they acquired in their
school-days.

John Blackwood to Rev. Lucas Collins.

EDINBURGH, *April* 3, 1868

Although I have not written to you I have been thinking a good deal about my scheme for popularising the Classics, and I am pretty sure that the scheme is a good one, and that you are the man to carry it out. Your preface indicates exactly the sort of thing I intended, and I like the specimen pages of Homer. A pleasant and readable exposition of what the great poems, dramas, &c., of antiquity are all about is what is wanted, and your style is as pleasant as can be, while your familiarity with the subject gives the proper scholarly tone and will impart the required knowledge. "Ancient Classics for Modern Readers" strikes me as pretty near the right kind of title.

Writing to Mr Delane, he thus describes his idea of the series :—

John Blackwood to John Delane.

EDINBURGH, *Dec.* 21, 1869.

The enclosed is prospectus of a series of little volumes which has been in my head for a great many years, and which, if I mistake not, will exactly jump with your humour. The first volume, containing the 'Iliad,' is sent to you along with this, and I wish you very much to read it, which you will find a very pleasant operation. I have often been conscious of the want of some such series myself, and I felt that if such was the case with one like myself who was educated up to the muzzle, what must it be with other busy men, and ladies or gentlemen who have not had a thorough education. My difficulty was to find a scholar who wrote a real easy popular style, and I fixed upon Collins as one of the very pleasantest writers I knew. Poor —— was to have done the 'Æneid,' but he had not the same ease and grace of style as Collins, who is one of my favourite contributors. I am certain that the idea of the series is a first-rate one, and that it fills a gap, hitting the wants of classicists or non-classicists.

In the scheme thus clearly propounded in the

VOL. III.   2 C

preceding letters the only point John Blackwood does
not touch upon—and this was rather important—
was the cost of the volumes : this he intended to
be a popular price, and fixed it at 2s. 6d. each, a
modest sum when we consider the "skilled labour"
employed upon them. But this was part of his intention, and formed, we believe, a new departure in
a line of publishing, the marked success of which
has called forth many imitations, the book world
having been flooded in recent years with attempts
to convey in a condensed form other literary nutri-
ment of a more ordinary kind — soldiers, sailors,
divines, all having been metaphorically boiled down
to meet the now universal demand for an ox in a
tea-cup.

The scheme was now fairly started, with the Rev.
Lucas Collins as editor of the volumes. One of the
interesting features in the series was the diversity of
pens employed in its production, many of the authors
who contributed being well known in widely different
fields of literature. Anthony Trollope, as we know,
wrote 'Cæsar's Commentaries' with right goodwill.
"It was a great pleasure to me to find Trollope so
good," John Blackwood writes to Mr Collins ; "and
what a relief it must have been to you to read his easy
well-turned narrative after the fiery furnace you have
been going through with poor ——'s proofs." Among
the other well-known names were those of Mr W. H.
Mallock, who wrote the Lucretius volume, and Sir
Theodore Martin, to whom naturally was given the
Horace—his well-known lyrical translation of the
poet already formed one of his numerous claims to
literary renown.

John Blackwood to Sir Theodore Martin.

STRATHTYRUM, *Oct.* 13, 1870.

You have done the 'Horace' excellently, and have grudged no pains on the work, and made a very delightful little volume. This hideous war interferes with literature, as it does with everything else. If this is felt a little in England, fancy the position of those dependent on literature in France.

Sir Alexander Grant, then Principal of Edinburgh University, did the Aristotle volume, which was one of the marked successes of the series.

John Blackwood to Sir Alexander Grant.

EDINBURGH, *June* 5, 1877.

In accordance with our arrangement, I have now the pleasure of enclosing you cheque for your Aristotle volume in our supplementary series of "Ancient Classics for English Readers." You have, I think, been wonderfully successful in making Aristotle both intelligible (as far as it is possible to make him to a certain class of English readers) and interesting, and the volume should be specially acceptable to many young students of philosophy. I know *I* should have been very glad of such a volume when I began to read Aristotle, and I might then have studied him a good deal more than I did and improved my knowledge of philosophy. A few of the principal newspapers have noticed the volume in highly complimentary reviews.

The names we have mentioned instantly suggest the combinations which were not so obvious in many instances. Sometimes a "young" hand was given a chance, as in the case of Mr Clifton Collins, the son of the editor of the series, who made a conspicuous first success with Sophocles, thus early fulfilling a prediction of John Blackwood's, who, after reading a prize essay written by him when a boy at Rugby, foretold he would one day follow in his father's footsteps as a contributor to 'Blackwood.' Another well-known name that occurs to me in connection with the series is that of Lord Neaves, who wrote for it the volume 'Greek Anthology.' This veteran contributor and trusted friend had not of late years been so often seen amongst the regular contributors, and my father hailed with pleasure this occasion that induced him once more to emerge from the scholarly retirement of his library, and give to readers the benefit of those stores of learning and culture, the full extent of which were known perhaps only to those nearest him—his daughters, with whom he used to read and talk in the quiet seclusion of his book-lined study.

John Blackwood to Lord Neaves.
                                        EDINBURGH, *Sept.* 17, 1873.

I have some pleasant notes from Collins, in one of which he expresses his belief that your volume "will be one of the best of the series." . . . I hope you are getting on well, and that your work on the Anthology fills up your time pleasantly. Is it advancing—Anthology I mean, not time?

In the next letter my father refers to a pleasant incident in connection with Lord Neaves's contribution to the series.

John Blackwood to Lord Neaves.
                                        EDINBURGH, *April* 28, 1874.

Everything is right with the Anthology, and I doubt not you will find a proof of the Appendix awaiting you. Pray give away as many copies as you wish, but we cannot think of allowing you to pay for them, especially after your very kind and handsome proposal that you should not be paid for the copyright. I cannot but feel it a very high and gratifying compliment that two men so distinguished and so different from each other as Anthony Trollope and you should have asked me to accept their labour in this series as a mark of friendship and esteem.

Lord Neaves's varied gifts had been shown in many brilliant contributions to the Magazine, and his friendship by the ever-ready aid he gave when consulted on any knotty point in literary or political matters which the Editor might wish to discuss with him. On one occasion John Blackwood wrote to him: "I and those who are gone before me have always looked upon you as one of our truest friends and advisers. Your letter suggests a long look back, to which at another time I would have responded more fully, but with God's blessing I hope there are many years before us of that kindly, and to me most beneficial, intimacy with you."

Lord Neaves's death a year or two later drew from John Blackwood, when writing to his old friend's widow, the following warm expressions of affectionate regret :—

John Blackwood to Mrs Neaves.
45 GEORGE STREET, *Feb.* 27, 1877.

My object has been to get a sketch of Lord Neaves which should interest the public in general, and make them feel for the man they have lost, although they did not know him personally, or even by name. But at heart I care most that the writer should please the family of one who was very dear to me. In the first I think I have succeeded, and I shall be very anxious to hear how this imperfect tribute to 'Maga's' dear old friend and contributor strikes you and the girls. The only outside comment I hear is from Theodore Martin to-day, who says, "I cannot help adding a line to say how much pleased I have been with 'Maga's' paper on Charles Neaves. It is beautiful in feeling and expression."

We are here reminded of another of the oldest of 'Maga's' supporters who passed away in 1877, Mr

Samuel Warren, the author of 'The Diary of a Late Physician' and 'Ten Thousand a-Year.' His death touched a chord in my father's heart, recalling the days of long ago when he first used to live in London, and Warren and Warren's house made the city seem home-like to him.

John Blackwood to William Blackwood.

STRATHTYRUM, ST ANDREWS, *July* 31, 1877.

It sits very near my heart to do justice to Warren in the Magazine, which the press never have done. There never was a more sworn Blackwoodian, and he was the first great author who publicly stated his acknowledgments to my father and thoroughly recognised his position, as you will see in the preface to the Diary. Send me over a copy of his works, also his letters, of which you will find no end. I remember them very vividly.

My father had always liked going to the Temple Church in old days when he was so much with Mr Warren, and up to the last it was Warren's name which always gained us admittance to the Bencher's seats. The first time I remember seeing him was in that church. My father whispered "There is Warren," and at that instant he started up in front of us, and, turning round, indicated for us with one admiring comprehensive gesture the whole church, the choir, and the clergy. The fun and drollery underlying his most serious utterances, which made his conversation so fascinating, have often been described. And even in these latter days when we saw him, an old man, he was still Warren, entertaining us all the evening, keeping us thoroughly amused, and leaving us in the bewildering and altogether delightful uncertainty whether we had laughed when he had intended us to cry, or the reverse !

One after another of John Blackwood's friends of the older generation kept dropping out of the ranks, every year making fresh blanks. In Edinburgh his literary associates were now principally Mr Hill Burton the historian and Mr John Skelton. With these old friends he still had much pleasant intercourse. The accomplished writer of Shirley's Letters had lately varied his more serious labours and historical researches by a very clever paper in the style of 'Dame Europa's School,' having for its object the necessary drilling required to put John Bull in a state of preparedness to meet his foes.

John Blackwood to John Skelton.

STRATHTYRUM, ST ANDREWS, *Aug.* 3, 1873.

I like the idea of your paper, "How John was Drilled," extremely, and I am so confident that it will suit me that I shall get it into type at once. Will you therefore send or take the MS. to Willie at 45 George Street. The Government seem determined to teach everybody how to suck eggs. I had a visit the other day from my old friend David Wingate, who I was glad to find had been appointed on a commission to see that none but qualified engineers were appointed to work at pits, &c. The smile on honest David's face was good when I said, "Don't you think that is a thing the employers should look after ? They will appoint committees to teach us how to conduct our various callings, as well as to tell us what to eat, drink, and avoid." The great golf match was really a treat. I walked round all the three days breathless amid a breathless crowd, and I never saw better play. It would require a fusion of old Homer and old Sutherland to do justice to the struggle. I still think Tommy [young Tom Morris] the best.

A few weeks later he wrote to Mr Skelton :—

I have the pleasure of enclosing a cheque in acknowledgment of your excellent paper "How John was Drilled." It was extremely good, and liked, I think, as much as I expected (which is saying a good deal). The vein is to be worked more, and I hope you are going on with what you talked of. I should much like that for December or January.

The next letters mention a much valued friend of my father's, whose name frequently occurs in his letters in connection with politics and the important events of the different Conservative Governments with which as Lord John Manners, before becoming Duke of Rutland, he had been so long associated. The acquaintance with him had begun in the early days when Lord John, to give him the name by which he was so long known, had conjointly with Mr Gladstone represented Newark in the Conservative interest, and by his efforts in opposition to the repeal of the Corn Laws in 1841 had met with the warm support of ' Blackwood.' The friendship born of political sympathies had a further bond in the refined and cultured tastes of Lord John, which lay in the direction of literature, to which in the days of his leisure he made various contributions in the form of original poetry and many admirable translations and adaptations from the German. In the latter he was ably seconded by the accomplished lady to whom my father frequently refers as "Lady John," now Duchess of Rutland, and herself the authoress of many charming poems. The references in the following letters show John Blackwood coming forward, in the best interests of literature, as witness on the Copyright

Commission (1876) before the House of Lords, Lord John being chairman on the occasion :—

John Blackwood to William Blackwood.

I had a most pleasant chat with Lord John yesterday. He says the demands of the three Powers on Turkey are too severe, and we could not assent. He told me the five points, and they are unreasonable. It is a serious business ; but as our Government know the Powers are quarrelling, and as jealous as the devil of each other on the subject, I daresay it will all come right. Their first intimation to us was a telegram totally unintelligible, to which we were asked to telegraph assent. He (Lord John) proposes to have me up for the Copyright exam. on Friday. He says Wolff and "Ginx's Baby" make speeches instead of asking questions, and Trollope too is rather in the speech-making line.

John Blackwood to his Wife.

I came back a little ago from an hour and half or ¾ examination before the Copyright Commission. I have given an account of it in my letter to Willie. . . . Lord John [Manners] was evidently pleased with his witness, and said, "You did capitally," and so said Trollope. . . . The weather is raw and cold, but my cold is nearly gone, and I am very fit and well. I go into the world so little that it really was a bother to me to go to the Commission to-day, and I was astonished to find what a very cool bird I was. At the end, when they thanked me for my evidence, I said, " My Lords and Gentlemen, I am so little in the way of being a witness in any public matter that I came down here with a lively recollection of Lever's remark, that next to being in the dock the next worst thing was being in the witness-box, but your courtesy has quite taken away that feeling."

This Copyright Commission is more fully described in a letter to my cousin William Blackwood. I re-

member Mr Anthony Trollope saying afterwards to
my mother in his hearty way, "Your husband was
the best man we had; he hit the nail on the head
every time he spoke."

John Blackwood to William Blackwood.

14 ARLINGTON STREET, *May* 26, 1876.

I have just returned from an hour and half exam. before
the Copyright Commission. Lord John was in the chair, and
the other members of Commission present were Trollope, Sir
Henry Holland, Sir Louis Mallet, Dr Smith ('Quarterly'), Mr
Daldy, and I think another, and I had nearly forgot to say
Drummond Wolff. Lord John of course was nice and judicious
as possible, and I think I made a very favourable impression on
the meeting, as I was clear and collected as man could possibly
be. I was under fire for an hour and $\frac{3}{4}$. It would have been
over in half the time had it not been for ——, who persisted in
asking questions about books being published at a high price
at first and then being published at a low price afterwards.
I had repeatedly to explain to him that publishers and authors
had to judge each individual case, and did so according to the
best of their lights, which were considerable, so no legislator
or legislation could interfere with them, and that he was
wandering away from the question of copyright. I was very
decided as to property in the work of a man's hand and brain,
and went strongly for extension after the life of the author.
I also put it most distinctly that the greatest boon to authors
and literature, English and American, would be international
copyright with the MS. I am to get my evidence to revise, of
course.

A letter to Mr Alex. Innes Shand, who was writing
in 1878 on the subject of "Correspondents to the
Press," led my father to state his views on that
hard-working and valorous portion of them who are
expected, when battles are the order of the day, to
supply for each morning a breakfast of horrors, and

a detailed account of the carnage, given with the minute accuracy that we are in the habit of seeing bestowed on the daily money article composed within
the peaceful seclusion of four walls.

John Blackwood to A. Innes Shand.

45 GEORGE ST., EDINR., *Nov.* 14, 1878.

The picture of the correspondents is extremely good. Having very considerable knowledge of the subject, I speak with
great confidence, and did I not feel rather tired I would enter
largely into comment. The public are chiefly to be blamed for
the false and hasty news, as they will take it rather than wait
a day. Von Moltke could not write a correspondent's letter
immediately, or indeed at any time, after a battle, and the
public would prefer the weakest correspondent's lucubrations
to a few well-considered sentences. Take it altogether, I think
you have hit the right key-note of praise and blame throughout,
and so I shall probably begin the number with the paper.

Mr Shand, who was writing these papers for the
Magazine, had been for some years a valuable contributor, and a member of the little band who constituted my father's intimate friends. He was, with
Hamley, Lockhart, and Kinglake, of later years a
regular frequenter of those pleasant gatherings at
the Burlington and Garrick which have been so
often described. A subsequent article by Mr Shand
on Quarterlies and Monthly Magazines drew from
John Blackwood a letter which, written as it was
near the close of his own life, gives a peculiar weight
and significance to the writer's words, particularly to
the list of names which he subjoined for Mr Shand's
guidance as being those which have given most lasting renown to the Magazine.

John Blackwood to A. Innes Shand.

45 GEORGE ST., EDINR., *Decr.* 30, 1878.

I had the pleasure of receiving yours of the 27th on Sunday evening, and the ladies join me heartily in sending all good wishes of the season to Mrs Shand and you. When I last wrote to you I should have put in a proviso that I quite saw your intention of following up the Quarterlies with the Magazine, and fully appreciate your devoted loyalty to 'Maga,' but I was writing in a hurry and felt the second title of the paper a misnomer. However, you will see that I have put it all in, and very good of its kind it is. I feel a delicacy of speaking of ourselves next month, as to how we should begin without seeming to brag; and, sticking to a quiet statement of facts, we make a vastly bigger brag than any other periodical could. The Magazine began in 1817, and has held its own at the head of the field ever since. Bulwer, Dickens, Thackeray, when at the highest wave of their popularity, all started or were employed to start periodicals, but they never touched 'Blackwood.' The most striking feature perhaps about the Magazine is the mass of books besides its own goodly volumes that it has contributed to the permanent literature of the country, and in that respect I think we may fairly challenge comparison not with one but with all the periodicals put together. Look at Wilson's Noctes, Recreations, and endless essays; the 'Tales from Blackwood,' including Aytoun's "Glenmutchkin," &c., &c.; 'The Diary of a late Physician' and 'Ten Thousand a-Year'; 'Tom Cringle's Log,' 'Cruise of the Midge,' with all the best of De Quincey except 'The Opium-Eater.'

He then passes on to those authors whose works he himself published, and which have, we may say, given a distinction to his life, and whom in many instances he introduced for the first time to the public :—

'The Caxtons' and all the series of novels which are now Bulwer's most lasting glory; 'The Scenes of Clerical Life,' which first made George Eliot famous, and have hardly ever been surpassed since. Aytoun's Lays all came first in 'Maga,' as did much of Mrs Hemans and Mrs Southey, also Mrs Barret Browning's "Cry of the Children," the best thing in my opinion she ever did. Lever, too, was an admirable contributor, and his "O'Dowds" were unique, quite a new feature in his reputation. Mrs Oliphant's 'Salem Chapel,' &c., &c. When we come nearer our own time it is awkward to name the contributors, as Trollope, Blackmore, Mrs Oliphant, &c.; but the Oliphants, Hamleys, Chesneys, Lockhart, yourself, Brackenbury, Andrew Wilson ('Abode of Snow'), Julian Sturgis, &c., &c., are no unworthy successors to those I have named in early days. We might come to last year, and amid all the periodicals that have been parading names from Gladstone downwards is there anything so likely to live as the anonymous contributions to 'Blackwood,' "Mine is Thine," "Irene Macgillicuddy," and "The New Ordeal"? I ought to write a volume, but I have been interrupted all day and my back is weary. Observe that nearly all the things that have first made a name in 'Blackwood' were by writers utterly unknown, and could not appear in periodicals that live by buying and advertising names. The only great exception is Bulwer, and he made a name for himself when he wrote for 'Blackwood.'

Amongst those above mentioned who were considered by John Blackwood to be worthily maintaining the literary reputation of the House appears the name of Julian Sturgis, author of 'John-a-Dreams,' 'An Accomplished Gentleman,' and other novels.

John Blackwood to Julian Sturgis.

45 GEORGE STREET, EDINR., *Dec.* 17, 1873.

I am happy to say that I think your story "The Philosopher's Baby" extremely good, and I shall put it into type for the Magazine. You will recollect that from the time of that famous idea of yours, when a young boy, of the funk a ghost would be in if it met a madman, I said that you would become an author; but I have met so many disappointments in the writing of clever young friends that I took up your MS. with a qualm, and was greatly relieved when I found it so good and amusing. The defect of the story is what I have often seen before in good first flights, that it wants filling out to make it more of flesh and blood and less of a skeleton of a tale. However, as one has much more often to complain of spinning out, the defect is a good one which will cure itself. I send no messages to your good father and mother, as I suppose you do not mean to tell them of your doings until you can show your bantling in full form.

The long train of literary celebrities who have passed before us in connection with John Blackwood's life and work have now fulfilled their part, as it were, in the moving scene, bringing us once more face to face with the man himself, the central figure of the group. His life will not afford us the picturesque contrasts of poverty and riches, for, thanks to the circumstances of his birth and parentage, his career began under the happy auspices that leave the mind free from worry and the monetary cares that have beset many men who have attained a high position by the work of their own intellect. Nor do we find later on any of the ups and downs which vary some careers, for the simple reason that his whole course tended in an upward direction, and that success seems almost invariably to have crowned even his most hazardous ventures,—for be it said that publishing is somewhat of a game of chance, nothing venture nothing win, but with this difference from ordinary play, that it is not always given to the publisher to know when he is holding trumps in his hand or the reverse. To the fact that John Blackwood possessed this intuitive knowledge to a remarkable degree may be ascribed much of his success, his keen literary insight rendering him secure where others might have blundered, and making him absolutely self-reliant and independent of the value of an author's name. This gave the weight and importance to his judgment which caused him to be regarded as a power in the publishing world, and amongst authors as a generous pioneer of fresh literary talent. His methods of gauging so accurately what was likely to find merit in the eyes of the public are given in these few characteristic sentences in a letter to George Eliot when some literary matter was under discussion :—

John Blackwood to George Eliot.

This forms another instance of many I have seen of how impossible it is, even with the best means of judging, to predict with certainty what the public will do about a book. The only principle is to publish, according to the best of one's judgment, nothing but good books, and if the public is sometimes a stupid beast, I am happy to say I have found him a most excellent beast in the main.

Referring to his dealings with authors, Colonel Lockhart says of him :—

He appears to have had the interests of his clients as much at heart as his own ; and his evidence before the Copyright Commission showed him to be the true friend of authors. So much so, indeed, that from the publishers' point of view he must have been somewhat heterodox; for certain it is that he did not look upon the filling of a publisher's pockets as the final cause of all literary creations. From the report of a speech which he delivered at the Scott Centenary Banquet at St Andrews we extract his account of his own relations with the author class: "Much was said of quarrels between authors and publishers, but he was happy to say that they were not within his knowledge; on the contrary, he could tell a very different tale. Authors had been his dearest friends and companions all the days of his life. To them he could turn in joy or sorrow for safe and certain sympathy." In the same speech he alluded to some of his special literary friendships, and paid a touching tribute to the memory of Aytoun, who was the dearest of all his intimates.

George Eliot's delight in this Centenary speech is quoted in the following letter from Mr Lewes to William Blackwood: "How capital your uncle's speech was! We heard him in every sentence; and when he came to that passage in which he said that his authors had been his friends, Mrs Lewes burst out in her fervid way, 'And I am sure it was *their* fault when they were not so.'"

Nearly all the letters of my father's correspondents during the year of 1879 contain a reference to his health—sometimes anxious, sometimes relieved, but always full of solicitude and asking for further tidings; for those who knew him were aware that he had never really regained strength after the severe illness he had at Rome in the preceding spring of 1878, and that though able to do his work and see his friends, any return of the chest and heart troubles would go hard with him. The golfing, which had been his great enjoyment, had to be given up; and that winter we find once, and once only, that he had been for a round at Musselburgh.

John Blackwood to Rev. G. R. Gleig.

Feb. 8, 1879.

I am going down to Musselburgh to golf for the first time these ten weeks, and the Lord President Inglis, when I met him yesterday, said, "If I can possibly get out of Court I'll meet you at the train at one." As it is Saturday I think he will.

His friend the President did not fail him, and I remember the cheerful return and discussion of the day's play, and the many friendly greetings that met him on his reappearing after so long an absence from the green. This is the last allusion I find to his playing golf, and this game must have been, I think, the last he played. The spring of 1879 was a particularly inclement one even for Edinburgh, and, in spite of all care, my father experienced another attack of pleurisy in the month of April, accompanied by the same heart symptoms which had occasioned him so much suffering in Rome the spring previous, and found him this time less able to resist it. When he recovered sufficiently from this severe illness we moved over to Strathtyrum in June. He of course had not been to London that spring, and his friends had been anxious and disappointed at not seeing him, and any improvement in his health was snatched at that held out hope of his complete recovery. On 16th July Mr Trollope wrote : "My dear Blackwood, I have just had a letter from Collins in which he says you are better. I need not say how glad we are to hear it." A week or two later he wrote again : "Do not trouble yourself to write about it [a business matter], but consider rather that though I receive no answer I shall consider my letter answered. Write to me a line simply to tell me how you are." Mr Trollope's kind considerate letter sent him off at once to his writing-table to answer it. He was always touched by any solicitude displayed on his behalf, and it invariably encouraged him to make some exertion to reassure the writer. Mr Trollope soon wrote again :—

Mr Trollope to John Blackwood.

FREIBERG, *Sept.* 9, 1879.

I have been very glad to get your letter, as I have been afraid that you were ill. Don't play golf too soon. Though there must be some of the salt of youth left to you, as somebody says somewhere to some one, it is not so much but that you should husband it after the illness you have had.

Yes, there was much of youth left to him, in that he remained to the last what the French call *jeune d'esprit*. No other expression could exactly describe his manner and mode of looking at life, which were in keeping with his slight well-knit figure, that never acquired the portliness of middle age, nor did he ever assume the solemn airs of a literary potentate. A certain quiet dignity and self-possession had always been his from the early days when he had been first left to his own resources in London. But this did not affect the half-humorous, half-deprecatory way he used to allude to himself as though he could never take himself quite seriously. There was a certain charm in being told that " he knew himself to be the most desperately careless fellow in the world," having that moment discovered, probably in a hotel, that he had left his money and watch on his dressing-table; or to read, as in a letter to Mr Collins, that nothing in the world would ever teach him " to keep his writing-table in order," but that fortunately he was surrounded by others who shone in those qualities where he felt himself deficient. " Mr Simpson, for example," he wrote, " is extremely methodical and orderly, and my nephew William has excellent habit of order."

Nor must we forget that besides this gay genial humour, which knew how to break down the barriers of reserve and the preconceived ideas of a stern editor, he possessed a far-reaching sympathy for others, which showed itself in numberless acts of tender generosity and courtesy that go unrecorded save in the memories of those that experience them, but that all tend to keep young the heart of the man who devises them. The summer passed very quietly, with only the companionship of his wife and children, and the members of our own family whom he most loved to see about him,—his nephews William and George Blackwood (the latter home on leave), and his nieces Bessie and Emma Blackwood, who came backwards and forwards from Edinburgh. A few intimate friends, whose society was beneficial and cheering without obliging him to make any great exertions to entertain them, were the only guests. Mr Wolfe Murray, an old golfing friend, was with us that summer, and James Logan White, the son of the Rev. James White, who used to spend a part of each summer at Strathtyrum. The gossip they brought from the Links was listened to with the same zest as of old, though, owing to the heart weakness I have alluded to, he never played golf now, but contented himself with walking out a hole or two to watch the incoming matches — "The next highest form of enjoyment," he would say, when his friends paused in their game to condole with him on not being able to join in his favourite sport. General Charles Thesiger, a man whose visits he had always particularly enjoyed, came over and stayed a couple of nights after inspecting the Fife Light Horse; and Mr Robert Mowbray, in whom my father felt much interested, he having recently written for the

Magazine a paper on a matter of public interest which he thought showed conspicuous ability. Later in the autumn, about the beginning of October, came Julian Sturgis for a day or two, and Mr Newdigate, who wrote that he "could not leave Fife without coming to see his old friend."

These visits afforded him as much pleasure as anything could in those days of languor and weakness, and nothing would have induced him to forego them. But when it came to the leave-taking, the hand-shake of each friend was like the snapping of another link that bound him to earth and earthly interests. The days that followed were sad and anxious, the house silent and hushed. Charles Reade would not have recognised the "Palais de Plaisir,"—its inmates hardly knew it themselves. One after another the friends and relations had gone, and only our four selves were left to face the last visitor, of whose coming we had had the warnings of which hearts bound up in the life that is threatened find it so impossible to realise the meaning. This going-about illness had yielded so many hopes of recovery that it was difficult to relinquish them even to the last, with the accustomed work and life going on around, the tide of letters and communications from all sides setting in around him as of old,—though the sight of a letter lying on his desk begun and never finished brought home, with a pang the present writer can never forget, the first sharp dread of impending separation, the fear that the beloved hand would never take up the pen again. Then the mournful conviction began to steal on us that as the days of autumn were drawing in, so were the days shortening of him whose life, like the year, had reached its fullest completion; that for him there was to be no winter of old age—he was to go down with all the bright powers of his intellect at their best, and in the full enjoyment of the success his life's toil was bringing him. A few more days of weakness and weariness, and then the call to the great Rest, to which he passed away suddenly and painlessly in the presence of his wife and his two children, of whom one, the young son so dear to him, was only two years later laid beside his father in the quiet grave.

To many of his friends his death came as an unexpected blow, though others, like George Eliot, had been dreading the worst for long before the end came. The letters written not only at the time when the first shock of grief was felt by his friends, but long afterwards up to the present, all tell the same tale,—not merely the regret for a good man gone out of the world, but the bitter sense of personal loss, as though each one felt that to him or her the world was a colder, drearier place without John Blackwood. Besides these private expressions of feeling, the numerous press notices of him, which contained many discriminating and able criticisms on his life and work, nearly all gave the same impression of having been written by those who either actually knew him personally, or who at all events wished to sketch him with the pleasant characteristic touches that only appear in the portraits of those who have influenced men's hearts as well as their heads. We may here be permitted to quote slightly from some of the notices which seem to have been particularly successful in portraying the characteristics by which his family and friends like to remember him.

"Brought up from his cradle in an atmosphere of letters, he became one of the boldest, most independent, and keenest critics of his time, and all the more by reason of a generosity and even enthusiasm of nature, over which a certain reserve drew the very thinnest of veils. He very seldom proved wrong in his judgments, and his judgments were invariably his own. Absolute independence of passing opinion, absolute impartiality towards friends and opponents, have been the consistent principles of 'Maga' under his rule; and as was the Magazine, such was the man—the very type of justice and generosity."

"He had also the rare merit of never shutting himself out by personal considerations from any literary success. He had his own special friends amongst authors. No publisher of the present day had probably a larger number of such friends. But he was always ready to welcome literary power in any quarter, and he lived to have the closest literary ties with many from whom he entirely differed. It was not merely that the instincts of his profession taught him what was right in such cases, but he felt a genuine intellectual attraction for all men of intellectual power. They in their turn, whether sympathising with his personal opinions or not, had the most sincere regard for him. They knew how sterling he was, how clearsighted, friendly, and manly in all his ways. His death will be deeply lamented by a host of warm friends scattered over the world; and many will think not only of his abilities and his loss to the publishing world—not easy to be repaired—but also, with moistening eyes, of his great kindness and his many personal virtues."

Colonel Lockhart, in his feeling and discriminating tribute to him in the Magazine, while dwelling on the position he held in the world of letters, thus emphasises his appreciation of his friend :—

I have before me the testimony of a man of letters of world-wide celebrity. He writes: "I have known no man—I think I may say there is no man left among us—in whom was found so much literary culture with so clear an understanding of the nature of his business. As a critic he was excellent, joining to the appreciation of what was good, the much rarer faculty of perceiving what was, for the occasion, good enough. Added to this there was an exquisite feeling of what a gentleman should, or should not, do in all emergencies. His loss will be very difficult to fill to the literary world at large."

Perhaps no more fitting expression of the general feeling that was shared by all his friends could be found than these touching words of Mrs Oliphant's, which were intended as an appreciation to follow Colonel Lockhart's tribute in the Magazine.

I suppose I may now rank myself among the oldest contributors to the Magazine, though it seems no very long time since, young myself, I made acquaintance with the young Editor, in all the genial force of early yet mature manhood, with eyes as blue as the sky, and life as prosperous and prospects as fair as any man could desire. Strangely enough, one of the things I remember best in my last interview with him, not yet two months ago, was those same blue eyes. The countenance had suffered change, — from youth to middle-age, from vigorous health to almost the last stage of illness—but the eyes were blue as ever. Between these two meetings seven-and-twenty years of almost constant intercourse had passed, during which a great part of my work had gone through his hands,—scarcely a page of it without some commentary, never a proof without annotation. I think of the absence of these now with a sickening of the heart. What lively little controversies, what friendly encounters, not without now and then a momentary disagreement that made the alliance all the stronger, went on upon those narrow fields of margin. Of the more serious support his good opinion was, I can scarcely speak. When I think that I have lost it, it is with a real pang. Many and many times I have sent my work to him, saying, "I think it is bad; I am too near it; I cannot judge," to be consoled and set on my feet by his ready understanding and the support of his judgment. Support is the word that occurs to me most readily. I am disposed to use it again and again. The strong and steadfast backing-up, the unfaltering verdict for good or evil, were invaluable to a writer still confused with the excitement of composition. This was John Blackwood's great power. If he made a mistake now and then it was by force of sympathy, and his warm and never-failing delight in brilliant workmanship; but his mistakes were few, and his approval a tower of strength. In the more private relationships of life, all his friends know what he was. Very happy and successful in his own career, he was never without a tender feeling for the sorrowful. Life was to me a very different matter, and full of trouble and sorrow, but I scarcely remember any moment of special darkness in which I missed the kind grasp of his hand held out to me, the ready help, the cheerful encouragement. And now all the friendly talks are done, the conferences over our children of the same age, the little outbursts of genuine humour, his somewhat slow elocution, helped by the eloquence of the lifted finger, the genial laugh, the fun in every feature. John Blackwood, kind captain and critic, friend and brother, farewell!

We who, through the medium of his letters, seem to have stepped back once more into the fresh wholesome atmosphere of his presence, are reminded again of his manly generous way of regarding others, always willing to see the best that there was in every one, and ever merciful to those who were less morally and intellectually gifted than himself. The knowledge and experience of life which he possessed seemed only to have given full weight to his understanding, without robbing him of those qualities of sympathy and trustfulness which too often get worn away by the world's hard contact. As we look back through the long years the rough places seem to be smoothed away, and the inevitable troubles of life have the tendency to shrink into insignificance in comparison with its brighter aspects. In his case, one of the most enduring of these lies in the recollection that friendship contributed so largely to his happiness, and that his loyalty to his friends reaped a rich harvest of love and devotion, which has left to those who come after him an inheritance of kindly traditions that will ever keep fresh the bright and happy memories that cluster round the name of John Blackwood.

INDEX.

THE END.

PRINTED BY WILLIAM BLACKWOOD AND SONS.

Lightning Source UK Ltd.
Milton Keynes UK
UKHW022151280720
367329UK00010B/198